THE COUNTRY
of the BLIND

THE COUNTRY

of the BLIND

THE SOVIET SYSTEM
OF MIND CONTROL

BY GEORGE S. COUNTS
AND NUCIA LODGE

The Riverside Press Cambridge   1949

HOUGHTON MIFFLIN COMPANY · BOSTON

The Riverside Press

CAMBRIDGE · MASSACHUSETTS

PRINTED IN THE U.S.A.

W<small>E HAVE LEARNT HISTORY</small> more thoroughly than the others. We differ from all others in our logical consistency. We know that virtue does not matter to history, and that crimes remain unpunished; but that every error has its consequences and venges itself unto the seventh generation. Therefore we concentrated all our efforts on preventing error and destroying the very seeds of it. Never in history has so much power over the future of humanity been concentrated in so few hands as in our case. Each wrong idea we follow is a crime committed against future generations. Therefore we have to punish wrong ideas as others punish crimes: with death. We were held for madmen because we followed every thought down to its final consequence and acted accordingly. We were compared to the Inquisition because, like them, we constantly felt in ourselves the whole weight of responsibility for the superindividual life to come. We resembled the great Inquisitors in that we persecuted the seeds of evil not only in men's deeds, but in their thoughts. We admitted no private sphere, not even inside a man's skull. We lived under the compulsion of working things out to their final conclusions.

A<small>RTHUR</small> K<small>OESTLER</small>, *Darkness at Noon* (New York, 1941).*

In our country there is but one **truth — state truth.** And our country is moving toward Communism.

Y. L<small>APTEV</small>, *Zaria* (Moscow, 1948).

* Copyright, 1941, by The Macmillan Company and used with their permission.

CONTENTS

PROLOGUE

THE MATERIALS presented in this volume are published for the purpose of helping the peoples of the free world to understand the Soviet Union. They tell the story in authentic detail of the operation of the Soviet system of mind control. No one who is unfamiliar with the reach and power of this system can pretend to an understanding of that strange land whose spokesmen are fond of calling "the first workers' republic in history."

The book could have many titles. At any rate, to the authors any one of several seemed at one time or another to be entirely fitting. As we read the charges of heresy and the endless recantations and confessions of error or guilt by leading writers, artists, and scientists, *The Return of the Inquisition* appeared to be a "natural" title. Then the substance of the resolutions of the Central Committee of the All-Union Communist Party suggested *The Assault Upon the West,* after Aurel Kolnai's volume on German Naziism which was published in 1938 under the title of *The War Against the West.* Also, because of their glorification of everything Soviet and even Russian, these resolutions and the responses which they evoked might well have been called *The Soviet Union Over All.* Even in his maddest moments Hitler rarely put on an exhibition of megalomania more impressive than the calculated policy of the Kremlin. Indeed *Da Zdravstvuet Stalin* or *Heil Stalin* would not have been inappropriate. *The Confident Men of the Kremlin* would have been wholly suitable and would have served to correct the widespread notion that these men are "scared." In view of the co-ordinated and concentrated power of

ix

the Soviet state, *The Soviet Leviathan* would have made an excellent title. In his last work, published shortly before his death, Charles A. Beard in all truth referred to Russia as "one of the most ruthless Leviathans in the long history of military empires." For reasons which the liberal and democratic revolutionary leaders of nineteenth-century Russia would have easily understood, the book could have been called *The Wages of Dictatorship*.

However, as the full picture unfolded in the documents, my mind turned with increasing frequency to a conversation of last spring. At that time there came into my office a European scholar who had taught languages in Soviet schools from 1939 to 1946, having entered the Union with passport and visa before the war started. In terms of intimate knowledge of life in Russia during the recent period, he far surpasses anyone else of my acquaintance. It should be said, too, that he left the Soviet Union with a feeling of deep friendship for the Russian people.

After we had talked for an hour or so, he asked me this question: "What is the best work ever written on the Soviet Union?" Knowing that he had something on his mind, I asked him to name it. He replied that it was a piece by H. G. Wells. This surprised me, because I could recall no work of Wells' on the Soviet Union. My visitor then told me that it was not a work on the Soviet Union, but one of his early short stories, a typical Wellsian fantasy, "The Country of the Blind." He said that the people of the Soviet Union, like the citizens of this negative Utopia, seemed not to see at all a thousand things that stood right before their eyes. Or, if they saw them, they remained silent.

With this challenge I turned to the short story which I only dimly remembered. Wells places the setting of his tale in a "mysterious mountain valley" in "the wildest wastes of Ecuador's Andes," to which there came a long time ago a "family or so of Peruvian half-breeds fleeing from the lust and tyranny of an evil Spanish ruler." In the course of the decades a vast volcanic upheaval dislodged a mountaintop and sent it crashing down to close the only entrance and thus to create a pocket sealed off forever to the wanderings of men.

Some time after this cataclysm the people of the valley were struck by a strange disease which eventually left a race completely and congenitally blind. In the fifteenth generation following the visitation of this malady, a stranger from the outer world gained access to the valley through one of those happy accidents of Wells' which contravene all the laws of nature. While exploring the higher Andes roundabout, he was carried down into the Country of the Blind, without serious injury, on an avalanche of snow.

After making his acquaintance with the inhabitants, Núñez, as he was called, proceeded to tell them of the great world beyond the valley, of the beauties of the landscape and the heavens, of the delights and wonders of sight. To his surprise his words were not well received because during fourteen generations of blindness these people had gradually lost those elements of their original heritage which had been derived from and had been dependent on vision. And as time passed, blind men of genius had appeared and fashioned a cosmology appropriate to their condition. According to this cosmology the little pocket in the Andes constituted the whole of the universe and its people the entire race of men. This universe was bounded by the enclosing mountain walls, a kind of "stone curtain," and by an overarching canopy of smooth rock in whose upper reaches the fluttering of the wings of angels could be heard.

At first Núñez, boasting of superior knowledge acquired through his powers of sight, ridiculed this simple conception of the world. Such talk, of course, outraged the citizens of the Country of the Blind, and he was declared to be both immature and ignorant, if not wicked. But gradually, through the pressure of hunger, argument, public opinion, and the love of a maid, he wavered in his beliefs and at last admitted them to be false.

"They asked him if he still thought he could 'see.'

" 'No,' he said. 'That was folly. The word means nothing — less than nothing!'

"They asked him what was overhead.

" 'About ten times ten the height of a man there is a roof above the world — of rock — and very, very smooth.' . . . He burst again into hysterical tears. 'Before you ask me any more, give me some food or I shall die.' "

Driven by his passion for the lovely Medina-saroté and by the demand of her parents that he become worthy of her, Núñez agreed to a surgical operation designed to remove the offending organs of sight and thus to raise him to the stature of a fully qualified citizen of the Country of the Blind — an operation rendered wholly safe by the marvellous advance of science in this land. Then, as "he lifted up his eyes and saw the morning, the morning like an angel in golden armor, marching down the steeps," he was torn by the most profoundly conflicting emotions. At last, Wells leaves his hero, who has decided that the gift of sight is precious beyond price, struggling laboriously but hopefully to conquer the unconquerable mountain wall barring his return to the world where men can see.

The so-called "iron curtain" which encloses the Soviet Union is of course by no means as impenetrable as the "stone curtain" of Wells' Country of the Blind. Yet it constitutes a formidable barrier to the free movement of persons and ideas. On the one hand, it reduces to a minimum the number of citizens of foreign countries allowed to enter and limits the contacts and movements of those admitted. Freedom of travel for visitors from other lands is now at the lowest point since the Revolution and freedom of communication is destroyed by fear on the part of the Russian people, born of experience, of the charge of being "too friendly with foreigners." On the other hand, the "curtain" closely controls the travel abroad of Soviet citizens. All who enjoy this privilege go as agents of the state and on government assignments. Moreover, because of the "desertion to the enemy" of such people as Ipatiev, Krivitsky, Barmine, Kravchenko, Gouzenko, Samarin, and Kasenkina, the candidate for foreign service is selected with meticulous care. His family and class origin must be above suspicion, his performance in school must be exemplary, his life as child and youth should be identified preferably with Pioneer and Young Communist organizations, and his record of loyalty to Party and government must be without blemish. If he has ever shown the slightest tendency toward independence of thought respecting prescribed doctrines and policies, if he has ever revealed any evidence of being endowed with the gift of sight in the realm of the mind, he is automatically rejected. On being placed among the elect, he is subjected to a rigorous training designed in part to test and strengthen his loyalties and to develop resistance to the temptations of the wicked "bourgeois world." And after he arrives at his post in a foreign land, he is placed, not only under the watchful eyes of his fellows, but also under the secret surveillance of Soviet agents whom he does not know. Efforts on the part of the American Government and American universities immediately following the war to enter into a program of exchange of students and professors received no encouragement whatsoever from the Kremlin.

Contact with the outer world is gradually being lost also by the passing of the prerevolutionary generation. The members of the intellectual class of old Russia were renowned for their knowledge of the languages, literatures, arts, sciences, and philosophies of other lands. Indeed the foremost leaders of the Revolution had not only been profoundly influenced by the thought of the West, they had also lived as exiles for years in Germany, Austria, Switzerland, France, England, and other countries. Mention may be made here of Lenin, Trotsky, Radek, Zinoviev, Kamenev, Bucharin, and Lunacharsky. When the survivors of this group were finally liquidated in the great purges of the thirties, they were sometimes referred to quite accurately as "Westerners." Stalin alone of the original leaders of the first rank knew almost nothing of the outer world through direct experience. His years of exile had all been spent within the borders of the empire. Unless policy changes drastically, the direction of the Soviet state will gravitate increasingly into the hands of men who know little if anything at first hand about other societies, civilizations, and peoples.

The "iron curtain" is fortified by a system of internal control of great reach and power. First of all, there is the Communist Party itself whose six million members constitute a kind of political army. Organized into a network of thousands of cells, it holds within its immediate grasp all factories, mills, shops, enterprises, collective farms, professional unions, and institutions of every description. The Party is re-enforced in its activities by organizations of children and youth which it leads and moulds. Then there is the political police, now known as the MVD, which is in actuality an agent of the central organs of the Party and "watches over" the entire population. It nips organized and even unorganized discontent in the bud and thus fills the forced-labor camps and detachments which probably contain from five to fifteen million persons. The MVD is assisted very effectively in the performance of its duties by the internal passport system which the Bolsheviks inherited from the Tsar and made more efficient. Every Soviet citizen, as he moves from place to place within the country, even for a brief visit, must register his passport with the police both on his departure and on his arrival. The school child is required to have his "pupil's card" always with him. And relatives may be held strictly accountable and severely punishable for certain mistakes and transgressions of the individual.

On the positive side this "country of the blind" makes the fullest possible use of tangible and intangible rewards to induce its citizens to follow the line laid down by the Party, whether in mining coal or growing sugar beets, whether in making shoes or composing an opera, whether in conducting Soviet foreign policy or waging a military campaign. Financial compensation in the form of wages, salaries, and bonuses is employed to the limit to encourage effort in the desired direction. But perhaps the most striking feature of this scheme of control is the vast system of honorifics which embraces practically all spheres of activity from student scholarship to motherhood. Millions of Soviet youth undoubtedly look forward to being awarded the highly coveted Order of Lenin or Order of Suvorov; and many more millions probably have their eyes fixed more modestly on the Badge of Honor or the Red Banner of Labor.

The people of the Soviet Union of course suffer from no physical malady such as afflicted the entire population of the Country of the Blind. Yet the all-inclusive system for the positive moulding of the mind, to be abundantly illustrated in the present volume, may well have comparable results in the course of time. Working through all conceivable agencies and methods, the All-Union Communist Party is engaged with great energy in systematically building, in the minds of young and old alike, two great myths — one about themselves and their country and the other about the rest of the world and the so-called "camp of capitalism." The nature and content of these myths are revealed with awful clarity in the documents which follow. Efforts thus to shape the mind of a people have been launched many times in history, but rarely, if ever, with such efficiency and ruthlessness. In the past those mighty instruments were lacking which science and technology have recently placed in man's hands. The thoroughness with which the two myths are being propagated probably derives largely from the fact that they rest on doctrines and dogmas of historical and philosophical interpretation which the leaders themselves believe to be absolutely true. Lord Acton observed long ago that power always tends to corrupt. It is equally true that power always tends to blind, and that absolute power tends to blind absolutely. The men of the Kremlin come as near possessing absolute power as any oligarchy in history.

As yet the Soviet people are not wholly blind. The affliction which is descending on them so relentlessly has still to run its course. In this respect they are much like the inhabitants of the Country of the Blind during the period immediately following the first visitation of the malady. As Wells puts it, "the old became groping and purblind, the young saw but dimly, and the children that were born to them saw never at all." One wonders how many men and women behind the "iron curtain" have refused to accept fully the two myths, how many Soviet soldiers and officers would like to follow their comrades who by the thousand have escaped to the West during postwar years, how many Soviet schoolteachers envy the fate of Kasenkina and long for the opportunity to jump to freedom from a third-story window onto concrete pavement below, or how many Soviet citizens would willingly join the ranks of their compatriots in the camps for displaced persons in Europe and become people without a country. These questions cannot be answered. Rumors reach the West from time to time that there are still many in the Soviet Union who retain their vision. But whether their number is large or small, only the renewal of communication with the outside world can save them.

It would be a mistake, however, to indulge in wishful thinking on this matter. The references to other countries contained in the documents presented in the present volume, even in those prepared by ministers of education and leading scientists, demonstrate clearly that Soviet spokesmen are already either purblind or under tremendous coercion. Their words suggest that they see beyond Russian borders but dimly. The European scholar referred to above believes that the people of the Soviet Union are overwhelmingly loyal to their country, as were the citizens of the Country of the Blind. He takes this view even though he taught for some time in a higher institution in Siberia in which he was the only member of a staff of eighty who had never served a prison sentence. These teachers had been caught in the purges, had been convicted on some charge or other, had been sent to prison or forced-labor camp for a period, had confessed their mistakes or sins, had promised to be good in the future, and had been placed on probation in a distant and undesirable location. Presumably it was hoped that under proper treatment, far removed from their old associations, they would either lose their sight, recover their blindness, or at least learn to conceal their vision.

But the purpose of this volume is not to foster complacency on the part of the free peoples of the earth respecting their own condition. We in America are blind to many of the realities of the world and to many of our own weaknesses. The very success of the Soviet formula is due to the fact that the myth about us which they have fashioned contains more than a grain of truth. The malady, moreover, from which the Russians are suffering in an extreme form is not new to this planet. In fact, it is as old as mankind and as wide as the world. If one looks back through the centuries of recorded history, one will find that men have always been blinded by ignorance and prejudice, by doctrine founded on error and proclaimed as final truth. One will find also that ruling cliques and classes, priests and lords and monarchs, have fostered ignorance and prejudice, and manipulated dogma for the purpose of consolidating and maintaining power and privilege. Also the ways of life and thought and feeling into which the member of any society is born and in which he is reared, be they good or bad, shape his mind from the moment of birth and draw a curtain of bias and prejudice over his eyes. The Russian example therefore is not unique. Yet it should disturb us because of its great power and aggressive character. The fortunes of ourselves and all mankind are closely linked with the course of Soviet foreign policy during the years ahead.

GEORGE S. COUNTS

ACKNOWLEDGMENTS

THE PREPARATION of the present volume was made possible by the active and generous co-operation of many people. We wish to express our appreciation particularly to the officers of the American Russian Institute of New York City and the staffs of the Slavic and Russian departments and sections of the Libraries of Columbia University, the Library of Congress, and the New York Public Library. They all assisted in tracking down elusive Russian materials.

We wish to thank the Macmillan Company for permission to quote from Arthur Koestler's *Darkness at Noon*, Crown Publishers for permission to quote from Franz Mehring's *Karl Marx*, Little, Brown & Company for permission to quote from Max Nomad's *Apostles of Revolution*, and the *Baltimore Bulletin of Education* for permission to quote from an article by Miss Anne C. Phillips.

We are greatly indebted to the authors of a number of scholarly studies of Russia and the Soviet Union. Mention should first be made of Thomas G. Masaryk's monumental *The Spirit of Russia*. Though written and published several years before the October Revolution of 1917, it is indispensable for an understanding of the course of Soviet development. The following recent works in English are invaluable: *The Russian Enigma* by W. H. Chamberlin, *World Communism Today* by Martin Ebon, *The Great Challenge* by Louis Fischer, *Stalin and German Communism* by Ruth Fischer, *The Life of a Chemist* by V. N. Ipatieff, *The Origins of Modern Russia* by Jan Kucharzewski, *Lenin* by David

Shub, *Forced Labor in Soviet Russia* by David J. Dallin and B. I. Nicolaevsky, and *Three Who Made a Revolution* by Bertram D. Wolfe. Dostoievsky's *The Diary of a Writer,* written three quarters of a century ago, is astonishingly relevant to the postwar mood and outlook of the Soviet leaders. The reading of these volumes will dispel much of the mystery surrounding Soviet practices, institutions, and policies.

As these lines are written the Soviet press conveys not the slightest suggestion that the Soviet assault on the West is being moderated. In fact that assault still seems to be gathering momentum, to be getting sharper, and to be turning increasingly against the United States of America.

GEORGE S. COUNTS
NUCIA LODGE

New York City
August 4, 1949

THE COUNTRY
of the BLIND

CHAPTER ONE

THE PARTY OF LENIN AND STALIN

THE FREE WORLD must understand the source and controlling purposes of Soviet foreign policy and world outlook. For the building of mutual sympathy and an enduring peace, it should also know far more than it does about the history, the ethnology, and the geography, the music, the art, and the literature, the education, the science, and the technology, the economy, the government, and the whole social order of this vast country that excites the hopes and the fears of so many millions today throughout the earth. But from the standpoint of the immediate future condition of mankind it is Soviet foreign policy and world outlook that must be understood at this time. That such understanding is far from easy was recognized by Winston Churchill when he dramatically characterized Russian policy as a "riddle wrapped in a mystery inside an enigma." But perhaps the problem is less difficult than he thought.

In seeking the key to this riddle one must turn first of all to the All-Union Communist Party of Bolsheviks, its origin, its history, its structure, its leadership, and its basic ideology. With its six million members, its Central Committee of seventy-two, its Politburo of fourteen, and its complex and far-flung apparatus it is the decisive *political* reality in the Soviet Union. Granted the power of the country, everything else dwindles into comparative insignificance. Under the popular designation of the "Party of Lenin and Stalin" it is officially hailed by the editor of *Pravda* as "the

1

organizer of the victory of the Great October Socialist Revolution," as "the inspirer and organizer of victory in the Great Patriotic War," as "the guiding force in all branches of the life of the Soviet land," as "the mind, the honor, and the conscience of our epoch," and as the agency that "will lead to the victory of Communism." [1] And by the "victory of Communism" Pospelov does not mean merely the triumph of the Soviet system and ideology within the borders of the country that embraces "one-sixth of the land surface of the globe."

As the Party stands today, it is of course the product of many minds, of many historical currents, and of many events and circumstances. Yet two men, two political giants, two powerful personalities differing profoundly in character, temperament, and talents, may rightly be regarded as its architects — Lenin and Stalin. The one, a Great Russian who spent years in foreign exile, and the other, a Georgian who passed a good part of his early manhood in the jails and prison camps of Great Russia — each has left his special stamp on the Party. But this institution was also and at the same time a creature of the union of two great cultural streams — certain traditions of the Great Russian people and certain doctrines of Marxian socialism. Consequently, as the present chapter will endeavor to show, the All-Union Communist Party which threatens to engulf all nations is of complex origin. It is the fruit of a strange union of Russia with Germany and the West, of Slavophilism with international revolutionary socialism, of Ivan and Peter and Bakunin with Marx and Engels, joined and molded by the genius of Lenin and Stalin. The forging of the Party as an instrument for the conquest of power, for the government of a country of two hundred million people, for the propagation of revolution throughout the world, and for the launching of an aggressive imperialism under the aegis of peace and progress was a process which came to its first fruition in 1917, but which already at that time had a long history and which has continued with unabated energy down to the present moment. The analysis may well begin with the Great October Revolution.

[1] P. N. Pospelov, *The Party of Lenin and Stalin* (Moscow, 1947). (In Russian.)

2

The Russian Revolution will doubtless be a subject of controversy as long as its records survive. But the Soviet system which it produced must be and can be appraised at this time. That system is now in its thirty-second year and may be regarded as having revealed its essential character. The Russian people who can recall distinctly the old régime now constitute a definite minority of the population. Moreover, in spite of the many obstacles confronting the student of Soviet affairs and the deficiencies of knowledge concerning many details of life under Communist rule, the broad outlines of the system itself stand out clearly and seem not likely to undergo fundamental change in the coming generation, in the absence of some profound social convulsion. No longer is there any excuse for misunderstanding either the nature of Soviet society or the long-range purposes of its rulers.

When the Revolution broke in February, 1917, the entire free world rejoiced. For had not men and women of democratic temper in all countries been looking forward for several generations, perhaps since the uprising of 1825, to the revolution which would sweep away one of the most despotic régimes to survive down to the nineteenth century and establish on the ruins of the empire a constitutional republic? Even when the revolutionary forces moved beyond the historical forms of political democracy and finally lodged on the so-called extreme left under the banner of the "dictatorship of the proletariat," many viewed this consummation either as a natural reaction to the tyranny of the tsar or as a hopeful advance of the forces of human liberation from politics to the realm of economics. And even if these friendly observers had fully grasped the true character and purposes of the new masters of the Kremlin, drawn from the attics and cellars and prisons of the Western World, they would have regarded the dictatorship as a temporary expedient and destined soon to pass away.

In 1917, Western man was still largely under the sway of the idea that political liberty was on the march and could not be halted.

As we look back now, we know that the great hopes inspired by the Revolution were not justified and have not been fulfilled. Few indeed are those who have sustained such hopes from 1917 down to the present time. The overwhelming majority of the onetime friends of the Soviet Union have dropped away as they have come to know the inner character and tendencies of Communist rule. This fact of course has not kept others from joining the ranks of the multitude looking to Moscow for leadership, until they in turn are disillusioned. An earlier generation of Americans, typified perhaps by Thomas Jefferson, had a similar experience in relation to the French Revolution of 1789. In 1791 he wrote to Sir John Sinclair: "We are now under the first impression of the news of the King's flight from Paris, and his recapture. It would be unfortunate were it in the power of any one man to defeat the issue of so beautiful a revolution. I hope and trust it is not, and that, for the good of suffering humanity all over the earth, that revolution will be established and spread through the whole world." Reluctantly, but gradually, under the hammer-blows of events that outraged his deepest convictions and loyalties, Jefferson abandoned utterly this first estimate of the Revolution. By 1815 he was writing to Lafayette that the French people had exchanged a limited monarchy "for the unprincipled and bloody tyranny of Robespierre, and the equally unprincipled and maniac tyranny of Bonaparte." The response to the Russian Revolution seems to have run a not dissimilar course.

The Russian Revolution inspired universal hopes because it was regarded by many, not merely as a *Russian* revolution, but also as the beginning of a beneficent revolution that would circle the earth. And the Soviet Union has continued to inspire such hopes in the uninformed because it was the child of this revolution. It claims to be sole heir to the mightiest and noblest popular movement of the nineteenth and the early twentieth century — international revolutionary socialism. Founded by Marx and Engels and elaborated by great political thinkers and leaders of many countries, this movement saw the salvation of mankind in the inevitable rise to power of the working class of all nations. Conceived in terms of the completion of the work begun by the English, American, and French Revolutions, it sought to combine in one grand and realistic synthesis all the liberating and humanizing tendencies of the human heritage. It saw war, misery, and injustice in the current age as the necessary fruit of the operation of capitalist institutions, and held before the peoples of the earth the vision of a world of peace, justice, security, and plenty. It promised to abolish once and for all the age-long exploitation of man by man.

With the passing of the years this movement gained great moral and political power in most of the nations of Europe, and cast its lambent glow in some measure to all the continents. It appealed to the idealism of youth, quickened the sense of right of many of the good and the great, and even touched the hearts of kings and emperors. The story of its advance is told with sympathy and understanding by Angelica Balabanoff, who as a girl of seventeen, child of wealthy parents, left her native Russia at the close of the nineteenth century to participate in this struggle for human liberation in Belgium, Italy, France, and other countries of the West. In her *My Life as a Rebel,* published in 1938, though horrified by the rise of fascism and the perversion of the revolution in the Soviet Union, she can still speak with passion of "an Idea" which "inspired whole generations to matchless heroism and enthusiasm." She quotes as an expression of her own spirit the immortal words of August Bebel, brilliant leader of German socialism: "And if, in the course of this great battle for the emancipation of the human race, we should fall, those now in the rear will step forward; and we shall fall with the consciousness of having done our duty as human beings, and with the conviction that the goal will be reached, however the powers hostile to humanity may struggle or strain in resistance. Ours is the world, despite all." [2] The Soviet leaders claim all of this as their inheritance. Many idealistic young men and women in America and throughout the

[2] Angelica Balabanoff, *My Life as a Rebel* (New York, 1938), p. v.

world, blinded by the brilliance of this vision, still regard as the essence of Communism the radiant mantle with which it is draped.

3

In their origins the doctrines of international revolutionary socialism bore the imprint of the minds which framed them and of the civilizations out of which they came. Although Marx and Engels lived much of their lives in Western Europe and England and although they were profound students of universal history, the stamp of German thought on their works is clearly evident. When these doctrines migrated to other countries they inevitably experienced change, slight or profound, depending on the nature of the new environment, the level of technology, the political habits and institutions, the great patterns of civilization. On crossing the English Channel they evolved into the moderate forms of Fabian Socialism, and they scarcely reached North America.

Marx himself recognized this fundamental truth. In addressing the Amsterdam branch of the First International in September, 1872, and after declaring that the worker "must overthrow the old political system," he said: "Of course I must not be supposed to imply that the means to this end will be everywhere the same. We know that special regard must be paid to the institutions, customs, and traditions of various lands; and we do not deny that there are certain countries, such as the United States and England, in which the workers may hope to secure their ends by peaceful means. If I mistake not, Holland belongs to this same category." [3] Moreover, shortly before his death in 1895, Engels subjected the more extreme positions of his earlier years to sharp criticism. Influenced by changes in the means of warfare and the development of democratic political institutions, particularly in Germany, he de-

[3] G. M. Stekloff, *History of the First International* (London and New York, 1928), pp. 240–41.

clared that "our former point of view has been proved an illusion" by "history," that "universal suffrage" is a "new weapon of the struggle, one of the most powerful," that "revolt of the old type . . . has now in significant measure become obsolete," that the time of "revolutions of unconscious masses led by conscious minorities is past," and that "we revolutionists" are "advancing more surely toward our goals by legal than by illegal methods." [4]

The year 1883 is generally regarded as marking the appearance of Marxism in Russia as an organized movement. From the very first it felt the molding power of Russian conditions, geography, ethnology, economics, politics, and history. Particularly was it influenced by Russian revolutionary traditions which were already at least two centuries old. From 1667 to 1671 Stenka Razin, a rough untutored Cossack leader without ideology or program, headed a bloody revolt in the valley of the Volga. A century later, from 1773 to 1775, another Cossack leader, Emilian Pugachev, led a rebellion in the same spirit and in the same region, proclaimed the abolition of serfdom, and for a time challenged the rule of Catherine the Great. Both of these popular uprisings were waged with savagery and put down with ferocity and brutality. In the nineteenth century the struggle against the autocracy took on a definitely revolutionary character, with more or less developed doctrines and programs. As the masses of the people, the peasantry, remained apathetic for the most part, there emerged a class of professional and dedicated revolutionists who fought in the name of the people. The conflict was conducted with violence and terror on both sides, and prison, exile, torture, and death were generally the price of the apparently never-ending defeat or failure.

It was in this soil that the doctrines of Marx and Engels were planted; and it was in this soil that they grew to maturity and shaped the Revolution of 1917. The fact must of course be recognized that these doctrines, even in the softest light, presented harsh and unlovely features. As developed in the West, Marxism

---

[4] Friedrich Engels, "Introduction" to Karl Marx, *The Class Struggle in France* (Odessa, 1905), pp. 7, 12, 13, 17, 18–19. (In Russian.)

rested on a wholly unsentimental and realistic analysis of history and society. It saw the human record in terms of the class struggle, and it saw the salvation of the human race achieved finally through the triumph of the working people in an irreconcilable war with their oppressors. The Communist Manifesto, the most sacred of the Marxian scriptures, breathes fire and brimstone, warns the "ruling classes to tremble," and calls for the "forcible overthrow of all existing social conditions." Although this militant and aggressive approach to the problem of political change was gradually moderated in the West, it found ready and eager champions in imperial Russia — men and women of boundless courage and fanaticism.

One of these was Lenin. Born Vladimir Ilich Ulianov in 1870, he grew to manhood in a land and an age seething with revolutionary ideas and deeds. His older brother, Alexander, was arrested, convicted, and hanged in 1887 for participating in a conspiracy to assassinate Tsar Alexander III. It was a time of violence and counter-violence, a time of bitter struggle in which the contending parties often neither asked nor gave quarter, a time of literal war between the revolutionists and the defenders of the old order. The longer one studies the Soviet Union the more one is forced to the conclusion that the key to understanding is found, not in orthodox Marxian doctrine, but in the history of this revolutionary struggle in old Russia.

The revolutionists, however, were divided into innumerable sects, each certain at least for a time that it alone possessed the secret of success. Some pinned their faith on the bourgeoisie; others on the peasants; others on the industrial working class; and still others on the intelligentsia. Some even thought that the road to justice lay in the conversion of the tsar or the nobility or the landlords or the rich to a voluntary surrender of their privileges. Others renounced the world and addressed their appeal to God. Some saw hope in the gradual processes of enlightenment; others in an idealistic policy of non-violence; others in the assassination of individual rulers; others in the organization of the masses for violent revolt; and yet others in the conquest of power by a conspiratorial élite and the establishment of a dictatorship. Few countries in history, if any, ever presented to the world such a phantasmagoria of revolutionary ideas, methods, persons, and movements. Into this apparently endless and hopeless struggle to overthrow a cruel and brutal despotism the energies and lives of many of the finest spirits of old Russia were enlisted from generation to generation. Often these people responded to the "call" of the revolutionary cause while they were little more than children. Many abandoned the fight and many fell in battle, but sooner or later, in the words of Bebel, those in the rear stepped forward and filled their places.

Amid the rivalry of revolutionary ideas and methods two contrasting strains may be discerned — the liberal strain which stressed education, political liberty, and law, and the absolutist strain which advocated conspiracy, violence, and dictatorship. Curiously enough, the two strains were sometimes found in the same individual. This was clearly true in the case of Lenin, if one may judge from his writings. It was also true in the case of a remarkable precursor of the founder of Bolshevism, an aristocrat by birth and a soldier by profession, Paul Pestel (1792–1826). Perhaps the foremost revolutionary figure of early nineteenth-century Russia, this man believed in political democracy, in constitutional government, and in many of the doctrines of pre-Marxian socialism. At the same time, as leader of the Southern Section of the secret society which planned the revolution of 1825, he believed in the seizure of power by a militant minority and the establishment of a temporary dictatorship. Also he conceived a revolutionary association modelled after the structure of an army with three levels of membership — at the top the fully initiated, in the middle the partly initiated, and at the bottom the wholly uninitiated, the common soldiers of the revolution committed to unquestioning obedience. Standing on the fringes of the association, without power or obligation, were sympathizers and in the language of today, "fellow travellers." Probably influenced by the French Jacobins and the Larbonari, as well as by conditions in absolutist Russia, Pestel articulated a conception of revolutionary method

which was destined to triumph in Russia and which today constitutes one of the major political realities in all nations.

In the course of the years, Pestel's conception was appropriated
and perfected by a dark and sinister strain in the struggle for
popular liberation — a strain reaching back through the most barbarous episodes of the Russian past to Pugachev, Razin, Ivan the
Terrible, and the Tatars — a strain of great vigor in Russian revolutionary circles in the years when the mind of the young Lenin
was being formed. Though easily understood in terms of historical conditions as a revolutionary version of Russian absolutism, it
nevertheless presents a forbidding and terrifying aspect to all who
cherish the hope of peace, justice, and reconciliation among men.
Its vengeful spirit is expressed in these lines from a revolutionary
proclamation of 1862 addressed to the younger generation:

> With complete faith in ourselves, in our strength, in the sympathy
> of the people, in the glorious future of Russia which is destined to be
> the first to achieve socialism, we shall cry: "to the axes" — and then
> strike the members of the imperialist party without mercy, just as they
> show no mercy toward us now, strike them in the public squares, if
> these depraved rogues dare to show themselves, strike them in their
> houses, strike them in the narrow alleys of the towns, strike them in
> the wide streets of the great cities, strike them in the villages and the
> hamlets! Remember that whoever is not with us is against us, that
> whoever is against us is our enemy, and that an enemy must be ex-
> terminated by all possible means.[5]

The most powerful and influential representative of this approach to revolution was the anarchist, Michael Bakunin (1814–
76), contemporary and adversary of Karl Marx. Assuming all
existing institutions to be evil, he elaborated a philosophy of
"pandestruction." He gave little thought to the question of construction or reconstruction which presumably should follow the
all-destroying revolution. "Let us put our trust," he said, "in the
eternal spirit which only destroys and annihilates because it is the
unsearchable and eternally creative source of all life. The desire

5 Vladimir Burtsev, *For a Hundred Years* (London, 1897), pp. 45–46. (In Russian.)

for destruction is also a creative desire!" This nonsense and much more of the same order would have no place here if Bakunin had not departed from his abstract defense of violence and anarchy to outline, suggest, or espouse a revolutionary method. He accepted both mass revolution and individual assassination, propagated the idea of the use of terror for its educative values, and advocated resort to deception and conspiracy in the pursuit of his revolutionary aims. He saw the process of social destruction guided and directed by a secret central committee whose members would be unknown to the revolutionary organization as a whole and whose absolute tsar would be Bakunin himself.[6]

Among Bakunin's many disciples was Sergei Nechaiev (1847–82), one of the most extraordinary and controversial figures in the whole history of Russia, whose career is thought to have inspired Dostoievsky to write *The Possessed*. With matchless zeal he took his mentor's teachings seriously and proceeded to create for himself a reputation for bold revolutionary leadership. Without the slightest regard for truth, he circulated the most fantastic and wholly false tales about his own exploits — tales deliberately designed to enhance his standing among the members of the revolutionary community. One was to the effect that he had been imprisoned for some terrible deed and had escaped from the impregnable fortress of St. Peter-Paul; another that he was the head of the Russian branch of the mythical all-powerful "Revolutionary Union of the World." Under the slogan, "Everything for the Revolution — the end justifies the means," he succeeded in recruiting some university students in a secret revolutionary society. As leader he persuaded his fellow conspirators to murder a comrade on the charge that the latter was a spy in the service of the tsar. Probably under his influence Bakunin composed the famous "Catechism of a Revolutionist." This extraordinary document is of more than historical interest. It preaches a Machiavellian morality and method of action which two generations later were to be carried in some of its parts to nearly all countries through the All-Union

[6] See Thomas G. Masaryk, *The Spirit of Russia* (London and New York, 1919), vol. 1, pp. 430–71.

Communist Party and the Communist International. The essence of the Catechism follows:

> The revolutionist is a doomed man. He has no personal interests, no affairs, sentiments, attachments, property, not even a name of his own. . . . He despises and hates the present-day code of morals with all its motivations and manifestations. To him whatever aids the triumph of the revolution is ethical; all that which hinders it is unethical and criminal. . . . All tender, softening sentiments of kinship, friendship, love, gratitude, and even honor itself must be snuffed out in him by the one cold passion of the revolutionary cause. . . .
>
> A revolutionist may feel friendship or attachment only for those who have proven themselves by their actions to be revolutionists like himself. . . . The fellow revolutionists who stand on the same plane of revolutionary understanding and ardor must, as far as possible, discuss all important matters jointly and decide them unanimously. . . . Each comrade must have at hand several revolutionists of the second and third degree, i.e., such as are not entirely initiated. He must consider them as part of the common revolutionary capital placed at his disposal. . . . When a comrade comes to grief, in deciding the question whether or not to save him, the revolutionist must take into consideration not his personal feelings, but solely the interests of the revolutionary cause. . . .
>
> For the purpose of ruthless destruction, the revolutionist may and frequently must live in society, pretending to be something entirely different from what he is. . . . The whole ignoble social system must be divided into several categories. . . . First of all, those men must be destroyed who are particularly harmful to the revolutionary organization. . . . The second category must consist of persons whose lives would be spared only temporarily. . . . To the third category belong a great many brutes in high positions. . . . It is necessary to exploit them in every possible way; trap them, confound them, and, getting hold of their dirty secrets as far as possible, turn them into one's slaves . . . the inexhaustible treasury and support of various revolutionary enterprises. . . . The fourth category consists of ambitious officeholders and liberals of various shades. One may conspire with them in accordance with their programs, making them believe that one follows them blindly, and at the same time one should take hold of them, get possession of all their secrets, compromise them to the utmost, so that

no avenue of escape may be left to them, and use them as instruments for stirring up disturbances in the State. . . . The fifth category — doctrinaires. . . . They must be continually pushed and pulled forward, towards practical neck-breaking statements, the result of which would be the complete destruction of the majority and the real revolutionary training of a few. . . .

The Association has no aim other than the complete liberation and happiness of the masses.[7]

A third leader of ability and influence who helped to formulate the doctrine of revolution by a minority of professional revolutionists proceeding by the method of conspiracy, violence, and dictatorship was Peter N. Tkachev (1844–85). In an article entitled "The People and the Revolution," published in 1876 when Lenin was six years old, he defined the rôle of the revolutionary minority in terms that the Bolsheviks were destined to fulfill in spirit in 1917 and to the letter during the later "great Stalinist epoch." A communist in social philosophy, he outlined with complete frankness the theory of the dictatorship both during and after the seizure of power. The following brief excerpts give the essence of his argument:

The people are incapable of building on the ruins of the old a new world that will develop in the direction of the communist ideal. In the building of this new world they therefore cannot and should not play a prominent or primary rôle. This task belongs exclusively to the revolutionary minority. . . .

Even in the matter of destruction the revolutionary force of our people can have only relative significance. . . .

In order to continue its destructive-revolutionary activity in those spheres where it can hardly hope for the active support and assistance of the majority of the people, the revolutionary minority must possess force, rule, and authority. The greater the force, the firmer and more vigorous will be the rule, the more fully will the ideas of the social revolution be realized in life, and the more easily will conflict with the conservative elements of the people be avoided.

[7] Max Nomad, *Apostles of Revolution* (Boston, 1939), pp. 228–33.

Thus the relation of the revolutionary minority to the people and the rôle of the people in the revolution can be defined as follows: the revolutionary minority, having liberated the people from the oppressive yoke of fear and terror of the constituted authorities, opens to them the opportunity of exercising their destructive-revolutionary force. Leaning on this force and artfully directing it toward the destruction of the immediate enemies of the revolution, it shatters their defenses and deprives them of all means of resistance and counteraction. Then, employing its force and exercising its authority, the revolutionary minority introduces new progressive-communist elements into the social order, moves this order from its century-old moorings, and breathes life into its numb and cramped forms.

In its work of reformation the revolutionary minority must not rely on the active support of the people.

The revolutionary rôle of the people ends at the moment when they shatter the institutions and destroy the exploiting tyrants immediately oppressing them. . . .

Thus, *by taking advantage of the destructive-revolutionary force of the people, the revolutionary minority will destroy the enemies of the revolution and, guided by the general needs and ideals of the people . . . lay the foundations of a new and rational social order.* . . .

Neither in the present nor in the future can the people, left to themselves, achieve a social revolution. Only we, the revolutionary minority, can do this, — and we *must* do it as soon as possible.[8]

Throughout the nineteenth century the great leaders of Russian revolutionary thought were compelled sooner or later to confront this question of method. Outstanding among those who repudiated the proposal of Pestel and his heirs, men with whom the Bolsheviks have sought increasingly to identify themselves, were such writers as Alexander Hertzen (1812–70), Nikolai Chernyshevsky (1828–89), and Peter Lavrov (1823–1900). The words with which they condemned the method of conspiracy and dictatorship almost a century ago sound tragically prophetic today. "We socialists above all," said Hertzen in 1867, "are profoundly con-

8 P. N. Tkachev, *Collected Works* (Moscow, 1933), vol. III, pp. 264–68. (In Russian.)

vinced that social progress is not possible without full republican
liberty, without full democratic equality. . . . A socialism which
would dispense with political freedom and equal rights would
swiftly degenerate into an authoritarian communism." [9] In his
famous "Letters to an Old Comrade" (Bakunin) in 1869 he rejected the method of *coup d'état* by a revolutionary minority
operating secretly and identified himself with the "power of reason
and understanding." "If we reject this power," he wrote, "we become outlaws from science and renegades from civilization." [10]
Chernyshevsky in 1856 "declared himself opposed to secret societies, saying that great and truly useful ends can be secured only
by straightforward and open procedures." [11] Lavrov in 1874 appealed to "Russian Social Revolutionary Youth" to repudiate
without qualification the idea of a self-constituted dictatorship:

History proves and psychology confirms that unlimited power or
dictatorship corrupts the very best men, and that even persons of
genius, thinking to benefit the people by means of decrees, are unable
to do so. Every dictatorship must surround itself with coercive power
and blindly obedient tools; every dictatorship is compelled to suppress
with violence, not only reactionaries, but also persons who merely
disagree with its methods of action; every dictatorship is compelled to
expend more time, effort, and energy on the violent struggle for power
with its rivals than on the realization of its program. . . .
A dictatorship can be wrested from the hands of dictators only by a
new revolution. . . .
These people . . . are ready to lie to everybody in order to organize a
strong party. . . . They are ready to exploit their own friends and
comrades in order to convert them into tools of their plans; they are
ready to defend with words the most complete independence and
autonomy of persons and groups, while at the same time they organize
a most resolute secret dictatorship and habituate their followers to the
most sheep-like unreasoning obedience. As if a social revolution could
be consummated by a union of exploiters and exploited, by a group of

9 Alexander Hertzen, *Complete Collection of Works and Letters* (Moscow, 1923),
vol. XX, p. 132. (In French and Russian.)
10 Thomas G. Masaryk, *op. cit.*, vol. I, p. 406.
11 *Ibid.*, vol. II, p. 40.

people who at every step repudiate by deed what they preach by word. . . .

The truth and solidarity of a new socialist order cannot be based on falsehood and hypocrisy, on the exploitation of some people by others, on the manipulation of the principles which must serve as the foundation of the new order, on the meek submission of groups to certain leaders. . . .

We remain true to the maxim: "Falsehood cannot be the means for the dissemination of truth, nor the authoritarian rule of a person the means for the realization of justice." [12]

These clear and honest democratic voices from the eighteen-fifties, -sixties, and -seventies are wholly silent in the Russia of today. They have been stilled by the political police, the prisons, and the forced-labor camps of the "new order" for which generations of revolutionists gave their lives. Hertzen, Chernyshevsky, Lavrov, and their associates have no articulate successors in the Soviet Union.

All of this and much more constituted the Russian revolutionary inheritance of Lenin. Then at eighteen years of age he began to study Marx and was entranced by the sweep, grandeur, and power of his ideas. He seems to have accepted without a struggle the Marxian theory of the universe, interpretation of history, conception of the state, doctrine of the class struggle, faith in the industrial proletariat, and vision of an ideal society. The unsentimental and inflexible realism of this body of thought, clothed in the authoritative terms and sanctions of science, appealed to him. And, although he made his selections from Russian traditions, he never renounced or surrendered his Russian inheritance. As Ruth Fischer has said, "Wherever he dwelt, Lenin lived in Russia."

That Lenin possessed one of the truly great creative minds of history is clear. But, in spite of the official Soviet view carefully cultivated in Moscow today, his greatness did not lie in the realm of profound theoretical analysis and thought. He was neither a great scholar nor an original thinker in the fields of history,

---

[12] Peter Lavrov, *To the Russian Social Revolutionary Youth on the Brochure — "Problems of Revolutionary Propaganda in Russia"* (London, 1874), pp. 42–46. (In Russian.)

science, and philosophy. He was essentially a practical man. He hated the tyranny of the old order with all of his being, possessed a deep passion for justice and equality, and dedicated his life to the seizure of power in the name and the interests of the masses of the people. He was a revolutionist. Here he was the master, standing head and shoulders over all his contemporaries. His mind was a powerful and discriminating magnet which drew to itself whatever was relevant to its purposes. Every idea, even the most abstract, was viewed from the standpoint of the revolution and was therefore espoused or combated with the heat of partisan politics. To him education, literature, art, science, and philosophy were "partisan" in the "Party" meaning of the term. From youth to the day of his death he lived, worked, battled, thought, and dreamed for the revolution. Nothing else really mattered to him, although he seems to have sustained a tender affection for the members of his immediate family through all the vicissitudes of the struggle to overthrow the old order and build the new. Also he seems to have had a capacity for friendship and human understanding. Lenin's genius resides in the fact that he mastered both his Russian revolutionary heritage and the doctrines of international revolutionary socialism, and brought them into a masterly synthesis which transformed and continues to transform his country, which shook and continues to shake the world.

His central achievement was the creation of the Bolshevik Party — a revolutionary instrument or weapon for the conquest of power without peer in history. Totally rejecting the anarchist doctrine of individual terror and completely disregarding the vague, violent, and undisciplined ideological sputterings of Bakunin, Lenin seized upon his idea and the idea of Pestel of a closely organized company of professional revolutionists and proceeded to arm it with the doctrines of Marx in their most extreme form. Or rather perhaps he proceeded to capture the All-Russian Social Democratic Labor Party with its Marxian ideology and to recast it in the organizational image of the proposals of the terrorists. Thus, although in life Bakunin and Marx quarrelled bitterly on almost every occasion that brought them together, in death they formed a close partnership, thanks to the genius of Lenin. The fact that the Soviet leaders seek to trace their ancestry back to the great liberal and humanist leaders of eighteenth- and nineteenth-century Russia, such as Radishchev, Hertzen, Belinsky, Chernyshevsky, and Dobroliubov, does not obscure the full lineage of Lenin. Although he undoubtedly was influenced by these men, he also expressed his admiration for Tkachev and even Nechaiev. The All-Union Communist Party in its operations constitutes a union of some of the most evil elements of the Russian revolutionary tradition under the banners of the best.

By the time Lenin was thirty-two years of age he had formulated the essence of what has since come to be known as Leninism. In his brochure, *What Is to Be Done*, published in 1902, and in his numerous other writings of the period, he laid the theoretical foundations of the Party which fifteen years later would seize power in Russia in the name of the proletariat and which under Stalin's direction would be forged into a mighty instrument for controlling the thought and action of the Soviet people and of the Communist Parties of the world. In this work he aligned himself definitely and finally with that Russian revolutionary tradition which placed faith in a highly compact minority of professional revolutionists who alone would be qualified to direct the struggle and build the new order. He argued that the working class is quite unable by itself to know its own interests and that consequently it must submit to the leadership and guidance of a self-chosen revolutionary élite. He saw this élite organized in hierarchical fashion with power at the centre.

With his ideas fully matured, Lenin proceeded to devote his indefatigable energies and his matchless genius for political manipulation to the capture of the All-Russian Social Democratic Labor Party. He laid his lines well and thoroughly to insure the triumph of his conceptions at the Second Congress of the Party which was held in Brussels and London in 1903. He made every effort to get as many delegates as possible devoted to himself and worked over his strategy and tactics to the last detail. Finding himself in a minority on early and crucial ballots, he succeeded in obtaining the passage of certain motions which so offended the members of two groups in the Congress that they withdrew. By these maneuvers, whose purpose was probably understood only by himself, he was able to triumph in the end. The result was the division of the Party into two factions, the Bolshevik and the Menshevik, two Russian terms meaning majority and minority respectively. The breach was never healed, and eventually Lenin built out of his fictitious majority the organization which he led to power successfully in 1917.

At the Congress, Lenin revealed certain traits which he transmitted in exaggerated form to his successor and which came to mark the Communist Party everywhere. He was absolutely sure of the correctness of his position, attacked his opponents with bitter invective, regarded any manipulation of persons or groups as justifiable, accepted a majority decision only when it was to his advantage, and knew that he and he alone spoke for the masses of the people. This meant that if he was in the minority in any counting of votes, he still was confident that his minority was in actuality the majority. He would have used the "veto" so dear to Molotov and Vishinsky without hesitation and with a clear conscience. He adjusted himself to the power factors in a situation, but only as a tactic, never modifying his ultimate objective, the seizure of power for himself. He tended to regard his political adversaries as enemies without rights. In spite of his acquaintance with the intellectual life of Western Europe, he was an absolutist in the tradition of the Russian autocracy. Incidentally it was at this Congress that by his methods he alienated forever his closest friend — Jules Martov. Yet to the end of his days, utterly unlike Stalin, he cherished an affection for his old comrade and could exclaim shortly before his death: "What a pity Martov is not with us! What a wonderful comrade Martov is!" He seemed to have retained a touch of "bourgeois" liberalism and humanity.

In that final struggle for power in 1917 he was guided by only one consideration — victory. He resorted to every stratagem, he made promises he never intended to keep, he preached loyalty to democratic processes when that was politically expedient, and frankly repudiated those processes when they did not serve his ends. By attacking the Provisional Government in the summer and autumn of 1917 for its tardiness in calling for the democratic election of a Constituent Assembly for the purpose of writing a constitution for the new republic, he rallied millions of people from all revolutionary elements to the Bolshevik standard. Then, after destroying the Provisional Government by force of arms and after reluctantly ordering the election, he dispersed the Assembly by the same means, because he found his Party in a decided minority. In this election of November 25, the only relatively free election ever held in Russia either before or after the Revolution, the Bolsheviks received but nine million out of a total of thirty-six million votes. The Social Revolutionary Party, the great peasant party, obtained a clear majority with almost twenty-one million. The Assembly convened according to schedule on January 18, but failed to survive through the second day.

The doctrine implicit in *What Is to Be Done* was now made utterly explicit by deed. Also at this time Lenin supplied the words in a language which no one could fail to understand. Having established the dictatorship, he proceeded to justify it. In April, 1918, he wrote: "There is absolutely no contradiction in principle between the Soviet (that is, socialist) democracy and the assumption of dictatorial powers by particular individuals. . . . *Absolute submission* to a single will, for the purpose of achieving success in work, organized on the pattern of large machine industry, is unquestionably necessary." [13] And again in the same statement: "We must learn to combine democratic discussion of the toiling masses with *iron* discipline during work, with *absolute obedience* to one person." [14] A year later, in October, 1919, in a message of "Greetings to Italian, French, and German Communists," he could say: "Only scoundrels and half-wits can think that the proletariat must first win a majority of votes in elections conducted under *bourgeois oppression*, under the *oppression of hired slavery*, and only then seek to win power. This is the height

13 V. I. Lenin, *Collected Works* (Moscow, 1921?), vol. XV, p. 218. (In Russian.)
14 *Ibid.*, pp. 220–21.

of stupidity and hypocrisy." [15] In defining dictatorship in the autumn of 1920 Lenin said that "dictatorship . . . means unlimited power resting on force and not on law." [16]

The strategy and tactics employed by Lenin in the entire struggle for power in the summer and autumn of 1917 recalled to more than one mind the violent and conspiratorial pattern of the Russian revolutionary tradition. Joseph Goldenberg, a former member of the Bolshevik Central Committee, doubtless expressed the thought of many when he responded in these words to one of Lenin's speeches:

> The place so long vacant, the place once occupied by the famous anarchist Bakunin, who has had no heir for decades, is now filled. Everything we have just heard here is a complete repudiation of the entire Social Democratic doctrine, of the whole theory of scientific Marxism. Here anarchism has been clearly and distinctly proclaimed. Its spokesman, the heir of Bakunin, is Lenin. Lenin the Social Democrat, Lenin the Marxist, Lenin the leader of our militant Social Democratic Party, is gone. A new Lenin has been born — Lenin the anarchist.[17]

After seizing power, Lenin was prepared to employ any methods whatsoever to hold it. In a pamphlet completed in October, 1917, he argued that if the Tsar could rule Russia with his 130,000 aristocrats and landlords, the Bolsheviks should be able to do so with their 240,000 members. As an instrument of rule he and his associates created the Cheka, or secret police, somewhat in the image of the Okhrana of the Tsar, and charged it with the double task of crushing every sign of organized opposition and of spreading panic among all dissident or hostile elements. While rejecting the method of individual terror of the nihilists, on grounds of expediency rather than of morals, the Bolsheviks in their struggle to seize and hold power supported and practiced mass terror. The policy was clearly stated by M. Latsis, one of the chiefs of the Cheka. "We are not waging war against particular individuals,"

15 *Ibid.* (Moscow, 1922), vol. XVI, p. 336.
16 *Ibid.* (Moscow, 1923), vol. XVII, p. 355.
17 Vladimir Bonch-Bruevich, *Lenin in Russia* (Moscow, 1925), p. 27. (In Russian.)

he said. "We are exterminating the bourgeoisie as a class. Don't look for evidence to prove that the accused acted by deed or word against the Soviet power. The first question you should ask him is: To what class he belongs, what is his origin, his education, his training, and his profession? This should determine the fate of the accused. Herein lies the meaning and the 'essence of the Red Terror.' " [18] Although the organization has changed its name a number of times, its functions, methods, and spirit have remained essentially unchanged down to the present moment. To be sure, it has increased in size until its members now constitute an army of half a million, thus making its forerunner under the tsars with its one thousand agents appear to be merely a terroristic gesture. And today, as the MVD, it extends its operations into almost all countries.

It has often been said that the Party and the men and women who founded the Soviet state had no ethics. This of course is incorrect. Their ethics was that of the conspiratorial tradition of Bakunin, Nechaiev, and Tkachev, given direction by the class-struggle conception of Marx and sanctified by an avowed passionate devotion to the cause of human liberation. Communist morality is the morality of war and conflict under which the enemy is to be literally destroyed. "We say," wrote Lenin, "that our morality is subjected entirely to the interests of the class struggle of the proletariat. Our morality is derived from the interests of the class struggle of the proletariat." [19] More specifically, "We say that morality is that which serves to destroy the old exploiting society and to unite all toilers around the proletariat which is creating the new Communist society." [20]

In responding to the question in April, 1920, "Should revolutionists Work in Reactionary Trade Unions?" Lenin declared that Bolsheviks must "work wherever the masses are." "One must be prepared," he said, "to make all kinds of sacrifices and over-

18 S. P. Melgunov, *"The Red Terror" in Russia 1918–1923* (Berlin, 1924), p. 72. (In Russian.)
19 V. I. Lenin, *Collected Works* (Moscow, 1923), vol. XVII, p. 321. (In Russian.)
20 *Ibid.*, p. 323.

come the greatest obstacles, in order to propagandize and agitate systematically, stubbornly, persistently, and patiently, precisely in those institutions, associations, and unions, even the most reactionary, where there is a proletarian or semi-proletarian mass. . . . One must be prepared . . . in case of necessity, even to resort to all kinds of tricks and ruses, to employ illegal measures, secretiveness, and concealment of truth in order to penetrate into trade unions, to remain in them, and to conduct Communist work in them at any cost." [21]

Applying these basic principles to the question of the world revolution, Lenin concludes: "If war is waged by the exploiting class with the object of strengthening its class rule, such a war is a criminal war, and 'defencism' in *such* a war is a base betrayal of socialism. If war is waged by the proletariat after it has conquered the bourgeoisie in its own country, and is waged with the object of strengthening and extending socialism, such a war is legitimate and 'holy'." [22] Communist morality is the morality of the tribe applied to a class, then to a party, and finally to a central committee or bureau. There is no reason whatsoever for believing that the present rulers of the Soviet Union have softened this ethics of the barricade and the battle in the slightest. Indeed, the founder of Bolshevism was probably much more sensitive to the rights of man in the eighteenth- and nineteenth-century sense than the collective mind of the Politburo today.

In 1918 the Bolshevik wing of the Russian Social Democratic Party reached maturity and became the All-Union Communist Party of Bolsheviks. The following year, having failed in its effort to capture the Socialist or Second International, it founded the Third International and through the various national parties carried this whole pattern of revolutionary action and morals, the pattern of Bakunin, Nechaiev, and Tkachev, the pattern of Lenin, the pattern of a Russified Marx, into nearly all countries of the earth. This tragic measure divided the labor and liberal forces of

21 *Ibid.*, pp. 144, 145.
22 V. I. Lenin, *Selected Works* (New York), vol. VII, p. 357. (In English. Translated by the Marx-Engels-Lenin Institute.)

the world and was probably responsible for bringing Hitler to power. As the International grew, its dependence on Moscow became ever more complete until by the end of the twenties it was little more than an organ of Soviet foreign policy. Indeed, from almost the very beginning the men of the Kremlin have been able to seat and unseat at will the leaders of the various national parties. That the case of Tito, head of a state and commander of his own army and police though he is, constitutes an exception remains to be proved. It would seem quite probable that the doctrine of centralism for which Lenin fought with such skill and tenacity has triumphed above his expectations. At any rate, the whole world is now paying for the age-old tyranny and stupidity of Russian absolutism.

The power of Lenin's genius has been felt far beyond the borders of his own country in yet another form. In a number of countries the conception of a closely organized party of revolutionists dedicated to the twofold task of seizing power and rebuilding the fatherland has taken root. Two outstanding examples are those of Mustafa Kemal in Turkey and Sun Yat Sen in China. And counter-revolutionists seemed to find the ideas of Lenin equally good. Both Benito Mussolini and Adolf Hitler borrowed heavily from the principles and the methods of the All-Union Communist Party. Under the reign of Stalin, the Bolsheviks in their turn have learned much from the fascist dictators. Thus has backward Russia, through the person and genius of Lenin and his successors, cast her lengthening shadow over the entire world.

4

Following the death of Lenin in 1924, the leadership of the Party passed swiftly and inexorably into the hands of Joseph Vissarionovich Djugashvili. Prior to 1917 and for several years thereafter, this man was looked upon as a secondary figure among the revolutionary leaders, scarcely to be compared with such giants as Trotsky, Radek, Bucharin, Zinoviev, and Kamenev. Indeed, he was regarded with a measure of scorn and contempt by these men, partly because he had shown little talent for theoretical formulation, partly because he had never lived abroad and participated in the intellectual life of European socialism, and partly because his methods of operation as a revolutionist suggested even to his scarcely supersensitive comrades the mentality of an ordinary bandit. For being implicated in a bank robbery in 1907 in the interests of the Revolution, he was actually forced out of the Party for a time. Moreover, by the side of the brilliant and arrogant Trotsky he appeared in sombre colors. A common estimation of Stalin's powers was given in private conversation in 1929 by one of the foremost intellectual members of the Party. When asked how this successor of the great Lenin was regarded, he replied: "We think he is above the average."

But Djugashvili had christened himself Stalin, meaning "steel." The entire world now knows that this was not a meaningless or boastful gesture. It would be difficult to find a more appropriate name for the man who stepped into the shoes of Lenin and in the course of time came, not only to overshadow the founder of the Soviet state, but also to re-create that man in his own image. In the bitter struggle for power after the death of Lenin and in the conduct of domestic and foreign policy during the most critical period of Russian and world history, he has shown himself to possess the strength, the hardness, and the resilience of tempered steel. Patient, tireless, cunning, bold, and ruthless, tenacious of purpose and persevering in effort, skilled in the uses of rewards and punishments, master of organizational strategy and tactics, avowed pupil and disciple of Lenin, Stalin quickly vanquished all his rivals. As Secretary of the Party he put Machiavelli to shame in the refinement of the art of grasping and holding power. Most of the men whom he sent to the execution chamber were more brilliant intellectually than he, but while they talked and debated in the manner of their doctrinaire past, he took the Party firmly into his hands. His central achievement, however, lies not in his

triumph as an individual, but rather in the new direction which
he gave to the Russian Revolution and the Soviet state.

The migration of Marxian doctrines to the land of the tsars, as
we have seen, led to the development of a unique revolutionary
movement — neither wholly Marxian nor wholly Russian, but an
amalgam of the two. Lenin took the harsher features of revolutionary socialism and linked them with the more violent and
tyrannical revolutionary traditions of old Russia. In a sense Stalin
continued the work of Lenin by taking the harsher features of his
teachings and completing the Russification of Marx and Engels.
It is a measure of Stalin's genius that he has achieved a synthesis
of Leninism with the two most powerful and dynamic political
tendencies of the old empire — national expansion and Messianic
vision. And as he accomplished this incredible feat, he not only
maintained but even strengthened the world Communist movement. He succeeded in transferring the loyalty of millions in
foreign lands from a noble international conception to the policies
of the Soviet Union and its leadership. And in the arena of world
affairs he pursued a policy, whether by chance or by design, that
led to the division of the "camp of capitalism" and the total
elimination for a period of the three most aggressive great "capitalist states" and the decisive weakening of two others. In his
speech at the meeting of representatives of European Communist
Parties in Poland toward the end of September, 1947, George
Malenkov, member of the Politburo and Secretary of the Central
Committee, announced boastfully: "The wise Stalinist foreign
policy of the Soviet state both before the war and during the war
enabled us to use correctly the contradictions within the camp of
imperialism. This was one of the important conditions of our
victory in the war." [23]

No sooner was Stalin firmly established in power than he
launched a program for the rewriting of Russian history. Naturally this involved first of all a revision of the account of the period
of the rise of the Bolsheviks and the growth of Soviet power, and

[23] George Malenkov, *Informational Report on the Activity of the Central Committee of the All-Union Communist Party* (Moscow, 1947), p. 34. (In Russian.)

particularly the glorification of Stalin and the degradation of his opponents. But the new policy went much further. The practice followed by the first leaders of the revolution of repudiating national patriotism and of presenting prerevolutionary Russia in darkest colors was gradually abandoned. The word for mother-land became one of the most sacred words in the language, love of country was raised to the exalted position of the most important element in the moral education of the young, and the entire Russian past was recovered and clothed in garments of grandeur. Every figure of that past, whether tsar, soldier, statesman or admin-istrator, explorer, scientist, educator, writer, or artist, who had shed lustre on Russian genius or increased the power of the Russian state, was brought into the gallery of heroes.

The measure and character of this reversal are clearly revealed in the unqualified rehabilitation of Ivan IV, who in life violated most of the Ten Commandments and in death was called the "Terrible," even under the despotism of the empire. The current interpretation is given briefly in an official history textbook pub-lished in 1945 and used throughout the country in the eighth grade. "Ivan IV," so runs the summation, "died . . . in 1584. He was a talented and wise man. He was well-educated for his time; he loved and knew how to write; he had a sharp and fine mind. In both domestic and foreign policy he formulated his aims cor-rectly and clearly, and pursued them with tenacity and persever-ance. His recognition of the necessity of possessing the shores of the Baltic reveals his great vision." The failure of the world-renowned moving-picture director, Sergei Eisenstein, to sense or at least to recognize in his work, this complete reversal in the estima-tion of Ivan IV led to his disgrace and possibly to his death.

All through the nineteenth century the question of the rôle of Russia in history weighed heavily on the hearts and minds of the great leaders of Russian thought. Looking out on Slavic isolation, backwardness, and tyranny and conscious of the cultural riches and political traditions of the West, they oscillated back and forth between irrational hope and irrational despair. On the one hand, some of these men saw salvation for their country only in complete

Westernization; while, on the other hand, certain of them were confident that Russia alone could bring salvation to Europe. Not infrequently the same individual would find himself in both camps at different times or moments in his life. The outlook of the Westerners was expressed in the early part of the century with a power that shook the entire intellectual and official world by Peter Chaadaev (1794–1856), a young writer and aristocrat. In a letter to a friend in 1829 he wrote despairingly:

Historical experience does not exist for us; generations and centuries have passed without profit to us. It would seem that the general law of mankind does not apply to us. We alone have given nothing to the world, and have taught it nothing. We have not added a single idea to the human heritage; we have assisted in no way the progress of the human mind; and we have distorted everything we have received from this progress. From the first moment of our social existence, we have done nothing for the general welfare of people; not one useful thought has been born on the barren soil of our motherland; not one great truth has issued from our midst; we have not produced a single invention, and from the inventions of others we have adopted only deceptive outward form and useless luxury.

It is a strange phenomenon: even in the world of science, which embraces everything, our history touches nothing, clarifies nothing, proves nothing. If the wild hordes, which troubled the world, had not passed through the land in which we live before sweeping on toward the West, scarcely one page in world history would have been devoted to us. If we were not spread from the Bering Straits to the Oder, we would not have been noticed.[24]

Many of the revolutionary leaders belonged in the camp of the Westerners. Hertzen, Chernyshevsky, and Lavrov could certainly be classed among them. Also of course the followers of Marx and Engels, the leaders of the Russian Social Democratic Labor Party, both the Mensheviks and the Bolsheviks, Axelrod, Plekhanov, and Martov, Lenin, Trotsky, and Bucharin. The October Revolution appeared to mark the definite triumph of the West.

[24] M. Gershenzon, *P. Ia. Chaadaev — Life and Thought* (St. Petersburg, 1908), p. 215. (In Russian.)

The contrary current, however, runs deep in Russian history. A sense of divine or historic mission seems to have brooded over Russia ever since she became aware of herself in the fifteenth century. In its religious form this Messianic note was struck by a Russian monk after the fall of Constantinople. "Two Romes have fallen and have passed away," he said, "the western and the eastern; destiny has prescribed for Moscow the position of the third Rome; there will never be a fourth." [25] The nineteenth century witnessed the flowering of this ancient tradition in "Slavophilism" and "Panslavism." Not a few of the first minds of Russia were attracted to these doctrines, were moved by a mystical faith in their land, proclaimed the Russians to be youthful in vigor and unspoiled by civilization, excoriated the "decadent" influences from the West, and declared that Russia would save the world. One of them, S. P. Shevyrev (1806–64), a literary historian, coined the formula, now a part of official Party doctrine: "The West is putrescent." In his eyes "Western civilization was poisonous, and the West was a predestined corpse whose deathlike odor already tainted the air." [26]

In the second volume of his celebrated "Diary," written in the late seventies, Dostoievsky turns again and again to the theme of Russia's glorious destiny in words which reflect the spirit of the pronouncements of the Central Committee of the Party in the present "great Stalinist epoch." He asserts that "the Slavic idea" is beginning "to kindle and shine with unprecedented and never-heard-of light" and that it will perhaps provide the "solution of European and human destinies." And he challenges the spokesmen of Europe: "Can they — these uppish, learned and strong ones — comprehend and presume, be it only in fantasy, that perhaps Russia has been predestined and created for their own salvation, and that it is she which, perhaps, will finally utter this word of salvation?"

The Slavophils, under the romantic spell of Rousseau and Herder, interpreted Russian backwardness as an asset and re-

25 Thomas G. Masaryk, op. cit., vol. I, p. 41.
26 Ibid., p. 309.

garded the Russians as "the chosen people, fresh and uncorrupted, competent with undiminished energies to carry on the task of civilization." To them the "Russian muzhik was the Messiah" embodying these qualities. Masaryk thus defines the essence of this powerful cultural strain:

The Russians were thoroughly competent to become leaders and saviours of mankind; the nations of Europe could follow Russia willingly; their needs would be fully understood by the Russians. In Dostoevskii's interpretation of Slavophil Messianism, Russian comprehensive humanity is to be something very different from a Babylonian welter of the nations. The one and only Russian people would be representative, leader, and saviour of mankind — and would naturally be master as well, for Europe must not forget that Russia is the sixth continent; and . . . before so very long will dispose of 500,000,000 men, destined in due course to become 1,000,000,000.[27]

Under the leadership of Stalin this sense of divine mission of Russia, which many thought was buried in 1917, has been recovered and incorporated into the Soviet apocalyptic vision. So today, when contemporary Soviet writers and political leaders speak of "the great historic mission of the Soviet people," as they do in an unbroken chorus, they are marching in an ancient and persistent Russian tradition. They never tire of quoting as a prophecy already fulfilled a statement attributed to the great Russian writer, Vissarion Belinsky, himself a Westerner, in 1840: "We envy our grandchildren and great-grandchildren who are destined to see Russia in 1940 standing at the head of the civilized world, giving laws to science and art, and receiving reverent tribute from all enlightened humanity." Stalin has succeeded in identifying the Marxian Party of Lenin, not only with Russian nationalism, but also with the Slavic sense of mission and high destiny. The documents presented in this volume are saturated with this Messianic outlook.

The instrument through which this curious amalgam of revolutionary and counter-revolutionary, national and international,

27 *Ibid.*, pp. 320–21.

purposes is being and is to be wrought is the All-Union Communist Party of Bolsheviks. And here again Stalin, while obviously continuing the work of Lenin, has placed on the Party his own peculiar and powerful stamp. When Lenin was establishing the dictatorship of the Party in the name of the "dictatorship of the proletariat," he never made wholly explicit his ultimate intentions or expectations. For how long a period he anticipated the dictatorship would endure, he failed to state. In the light of the entire record of his thought, which of course contained many contradictions, one is justified in concluding that he regarded it only as the instrument for seizing power and consolidating the revolutionary position. It seems quite unlikely that he ever considered it an enduring feature of the new socialist society. In fact, in 1905 he took this stand without qualification. "He who wishes to proceed to Socialism by any path, other than political democracy," he wrote, "inevitably arrives at absurd and reactionary conclusions, both in the political and the economic sense." [28] Also, "without political freedom," he said, "all forms of workers' representation will continue to be a fraud. The proletariat will remain as heretofore in prison." But all this perhaps merely means that Lenin was either in conflict with himself or did not really know what kind of seed he was planting in those early years when he was elaborating his revolutionary ideas.

During the sharp crisis following the Congress of 1903, Trotsky, in a bitter attack on the apparent tendency of Lenin's position, wrote prophetically: "The organization of the Party takes the place of the Party itself; the Central Committee takes the place of the organization; and finally the dictator takes the place of the Central Committee." [29] Under Stalin this prophecy of Trotsky seems to have been fulfilled. At any rate, for all practical purposes the Party dictatorship now appears to be a permanent feature of the Soviet system. It is the instrument by which Stalin and his associates maintain themselves in power, exercise control over the

28 V. I. Lenin, *Works* (Moscow, 1935), vol. VIII, third edition, p. 41. (In Russian.)
29 Bertram Wolfe, *Three Who Made a Revolution* (New York, 1948), p. 253.

entire Soviet people, and drive the Russian state and the world Communist movement toward some unknown destination.

The grip of the high command on the Party membership and on the Soviet people generally has been immeasurably increased since Stalin came to power. The Party has been purged, is being purged, and will be purged of all "unstable and disloyal elements." The political police has been vastly enlarged and organized into a network which holds the entire population, and particularly the armed forces, under close surveillance. The internal passport system has been greatly tightened and movement from place to place and from occupation to occupation put under severe restrictions. The camps of forced or slave labor to which political dissidents, along with common criminals, are sent for "re-education in the spirit of socialist labor" have been expanded beyond recognition and have become an integral and important part of Soviet economy. So carefully is travel controlled and limited that the full reach and magnitude of this system remain obscure even to the average Soviet citizen. But by piecing together scraps of evidence from this source and that, and particularly from the repatriated Poles who in 1939 and 1940 were arrested and sent to these camps in hundreds of thousands, the student may safely place the estimate of prisoners between five and fifteen millions.

The ancient practice of tyranny of holding the members of a family responsible for the acts of one another was introduced by governmental decree on June 8, 1934. This decree was directed at preventing "desertion or flight across the border by a member of the military services." The substance of the decree reads as follows:

All members of his family who are of age, provided they in any way aided the contemplated or accomplished treason, or even knew of it and failed to notify the Soviet authorities, are punished by imprisonment for five to ten years and confiscation of all their property.

The remaining members of the family of the traitor who are of age and reside with him or were dependent on his support at the time of the commission of the crime are deprived of electoral rights and are subject to exile for five years to remote regions of Siberia.[30]

The All-Union Communist Party of course is not a political party at all in the sense in which the term is used in democratic states. It rules neither on the authority nor with the consent of the people. Like its predecessor of the empire, it can be dislodged only by violent revolution. In general structure and mode of operation it is a kind of political army. Following the plan of Pestel with amazing precision, it has its three levels or circles of membership: it has its common soldiers, its commissioned and non-commissioned officers, its high command. The duty of the soldiers and officers is to carry out the orders of the high command. The latter consists of the fourteen members of the Politburo and the seventy-two members of the Central Committee. In Lenin's time the operation of the Party was supposed to proceed under the principle of "democratic centralism." According to this principle all policies would be fully discussed by the rank and file in the thousands of cells which constitute the base of the organization. Thereafter delegates would be chosen presumably to represent the members at regularly called Party congresses and the policies adopted would be binding on the entire membership. Under Stalin this entire process has been abandoned, and even reversed. The last congress convened in the spring of 1939. And if another congress should be called in the near future, as promised, one may be certain that every delegate will be carefully picked by the leadership and will support without qualification the basic policies of Stalin and the Politburo.

Under this system of control there can be no *public* discussion of grand policy, either foreign or domestic. Such policy is discussed and formulated by the Party high command, and is then commonly given to the world in the form of a resolution by the Central Committee. It is thereafter the function of the other members of this political army to carry the policy to the people, to explain and argue, to persuade and cajole, to secure the adop-

[30] *Izvestia*, June 9, 1934.

tion of resolutions of approval, and to prevent the emergence of any kind of organized opposition. The press, the radio, and all media of communication, education, literature, art, and the entire cultural apparatus are made to serve the same purpose. The Soviet citizen reads and listens in vain for the slightest criticism of any policy adopted by the central organs of the Party. This monolithic system of control will be laid entirely bare in the materials to be presented in subsequent chapters.

The system constitutes a remarkably effective instrument for controlling the thought of the two hundred million people of the Soviet Union and of the other millions of Party members and fellow travellers throughout the world. It is at the same time an equally effective instrument for waging the present cold war against the West in general and the United States in particular. The Soviet leaders need never take the Soviet people into their confidence on any matters which they desire to conceal from the rest of the world. They can reverse their policies in an instant, without any prior explanation or preparation whatsoever, and carry their people with them. Their ability to do this was demonstrated beyond question in the case of the Soviet-Nazi Pact. A position that had been propagated for years through the entire cultural apparatus was reversed without warning and apparently with complete success. The Soviet leaders can march right up to the edge of the precipice of war and then draw back without the slightest fear of public opinion. The entire population is thoroughly indoctrinated with the idea that Stalin and the Party are never wrong. In the present cold war the necessarily clumsy, faltering, and public methods of a democracy place it at a great disadvantage. It can have really no inkling of what the policy of its adversary will be tomorrow morning, yet it must expose its own motives and plans to the gaze of the whole world.

In some fundamental respects the Russian Revolution appears now to have traversed a full cycle. In 1833 the Russian minister of education, Count Uvarov, announced that the work of the schools should be governed by three great ideas or conceptions — *Ortho-*

doxy, autocracy, and *patriotism.* Though the content of these terms has changed, the pattern remains remarkably the same. Certainly neither loyalty to Russia nor loyalty to the Church was propagated as fiercely and systematically under the empire as loyalty to the Soviet motherland and loyalty to the Party are propagated today. And the cultivation of utter devotion to "our dear father and teacher, our own beloved Comrade Stalin," far exceeds anything to be found under the old régime. An aura of ineffable sanctity surrounds the name and person of Stalin. And by the rewriting of history the doctrine of purity of motive and infallibility of substance is attached to his every utterance.

5

The issue of war or peace and so the fate of all mankind rest in no small measure in the hands of the members of the high command of the All-Union Communist Party. This means the seventy-two members of the Central Committee, the fourteen members of the Politburo and, probably above all, Stalin himself. If the leaders of the democracies of the world could penetrate their secret councils and thus learn of their long-range plans and intentions, they could develop counter-measures in the light of wholly trustworthy knowledge. This of course is not possible. Yet from the record of these men it is not difficult to derive their basic traits of character and their controlling purposes. The literal survival of freedom on the earth may well depend on a correct analysis of the qualities of the members of the Politburo, by far the most powerful oligarchy of the contemporary world and one of the most powerful in history. Not only does decision rest with them; they also set by example the pattern of the "new Soviet man." Doubtless every younger member of the Central Committee, as well as many a youthful Communist, dreams fondly of being called to join this select company of men who hold the destiny of Russia and world Communism in their hands.

The members of the Politburo obviously possess in high degree four fateful traits of character. In the first place, they are able and vigorous. Though not as young as they were ten years ago, they are still, in comparison with men of corresponding responsibility in America, relatively youthful. Most of them were born into poor families and have had to work hard and endure from childhood. Also most of them were just reaching maturity at the time of the Revolution. They are consequently wholly identified with the Soviet order and know little of any other, past or present. They have achieved their positions of power first of all by hitching their wagons to Stalin's star, and also by dint of energy, industry, and ability. They are dangerous adversaries.

In the second place, they are thoroughly devoted to the cause of Soviet Communism. A much stronger word is probably more precise. Like the thousands who went before them in the revolutionary struggle, they are fanatics. They have no doubts regarding the truth of their doctrines of historical interpretation. By these doctrines and without examination they know that all current forms of "bourgeois" culture from humor to science are "decadent," simply because they must be. They know, too, that "capitalism" as a social system is on the way out and Communism is on the way in. They have no doubt of the righteousness of the cause in which they fight. They know that "capitalism" in its present stage is "putrid" and evil, and that Communism is good beyond anything that man has known. Indeed, they know that Communism is the perfect and final form of social organization and way of life. This means that they have no tolerance for contrary ideas and that they are ready to give everything they possess for the triumph of their cause. They regard both Lenin and Stalin as their models, of each of whom it could be said, as it was said of Lenin by his Menshevik opponent, Axelrod: "There is no other man who is absorbed by the revolution twenty-four hours a day, who has no other thoughts but the thought of revolution, and who, even when he sleeps, dreams of nothing but the revolution." [31]

[31] Bertram Wolfe, *op. cit.*, p. 229.

In the third place, these men are ruthless. Indeed, their fanaticism, which is complete, is only matched by their ruthlessness. Not infrequently in human history has the latter been associated with the former. Human life when put in the balance against Party doctrine and purpose means nothing to them. Knowing themselves to be absolutely right, they do not hesitate to resort to the most extreme measures. They did not hesitate at the time of the Revolution and later to invoke the "red terror"; they did not hesitate in the middle thirties to arrest and execute their former comrades-in-arms; they did not hesitate, following the recent war, to scatter several nationalities whose members had been insufficiently loyal at the time of the Hitler invasion — the Tatars of the Crimea, the Kalmucks of the lower Volga, and the Chechen and Ingushi of the North Caucasus. In the words of a resolution of the Supreme Soviet of the RSFSR (Russian Socialist Federated Soviet Republic) on June 25, 1946, "the Chechen and the Crimean Tatars were resettled in other regions of the USSR." The total population of the two autonomous republics was almost two million.

A most extraordinary exhibition of ruthlessness occurred in the early thirties as a part of the powerful drive toward the collectivization of agriculture. Millions of peasants were bitterly opposed to this measure, but they apparently could do nothing. They possessed neither bullets nor ballots, and of course they could not organize. One thing, however, they could do: they could and did refuse to plant their crops. The result was widespread starvation in some of the richest agricultural regions of the country. The Politburo let many of these recalcitrant peasants die as a disciplinary measure, and under the slogan of the "liquidation of the kulaks as a class" shipped vast numbers off to the labor camps of the North and East. Also they could and did slaughter their farm animals. And before the Party leadership relented, the peasants had reduced the number of horses by almost sixty per cent, the number of cattle by approximately fifty, the number of goats and sheep by more than sixty-five, and the number of hogs by over fifty-five.[32] Men who would thus pursue a policy to the very brink of disaster are not easily frightened — nor are they easily persuaded that they are wrong or mistaken.

This quality of ruthlessness combined with fanaticism is so crucial, and at the same time so difficult to comprehend in its fullness, that the case of the uprising in Warsaw in the summer of 1944 merits full recall by the entire free world. Perhaps no other incident in the history of Soviet Communism reveals more clearly the extremity to which the Politburo will go in the pursuit of its goals. The essential facts seem to be well established.

Toward the end of July, 1944, the Russian armies reached the outskirts of Praga, an eastern suburb of Warsaw. The leaders of the Polish underground in the city naturally saw the hour of liberation at hand and eagerly elaborated plans for an insurrection. But they hesitated because they believed that the uprising, if initially successful, could not be sustained longer than a week or ten days without assistance from the outside. This of course meant contact with the Soviet forces. Then on the evening of July 29, a three-hundred-word message in the Polish language was broadcast from a Moscow station. The message began as follows: "Appeal to Warsaw: Fight the Germans. No doubt Warsaw already hears the guns of the battle which is soon to bring her liberation." [33] The broadcast was made in the name of the Union of Polish Patriots, a Communist- and Moscow-dominated organization, and undoubtedly with the knowledge and on the authority of the Soviet Government. The following day, July 30, a second broadcast from Moscow renewed the appeal. "People of Warsaw, to arms!" it called. "The whole population should gather round the National Council and underground army. Attack the Germans. . . . Assist the Red Army in crossing the Vistula. Give it information and show it the best fords." [34]

With these assurances and with high hopes the people of War-

---

[32] *Sotsialisticheskoe Stroitelstvo SSSR* (Moscow, 1936), p. 354.
[33] Copy of the transcript is in the possession of the authors.
[34] *Manchester Guardian*, August 22, 1944.

saw and the Polish Home Army under the command of General Bor-Komorowski rose against the Germans at five o'clock on the afternoon of August 1. In the meantime Molotov had told the Polish Premier Stanislaw Mikolajczyk, then in Moscow, that the Red Army would enter Warsaw on August 6. Under such auspices it seemed that the uprising would certainly be crowned with success. But the Soviet forces stood immobile at the gates of Warsaw, watched the slaughter of a quarter-million men, women, and children, and prevented the British and American air forces from bringing more than symbolic aid to the defenders of the city. With unsurpassed valor and heroism the Poles fought until October 3, 1944, when lack of food and supplies forced capitulation. There can be only one explanation of this extraordinary behavior of the Russian "Ally": The Politburo actually desired the destruction of the Polish Home Army so that the way would be cleared for the triumph of the Soviet-dominated Lublin Committee of National Liberation. By this maneuver the Nazi armies were employed to remove one of the obstacles to the march of Soviet power to the Elbe and beyond.[35]

In the fourth place, the members of the Politburo are realistic. At any rate, they claim realism as one of their virtues. By this they mean one thing and one thing only. They will change a policy when and only when, if and only if, the power factors in the situation change. This trait is revealed clearly in the great shifts in both foreign and domestic policy since the Revolution. The principle of course works both ways. If the power factors turn against them, they will make concessions; but if the power factors shift in their favor, they will expect to reap a corresponding reward. Apparently a major reason for the falling-out between Hitler and Stalin in the autumn of 1940 was the fact that the latter demanded a revision of their Pact to his advantage because the power factors had changed in his favor, Britain having survived the Nazi air attack. But it must be remembered that these

---

[35] See Arthur Bliss Lane, "The Incredible Crime," chapter III in *I saw Poland Betrayed* (New York, 1948).

men are the foremost students of power in the world today and are therefore not likely to be fooled to their detriment. The danger lies in the possibility that their ignorance of the outside world and their fanatical devotion to doctrine may blind them to the realities in the international situation.

CHAPTER TWO

THE SOVIET APOCALYPSE

THE MEN who shape the policies of the Soviet Union are able, fanatical, ruthless, and realistic. Offspring of a strange union of historic conditions and forces, including Russian absolutism, Russian nationalism, Russian Messianism, Russian revolutionary traditions, and Marxian ideas and doctrines, they were badly misunderstood before the war, during the war, and after the war by American statesmen and even by the more sophisticated political leaders of the countries of Western Europe. If the free world is to survive, its representatives must understand these men, not only their traits of character, but also their controlling ideas, fundamental allegiances, and ultimate purposes. At present, owing in part to sheer ignorance and in part to Communist manipulation, the American mind is confused on the "Russian question." A retrospective glance may prove instructive.

From 1917 to 1941 the common American attitude toward the Russian Revolution and the Soviet system embraced conflicting elements of fear, suspicion, and hostility, wonder, condescension, and contempt. During the war years this attitude was swiftly transformed. Organizations for sending relief to the Russian people and for promoting friendship between the two countries were launched under most benign auspices. Ardent defenders of the Soviets appeared in the most unexpected places and good will flourished. Joseph Stalin became "good old Uncle Joe," the Soviet Union "our great Russian ally," and even the American Communist Party a "dependable fighter against fascism." After the Teheran Conference, Earl Browder was "prepared to clasp the hand" of J. P. Morgan, even though the Wall Street banker was in his grave at the time. And apparently most thoughtful men and women hoped and believed that the old rift between America and Russia, which had played its rôle in the bringing of the war, was at last being closed.

Today, in the fourth year after the defeat of Germany and Japan, one can scarcely recapture the spirit of good will which prevailed so generally as the armies of Hitler were being ground to bits under co-ordinated blows from the East and the West. The "Fortune Survey" for January, 1945, reflects not only this spirit, but also the strong optimism then prevalent regarding the post-war years. According to this poll almost fifty per cent of the American people thought that relations with Russia would be better in the future than in the past, twenty that they would remain "about the same," and twenty-two that they would get worse. About ten per cent had no opinion. The corresponding figures reflecting American opinion on England were thirty-one, forty-three, nineteen, and seven per cent. Difficult to comprehend under the Marxian formula is the fact that optimism was highest in the two upper income groups. Fifty-six per cent of proprietors of business and sixty-one per cent of professional and executive people expected relations with Russia to improve. A more detailed survey reported in September of the same year showed Russia to have most friends among American businessmen and fewest among the "proletariat." A study of the press based on the method of balanced sampling for the period from February to June revealed sixty per cent of the relevant editorials to be "favorable" toward the Soviets. In commenting on this point, *Fortune* observed that "such a margin, Russians should learn, is a landslide."

The situation now is profoundly changed, and most Americans are puzzled over what has happened. The extremely pessimistic mood of the brief period of the Soviet-Nazi Pact has returned. A general state of fear, suspicion, and distrust toward Russia has replaced the good will. What is the source of this change? Not a few

Americans place the blame squarely on their own Government. They say that Russia was terribly weakened by the war, that the "men of the Kremlin" are badly frightened, and that Soviet policy is motivated wholly by a desire to achieve military security. They say further that the shaping of our foreign policy following the death of Roosevelt fell into the hands of a clique of imperialists composed of military men and representatives of big business who seek world domination in the style of Hitler and regard war with the Soviet Union as both inevitable and desirable. To them what appears to many other Americans as Russian intransigence is merely the natural response on the part of a proud people to the aggressive policies expressed in the Truman Doctrine and the Marshall Plan. A genuine understanding of the ideology of the Soviet leaders will throw light on this all-important question.

2

It has become increasingly clear since the Russian Revolution that the Communist movement throughout the world, as directed and moulded by the Kremlin, is essentially religious in its psychology. It is marked more and more by that fanaticism and dogmatism, that emphasis on ceremonial and worship, which in the past have characterized great religious movements during their periods of maximum vitality and aggressiveness. At the very heart of this materialistic religion is an apocalyptic vision or revelation of the future. It is this vision that provides the drive of Soviet Communism everywhere.

If the All-Union Communist Party and its central organs constitute the decisive *political* reality in Russia today, the Soviet apocalypse is the decisive *ideological* reality. The essence of this apocalypse is the certainty of the ultimate triumph of Communism in all countries under Russian direction and leadership. The true Communist believes as firmly in the coming of Communism as the early Christians ever believed in the "second coming" of

Christ. And the power of this vision rests in the last analysis on the conviction that it is an authentic deliverance of "science" and not the dream of some Utopian stargazer. To the Soviet leaders it is derived from the monumental studies of two of the greatest geniuses of mankind, Marx and Engels, as elaborated and interpreted by their two greatest successors, men of equal or even superior brilliance, Lenin and Stalin. Indeed, as one reads contemporary Soviet literature, one gains the impression that these men are being elevated to the realm of the demigods. Their utterances, as selected, interpreted, and formulated by the last of them, have already taken on the garb of absolute authority.

That the studies of society, history, and philosophy by Marx and Engels were of monumental proportions has long been recognized by both European and American scholars. They sought to bring the entire human adventure, future as well as past, within the compass of a single comprehensive conception. According to this conception, known in the Soviet Union today as historical materialism, which is the application to human society of their all-embracing philosophy of dialectical materialism, the basic reality from which everything else derives is the modes of production and exchange. As a "reflection" of this reality, emerge all social relations, family patterns, class structures, property rights, political institutions, and even education, literature, art, music, science, and philosophy. Only as the economic base changes do modifications appear in the other realms.

The application of these fundamental postulates to the human past brought forth certain broad generalizations which have assumed the rigidity and the sanctity of religious dogmas. As the modes of production and exchange have been transformed in history one social system has followed another inevitably, each being superior to its predecessor in terms of the release and harnessing of productive energies. Thus an assumed primitive communism was superseded by the slave system, which gave way in time to the feudal order, which, in its turn, was followed by capitalism. Under each of these three systems, all of which were founded on the institution of private property, society was divided into two classes, the ruler and the ruled, the master and the servant, the exploiter and the exploited. The dynamic of history is found in the struggle between these two classes in a given epoch — a struggle which inevitably is rendered acute and irreconcilable, not merely by the fact of exploitation, but also by the emergence of contradictions in the economy which the ruling class is unable to resolve. The rising class unseats the old when the basic economic changes have advanced to the point where its intersts are in harmony with the fundamental need of society for the full release of its productive energies — human and technical. But before the old order passes away the two opposing classes engage in a more or less prolonged conflict marked by violence and bloodshed. The triumph of the new class results in the setting up of a dictatorship which continues until the last vestiges of the old order have been destroyed and the new order established.

This succession of social systems and the cycle of a period of violence and dictatorship leading in time to another period of violence and dictatorship will be broken only when the institution of private property in the means of production is abolished and a society without classes inaugurated. This point is reached, according to the revelation, with the final overthrow of capitalism by the proletariat under the leadership of the Communist Party and with the building of a socialist order which in time will be transformed peacefully into Communism — the final and perfect form of human association. And capitalism today stands in its final stages, decadent and evil, shaken by crisis after crisis, and driven by its inner nature to seek to put off the day of its demise by resort to imperialism and war. When the Soviet leaders say confidently, as they do, that all roads now lead to Communism, they mean that the apocalyptic vision is to be fulfilled in the present epoch. To them the laws of history and human society are working inexorably and swiftly on their side.

The American reader should know that this apocalypse, as a practical conception, is now passing its centenary. Its creators, Marx and Engels, were firmly convinced of the soundness of their analysis and the validity of their conclusions. In 1848 they believed that history was about to deliver their revolution, and not a revolution in one country only but a revolution embracing the world, or at least that part of the world which they were inclined to identify with the whole — the continent of Europe. And when it failed to come off, they did not lose faith and abandon the doctrine. They merely postponed the dawn of their millennium to some indefinite point in the future. When troubles descended on Europe again in 1857 Engels wrote to Marx: "In 1848 we thought our time was coming and in a certain sense it did, but this time it is really coming and everything is at stake."

The mentality of these men, and of all true revolutionists, including those who sit in the Kremlin today, is revealingly portrayed in the correspondence between Marx and Engels at that time. On the thirteenth of November the former, replying to an earlier letter from his friend, confessed: "Although I am in serious financial difficulties myself, I have not felt so happy since 1849 as I do to-day in face of this eruption." It should be added that he had been suffering from liver trouble and that his wife had just delivered a still-born child. Engels responded in similar vein:

I think it would be better that the crisis "improve" until it assumes a chronic character, before any second and decisive blow follows. Chronic pressure is necessary for a while in order to warm up the people. The proletariat would then fight better and with a better knowledge of the situation and more unison, just as a cavalry attack has greater élan if the horses must first trot 500 paces before coming within charging distance of the enemy. I shouldn't like anything to happen too soon, before the whole of Europe is completely involved, for then the struggle afterwards would be more severe, more tedious and more fluctuating. May or June would be almost too early. The masses must have become damned lethargic after the long period of prosperity. . . . By the way, I feel just as you do. Once the swindle collapsed in New York, I no longer had any peace in Jersey and now I feel in splendid form in the general collapse. The bourgeois mud of the past few years had stuck to me to a certain extent after all, but now it will be washed off and I shall feel a new man. The crisis will do my health as much good as a seaside holiday. I can feel that already.[1]

[1] Franz Mehring, *Karl Marx* (New York, 1935), p. 281.

3

As Marx and Engels approached old age, their hopes for "their revolution" grew somewhat dim. But many of their successors inherited their vision with all the vigor and enthusiasm of the new convert. This was particularly true in the case of the Russian Bolsheviks who had eagerly accepted Marxian doctrine in its most extreme and uncompromising form.

So when the Revolution broke in 1917 Lenin and those around him thought of it, not as a Russian revolution, but as the beginning of the "world revolution," of the fulfillment of the Marxian revelation. And it did seem in the months that followed that it would spread to a large part of Europe. It broke in Hungary and Bavaria, and for a period the whole of Germany teetered on the brink of a vast convulsion. In fact, Lenin was of the opinion that the Soviet régime would not endure if the Revolution failed to advance beyond the borders of backward Russia. On November 11, 1918, he exultingly proclaimed, "the International World Revolution is near." To assist the processes of history and hasten the inevitable, the Third or Communist International was launched in March, 1919. Three months later, Gregory Zinoviev, first chairman of the organization, intoxicated by great events, announced that "before long the whole of the civilized world will become Communist." The founding of the American Communist Party in the autumn threw him into ecstasies. In this event he saw "the first swallow which foretells the coming of a world-wide Communist spring." In the meantime the Executive Committee of the new organization announced to the world: "The Great Communist International was born in 1919. The Great International Soviet Republic will be born in 1920."

But these hopes were not fulfilled. The "International World Revolution" did not come off, and the "Great International Soviet Republic" did not materialize. As a matter of fact, the Communists were routed in both Germany and Hungary, the Red Army was repulsed in Poland, the new Soviet Republic encountered unforeseen difficulties, and the revolutionary wave began to recede everywhere. Forthwith the doctrine of the "temporary stabilization of capitalism" was formulated and efforts were made to improve diplomatic relations with "bourgeois states." Under Lenin's leadership the revolution also conducted a retreat on the domestic front. The extremes of "military communism" were abandoned and the New Economic Policy was launched in 1921. Among the more naïve political leaders of the West all of these changes were interpreted as meaning that the Bolsheviks, having discovered the impracticability of their doctrines of socialism and world revolution, had come to their senses and were on their way back to time-tested practices and ideas in both domestic economy and foreign affairs.

This interpretation of the actions of the Soviet leaders was soon discovered to be false. In 1928, having recovered from the ravages of revolution and civil war under the New Economic Policy, they launched a gigantic program of socialization and within eight years practically abolished the institution of private property in both land and the tools of production. At about the same time, as the capitalist world was shaken to its very foundations by a great depression, they began to think again in terms of revolution beyond the Soviet borders. Viewing fascism as merely capitalism in its final stages and certain of Hitler's inability therefore to "resolve the contradictions of capitalist economy," they pursued a policy of weakening the truly democratic elements in Germany and even collaborated with the Nazis in the overthrow of the Weimar Republic.[2] But realizing by 1935 that they had been mistaken, they proceeded with unseemly haste but without embarrassment to reverse the policy of the preceding five or six years. They called for a "united front" of all "democratic elements" against fascism, giving the most honored place among these elements to the Social Democrats whom they had just been calling

[2] See Max Beloff, *The Foreign Policy of the Soviet Union* (New York, 1947), vol. I, chap. V.

"social fascists," a peculiarly offensive and dangerous variety of the species. They also proposed a union of all "democratic states" and "freedom-loving peoples" to oppose the aggressions of fascism, the "enemy of all progressive mankind." This period lasted until 1939 when the Soviet-Nazi Pact was formed, fascism became merely a "matter of taste," and the "great democracies of the West" were demoted to the rank of "imperialistic states." They returned frankly and volubly to Lenin's position of 1914, characterized the war as a struggle between rival imperialisms, and hoped to see the "imperialistic war" converted into a "civil war" under their leadership. But this policy too was doomed to be short-lived. As soon as the Nazis invaded the Soviet Union, the "imperialistic states" of Britain, France, and America became again the "great democracies of the West" thickly inhabited by "freedom-loving peoples." And fascism was reduced to its former status as the "enemy of all progressive mankind."

The meaning of these zigs and zags, these twists and turns, these advances and retreats in Soviet policy from 1917 to 1941 was a subject of endless speculation throughout the period. Many saw in the Lenin New Economic Policy, the Stalin policy of building socialism in one country, or the Litvinov policy of collective security against aggressors, an abandonment of the apocalyptic vision of the universal triumph of Communism. In each case events sooner or later proved them mistaken. But since man is ever hopeful, the forced collaboration between East and West in the defeat of the Axis Powers nurtured the conviction among millions in America, Britain, France, and other countries that at long last the breach between the two camps had been healed.

During the war there were some grounds for this optimism. The extension of Lend-Lease to Russia, the twenty-year Anglo-Soviet alliance pact, the acceptance by all three Powers of the principles of the Atlantic Charter, the good will generated by the struggle with a common enemy, the launching of the United Nations at San Francisco, the vast concessions made to the Kremlin at Teheran, Yalta, and Potsdam, and the conviction of Roosevelt and others that they could "get along with Stalin" — all of these and numerous events and circumstances in addition naturally led many to believe that the pre-war differences between Russia and the Western democracies had been due fundamentally to misunderstandings and to an evil heritage dating from the days of civil war and intervention, following the seizure of power by the Bolsheviks and their raising the banners of world revolution. It was confidently assumed that these misunderstandings had been cleared away and the heritage liquidated by the shedding of blood in a common cause.

Various developments within the Soviet Union during the war years suggested that Stalin and his associates were expecting to maintain friendly relations with the West after the achievement of victory. On May 22, 1943, the Communist International, always a source of irritation to other countries and a grievous violation in spirit on the part of Russia of the laws of nations, was dissolved with ostentatious professions of good will. On October 9, 1943, through an order creating a Council for Russian Orthodox Affairs, the Soviet authorities seemed to be announcing to the Western World that the war against religion was halted and that another source of friction was being removed. The case of Eugene Varga suggests that in the midst of the war the Party leaders were expecting to continue on terms of friendship with "capitalist" states in the postwar years. As the foremost Soviet economist, director of the World Institute of Economics in Moscow, and editor of *World Economics and Politics,* he was commissioned to make a comprehensive study of "Changes in the Economy of Capitalism Resulting from the Second World War." The outcome was a volume bearing the above title which was completed about the time the war ended. In this work Varga concluded that world capitalism would be strong, that capitalist states would have learned to plan and control depressions, and that the relations between imperial states and their colonies would have changed in the interests of the latter. All of these positions constituted a repudiation of certain of the "laws of capitalist development," as formulated by Marx and Lenin. During these same years Earl Browder was announcing the conversion of the American Communist Party into the Communist Political Association and proclaiming, in the "spirit of Teheran," the indefinite peaceful collaboration between America and Russia and the end of the class struggle in the United States!

The course of this friendly policy can be traced in the utterances of Stalin. In a radio address on July 3, 1941, just eleven days after the Nazi attack, he announced that "in this war of liberation we shall not be alone," that "we shall have faithful allies in the peoples of Europe and America," that "this will be a united front of peoples defending freedom against enslavement and threats of enslavement by the fascist armies of Hitler," and that the promise of aid from the Prime Minister of Great Britain and the Government of the United States "can evoke only a feeling of gratitude in the hearts of the peoples of the Soviet Union." [3] In an order of the day for May 1, 1942, Stalin placed America unequivocally among the "freedom-loving" countries:

The international relations of our Motherland have been strengthened recently as never before. All freedom-loving peoples have united against German imperialism. Their eyes are turned toward the Soviet Union. The heroic struggle, which the peoples of our country are conducting for liberty, honor, and independence, calls forth the admiration of all progressive mankind. The peoples of all freedom-loving countries look to the Soviet Union as the force capable of saving the world from the Hitlerite plague. Among these freedom-loving countries first place belongs to Great Britain and the United States of America with which we are linked with bonds of friendship and alliance, and which extend to our country ever more and more military aid against the German-fascist robbers.[4]

On June 13, 1944, in reply to a question from a correspondent of *Pravda*, asking him to appraise the landing in Normandy, Stalin paid a matchless tribute to his British and American allies. Since this statement probably represents the most favorable commentary on the "bourgeois states" of the West ever made by a Soviet leader, it merits publication in full:

3 I. Stalin, *On the Great Patriotic War of the Soviet Union* (Moscow, 1947), p. 16. (In Russian.)

4 *Ibid.*, p. 54.

Summing up the seven-day battle of the liberating forces of the allies in the invasion of Northern France it can be said without hesitation that the wide forcing of the Channel and the mass landing of allied troops in the north of France has been entirely successful. This is undoubtedly a most brilliant achievement of our allies.

One must acknowledge that the history of warfare knows no other undertaking comparable in breadth of conception, grandeur of scale, and mastery of execution.

The "invincible" Napoleon in his day failed ignominiously in his plan to force the Channel and seize the British Isles. The hysterical Hitler, who boasted for two years that he would force the Channel, did not dare even to attempt to fulfill his threat. Only the British and American armies succeeded in fulfilling with honor the grandiose plan of forcing the Channel and of achieving a mass landing of troops.

History will mark this deed as an accomplishment of the highest order.[5]

At a meeting celebrating the twenty-seventh anniversary of the Revolution on November 6, 1944, in Moscow, Stalin reviewed the course of the war during the year just ending. Although he placed emphasis quite naturally and justly on the achievements of Soviet arms and industry, he made many friendly and even generous references to the allies. He praised the "unity of views and accord of action of the three great powers at the Teheran Conference" and spoke lightly of "differences of opinion among the three powers on questions of security." While recognizing the existence of such differences, he said that "one should be surprised, not that differences of opinion exist, but that they are so few and are being resolved in almost every instance in a spirit of unity and accord." The failure of the fascist leaders to disrupt the alliance of the three Powers, he said, was due to the fact that "the union of the Soviet Union, Great Britain, and the United States" is based, "not on casual and fleeting motives, but on vital and lasting interests." He saw the "militant union of democratic Powers," tested by "three years of war" and "sealed with the blood of peoples," enduring the "ordeal of the concluding stage of the war."[6] This prediction was greeted with "prolonged applause."

5 *Ibid.*, pp. 148–49.   6 *Ibid.*, pp. 163–67.

That the policy of friendly relations with the West was regarded at the time as more than a maneuver for the winning of the war is suggested by the fact that it found expression in diverse cultural activities. On May 26, 1943, under the sponsorship of the highest authorities, a concert of English music was given in the Large Hall of the Moscow Conservatory. The event "was received with all the warm feeling that is accorded to music that need be heard but once to touch and convince." Then very appropriately on July 4, American music was honored in the same way. A Soviet journal proudly announced that this concert was "perhaps the first concert of national American music on the European continent" and that it "bore witness to the lively interest always felt by the Soviet public for American culture." [7] The account of the concerts noted not the slightest taint of "bourgeois decadence" in either the English or the American music.[8] But modifications of the program of the schools are probably more significant. The nature of such changes is suggested in an article by Professor A. Pankratova, a Soviet historian who for a number of years has played a central rôle in the editing of history textbooks for use in the secondary school. This article was published in 1943 for the guidance of teachers of history and contained an interpretation of the Western democracies never before permitted in Soviet schools:

The Soviet history teacher pays particular and detailed attention to the American constitution of 1787–89, to the French constitution of 1791–93, to the struggle for the democratization of the English Parliament by means of the reforms of 1832, 1867, 1884, to the workers' legislation of leading European countries, especially England and France. All this material makes it possible to show why the people of freedom-loving, democratic countries, particularly England and the U.S.A. are now fighting together with the U.S.S.R. for freedom and democracy against Hitlerite barbarism. . . .

The history of the relations between Russia and the United States presents particular interest. These mutual contacts are marked by an

[7] To grasp the significance of these events the reader should turn to chapter V of this volume: "Music as a Weapon."

[8] "Concerts of English and American Music," *VOKS Bulletin*, No. 7, 1943, pp. 44–45.

unfailing community of interests, commencing with the "armed neutrality" of Catherine II, and continuing through the lively interest in America displayed by the liberal-minded element of Russian society during the reign of Alexander I (the correspondence between Alexander I and Thomas Jefferson; the study of the American Constitution by Speransky and the Decembrists, etc.), and, in particular, at the time of the Civil War in the United States when the emancipation of the serfs in Russia coincided with the struggle of the Northern States against the slave-holding South. Russian diplomacy supported the Federal government and the inviolability of the Union. The sale of Alaska to the United States in 1867 served to strengthen the friendly bonds between the two countries.[9]

Toward the end of the war new textbooks were coming from the press which expressed with moderation the new viewpoint. A history of the Soviet Union, covering the period since 1890 and designed for the last year of the high school, was published early in 1945. Being an "officially approved" textbook it expressed the Party "line" at the time and enjoyed a monopoly position for the grade. Although the volume gives relatively little attention to the contribution of the Allies to the winning of the war, it is friendly throughout and quotes in full Stalin's appraisal of the landing in Normandy. The author then added these words:

The brilliantly executed invasion of Northern France by the British and American armies led to further military successes by the allies who by September 15, 1944, had already cleared almost all of France and Belgium of German troops and had crossed the German frontier, occupying the first German city — Trier, the birthplace of Marx.[10]

The textbook also gives a fairly full account of the "dissolution" of the Third International in May, 1943.

9 *VOKS Bulletin*, No. 1–2, 1943, pp. 27–28.
10 A. M. Pankratova, Editor, *History of the USSR* (Moscow, 1945), vol. III, p. 327. (In Russian.)

4

By the time the war ended, a profound shift in foreign policy was already clearly under way. Never again after November 6, 1944, did Stalin pay high tribute to the Western democracies, or suggest that the union of the three Powers would be sustained in the years to come by enduring common interests. The mood and outlook of 1917 returned with incredible swiftness and power, with one striking difference. The apocalyptic vision of Marxian socialism was now joined with the expansionism and the Messianism of the Great Russians. Thus did the Communist apocalypse of Marx and Lenin become the Soviet apocalypse of Stalin. This new development, which has gained great strength in the meantime, was heralded by "our dear father and teacher" in a speech on May 24, 1945, at a reception in honor of Red Army commanders in the Kremlin. Drinking toast after toast to the Great Russians, he declared them to be the "most outstanding nation of all the nations composing the Soviet Union," to merit recognition "as the leading force of the Soviet Union among all the peoples of our country," to possess a "clear mind, steadfast character, endurance . . . and faithfulness." [11] This estimate of the Great Russians has permeated the entire cultural apparatus.

The great change brought many casualties, some of which will be reported from document to document in the present volume. Two personal tragedies should perhaps be mentioned here. Earl Browder, who had assumed the indefinite continuation of the friendly spirit of the middle war years, found himself under attack in May, 1945, from Jacques Duclos, a French Communist leader who had just returned from Moscow. Although he attempted to correct his mistakes, he was thrown out of office and

---

[11] I. Stalin, *On the Great Patriotic War of the Soviet Union* (Moscow, 1947), p. 196. (In Russian.)

expelled from the Party. Fortunately for him he was still an American citizen and enjoyed the safeguards of the Federal Constitution. Eugene Varga, having prepared a report on postwar capitalist economy in accord with the outlook of 1943 and 1944, discoverd in 1945 that the "line" had changed and that his services as the foremost Soviet economist were no longer needed. The World Institute of Economics of which he was director and the journal *World Economy and World Politics* of which he was editor were both liquidated and he was demoted to a minor post. In a half-hearted defense of his report at a conference in May, 1947, he naïvely pointed out that he could have written the report "more sharply," but had thought that the "international situation" at the time required him "to manifest 'discretion' in the choice of terminology."[12] The fall of Varga is the more impressive because he was generally reputed to be able to bring his statistical analyses into precise correspondence with the latest Party resolutions. Trotsky once called him the "theoretical Polonius of the Comintern" who was "always ready to prove statistically that the clouds in the sky look like a camel's back, but if you prefer, they resemble a fish, and if the Prince desires it, they bear witness to 'socialism in one country.' " On April 27, 1949, Varga retracted his "errors" fully with the sensible observation that such retraction is "better late than never."

The textbooks used in the schools also began to change immediately after the war. The 1945 edition of Volume 3 of *The History of the USSR,* referred to above, was replaced almost at once by a new edition which carries the account through February, 1946. The reader should know that a new edition of any textbook means either that knowledge has advanced notably or that the "line" has changed appreciably. It is very unusual to keep an edition for only one year. But a mere glance through the pages of this book dealing with the war reveals the occasion for this extraordinary haste. Two items appearing in the 1945 edition are gone

---

[12] *Soviet Views on the Post-War World Economy* (Washington, 1948), p. 5. (English translation.)

without leaving a trace. Stalin's generous tribute to the landing in Normandy is no more, and the entire account of the "dissolution" of the Third International has disappeared. And strangely enough Shura Chekalin, a member of that heroic band of partisans who fought behind the German lines and died quietly at the hands of the Germans in the 1945 edition, dies singing the "Internationale," the anthem of revolutionary socialism, in the 1946 edition. It seems rather improbable that this change was due to the advance of historical knowledge.

In the account of the war there is no reference to Lend-Lease, to the battle of the oceans, or to the bombing of German industrial cities by the Allied air force. The entire contribution of British and American arms to the winning of the war is reported in the following lines:

The victories of the Red Army played a decisive rôle in insuring the military successes of the allies in North Africa and in Italy. The drawing of the basic strategic reserves of the Germans from the West and the annihilation of the best German divisions on the Soviet-German front made possible the successful development of large offensive operations of the allies in Europe. On June 6, 1944, allied armies achieved a landing in the north of France. The second front held 75 Hitler divisions and to a definite degree facilitated the fulfillment by the Red Army of its task of finally defeating the German troops. Thus, the fourth year of the war was a year of decisive victories of the Soviet armies and the armies of our allies over the German forces. [13]

The postwar Soviet outlook is further revealed in the following summation of the struggle:

The victory of the Soviet Union in the Great Patriotic War called forth the admiration of all progressive mankind. The entire world acknowledged the great service of the Red Army which, through its heroic, self-sacrificing struggle, rescued civilization from the German-fascist barbarians and from the Japanese imperialists. The Red Army appeared before the whole world as an army of liberation and the

[13] *Op. cit.*, p. 381.

Soviet Union as the savior of civilization and progress in Europe and throughout the earth.[14]

The change in orientation of the Soviet leaders was heralded in moderate tones by Stalin in a speech [15] at a pre-election meeting of voters in the Stalinist election district in the city of Moscow on February 9, 1946. The reader should know that the expression by Stalin of the slightest whim is taken at once as a command to move extravagantly and without restraint in the direction indicated. If he pays a compliment to Glinka, then a movie of Glinka's life must be produced. If he hangs a portrait of Suvorov in his office in the Kremlin, then everybody who hopes to be somebody must display a portrait of Suvorov. So the two emphases contained in Stalin's speech were destined in the months ahead to be carried to their logical extremes with the blindness and fanaticism characteristic of Communist behavior both inside and outside the Soviet Union. The first was the unqualified revival of the Marxian interpretation of the present epoch and the implication that wars will continue as long as the system of "capitalism" endures. The following extracts from the speech give the essence of Stalin's thought:

It would be incorrect to think that the war arose accidentally or as a result of the mistakes of these or those statesmen, even though mistakes unquestionably were made. In reality the war arose as the inevitable result of the development of world economic and political forces founded on contemporary monopoly capitalism. More than once Marxists have declared that the capitalist system of world economy conceals within itself elements of general crisis and war, that the development of world capitalism in our time advances not on a smooth and even course, but through crises and military clashes. The fact is that the uneven development of capitalist countries leads habitually in the course of time to a sharp disturbance of the equilibrium within the world system of capitalism, and that a group of capitalist countries which regards itself as least well provided with raw materials and markets generally makes efforts to change the situation and to divide

[14] *Ibid.*, p. 390.   [15] *Pravda*, February 10, 1946.

anew "spheres of influence" to its advantage by the use of armed forces. As a result the capitalist world is split into two hostile camps and war between them arises.

Of course it would be possible to avoid military catastrophes if periodically raw materials and markets could be redistributed among countries according to their economic weight through the acceptance of negotiated and peaceful decisions. But this is not possible under present capitalist conditions of the development of world economy.

Thus, as a result of the first crisis of the capitalist system of world economy the first world war occurred; as a result of the second crisis, the second world war.

The second emphasis in Stalin's speech, which seems to have been taken as a directive for the purging of the entire cultural apparatus, was the unquestioned superiority of all things Soviet. In the excerpts below he portrays the broad outlines of this superiority:

For our country this war was the most savage and terrible of all the wars ever experienced in the history of our Motherland.

But the war was not only a curse. It was also a great school of experience and a test of all the forces of the people. The war laid bare all facts and events in the rear and at the front, it pitilessly snatched away all the covers and veils which concealed the actual face of the state, the government, and the Party, and exhibited them on the stage without masks, without embellishments, with all their faults and merits. The war arranged a kind of examination for our Soviet order, our state, our government, and our Communist Party, and summed up the results of their work, as if saying to us: here they are, your people and organizations, their works and their days — examine them attentively and reward them according to their deeds.

This is one of the positive aspects of the war. . . .

Our victory means, first of all, that our Soviet *social* order was victorious, that the Soviet social order passed successfully the test in the fires of war and demonstrated fully its vitality . . .

Now we know that the Soviet social order has shown itself to be more vigorous and stable than the non-Soviet social order, that the Soviet social order is a better form of social organization than any non-Soviet social order. . . .

Our victory means, in the second place, that our Soviet *political* order, that our multi-nation state, passed all the tests of war and proved its vitality.

Now we know that the Soviet political order has shown itself to be a model of the multi-nation state, that the Soviet political order is a political system in which the question of nationalities and the problem of the cooperation of nations have been resolved better than in any other multi-nation state. . . .

Our victory means, in the third place, that the Soviet armed forces were victorious, that our Red Army was victorious, that the Red Army endured heroically all the horrors of war, completely smashed the armies of our enemies, and emerged from the war as a conqueror. . . .

The war showed that the Red Army is no "colossus with feet of clay," but a first-class army of our times with an entirely modern equipment, with a most experienced staff of officers, and with high moral fighting qualities. One must not forget that the Red Army is the very army that completely destroyed the German army which only yesterday brought terror to the armies of the European states. . . .

Everyone knows that, in the matter of provisions and equipment, the Red Army not only experienced no deficiencies whatsoever, but even had the needed reserves.

Following this speech by Stalin, the harsh Leninist doctrine of bitter and mortal hostility toward the entire "bourgeois" world seems to have been revived completely. One looks almost in vain in postwar Soviet literature for any sign of hope of peaceful relations between the "two systems." "We are living," said Lenin, "not merely in a state, but in a *system of states;* and it is inconceivable that the Soviet Republic should continue to exist for a long period side by side with imperialist states. Ultimately the one or the other must conquer. Meanwhile, a series of frightful clashes between the Soviet Republic and the bourgeois states is inevitable." [16] This point of view, identifying the Communist with the Soviet apocalypse, is repeated and expanded in a recent authoritative work by Nikolai A. Voznesensky, Deputy Premier of the

16 V. I. Lenin, *Works* (Moscow, 1932), vol. XXIV, third edition, p. 122. (In Russian.)

USSR, Head of the State Planning Commission, and member of the Politburo:

Lenin and Stalin warned the socialist Motherland again and again of the inevitability of historic battles between imperialism and socialism and prepared the peoples of the USSR for these battles. Lenin and Stalin explained that wars which the working class, having conquered the bourgeoisie at home, wages in the interests of its socialist Motherland and in the interests of strengthening and developing socialism, are lawful and holy wars.

Lenin's great companion in arms and successor, Stalin, teaches that the duty of every revolutionary is to protect and guard the USSR which is the first socialist state in the world. Only he who unconditionally defends the USSR is an internationalist, for it is impossible to resolve the question of the international revolutionary workers' movement without defending the Union of Soviet Socialist Republics.

Lenin taught that the fate of all revolutions heretofore has been decided by a long series of wars, that with the period of the Civil War we concluded only one phase of the wars, and that we must be prepared for a second phase. The continuing existence of the Soviet Union alongside aggressive imperialist states involves a series of great conflicts. As long as capitalist encirclement remains, there exists the danger of attack by imperialist states on the land of socialism.[17]

Extremely relevant to this discussion was the re-publication in January, 1947, of one of Stalin's early pamphlets in an edition of two hundred thousand copies. Entitled *The October Revolution and the Tactics of the Russian Communists,* the pamphlet first appeared in December, 1924. In it Stalin develops at some length the question of the relation of the Russian Revolution to the world revolution. He says without qualification that the Russian Revolution "is at the same time the beginning and the premise of the world revolution" and should regard itself "as a means for the hastening of the victory of the proletariat in all countries." After stating categorically that the "victorious proletariat" should "aid

[17] Nikolai A. Voznesensky, *The Economy of the USSR during World War II* (Moscow, 1947), pp. 5–6. (In Russian.)

the workers and toiling masses of all remaining countries," he proceeds to indicate the forms of assistance to be given. Then he quotes Lenin to the effect that the "victorious proletariat" of one country, "expropriating the capitalists and organizing its own socialist production, should rise ... *against* the remaining capitalist world, drawing to itself the oppressed classes of all countries, inciting them to rebellion against the capitalists, and in case of necessity even moving with armed force against the exploiting classes and their governments." This pamphlet would not have been brought out in such a large edition in 1947 if its basic argument had not been in complete harmony with the Party "line." [18]

Not only are there to be wars between "socialist" and "capitalist" states. The doctrine is proclaimed also that the course of events in all "capitalist" countries must invariably follow the violent pattern of the Russian Revolution to the fulfillment of the apocalyptic vision of Marx and Lenin. This position is expounded frankly in the September 15, 1948, issue of *Bolshevik*, the theoretical and political organ of the Central Committee of the All-Union Communist Party. "The assertion," says this article, "that every country travels toward socialism along its own and entirely original path, and that there are as many paths as there are countries, is incorrect. To speak thus is to deny the international significance of the experience of Bolshevism. The general laws of transition from capitalism to socialism, revealed by Marx and Engels, tested, applied, and developed by Lenin and Stalin on the basis of the experience of the Bolshevik Party and the Soviet state, are obligatory for all countries." Then the article adds: "The great historic experience of the Bolshevik Party is a guide for the action of Communists and toilers of all countries." [19] In these words is revived the high mission of Russia as conceived by the Slavophils of the mid-nineteenth century. To find anything comparable to such dogmatism one must turn to the teachings of the more primi-

[18] I. Stalin, *The October Revolution and the Tactics of the Russian Communists* (Moscow, January, 1947), pp. 43, 46. (In Russian.)
[19] *Bolshevik*, September 15, 1948, p. 51.

tive and authoritarian religious sects concerning the road to individual salvation.

5

Perhaps the most important question regarding Soviet foreign policy is this: What are the considerations that lead the members of the Politburo to make those radical shifts which have marked their policy since 1917? The evidence now at hand over a period of a generation makes possible a wholly trustworthy answer to this question. In the first place, there is no reason today for believing that either Lenin or Stalin ever seriously questioned the truth of his own interpretation of the Marxian analysis or the apocalyptic vision of the coming of Communism throughout the world. Their changes in policy have been merely shifts in strategy and tactics with the ultimate goal remaining ever the same. In the second place, these twists and turns and reversals have always been dictated by the power factors in either the domestic or the world situation. So it was in 1920, in 1928–29, in 1935, in 1939, and in 1941. So it was too in 1945–46, and so it is today.

The fact is that in terms of their revolutionary ideology the Soviet leaders found themselves at the close of the war in a position of power far exceeding their fondest dreams of the nineteen-thirties and the middle war years. As they shaped and followed the course of events, as they won one brilliant military or diplomatic victory after another, particularly in 1944 and 1945, they must have been almost overcome with excitement. They saw their onetime enemies, the enemies of their revolution, fall one by one, they saw their own power as revolutionists at home and abroad grow by leaps and bounds; and they saw history marching with rapid pace at their side. A cool review of events suggests that the Soviet shift of policy, a shift which was certainly consummated in idea long before the Truman Doctrine or Marshall Plan was ever

thought of, was based on a full and careful calculation of power
factors by the world's most eminent students and ardent devotees
of power.

If all the facts are placed side by side the above conclusion is in-
escapable. First, when the war was over Soviet arms stood on a
line beyond the Elbe, certainly a position which in 1943 the
Kremlin was hardly expecting to occupy. Fundamental here was
the destruction of the Polish Home Army in the Warsaw rising of
1944, which gave Russia complete control of all of East-Central
and Eastern Europe. The agreement on the division of Germany
was reached tentatively by the European Advisory Council in the
autumn of 1944 and was concluded at Yalta in February, 1945.
But for this agreement the armies of the Western Allies could have
and would have liberated and held a large part of East-Central
Germany. Second, the greatest military establishment in history
under the command of General Eisenhower was dismantled "as
rapidly as possible." By the summer of 1946 it had been reduced
to police strength. This abandonment of Europe was carried
through as a response to the natural desires of the American and
British people, but the process was accelerated by the organized
propaganda of the Communist Parties and their fellow travellers.
Third, the withdrawal of Allied armed forces left a power vacuum
unequalled in history. All the great states on the Eurasian continent had been destroyed, except the Soviet Union. Indeed after
the war the United States was the only rival power of first rank in
the entire world. Fourth, in order to bring Russia into the war
against Japan, as the Allied statesmen thought, incredible concessions were made to the Kremlin. The losses suffered in the
Russo-Japanese War were recouped with interest, and China was
partly dismembered and greatly weakened. Fifth, the Soviet
leaders assumed that the American economy was unstable, that
this instability would lead to a profound and prolonged crisis,
and that this crisis would force the United States to lose interest
in Europe and Asia. Sixth, the undoubted heroic achievements of
Soviet arms, economy, and people during the war radically raised

the prestige of the Kremlin everywhere in the world. No longer could anyone say that the Soviet system was a house of cards that would come crashing to the earth at the slightest push.

One further and peculiarly decisive consideration must be placed in the record. When the bombs had ceased falling and the smoke of war had cleared away, it was evident to any high-school student that practically the whole of the Old World, outside of Britain and the Soviet Union, was in a revolutionary state. First, a general condition of economic, political, and moral paralysis prevailed almost everywhere from the English Channel to the China Sea. Second, the old political parties, having been thoroughly discredited and shattered, were quite unable to halt the spread of misery and meet the challenge of revolution. Third, in almost every country of Europe a revolutionary party, well organized and disciplined, experienced in the use of arms, and eager to take power, emerged from the war, several times stronger than it had been in 1939 — the national Communist Party. In a word, the conditions essential to a successful revolution, according to Lenin, had become almost universal. If the "men of the Kremlin" had not been tempted to take full advantage of this situation, they would not have been the "men of the Kremlin."

In September, 1947, Andrei Zhdanov, the man who at the time was generally regarded as the probable successor of Stalin, was commissioned to attend a meeting in Poland of representatives of European Communist Parties and to assume leadership in the open reconstitution of the Communist International under the name of the Cominform. At this meeting he delivered an address [20] in which he made a dispassionate analysis of the world situation from the Communist standpoint and outlined certain phases of Russian foreign policy which obviously had been maturing since Yalta days. The address was one of the two or three most important pronouncements made by any Soviet leader since the war. The major part of his powerful and triumphant analysis follows:

[20] A. Zhdanov, *On the International Situation* (Moscow, 1947). (In Russian.)

The conclusion of the second world war brought substantial changes in the entire international situation. The military defeat of the bloc of fascist states, the anti-fascist liberating character of the war, and the decisive rôle of the Soviet Union in the victory over the fascist aggressors sharply changed the power relations between the two systems — the socialist and the capitalist — to the advantage of socialism.

What is the essence of these changes?

The primary result of the second world war was the military defeat of Germany and Japan, the two most militaristic and aggressive countries of capitalism. Reactionary imperialist elements throughout the world, and particularly in England, the United States, and France, placed special hopes on Germany and Japan, and above all on Hitlerite Germany: first, as the force most capable of striking a blow against the Soviet Union in order, if not to destroy, then at any rate to weaken it and to undermine its influence; and, second, as the force capable of shattering the revolutionary labor and democratic movement in Germany itself and in all countries, which was the object of Hitlerite aggression, and thus of strengthening the general position of capitalism. This constituted one of the chief causes of the prewar, the so-called Munich, policy of "appeasement" and of the encouragement of fascist aggression, a policy which was conducted consistently by the ruling imperialist circles of England, France, and the United States.

But these hopes of the Anglo-French-American imperialists were not fulfilled. The Hitlerites proved to be weaker, and the Soviet Union and freedom-loving peoples stronger, than the men of Munich had supposed. As a result of the second world war the major forces of militant international fascist reaction were beaten and weakened for a long time.

At the same time the system of world capitalism as a whole suffered yet another serious loss. If the chief result of the first world war was the breaking of the united imperialist front and the withdrawal of Russia from the world system of capitalism, and if as a result of the victory of the socialist order in the USSR, capitalism ceased to be a unified all-embracing system of world economy, then the second world war and the shattering of fascism, the weakening of the world position of capitalism, and the strengthening of the anti-fascist movement led to the withdrawal from the imperialist system of a number of countries of central and southeastern Europe. In these countries arose new people's democratic régimes. The great example of the Soviet Union in the Patriotic War and the liberating rôle of the Soviet Army were linked with the rise of a mass national-liberating struggle of freedom-loving peoples against the fascist robbers and their allies. In the course of this struggle the pro-fascist elements which had collaborated with Hitler — the most influential large capitalists, the landlords, the higher bureaucracy, and the monarchist officer class — were exposed as traitors to the national interests. In the countries of the Danube the liberation from German-fascist slavery was accompanied by the removal from power of the top bourgeois-landlord leaders who had engaged in compromising collaboration with German fascism and by the coming to power of new forces of the people which had revealed themselves in the struggle against the Hitlerite enslavers. In these countries representatives of the workers, the peasants, and the progressive intelligentsia rose to power. Since the working class had exhibited everywhere the greatest heroism and the greatest consistency and irreconcilability in the anti-fascist struggle, its authority and influence among the people grew immeasurably.

The new democratic power in Yugoslavia, Bulgaria, Rumania, Poland, Czechoslovakia, Hungary and Albania, by leaning on the support of the popular masses, was able to achieve in the shortest time progressive democratic reforms of which bourgeois democracy had been incapable. Agrarian reforms transferred the land to the peasants and led to the liquidation of the class of landlords. The nationalization of large industry and banks and the confiscation of the property of traitors who had collaborated with the Germans blasted at the root the positions of monopolistic capital in these countries and delivered the masses from imperialist slavery. At the same time a basis for the public ownership of property was established and a new type of state, *a people's republic*, was created, in which power rests with the people, large industry, transport, and banks belong to the state, and a bloc of the toiling classes guided by the industrial workers constitute the leading force. Consequently the people of these countries not only escaped from the jaws of imperialism, but also laid the foundation for a transition to the road of socialist development.

As a result of the war the international importance and authority of the USSR grew immeasurably. The Soviet Union was the leading force and spirit in the military defeat of Germany and Japan. The democratic progressive forces of the entire world rallied around the Soviet Union. The socialist state had passed the supreme test of war and had emerged victorious from the deathly encounter with the strongest enemy. Instead of being weakened, the Soviet Union emerged stronger than ever.

The face of the capitalist world was also essentially changed. Of six so-called great imperialist powers (Germany, Japan, England, the United States, France, and Italy) three (Germany, Italy, and Japan) disappeared as a result of military defeat. Also France was weakened and lost its former significance as a great power. Thus only two "great" world imperialist powers, the United States and England, remained. But the position of one of these, England, was undermined. During the war English imperialism showed itself to be weak in both military and political relations. In Europe, England proved to be weak in the face of German aggression. In Asia, as the greatest imperialist empire, she was unable to hold her colonial possessions with her own power. Having lost temporarily her connection with the colonies, which had supplied her with food and raw materials and which had consumed a substantial part of her industrial production, England found herself in a state of military-economic dependence on America for food and manufactured goods. Following the war the financial-economic dependence of England on America continued to grow. Though successful in regaining her colonies, England was confronted with strong American influence in the colonies, which during the war had reached into all of those regions which in pre-war days had been regarded as the monopolistic sphere of English capitalism (the Arabian East and South-East Asia). Also the influence of America was strengthened in the British dominions and in South America where the rôle of the former is passing significantly and in ever growing measure to the United States of America.

As a result of the second world war the sharpening of the crisis of the colonial system was expressed in a powerful drive for national liberation in colonial and dependent countries. Thus the rear of the capitalist system was threatened. Colonial peoples no longer wish to live in the old way. The ruling classes of the home countries can no longer govern the colonies as before. Attempts to suppress the movement for national liberation by military force meet now with ever-growing armed resistance by the colonial peoples and lead to prolonged colonial wars (Holland and Indonesia; France and Viet-Nam).

The war brought a further sharpening of that inequality which is characteristic of the development of capitalism in different countries. Of the capitalist empires only one, the United States of America, emerged from the war not weakened, but significantly strengthened both economically and militarily. American capitalists enriched themselves substantially in the war. At the same time the American people did not experience the privations which accompany war, the oppression of occupation and aerial bombardments; and the human losses of the United States, since she entered the war, as a matter of fact, in its final stages and after its fate had been decided, were comparatively insignificant. For the United States the war served above all as an incentive for the broad expansion of industrial production and for the decisive strengthening of export trade (for the most part to Europe).

The conclusion of the war placed before the United States a number of new problems. Capitalist monopolies strove to preserve their profits at the high level attained during the conflict. With this in mind they endeavored to prevent a decrease in the volume of trade. But to accomplish this it was necessary for the United States to hold those external markets which had consumed American production during the war. Also, since the purchasing power of most states had been sharply lowered as a result of the war, it was necessary to conquer new markets. At the same time the financial-economic dependence of these states on America had been increased. The United States extended credits abroad in the sum of nineteen billion dollars, not counting contributions to the international bank and the international stabilization fund. The disappearance from the world market of America's chief competitors, Germany and Japan, opened up new vast opportunities for the United States.

If prior to the second world war the most influential circles of American imperialism subscribed to the policy of isolationism and refrained from active intervention in the affairs of Europe or Asia, under the new postwar conditions the masters of Wall Street shifted to a new policy. They advanced a program for the utilization of the entire military and economic might of America, not only to hold and strengthen the positions conquered abroad during the war, but also to extend these conquests to the maximum and to occupy the place of

Germany, Japan, and Italy in the world market. The sharp weakening of the economic power of other capitalist states created an opportunity for the speculative exploitation of postwar economic difficulties which facilitate the subjection of those countries to American control, and in particular the exploitation of the postwar economic difficulties of Great Britain. The United States proclaimed a new and frankly grasping expansionist course.

The new and frankly expansionist course of the United States set as its aim the establishment of the world-wide domination of American imperialism. For the purpose of strengthening the monopoly position of the United States in the markets created by the disappearance of America's two greatest competitors, Germany and Japan, and the weakening of America's capitalist partners, England and France, the new course of American policy is calculated on a broad program of military, economic, and political measures. The object of this program is the establishment, in all countries which are the objects of American expansion, of the political and economic rule of the United States, the reduction of those countries to the position of satellites of the United States, and the founding of internal régimes which will remove all opposition on the part of labor and democratic movements to the exploitation of these countries by American capital. An attempt is being made now to extend this new policy, not only to the military enemies and neutral states of yesterday, but also in very large measure to the wartime allies of the United States.

Particular attention is being devoted to the exploitation of the economic difficulties of England — an ally and at the same time an old capitalist rival and competitor of the United States. The American expansionist course stems from the necessity not only of not releasing England from the jaws of economic dependence on the United States established during the war, but, on the contrary, of strengthening the pressure on England in order gradually to take away her control over her colonies, to force her out of her sphere of influence, and to reduce her to the position of a vassal empire.

Thus the new policy of America is directed toward the strengthening of her monopolist position and is designed to place her capitalist partners in a submissive and dependent position.

But on the road of the aspiration of the United States for world domination stands the USSR with its growing international influence.

Also, as a bulwark of anti-imperialist and anti-fascist policy, stand the countries of the new democracy which have escaped from the control of Anglo-American imperialism, stand the workers of all countries, including the workers of America herself, who wish no new wars in behalf of the rule of their oppressors. Therefore the new expansionist reactionary course of American policy is designed for a struggle against the USSR, against the countries of the new democracy, against the labor movement in all countries, against the labor movement in the United States, against liberating anti-imperialist forces throughout the world.

American reactionaries, disturbed by the successes of socialism in the USSR, by the successes of the countries of the new democracy, and by the growth of the labor and democratic movement in all countries of the world following the war, are disposed to assume the rôle of "saviors" of the capitalist system from Communism.

Thus the frankly expansionist program of the United States is extremely reminiscent of the hazardous program of the fascist aggressors who, ingloriously vanquished, as is well known, recently aspired to world domination.

Just as the Hitlerites, while preparing for military aggression, cloaked themselves in anti-Communism in order to oppress and enslave all peoples, and in the first instance their own people, so the contemporary ruling circles of the United States mask their expansionist policy and even their attack on the vital interests of a weaker imperialist rival, England, by pseudo-defensive anti-Communist aims. The feverish armament race and the construction of new military bases for American armed forces in all parts of the world are falsely and hypocritically rationalized as measures of "defense" against a fantastic war threat on the part of the USSR. American diplomacy, employing the methods of intimidation, bribery, and blackmail, easily obtains from other capitalist countries, and first of all from England, consent to the legal strengthening of the superior American positions in Europe and Asia — in the western zones of Germany, in Austria and Italy, in Greece and Turkey, in Egypt, Iran, and Afghanistan, in China and Japan, and so forth.

American imperialists look upon themselves as the chief force opposing the USSR, the countries of the new democracy, and the labor and democratic movement in all countries of the world, as the bulwark of reactionary and anti-democratic forces throughout the earth.

Literally, therefore, on the second day after the conclusion of the second world war they moved to restore the hostile front against the USSR and world democracy. They began to encourage anti-people's reactionary forces — collaborationists and former capitalist protégés — in European lands which had been freed from the Hitlerite yoke and had begun to build a life according to their own choice.

The most vicious imperialist political leaders, having lost their sanity, and following Churchill, began to promote plans for the speedy launching of a preventive war against the USSR and openly called for the utilization against the Soviet people of the temporary American monopoly of atomic weapons. The firebrands of the new war are attempting to frighten and blackmail not only the USSR, but also other countries and particularly China and India. They slanderously represent the USSR as a possible aggressor and portray themselves as "friends" of China and India and "saviors" from the Communist peril, called "to aid" the weak. In this way India and China are held in submission to imperialism and are subjected to further political and economic enslavement. . . .

The radical changes in the international situation and in the position of individual countries which occurred as a result of the war altered the entire political map of the world. A new ordering of political forces was created. The farther we move from the end of the war, the more sharply will the two basic tendencies in postwar international politics be distinguished — tendencies which correspond to the distribution of political forces operating in the world arena in two fundamental camps — the imperialist and anti-democratic camp on the one hand and the anti-imperialist and democratic camp on the other. The principal leading force of the imperialist camp is the United States of America. In union with the United States are England and France, since the presence of the labor government of Attlee and Bevin in England and the socialist government of Ramadier in France does not prevent England and France from moving in the current of the imperialist policy of the United States as its satellites on all basic questions. The imperialist camp is supported also by such colonial states as Belgium and Holland, by such countries with reactionary régimes as Turkey and Greece, and by such lands as the Near East, South America, and China which are politically and economically dependent on the United States of America.

The fundamental aim of the imperialist camp is the strengthening of imperialism, the preparation of a new imperialist war, the struggle against socialism and democracy, and the universal support of reactionary and anti-democratic pro-fascist régimes and movements.

In the resolution of these tasks the imperialist camp is ready to lean upon reactionary and anti-democratic forces in all countries and to support yesterday's war-time adversaries against its war-time allies.

The anti-imperialist and anti-fascist forces compose the other camp. The foundation of this camp is the USSR and the countries of the new democracy. Into this camp there enter also such countries as Rumania, Hungary, and Finland, which have broken away from imperialism and are standing firmly on the road of democratic development. Indonesia and Viet-Nam are joining the anti-imperialist camp, and India, Egypt, and Syria are sympathetic. This camp leans on the labor and democratic movement everywhere, on the fraternal Communist Parties in all lands, on the warriors of the movement for national liberation in colonial and dependent countries, on the support of all democratic forces existing in each country. The aim of this camp is the struggle against threats of new wars and imperialist expansion, the strengthening of democracy, and the eradication of the remnants of fascism. . . .

The exposure of the American plan for the economic enslavement of European countries is the indisputable merit of the foreign policy of the USSR and the countries of the new democracy.

In this connection it is necessary to keep in view the fact that America herself is under the threat of an economic crisis. The official bounty of Marshall has its own weighty causes. If the European countries do not receive American credit, the demand of these countries for American goods will drop, and this will accelerate and strengthen the approaching crisis in the United States of America. Therefore, if the European countries exhibit the necessary firmness and readiness to resist the American enslaving conditions of credit, America can be forced to retreat.

The reader should note the stress which Zhdanov places on the power factors. It is obvious that his analysis of these factors is profoundly correct, and it is obvious too that the "men of the Kremlin" are not scared. Why should they be? One must remember who they are. They are not playboys, devoted to the fleshpots. Neither are they businessmen with their eyes glued on the stock markets. Nor are they doctrinaires "talking idly in groups." Nor yet are they humanitarians who quail at the thought of war, bloodshed, and human misery. On the contrary, they are men of action, of violent and ruthless action. They are as hard and unsentimental as any band of political leaders or conspirators ever gathered together on the planet. Molotov once boastfully proclaimed to the world in a calculated understatement that Bolsheviks are not "pacifists." In their younger years they did not hesitate to risk everything they possessed, including their lives, on their analysis of revolutionary forces or on a single throw of the dice of history. They are inured to adventure, struggle, and battle. They can all remember the days in 1918 and 1919 when they held Moscow and not much territory to the south and west, when they were threatened with annihilation by counterrevolution and foreign armies. They can also recall the days of Stalingrad when they saved themselves only by the skin of their teeth. In the light of Zhdanov's analysis and in the words of Engels they must indeed feel that at last "their time has come."

6

This consideration of the Soviet apocalypse may be concluded very fittingly with "the great vow of Stalin" which appears repeatedly in the history textbooks. Russian school children today are taught this vow and are told that "it has become the program of action of the Party and the Soviet state, guaranteeing the victorious development of our country on the road to socialism." Five days after the death of the creator of Bolshevism, Stalin vowed to fulfill the "commandments of Lenin." Speaking ostensibly in the name of the Party and the entire Soviet people at the Second Congress of Soviets of the USSR on January 26, 1924, he said in part:

Departing from us, Comrade Lenin bequeathed to us the duty of holding high and preserving in its purity the great title of member of the Party. We swear to thee, Comrade Lenin, that we will fulfill with honor this thy commandment! . . .

Departing from us, Comrade Lenin bequeathed to us the duty of preserving and strengthening the dictatorship of the proletariat. We swear to thee, Comrade Lenin, that we will not spare our energies in also fulfilling with honor this thy commandment! . . .

Departing from us, Comrade Lenin bequeathed to us the duty of strengthening with all our energies the union of workers and peasants. We swear to thee, Comrade Lenin, that we will also fulfill with honor this thy commandment! . . .

Departing from us, Comrade Lenin bequeathed to us the duty of strengthening and expanding the Union of Republics. We swear to thee, Comrade Lenin, that we will also fulfill with honor this thy commandment! . . .

Lenin often pointed out to us that the strengthening of the Red Army and the improvement of its condition is one of the most important tasks of our Party. Let us also swear, Comrades, that we will not spare our energies in strengthening our Red Army and our Red Navy. . . .

Departing from us, Comrade Lenin bequeathed to us fidelity to the principles of the Communist International. We swear to thee, Comrade Lenin, that we will not spare our lives in strengthening and expanding the union of the toilers of the entire world — the Communist International.[21]

This great vow, couched in the ceremonial language of religion, is more in harmony with the spirit of the present time than on the day Stalin made it, twenty-five years ago. Immediately after the war it was made the basis of an extravagant film, entitled *Kliatva* (The Vow). This picture glorifies Stalin without restraint and was constructed on the assumption that the "most truthful outward likeness of the beloved leader was not enough." But, good as it is, the task remains of "finding the means of portraying . . . the

[21] A. Pankratova, Editor, *History of the USSR* (Moscow, 1946), vol. III, pp. 310–11. Official textbook for the tenth grade, the last year of the high school. (In Russian.)

personality of this greatest man of all times and peoples." [22] The film also stresses the "commandments" and shows how the "words of Stalin's vow became a pledge for the fulfillment of all the hopes of the Soviet people and the ideological foundation of all our victories." [23] The picture was awarded a Stalin prize in 1947.

As school children are told, the great vow is indeed the "program of action of the Party and the Soviet state." Calling for the indefinite expansion of the Union of Soviet Republics and the indefinite strengthening of the Communist International, it constitutes a kind of unqualified and unlimited declaration of war on the entire "bourgeois world." And the Western democracies may be certain that the militant spirit and the apocalyptic substance of this document will dominate Soviet foreign policy until the tides of history turn again, until the power relations of the world change, as Zhdanov would say, to the disadvantage of "socialism." The Kremlin will honor its commitments with "bourgeois" states only as long as such commitments are in harmony with the distribution of economic and military force in the world.

Clearly, after the experience of 1917, 1920, 1928–29, 1935, 1939, 1941, and 1945–46, no democratic statesman should be fooled by the political maneuvers of the Kremlin. Soviet policies come and go, Soviet tactics change from moment to moment, but Soviet goals are today the same as yesterday, and doubtless will remain the same tomorrow, and perhaps the day after tomorrow. No loyal and wise leader of the free forces of the world will fail to hold ever in mind the guiding star of Soviet policy — the Russian version of the Communist apocalypse.

22 *Iskusstvo Kino* (January, 1947), No. 1, p. 7.
23 *Ibid.* (July–August, 1947), No. 5, p. 1.

CHAPTER THREE

LITERATURE AS A WEAPON

In the late summer and early autumn of 1946 the American people began to receive brief dispatches from Moscow suggesting that certain writers, dramatists, and moving-picture directors were in trouble. It appeared that the Central Committee of the Party of Lenin and Stalin had pointed the finger of criticism at these people and had asked them to mend their ways. Since most Americans were wholly unfamiliar both with the names mentioned in the dispatches and with the rôle of the Party in the Russian state, they tended to dismiss the reports as beyond their comprehension or to regard the events involved as humorous episodes to be treated with levity. They failed utterly to sense the personal tragedies lying behind the news stories and the world tragedy implicit in these strange actions of the All-Union Communist Party.

As a matter of fact, the dispatches were reporting the first battles in a gigantic and carefully planned offensive against the West and the entire free world. The attack of the Party on the literary arts was the beginning of a campaign to bring the entire cultural apparatus to the vigorous and unqualified support of the new foreign policy which the Politburo was maturing as the war drew to its close and which is outlined frankly in Zhdanov's address in Poland. Apparently the first object of the attack was to erase completely from the mind of the Soviet people all favorable impressions of the West and particularly of America gained during the struggle. But the controlling purpose apparently was and is the support of a stupendous and co-ordinated effort, armed with the full might of the Russian state and the Third International, to stir people to revolt everywhere, to extend the Soviet system to the utmost, and to fulfill the apocalyptic vision of Marx, Lenin, and Stalin.

The theoretical foundation of this action of the Party was laid by Lenin. Standing on the Marxian conception of the state, with all of its organs and powers, as the instrument of the ruling class, he proceeded logically to the position that the first duty of every division of Soviet culture is the education of the people in Party doctrine and policy. In a passage which is quoted more widely today than in Lenin's time he expressed himself as follows: "In the field of public education the Communist Party sets itself the aim of concluding the task begun by the October Revolution of 1917 of converting the school from a weapon for the class domination of the bourgeoisie into a weapon for the destruction of this domination, as well as for the complete destruction of the division of society into classes. The school must become a weapon of the dictatorship of the proletariat." [1] Stalin, as is his habit, put the matter even more bluntly in a conversation with H. G. Wells. "Education is a weapon," he said, "whose effect depends on who holds it in his hands and at whom it is aimed." And when the term "education" is employed in the Soviet Union today it is made to embrace all the influences and agencies for the informing and molding of the mind. In the measure that these influences and agencies can be organized and controlled, they constitute a weapon or a battery of weapons of fabulous power which the Communist Party holds in its hands and points at whomsoever or whatsoever it wishes.

The process of shifting the aim and of adjusting the sights of this powerful battery of weapons began in earnest on August 14, 1946, with a resolution [2] of the Central Committee of the Party on two literary journals published in Leningrad. Most famous of all the resolutions, because it was the first and therefore set the

[1] Lenin, *Works*, vol. XIII, p. 63.
[2] The Russian word may also be translated "decree."

pattern, it was called the "Resolution on the Journals *Zvezda* and *Leningrad.*" It was followed by resolutions on the drama, the cinema, music, genetics, humor, and other phases of cultural activity. Along with some of their consequences and reverberations in Soviet life, these resolutions will be presented in the pages and chapters that follow. Taken together they are known in the Soviet Union as the "resolutions on ideology." They reveal clearly the Soviet system of mind control.

2

The "Resolution on the Journals *Zvezda* and *Leningrad,*" like all other pronouncements of the Central Committee of the Party, the reader should note, is not the voice of a literary critic, or the editor of a magazine. Neither is it the voice of a rich patron, nor even of a congressional committee whose chairman may be haled before a court on a charge of defrauding the Government. In the Soviet Union today it is the voice of absolute and ruthless power lying utterly beyond the reach of the people or public opinion. Indeed it *makes* public opinion according to its desires. The entire resolution, as published in the journal of the Central Committee of the All-Union Communist Party, follows: [3]

The Central Committee of the All-Union Communist Party notes that the literary journals, *Zvezda* and *Leningrad,* published in Leningrad, are conducted in an entirely unsatisfactory manner.

In the journal *Zvezda* in recent times, along with significant and successful works by Soviet writers, ideologically harmful works have appeared. The gross mistake of *Zvezda* is the placing of a literary tribune at the disposal of the writer Zoshchenko, whose works are alien to Soviet literature. The fact is well known to the editors of *Zvezda* that for a long time Zoshchenko has specialized in writing shallow, empty, and vulgar stories, in preaching decadent banality and neutrality in ideology and politics, designed to confuse and poison the

---

[3] *Partiinaia Zhizn,* No. 1 (1946), pp. 59–61.

consciousness of our youth. The last of Zoshchenko's published stories, "The Adventures of a Monkey" (*Zvezda*, Nos. 5–6, 1946), is a vulgar parody on Soviet life and Soviet people. Zoshchenko presents the Soviet order and the Soviet people in the form of an ugly caricature, slanderously depicting Soviet people as primitive, uncouth, stupid, and narrow-minded in tastes and morals. His maliciously hooliganistic portrayal of our society is accompanied by anti-Soviet attacks.

The placing of the pages of *Zvezda* at the disposal of such vulgarians and dregs of literature is the more inadmissable because the editors of the journal know well the physiognomy of Zoshchenko and his unworthy behavior during the war. He gave no aid to the Soviet people in their struggle against the German robbers and wrote a loathsome story entitled "Before Sunrise." The appraisal of this story and of the entire literary "creative work" of Zoshchenko has been presented in the pages of the journal, *Bolshevik*.

The journal *Zvezda* also popularizes in every way the works of the writer Akhmatova, whose literary and socio-political physiognomy has been known time out of mind to Soviet society. Akhmatova is a typical representative of a form of poetry that is empty, neutral ideologically, and foreign to our people. Her verses are saturated with a spirit of pessimism and melancholy, and express the tastes of the old poetry of the salon. This poetry is frozen in the attitudes of bourgeois-aristocratic estheticism and decadence, of "art for art's sake"; it refuses to march in step with its own people, brings harm to the cause of the education of our youth, and is intolerable in Soviet literature.

The offering to Zoshchenko and Akhmatova of an active rôle in the journal undoubtedly has brought elements of ideological confusion and disorganization among Leningrad writers. Works which cultivate a non-Soviet spirit of servility before the contemporary bourgeois culture of the West have appeared in the journal. Compositions saturated with gloom, pessimism, and disillusionment with life have been published (the verses of Sadofiev and Komissarova, No. 1, 1946, etc.). By printing these works the editorial board has aggravated its mistakes and lowered yet further the ideological level of the journal.

While permitting the penetration into the journal of ideologically alien works, the editorial board also lowered the demand for artistic quality in the literary material published. The journal was soon filled with plays and stories of little artistic value ("The Road of Time" by Yagdfeld, "Swan's Lake" by Stein, etc.). Such carelessness in the selection of materials for publication has led to the lowering of the artistic level of the journal.

The Central Committee notes that the journal *Leningrad,* which has constantly offered its pages to the vulgar and slanderous attacks of Zoshchenko and to the empty and non-political verses of Akhmatova, is especially badly conducted. Just as the editorial board of *Zvezda,* so the editorial board of the journal *Leningrad* has tolerated grievous mistakes by publishing a series of works saturated with the spirit of servility toward everything foreign. It printed a number of faulty compositions ("Accident over Berlin" by Varshavsky and Rest, "At the Gate" by Slonimsky). In the verses of Khazin, "The Return of Onegin," under the guise of literary parody, contemporary Leningrad was slandered. For the most part the literary materials appearing in the journal are empty and inferior.

How could it happen that the journals *Zvezda* and *Leningrad,* published in Leningrad, a city of heroes, celebrated for its advanced revolutionary traditions, a city which has always been the home of advanced ideas and culture, permitted the surreptitious introduction. into their pages of works marked by ideological and political neutrality and alien to Soviet literature?

What is the meaning of the mistakes of the editorial boards of *Zvezda* and *Leningrad?*

The leading workers of the journals and in the first instance the editors, Comrades Saianov and Likharev, have forgotten the thesis of Leninism that our journals, whether scientific or literary, cannot be non-political. They have forgotten that our journals are a mighty instrument of the Soviet state in the cause of the education of the Soviet people, and Soviet youth in particular. They must therefore be controlled by the vital foundation of the Soviet order — its politics. The Soviet order cannot tolerate the education of the young in the spirit of indifference to Soviet politics, in the spirit of a devil-may-care attitude and ideological neutrality.

The power of Soviet literature, the most advanced literature in the world, consists in the fact that it is a literature which has not and cannot have interests other than the interests of the people, the interests of the state. The task of Soviet literature is to aid the state to educate the youth correctly and to meet their demands, to rear a new generation strong and vigorous, believing in their cause, fearing no obstacles and ready to overcome all obstacles.

Consequently any preaching of ideological neutrality, of political neutrality, of "art for art's sake" is alien to Soviet literature and harmful to the interests of the Soviet people and the Soviet state. Such preaching has no place in our journals.

Also as a result of their ideological deficiency the leading workers of *Zvezda* and *Leningrad* placed at the base of their relations with literary writers, not interests related to the correct education of the Soviet people and to the political direction of the activity of literary writers, but personal interests of friendship. Because of reluctance to mar friendly relations, criticism was dulled. Because of fear of offending a friend, obviously worthlesss works were published. The results of such a brand of liberalism, under which criticism is silenced, the interests of the people and the state are sacrificed, and the correct education of our youth is subordinated to considerations of friendship, are obvious: writers cease to perfect themselves and lose their sense of responsibility to the people, to the state, and to the Party: they cease to move forward.

Everything mentioned above bears witness to the fact that the editorial boards of the journals *Zvezda* and *Leningrad* did not carry out the work intrusted to them and tolerated serious political errors in the leadership.

The Central Committee has ascertained that the Administration of the Union of Soviet writers and particularly its president, Comrade Tikhonov, undertook no measures for the improvement of the journals *Zvezda* and *Leningrad*. They not only did not conduct a struggle against the harmful influences of Zoshchenko and Akhmatova, and non-Soviet writers like them, but even encouraged the penetration into the journals of tendencies and morals alien to Soviet literature.

The Leningrad City Committee of the All-Union Communist Party overlooked the outstanding mistakes of the journals, neglected the leadership of the journals, and offered an opportunity to people alien to Soviet literature, like Zoshchenko and Akhmatova, to assume a leading position in the journals. More than this, while knowing the attitude of the Party toward Zoshchenko and his "creative work," the Leningrad City Committee of the Party (Comrades Kapustin and Shirokov) exceeded their authority and on June 26 of this year approved the new staff of the editorial board of the journal *Zvezda* which included Zoshchenko. By this action the Leningrad City Committee was guilty of a grievous political error. Leningrad *Pravda* committed a mistake by publishing a suspiciously eulogistic review of the creative work of Zoshchenko by Uri German in the issue of June 6 of the current year.

The Administration of Propaganda of the Central Committee of the All-Union Communist Party has not provided the needed supervision of the work of the Leningrad journals.

The Central Committee of the All-Union Communist Party resolves:

1. To oblige the editorial board of the journal *Zvezda,* the Administration of the Union of Soviet Writers, and the Administration of Propaganda of the Central Committee of the All-Union Communist Party to undertake measures for the unconditioned removal of the mistakes and shortcomings of the journal mentioned in the present resolution, to correct the line of the journal, and to insure a high ideological and artistic level of the journal, putting a stop to the appearance in the journal of the works of Zoshchenko and Akhmatova and their ilk.

2. In view of the fact that at the present time the necessary conditions for the publication of two literary journals in Leningrad do not exist, to discontinue the publication of the journal *Leningrad,* concentrating the literary forces of *Leningrad* on the journal *Zvezda.*

3. For the purpose of introducing the necessary order into the work of the editorial office of the journal *Zvezda* and of radically improving the content of its pages, to appoint an editor-in-chief and an editorial board. To have the editor-in-chief assume full responsibility for the ideological and political direction of the journal and for the quality of the works published therein.

4. To appoint Comrade A. M. Yegolin as editor-in-chief of the journal *Zvezda* without relieving him of the duties of Acting Director of the Administration of Propaganda of the Central Committee of the All-Union Communist Party.

3

On August 21, 1946, Andrei Zhdanov, speaking at the First All-Union Congress of Soviet Writers, interpreted the resolution of the Central Committee in a powerful speech [4] of ten thousand

[4] *Literaturnaia Gazeta,* September 21, 1946.

words. This address, like the one given a year later in Poland before representatives of the Communist Parties of Europe, was one of the two or three most important pronouncements of the Party leadership since the war. Along with the several resolutions on ideology it is regarded in the Soviet Union today as an authoritative guide in the shaping of policy and practice in all departments of the cultural apparatus. The death of Zhdanov in September, 1948, has not been followed by the slightest weakening of the policy which he proclaimed.

The first part of his speech is devoted to a perfectly savage attack on a number of writers and particularly on Zoshchenko and Akhmatova. And the American reader should be reminded once more that from such an attack the individual in all probability "will never rise again," in the words Hitler once applied to the defeat of Russian arms. If he should "rise again," it would be only after he had grovelled before the Party, renounced his past, and demonstrated by *deed* a genuine state of contrition. All who heard Zhdanov knew that his indictment was final, that in his voice the court of last resort had spoken. His judgment on Mikhail Zoshchenko, one of the most popular of Russian writers at the time, may be summarized in these sentences from his address:

Zoshchenko takes absolutely no interest in the labor of the Soviet people, their struggles and heroism, their high social and moral qualities. With him this theme is always absent. Zoshchenko, like the Philistine and vulgarian that he is, chose as his permanent theme digging into the basest and pettiest sides of life. . . . Only the dregs of literature could produce such "works." But how could a journal . . . give shelter to such a vulgarian and un-Soviet writer as Zoshchenko? . . . In this tale Zoshchenko turned his vulgar and mean little soul inside out. . . . With complete justice Zoshchenko was publicly spanked in *Bolshevik* as a libeler and vulgarian alien to Soviet literature.

He spat on public opinion. . . . The thoroughly putrid and corrupt socio-political and literary physiognomy of Zoshchenko was not formed in the most recent period. . . . If Zoshchenko does not like Soviet ways, what is your command: to adjust ourselves to Zoshchenko? It is not for us to reform our tastes. It is not for us to reform our life and our social order according to Zoshchenko. Let him reform. But he does not want to reform. Let him get out of Soviet literature. In Soviet literature there can be no place for putrid, empty, vulgar, and ideologically indifferent works.

He depicts Soviet people as loafers and monsters, as stupid and crude people. . . . He is incapable of finding in the life of the Soviet people one positive thing, one positive figure. . . . Zoshchenko habitually mocks at Soviet life, Soviet institutions, Soviet people. . . . In his "The Adventures of a Monkey" he gives a deliberately deformed and vulgar caricature of the life of the Soviet people in order to insert into the mouth of a monkey the vile, poisonous, anti-Soviet maxim that it is better to live in a zoo than at liberty, and that it is easier to breathe in a cage than among Soviet people. . . . How can the people of Leningrad tolerate on the pages of their journals such filth and obscenity?

With cynical frankness he continues to remain a preacher of ideological indifference and vulgarity, an unprincipled and unscrupulous literary hooligan.

Zhdanov's "tribute" to Akhmatova is of the same order. It is not impossible that the vitriolic quality of his estimate is due in part to the fact that Akhmatova in one of her studies traced the theme of one of Pushkin's most celebrated poems, "The Golden Cock," to a story by Washington Irving. This must have been regarded as a wholly inadmissible instance of "grovelling before the West." Zhdanov's judgment on Anna Akhmatova, a poet surviving from the old régime, is expressed in these words:

Akhmatova is a representative of this ideologyless reactionary swamp. . . . She preaches the theory of "art for art's sake," of "beauty for beauty's sake."

The subject-matter of Akhmatova is individualistic to the core. Her poetry is poverty-stricken — the poetry of a frantic little lady, rushing back and forth between the boudoir and the chapel. Basic with her are amorous-erotic motifs, interlaced with motifs of sadness, anguish, death, mysticism, and doom. . . . Not quite a nun and not quite a fornicatrix, but rather a fornicatrix and a nun in whom fornication is mingled with prayer.

Such is Akhmatova with her petty, narrow personal life, her trivial emotional experiences and her religious-mystical eroticism. . . . Moods of loneliness and hopelessness, alien to Soviet literature, characterize the entire historical course of the "creative genius" of Akhmatova. . . .

What has this poetry in common with the interests of our people and state? Nothing whatsoever. Akhmatova's creative genius belongs to the distant past. It is alien to the realities of contemporary Soviet life and cannot be tolerated in the pages of our journals. Our literature is not a private undertaking designed to please the diverse tastes of a literary market. We are under no obligation to provide space in our literature for tastes and tempers which have nothing in common with the morals and qualities of the Soviet people. What of instruction can Akhmatova's works give to our youth? Nothing but harm. These works can only sow despondency, depression, pessimism, and an inclination to run away from the urgent questions of society, to leave the broad highway of social life and action for the narrow little world of personal experiences. How is it possible to put into her hands the rearing of our youth? And yet Akhmatova has been published with great readiness, now in *Zvezda*, now in *Leningrad*. She has even been printed in separate collections. This is a crude political error.

The second half of Zhdanov's address before the First All-Union Congress of Soviet Writers is devoted to the presentation of the views of the Party on Soviet literature. It is this part of the address that develops the new orientation, relates the entire subject to the essence of the teachings of Lenin, and outlines the duties and functions of the Soviet intelligentsia. An unabridged translation of this portion of the speech, as published in *Literaturnaia Gazeta*, follows:

What is the root of these errors and shortcomings?

The root of these errors and shortcomings lies in the fact that the editors of the journals, leading figures in our Soviet literature and on our ideological front in Leningrad, have forgotten certain fundamental theses of Leninism on literature. Many writers, including those who work as responsible editors or hold important posts in the Union of Soviet Writers, think that politics is the business of the government and the Central Committee. As for writers, politics is not their concern. A person has written well, artistically, beautifully — give him a start, regardless of the fact that his work contains putrid passages which confuse and poison our youth. We demand that our comrades, both as leaders in literary affairs and as writers, be guided by the vital force of the Soviet order — its politics. Only thus can our youth be reared, not in a devil-may-care attitude and a spirit of ideological indifference, but in a strong and vigorous revolutionary spirit.

It is known that Leninism incarnated all the best traditions of the Russian revolutionary democrats of the nineteenth century and that our Soviet culture has risen, developed, and flowered on the basis of a critical working over of the cultural heritage of the past. In the sphere of literature our Party, through the words of Lenin and Stalin, has recognized more than once the tremendous significance of the great Russian revolutionary-democratic writers and critics — Belinsky, Dobroliubov, Chernyshevsky, Saltykov-Shchedrin, and Plekhanov. Beginning with Belinsky, all of the best representatives of the revolutionary-democratic Russian intelligentsia repudiated so-called "pure art" and "art for art's sake." They were heralds of art for the people, of art of high ideological and social significance. Art cannot separate itself from the fate of the people. Recall Belinsky's famous "Letter to Gogol," in which the great critic, with all the passion that was in him, lashed Gogol for his attempt to forsake the cause of the people and go over to the side of the tsar. Lenin called this letter one of the best products of the uncensored democratic press. It retains to this day vast literary significance.

Recall the literary-journalistic articles of Dobroliubov, in which the social significance of literature is revealed with such power. All of our Russian revolutionary-democratic journalism was saturated with mortal hatred of the tsarist order and permeated with the noble impulse of fighting for the basic interests of the people, for their enlightenment, for their culture, and for their liberation from the fetters of the tsarist régime. A militant art, leading the struggle for the finest ideals of the people — thus were literature and art understood by the great representatives of Russian literature. Chernyshevsky, who of all utopian socialists approached closest to scientific socialism and whose works, as Lenin pointed out, "breathed the spirit of the class struggle," taught that the task of art is, besides the perception of life, the teaching of people to evaluate correctly this or that social phenomenon. As his closest friend and companion in literature, Dobroliubov, pointed out, "life does not proceed according to literary norms, but literature conforms to the tendencies of life." He propagated vigorously the principles of realism and populism in literature. He thought that reality is the foundation of art and the fountain of creative genius, that art has an active rôle to play in social life, in the molding of social consciousness. According to Dobroliubov, literature must serve society, must give the people answers to the most crucial questions of contemporary life, must keep abreast of the ideas of its epoch.

Marxist literary criticism, carrying on the great traditions of Belinsky, Chernyshevsky, and Dobroliubov, has always been the advocate of realistic and socially directed art. Plekhanov did much to expose idealistic and anti-scientific ideas concerning literature and art and to defend the theses of our great Russian revolutionary democrats who taught that literature is a powerful means for serving the people.

V. I. Lenin was the first to formulate with utmost precision the attitude of advanced social thought toward literature and art. I remind you of Lenin's well-known article "Party Organization and Party Literature," written at the end of 1905, in which he showed with characteristic force that literature cannot be non-Party, that it must be an important component part of the general proletarian cause. In this article Lenin lays the foundations on which the development of our Soviet literature is based. He wrote as follows:

"Literature must become Party. As a counterpoise to bourgeois morals, to the bourgeois commercial press, to bourgeois literary careerism and individualism, to 'manorial anarchism' and the pursuit of gain, the socialist proletariat must promote and develop the principle of *Party literature* and bring this principle to life in the most complete and integral form possible.

"In what does this principle of Party literature consist? Not merely in the fact that for the socialist proletariat the literary cause cannot be a means of profit to persons or groups, and that it cannot be generally an individual cause, independent of the proletarian cause as a whole. Down with non-Party writers! Down with supermen writers! The literary cause must become *part* of the general proletarian cause. . . ."
And further on in the same article:

"To live in society and be free of society is impossible. The freedom of the bourgeois writer, artist, or actress is only a disguised (or hypocritically masked) dependence on the money-bag, on the bribe, on the salary."

Leninism proceeds from the fact that our literature cannot be politically indifferent, cannot be "art for art's sake." On the contrary, it is called upon to play an important leading rôle in social life.

From this position issues the Leninist principle of partisanship in literature — a most important contribution of V. I. Lenin to the science of literature.

Consequently, the best tradition of Soviet literature is a continuation of the best traditions of Russian literature of the nineteenth century, the traditions created by our great revolutionary democrats, Belinsky, Dobroliubov, Chernyshevsky, and Saltykov-Shchedrin, carried on by Plekhanov, and scientifically elaborated and grounded by Lenin and Stalin.

Nekrasov called his poetry "the muse of vengeance and sorrow." Chernyshevsky and Dobroliubov regarded literature as a sacred service to the people. Under the conditions of tsarism the best representatives of the Russian democratic intelligentsia perished for these noble and lofty ideas, went into penal servitude and exile. How is it possible to forget these glorious traditions? How is it possible to scorn them? How is it possible to permit Akhmatovas and Zoshchenkos to propagate surreptitiously the reactionary slogan of "art for art's sake," and to intrude ideas alien to the Soviet people under the mask of ideological neutrality?!

Leninism recognizes the tremendous socially-transforming significance of our literature. For our Soviet literature to permit a lowering of its vast educational rôle would mean a development backward, a return "to the stone age."

Comrade Stalin called our writers engineers of human souls. This definition has profound meaning. It speaks of the enormous responsibility of Soviet writers for the education of the people and for the education of Soviet youth. It says that wastage in literary work is intolerable.

Some wonder why the Central Committee adopted such severe measures on a literary question. They have not become accustomed to this. They think that if wastage is permitted in industry, or if a production program for commodities is not fulfilled, or if a plan for the supplying of lumber is not executed, the administration of a reprimand is a natural act [*laughter of approval in the hall*]. But if wastage is permitted in the education of human souls, if wastage is permitted in the business of rearing the young, here one must be tolerant. Yet actually, is this not a worse fault than the non-fulfillment of a production program or the disruption of a production task? By its decision the Central Committee proposes to bring the ideological front along with all other sectors of our work.

Recently large gaps and weaknesses have been exposed on the ideological front. It suffices to remind you of the backwardness of our cinema, of the littering of our theatrical-dramatic repertoire with inferior productions, not to mention what happened in the journals *Zvezda* and *Leningrad*. The Central Committee was compelled to interfere and introduce decisive corrections. It had no right to soften its blow against those who forget their obligations to the people and for the education of the young. If we want to turn the attention of our active members to questions of ideological work and bring order here, if we want to give clear direction in this work, we must be quick, as befits Soviet people and Bolsheviks, to criticize mistakes and weaknesses in ideological work. Only then will we be able to correct matters.

Other writers reason thus: since the people were starving for literature during the war and since few books were published, the reader will swallow anything, even though it is rotten. But actually this is altogether incorrect. We cannot tolerate any literature which is passed off on us by unscrupulous writers, editors, and publishers. The Soviet people expect from Soviet writers genuine ideological armament, spiritual nourishment that will aid in the fulfillment of the plans of great construction, the plans for the restoration and further development of the public economy of our country. The Soviet people make high demands on writers, they want their ideological and cultural needs to be satisfied. Because of the situation during the war we were unable to meet these urgent demands. The people want to understand the events which have taken place. Their ideological and cultural level has been raised. Frequently they are not satisfied with the quality of the literary and artistic works which we produce. Some workers in literature and on the ideological front have not understood and do not want to understand this.

The level of the demands and tastes of our people has risen very high, and he who does not want to rise or is incapable of rising to this level, will be left behind. Literature is called upon not only to keep abreast of the demands of the people, but more than that — it must develop their tastes, raise higher their demands, enrich them with new ideas, and carry them forward. He who is incapable of marching in step with the people, of satisfying their growing demands, of keeping abreast of the tasks of the development of Soviet culture, will inevitably be retired.

A second large mistake flows from the ideological deficiency of the leading workers of *Zvezda* and *Leningrad*. This mistake consists in the fact that some of them have set up as the criterion of their relations with writers, not the political education of the Soviet people and the political direction of writers, but interests of personal friendship. It is said that many ideologically harmful and artistically weak works have been published because of reluctance to offend this or that writer. According to such a point of view it is better to sacrifice the interests of the people and of the state than to displease somebody. This is an entirely incorrect and politically mistaken position. It is just like exchanging a million for a penny.

In its decision the Central Committee of the Party points out that it is extremely harmful in literature to substitute relations of friendship for relations of principle. Among some of our writers irresponsible relations of friendship have played a profoundly negative rôle, have led to the lowering of the ideological level of many literary works, have facilitated the admission into literature of persons alien to Soviet literature. The absence of criticism on the part of leaders of the ideological front in Leningrad, on the part of leaders of the Leningrad journals, and the substitution of relations of friendship for relations of principle at the expense of the interests of the people have brought very great harm.

Comrade Stalin teaches us that, if we want to conserve, teach, and educate people, we must not be afraid of offending anyone, we must not be afraid of responsible, bold, frank and objective criticism. Without criticism, any organization, including a literary organization, can decay. Without criticism, any illness can be aggravated and made more difficult to cure. Only bold and frank criticism helps our people to perfect themselves, incites them to march ahead and overcome shortcomings in their work. Where there is no criticism, mold and stagnation take root and there is no room to move forward.

Comrade Stalin frequently points out that a most important condition of our development is the necessity for every Soviet person to take stock of his activity each day, to check himself fearlessly, to analyze his work, and to labor continuously on his own improvement. This applies to writers quite as much as to any other workers. He who fears criticism of his own work is a contemptible coward, not worthy of the respect of the people. [*Tumultuous applause.*]

An uncritical attitude toward one's own work and substitution of relations of friendship for relations of principle with writers are widespread also in the Administration of the Union of Soviet Writers. The Administration of the Union and especially its president, Comrade Tikhonov, are guilty of the very mistakes disclosed in the journals *Zvezda* and *Leningrad*. They are guilty not only of not opposing the penetration into Soviet literature of the harmful influences of Zoshchenko, Akhmatova and other non-Soviet writers, but even of conniving at the saturation of our journals with tendencies and morals alien to Soviet literature.

Among the shortcomings of the Leningrad journals the system of irresponsibility that developed in the leadership of the journals played its rôle. Because of the situation on the editorial boards of the journals, it was not known who was responsible for the journal as a whole and for its departments. Elementary order could not exist. This weakness must be corrected. It was for this reason that the Central Committee in its resolution appointed an editor-in-chief for the journal *Zvezda,* who must be responsible for the tendency of the journal, for the high ideological and artistic qualities of the works placed in the journal.

In a journal, as in any business, disorder and anarchy are intolerable. Responsibility for the tendency of a journal and the content of published materials must be clear.

You must restore the glorious traditions of Leningrad literature and the Leningrad ideological front. It is painful and offensive that the journals of Leningrad, which had always been seed-beds for advanced ideas and advanced culture, should have become a refuge for ideological indifference and vulgarity. It is necessary to restore the honor of Leningrad as an advanced ideological and cultural center. It is necessary to remember that Leningrad was the cradle of the Bolshevik Leninist organizations. Here Lenin and Stalin laid the foundations of the Bolshevik Party, the foundations of the Bolshevik world-view and of Bolshevik culture.

It is a matter of honor for Leningrad writers and Leningrad Party activists to restore and develop further these glorious traditions of Leningrad. The task of workers on the ideological front in Leningrad, and principally of the writers, is to drive ideological indifference and vulgarity out of Leningrad literature and to raise high the banner of advanced Soviet literature. They must not overlook a single opportunity for their own ideological and artistic growth, nor lag behind contemporary themes or the demands of the people. In every way they must develop a forthright criticism of their own shortcomings, a criticism that is neither servile nor based on cliques or friendships, but a genuine, bold, independent, and ideological Bolshevik criticism.

Comrades, by now it should be clear to you how crude was the blunder permitted by the Leningrad City Committee of the Party, especially by its Department of Propaganda and Agitation and the Secretary for Propaganda, Comrade Shirokov, who was placed at the head of ideological work and with whom in the first place is lodged responsibility for the failure of the journals. The Leningrad Committee of the Party permitted a crude political error by adopting at the end of June a decision on the composition of the new editorial board of the journal *Zvezda* which even included Zoshchenko. The fact that the Secretary of the Party's City Committee, Comrade Kapustin, and the Secretary of Propaganda of the City Committee, Comrade Shirokov, approved such a mistaken decision can be explained only by political stupidity. I repeat that all these errors must be corrected as speedily and decisively as possible, so that the rôle of Leningrad in the ideological life of our Party may be restored.

We all love Leningrad. We all love our Leningrad Party organization as one of the advance detachments of our Party. In Leningrad there should be no refuge for literary parasites and rogues who want to use Leningrad for their own purposes. Soviet Leningrad is not dear to Zoshchenko, Akhmatova, and their ilk. They want to see in it the incarnation of different socio-political forms and a different ideology. Old Petersburg, the Bronze Horseman as the image of this old Petersburg — that is what looms before their eyes. But we love Soviet Leningrad, Leningrad as an advanced center of Soviet culture. The glorious cohort of great revolutionary and democratic figures that issued from Leningrad — these are our direct ancestors, from whom we derive our genealogy. The glorious traditions of contemporary Leningrad are the continuation of the development of these great revolutionary democratic traditions, which we will exchange for no other. Let the Leningrad activists boldly, without a backward glance, without "cushions," analyze their errors, so as to correct them as completely and as rapidly as possible and move our ideological work forward. Leningrad Bolsheviks must assume again their place in the

ranks of pioneers and advanced workers in the cause of the forming of
Soviet ideology and Soviet social consciousness. [*Tumultuous applause.*]

How could it happen that the Leningrad City Committee of the
Party tolerated such a situation on the ideological front? Obviously it
was distracted by current practical work on the restoration of the
city and the raising of its industry and forgot about the importance of
ideological-educational work. This forgetfulness cost the Leningrad
organization dearly. Ideological work must not be forgotten! The
spiritual wealth of our people is no less important than the material.
To live blindly, without care for the morrow, either in the sphere of
material production or in that of ideology, is forbidden. Our Soviet
people have grown to such an extent that they will not "swallow" just
any spiritual product that might be passed off on them. Workers in
culture and art who do not reform themselves and fail to satisfy the
growing demands of the people could quickly lose their confidence.

Comrades, our Soviet literature lives and should live by the interests
of the people, the interests of the Motherland. Literature is a matter
near to the people. This is why every success of ours, every significant
work, is regarded by the people as their own victory. This is why
every successful work can be compared with a battle won or with a
great victory on the economic front. Inversely, every failure in Soviet
literature is deeply offensive and painful to the people, the Party, and
the state. The resolution of the Central Committee, which looks after
the interests of the people and their literature, and is extremely disturbed by the state of affairs among Leningrad writers, has precisely
this in mind.

If ideologically indifferent people want to deprive the Leningrad
workers in Soviet literature of its foundation, if they want to undermine the ideological side of their work and rob the creative genius of
the Leningrad writers of its socially transforming significance, then the
Central Committee hopes that the Leningrad writers will find in themselves the strength to block all attempts to divert the literary detachment of Leningrad and its journals into the channel of ideological
indifference, lack of principle, and political neutrality. You stand on
the advanced line of the ideological front and you have enormous tasks
of international significance. This should heighten the sense of
responsibility of every genuine Soviet writer toward his people, his
state, and his Party, and the consciousness of the importance of doing
his duty.

Our successes within our country as well as in the international arena do not please the bourgeois world. As a result of the second world war the positions of socialism have been strengthened. The question of socialism has been placed on the order of the day in many countries of Europe. This is unpleasant to imperialists of all colors. They are afraid of socialism. They fear socialism and our socialist country, which is a model for all progressive mankind. Imperialists and their ideological servants, their writers and journalists, their politicians and diplomats, strive in every way to defame our country, to present it in a wrong light, to slander socialism. Under these conditions the task of Soviet literature is not only to reply, blow for blow, to all this base calumny and to the assaults on our Soviet culture and on socialism, but also to lash out boldly and attack bourgeois culture which is in a state of emaciation and depravity.

However outwardly beautiful the form that clothes the creative work of the fashionable contemporary bourgeois West-European and American writers, and also film and theatrical producers, still they can neither redeem nor lift up their bourgeois culture. That culture is putrid and baneful in its moral foundations. It has been put at the service of private capitalist property, at the service of the egoistic and selfish interests of the highest stratum of bourgeois society. The entire host of bourgeois writers, of film and theatrical producers, is striving to divert the attention of the advanced strata of society from acute questions of the political and social struggle and to shift attention into the channel of vulgar and ideologically empty literature and art, crowded with gangsters, chorus girls, praise of adultery, and the affairs of adventurers and rogues of every kind.

Is the rôle of worshipers or pupils of bourgeois culture becoming to us, Soviet patriots and representatives of the most advanced Soviet culture? Certainly our literature, which reflects a social order higher than any bourgeois-democratic order and a culture many times higher than bourgeois culture, has the right to teach others this new universal morality. Where will you find such people and such a country as ours? Where will you find the magnificent qualities which our people displayed in the Great Patriotic War and which they display in their daily work as they pass to the peaceful restoration and development of economy and culture? Every day our people rise higher and ever higher. Today we are not what we were yesterday, and tomorrow we shall not be as we are today. Already we are not the same Russians we were before 1917, our Russia is different, our character is not the same. We have changed and grown along with the great reforms which have profoundly changed the face of our country.

To reveal these new high qualities of Soviet persons, not only to reveal our people in their today, but also to give a glimpse of them in their tomorrow, to help light the way ahead with a searchlight — such is the task of every conscientious Soviet writer. The writer cannot trudge along at the tail of events; he must march in the front ranks of the people, pointing out to them the road of their development. Guided by the method of socialist realism, studying conscientiously and attentively our reality, striving to penetrate more deeply into the essence of the processes of our development, the writer must educate the people and arm them ideologically. While selecting the best sentiments and qualities of Soviet man and revealing his tomorrow, we must at the same time show our people what they must not be and scourge the vestiges of yesterday, vestiges which hamper the Soviet people in their forward march. Soviet writers must assist the people, the state, and the Party in the education of our youth to be cheerful, confident of their own strength, and fearful of no difficulties.

However bourgeois politicians and writers may strive to conceal from their own peoples the truth about the achievements of the Soviet order and Soviet culture, however they may endeavor to erect an iron curtain, to render impossible the penetration abroad of the truth about the Soviet Union, however they may strain themselves to disparage the actual growth and sweep of Soviet culture — all these efforts are doomed to failure. We know very well the power and the superiority of our culture. Suffice it to recall the stupendous successes of our cultural delegations abroad, our physical-culture parades, and so on. Are we to grovel before every foreign thing or be put passively on the defensive?

If the feudal system and then the bourgeois in the periods of their flowering could create an art and a literature which affirmed the establishment of the new order and sang the praises of its flowering, then we, who represent the new socialist order, the embodiment of all that is best in the history of human civilization and culture, are all the more entitled to create the most advanced literature in the world, which will leave far behind the best models of the creative genius of former times.

Comrades, what does the Central Committee want and demand?

The Central Committee of the Party wants the Leningrad activists and the Leningrad writers to understand well that the time has come when it is necessary to raise our ideological work to a high level. It is for the younger Soviet generation to strengthen the power and might of the socialist Soviet order, to make full use of the dynamic forces of Soviet society for a new and unheard-of blossoming of our material welfare and culture. For these great tasks the younger generation must be educated to be steadfast, cheerful, unafraid of obstacles, eager to meet and able to overcome these obstacles. Our people must be educated people possessing high ideological, cultural, and moral standards and tastes. This means that our literature and journals must not stand aside from the tasks of contemporary life, but must assist the Party and the people in the education of the young in the spirit of supreme devotion to the Soviet social order, in the spirit of supreme service to the interests of the people.

Soviet writers and all of our ideological workers are standing today in the advanced line of fire. This is due to the fact that under the conditions of peaceful development the tasks of the ideological front and especially of literature are not decreasing but on the contrary are growing. The people, the state, and the Party want, not the withdrawal of literature from the contemporary world, but active intrusion of literature into all aspects of Soviet life. Bolsheviks value literature highly. They see clearly its great historical mission and rôle in the strengthening of the moral and political unity of the people, in the solidifying and the educating of the people. The Central Committee of the Party wants us to have an abundance of spiritual culture, for in this wealth of culture it sees one of the principal tasks of socialism.

The Central Committee of the Party is confident that the Leningrad detachment of Soviet literature is morally and politically healthy and will speedily correct its errors and assume its proper place in the ranks of Soviet literature.

The Central Committee is confident that the deficiencies in the work of the Leningrad writers will be overcome and that the ideological work of the Leningrad Party organization will, in the shortest period, be raised to the height now needed in the interests of the Party, the people, and the state. [*Tumultuous applause. All rise.*]

4

Following the resolution of the Central Committee of the Party and the address by Zhdanov, the Presidium of the Administration of the Union of Soviet writers met in formal session during the first week of September, 1946. An account of the meeting appeared in *Literaturnaia Gazeta,* the official organ of the Union, on September 7. The pattern of the proceedings is familiar to all students of Soviet life and institutions. Those present were expected to applaud the wisdom of Stalin and the Party, confess their mistakes, promise to do better in the future, and take practical steps to carry out the directives or orders contained in the resolution. The remarks of four of the leading members of the Presidium, as published in the journal, will convey a trustworthy idea of the sentiments expressed at the session.

Nikolai Tikhonov, one of the foremost Soviet poets, was on the spot. As President of the Union of Soviet Writers, he had been charged in the resolution of the Party with having been responsible in very considerable measure for the sad state of affairs in the two journals. Eagerly and emphatically admitting his guilt, he behaved as a "good Bolshevik" should. The full account of his speech follows:

Opening the session of the Presidium of the Union of Soviet Writers of the USSR, N. Tikhonov emphasizes the tremendous significance of the resolution in the life of the Union of Writers and of all Soviet literature.

A careful study of the work of the journals *Leningrad* and *Zvezda,* says Comrade Tikhonov, reveals that their leading workers, and in the first place the editors, Comrades V. Saianov and B. Likharev, have forgotten that the journals could not be neutral in politics, that they are a powerful means for the education of the Soviet people, and particularly the youth, and therefore must be guided by the politics of the Soviet state. The resolution justly points out that the Administration of the Union of Soviet Writers and I, as its president, undertook no measures for the improvement of the journals, *Zvezda* and *Leningrad*. We not only did not carry on a struggle with the harmful influences of Zoshchenko and Akhmatova and other non-Soviet writers like them, but permitted the penetration into the journals of tendencies and morals alien to Soviet literature.

How could these unprecedented mistakes have occurred which have now shaken every Soviet writer to the depth of his soul? It seems to me that the cause of this lies in the fact that the Administration of the Union of Writers in its daily work had forgotten the most important thing — the way of the development of Soviet literature. Concerned with individual tasks and the solution of private problems of literary life, we forgot about the grand historical significance of Soviet literature which has become the leading literature of the world. We must recognize that the mistakes which we permitted bear witness to the dulling of the sense of responsibility before the people, before our Soviet state, before the great Stalinist epoch.

A thoughtful analysis of the significant works appearing during the war years, and of the business of the journals and publishing houses, did not occupy the centre of attention of the Administration and the Presidium of the Union of Writers. This is my greatest weakness and fault as organizer and leader.

We should understand the resolution of the Central Committee of the Party not merely as a directive relating to the mistakes of certain journals and editors who provided a tribune for Zoshchenko and Akhmatova. The meaning of the resolution is much broader. It consists in the fact that Soviet literature — forward-looking and powerful — must grow and constantly reveal the new and ever new phenomena of the life of a victorious people, of its spiritual process of perfecting itself. Only such an understanding of the rôle of Soviet literature can assist us in seeing the essence of its development, in avoiding political errors, and in conducting our work correctly. From a responsible and ideological height all the phenomena of our literary life will be seen more clearly.

N. Tikhonov subjects to criticism the work of the Presidium of the Union of Soviet Writers during the past two years. In his opinion, the basic failing was the absence of a sense of responsibility on the part of the Presidium as a whole and of every member of the Presidium in particular for the work assigned to him. The daily work of the

Presidium was concentrated for the most part on questions of secondary importance.

Our sessions, continues N. Tikhonov, regardless of the matters we gathered to discuss, were conducted "within a narrow circle." When the question arose, let us say, about *Literaturnaia Gazeta,* we criticized it as if the paper were not ours and as if someone else and not we were at fault for its shortcomings.

The resolution of the Central Committee speaks of the spirit of servility before the bourgeois West which appeared in the journals *Zvezda* and *Leningrad.* This spirit also found other expressions in our literary life. It is well known how one dramatist took a foreign novel and converted it into a contemporary play on our life, exhibiting in so doing his complete ignorance of Soviet man and an irresponsible attitude toward his own literature. Although another writer does not work over foreign compositions, you feel in his writings an imitation of vicious models of the West. This is particularly noticeable in the sphere of the drama. Regardless of the form in which the ideological thrust of the capitalist world is expressed, we cannot encourage this. Recently in America there was published an article entitled "The future world domination of American literature in the Age of Atomic Energy" "The future world domination!" — so it said. The theory of the "right to make mistakes," which was formulated by certain writers in the Ukraine, disarms us in the face of foreign ideology.

Samed Vurgun could tell us how a writer in Azerbaidjan preaches that one should write only in black colors, that the ray of a literary project should be focused on ignorant people and scoundrels, and that one should write for the most part about them. This writer depicts unlovely types in such a way as to show their successes and their elements of strength; he exaggerates their significance in life.

In the sphere of historical writing at first glance all seems well: there are many novels and plays. But the trouble is that on closer examination these works do not seem so beautiful. Estheticism, which is often present in "novels of chivalry," veils the historic reality.

The writers of sixteen republics create our literature. In each republic literary processes evolve about which we are often ignorant. This leads to a whole series of mistakes. The Commission of Nationalities of the Union of Soviet Writers of the USSR does not respond fully to its assignment; other forms of work must be found for it. After the editorial staffs of the journals *Leningrad, Zvezda, Znamia,* and

Oktiabr were organized, we ceased to follow their activity. A journal is a high tribune and access to this tribune must be governed by the principle of strict ideological-artistic selection.

Only because the journals were not in the center of the attention of the Presidium did all these serious ideological failings appear. Why were verses published in *Novii Mir* which were saturated with the spirit of complacency and placidity, why were the verses of Akhmatova printed now in one and now in another journal, why was a poem by Kirsanov about *Alexander Matrosov* with a formalistic perversion published in *Oktiabr?* The latter poem is incorrect, not from the point of view of my taste, but from the point of view of an adequate understanding of the tasks of literature, and of the attitude toward such a significant theme as the heroism of Soviet man. Why did not Panferov sense the depravity of this work and why did he publish it?

Further N. Tikhonov pauses on the work of the publishing house, *Sovietskii Pisatel,* to which the Administration of the Union of Soviet Writers also devoted insufficient attention. He criticizes the Section of Poets. It labored actively, he says, but that should not be the essence of its work. It should have given to us some conception of the ideological condition of our poetry today and organized discussions on the creative work of the great poets. It should have analyzed the compositions of young authors and aided their growth, not through a simple critique of their books, but by a serious definition of the tendencies of their development.

All has not been well also in the Section of Dramatists. The resolution of the Central Committee of the Party on the theatre and the drama speaks correctly about our weakness in this field. Badly and superficially we have occupied ourselves with the drama; we have not analyzed for quality. The resolution should awaken in dramatists a deep sense of responsibility for this sector of our ideological front.

We must recognize our failures in the field of the moving picture, because this is also the business of writers. For the failure of *Bolshaia Zhizn* by P. Nilin, not he alone, but all of us, must bear responsibility. This picture is the failure of the entire line in the field of the kino-drama. The question here relates to the misunderstanding of the significance of the contemporary Soviet theme in literature. The kino-scenarist or dramatist, working on the contemporary theme, must not see life in "his own way," as Nilin imagined the restoration of the Don Basin. The film did not correspond to life. The restoration of the

Don Basin is a heroic theme. The liberation of the Don Basin and its restoration were achieved, not by individuals, but by the masses of the Soviet people through battle and labor. In the imaginary people portrayed by Nilin there is no power of enthusiasm, no knowledge, no culture, which the Soviet man in the ranks, who matured during the years of the mighty growth of our state, bears within himself.

N. Tikhonov criticizes further the work of the Section of Historical Literary Writers, the Department of the Press of the Presidium of the Union of Soviet Writers, the Section of Children's Literature, and so on.

The resolution of the Central Committee of the Party, N. Tikhonov concludes, is the program for our further activity. It states directly that the task of Soviet literature is to aid the state to educate correctly the youth, the new generation. If we proceed energetically to remove the mistakes which we have allowed, if we struggle for the high principles of Soviet literature, if we regard our journals as great tribunes, if we raise the contemporary theme to the needed height, if finally we know how to become deeply aware of the world significance of Soviet literature and of our responsibility before the Soviet people and before the whole world — I do not doubt that we shall advance the entire cause of the development of our literature.

As a result of the resolution of the Central Committee, Nikolai Tikhonov was deposed as President of the Union of Soviet Writers and the position itself was abolished. The man destined to take his place and become Secretary-General of the organization was Alexander Fadeev, a novelist who always kept close to the Party "line" and who, according to report, nourishes the hope of becoming a kind of proletarian Tolstoy. He it was, as we shall see later in this volume, who was commissoned to represent Soviet literature and thought at the "world conferences of intellectuals" held in Vroslav in August, 1948, and in New York and Paris in March and April, 1949. Below appear the more significant portions of his speech before the Presidium:

The resolution of the Central Committee of the All-Union Communist Party found a deep response in the hearts of writers. It broaches questions which must force us to re-examine much in all of our work. It justly charges that our Administration and its President N. Tikhonov, that all of us gave to such writers as Akhmatova and Zoshchenko the opportunity to propagandize alien views. In the pre-revolutionary period of development Akhmatova was a fairly dull representative of that movement of "art for art's sake" against which Bolshevism and the literature expressing the ideas of Bolshevism have always fought. We are the heirs of forward-looking Russian social thought beginning with Belinsky, Chernyshevsky, and Dobroliubov. Literary theory received its consistent and fundamental development in the teachings of Lenin and Stalin. We are warriors for the finest progressive ideals of mankind. That ideology which has opposed and continues to oppose our movement asserts that an artist is outside of politics and outside of the ideological struggle. We as Soviet writers were born in the struggle against such individualism and decadence. How then has it happened that, after a war in which the basic principles of our order were victorious, certain Soviet writers have lost the feeling of constitutional hatred toward manifestations of political and ideological neutrality? How did it happen that some of our writers began to squander our inheritance? How could it have happened that people could be found in our organization who thought that Akhmatova, a person from an alien camp, should appear on the pages of our journals?

The causes of such ideological failures are thoroughly exposed by the resolution of the Central Committee. . . .

N. Aseev has expressed here many beautiful thoughts. But take his attitude toward Pasternak. Here is an example of what happens when we make concessions because of relations of friendship. B. Pasternak is not as old as Akhmatova. He is almost our contemporary. He grew up under the Soviet order, but in his creative work he represents that individualism which is profoundly alien to the spirit of our society. For what reason, then, do we fawn upon a man who during the course of many years has refused to accept our ideology? Because he is not exposed in his true colors, his poetry can confuse some young people, can appear to them as a model, can seem to be surrounded with an eccentric "halo." And what sort of "halo" is it, when in the cruel war, in which millions of our people shed their blood, the poet in no way participated? The war came to an end, and aside from a few poems which no one could regard as Pasternak's best, he contributed nothing. Was not my address in 1943 correct when I said that, although translations of Shakespeare constitute an important cultural work, retirement into translations in time of war represents a definite position.

Some writers think: we hold power, and we can be kind toward an alien ideology. But we are surrounded by enemies who in order to disarm us deliberately strive to inoculate our people with an alien ideology.

It seems to me that among some of the students of the Leningrad Institute and some young persons in the poetry division of the Union of Writers tastes are being cultivated which we should have combated.

The works of Zoshchenko contain skepticism, nihilism, and lack of faith in the idea that man can be man, that within him can live and develop the best qualities for which our people have fought and which we cultivate in our people with such love and care. Zoshchenko lives among us and believes in nothing. He sees only the base and the vile, that which lives within him himself. Encouraging Zoshchenko and slapping him on the back have led to the present situation.

N. Aseev has rightly said that the address of N. Tikhonov did not reveal the full gravity and depth of the resolution of the Central Committee. As yet he has not pondered these questions to the end. Inability to grasp the main ideas is still evident in the speech which he made here in the Presidium.

At present among some of the writers there is a feeling of uneasiness lest certain people discredit and condemn everything indiscriminately. Without doubt such people will be found. But we must not fear self-criticism. We must have the courage necessary for self-criticism in order to understand literary phenomena correctly.

Our criticism must help us in this. It must be able to see the good too. But take, for example, the articles by Gurvich. Aside from the subjectivism, the esthetic subjectivism of his evaluations, it is difficult to recall in the entire course of Soviet literature even one article where he praises anything. . . . This can hardly be fair. . . .

We must all draw very important ideological, moral, and organizational inferences from the resolution of the Central Committee, inferences which would guarantee that in the future we would not have to blush for our mistakes before the people, before the Central Committee of the Party, before Comrade Stalin.

I would be much chagrined if my address were to be interpreted by some comrades as follows: "Is Fadeev here to teach people, is he not evading his responsibility for ideological failures in the Union of Writers?" On the contrary, throughout the course of the development of Soviet literature, I have always felt great personal responsibility for everything that takes place among us. I was directly involved in the leadership of the Union of Writers, and I personally share in and feel deeply my responsibility for those ideological failures which occurred under the present leadership of the union.

Another Soviet writer, a popular poet, who felt the sting of the resolution of the Central Committee, was Alexei Surkov. During the war he distinguished himself by writing poetry on the themes of the struggle, including "I Sing Hate." As editor of the literary magazine *Ogonëk,* he occupies an important place in shaping the policy of Soviet literature. Of all the speakers at the session of the Presidium he alone struck a humorous or quasi-humorous note. Here are his remarks as published in *Literaturnaia Gazeta:*

Besides the many faults enumerated here, we have one more — a short memory. Even before the war sharp and direct words about Anna Akhmatova were uttered; during the war, on the occasion of the publication of Zoshchenko's "Before Sunrise," sharp and direct words were said. But several months pass and again all is quiet, all is quiet and tranquil in our little literary world, until someone throws into our quiet creek a timely verbal stone.

Why then is it especially bitter for me to appear? There were times when I personally did not have to recant, when I listened ironically to people who asserted in the lobbies that Zoshchenko was a profound psychologist and that under his clowning was concealed a genuine soul. The same was said with respect to Anna Akhmatova. And now I find myself an editor of *Ogonëk* and its supplements, a man who only recently published a little book by Zoshchenko and included therein the infamous story "The Adventures of a Monkey." In the capacity of editor of *Literaturnaia Gazeta,* I along with the entire editorial staff more than a year ago published under the rubric of "Coming Books" an interview with Anna Akhmatova with her portrait. I ask myself now when everything has become clear, I ask myself how and why this happened? Without singing of praises and without throwing words to the wind, I must acknowledge that I lost the vigilance essential to the ideological evaluation of literary phenomena.

The resolution of the Central Committee of the Party contains an objective, sharp, and Bolshevik analysis of the state of affairs in literature as it applies to what has occurred in Leningrad.

It would not have been greatly harmful if Surkov alone had shown political blindness. No, this is a much more widespread disease. How many Leningradists have shown this same weakness! Yes, and in Moscow am I alone? Here is Comrade Vishnevsky. He also is an editor. Whether he wanted it or didn't want it, in the capacity of editor he published a series of verses by Anna Akhmatova. In some articles, devoted to literary reviews, the journal *Znamia* returned to the works of Anna Akhmatova and placed her among the first five or eight people who had established the level and the direction of our poetry.

But I speak about myself, about *Literaturnaia Gazeta,* about *Ogonёk,* about *Znamia.* And if we captiously read what we have had no time to read, it would seem that not only I, Vishnevsky, and the Leningradists exhibit the dulling of ideological vigilance. The sickness of ideological "chicken blindness" has been widely disseminated in our literature; and not all are free from it yet.

How then shall we work in the future? First of all, literary writers must understand how they should respond to the resolution of the Central Committee of the Party on the Leningrad journals and to the extremely profound and meaningful resolution on the theatre and the drama which contains many remarkable and fertile thoughts which are related not only to the drama. We must respond to these resolutions not only with self-criticism, but also with deeds and work.

If we fail to put our house in the Union of Writers in order, nothing will come of it. I regard as our misfortune the fact that the Presidium of the Union, consisting of twenty-seven persons, did not represent itself as the unified staff of Soviet literature. Lack of leadership and interest was revealed in our press, particularly in *Literaturnaia Gazeta.* I do not recall an instance when a single one of the great writers on any occasion came himself and proposed to publish in the pages of the paper.

It is necessary to emphasize that the people who were elected as members of the Presidium of the Union of Soviet Writers assumed responsibilities as well as rights. But we have not even made use of our own sacred right to come and say that the work of the union goes badly.

And regardless of how much we say today, how much we criticize ourselves and those around us, if we do not feel our responsibility for the general condition of affairs in literature before the people and before the writers who intrusted the work of the Union to us, we will not advance and we will repeat one and the same mistake.

The brief remarks of yet another member of the Presidium will be brought to the reader — Vsevolod Vishnevsky. Known as the "sailor-author," he is a playwright who during the war played a leading rôle in persuading Soviet writers to devote their talents to the production of works which would foster patriotism and a martial spirit among the people and in the Red Army. As editor of the literary journal *Znamia,* he also was involved personally in the criticism contained in the resolution of the Central Committee. The account of his attempt to seek absolution follows:

Vs. Vishnevsky dwelt in detail on the significance of the resolution of the Central Committee of the Communist Party for every literary writer as an individual and for the Union of Writers as a whole:

The transition to literary work after the terrific tension of wartime was not achieved by the writer at once. We had lived and talked of war. We did not meditate on poetry, we did not ponder particularly over certain critical articles, of which incidentally there were very few.

I recall this in order to see clearly why many errors occurred. No one needs formal confessions, and no one demands them, by the way. We must give ourselves an account of mistakes in order to move forward and do better work.

Now after the war we can give closer attention to the practice of literary art. We have noted the filthy writings of Zoshchenko. We have listened to the addresses of Samed Vurgun, Maxim Rilsky, and Nairi Zarian from which we have learned that mistakes are not confined to Leningrad. We have looked into the state of literary affairs in Moscow.

The Party has always come to our aid. In 1932 it intervened in literary debates and showed writers the way. What significant talks on literature were those of Alexey Maximovich Gorky with Comrade Stalin! Then recall the First Congress of Soviet Writers in 1934. Recall the extremely valuable directives on history made by Comrade Stalin, together with Comrades Kirov and Zhdanov, and then the resolution of the Central Committee of the Communist Party on criticism in 1940. We witness the continuous concern and attention to what takes place in literature.

I wish to say a few words about certain mistakes. A. Surkov said here that his "hearing and vision had been dulled." But I recall when in 1934, in his address at the congress of writers he raised his voice against Zoshchenko and warned against the "swampy" beginning of his creative work. After twelve years Surkov, unfortunately, made the mistake of publishing a volume by Zoshchenko. He made a blunder. One must analyze — wherein lies the error? This applies not only to him. As leader of the journal *Znamia*, I too permitted a mistake. Poems by Akhmatova were published in the journal (No. 4, 1945). I bear full responsibility for this. Her poems should not have appeared in our journal.

As editor and member of the Union of Soviet Writers, I am amazed that Akhmatova is silent now. Why does she not respond to the judgment of the people, to the judgment of the Party? She behaves incorrectly, individualistically, and in a hostile manner. I presume that the question must be raised about the continued presence in the union of Akhmatova and Zoshchenko. Their practice manifestly contradicts our statute, adopted at the First Congress of Soviet Writers.

Vs. Vishnevsky then sharply censured the work of the critic U. Usovsky, who in his opinion takes a purely esthetic position in the field of the theatre and theatre management.

Our discussion bears witness to the fact that the majority of writers judge the phenomena of literature correctly; but, at the same time, there are hasty, thoughtless, and unbalanced judgments.

A critical mention of Leites in the leading article of *Literaturnaia Gazeta* was made by the editor's office thoughtlessly. In his article of two printed pages Comrade Leites exposed the reactionary Anglo-American theories of "art for art's sake."

The resolution of the Central Committee mobilizes the writers. I say this in reply to those engaged in literary pursuits who begin to crawl into crevices, who state that one must "stop writing for say, about half a year," who are afraid to bear responsibility and thus hamper our work. The Party gathers and mobilizes the writers; it moves them ahead. The resolution of the Central Committee of the Communist Party is bright, invigorating, and leads us forward.

5

The Presidium of the Union of Soviet Writers concluded its session with a resolution which accepted in full and without question the criticism and the directives of the Central Committee. Presumably with this resolution the energies and talents of Soviet writers have been, are being, and will be mobilized behind the broad domestic and foreign policies of the Party, that is, until and unless the "line" changes. If that line should change, the American reader should know that the entire process reported in these pages will be repeated. The following resolution was adopted on September 4, 1946:

The resolution of the Central Committee of the All-Union Communist Party of August 14 of this year on the journals *Zvezda* and *Leningrad* designated quite correctly the ideological mistakes in the work of the editors of the journals, the outstanding defects in the life of writers' organizations, and the perversion of the work of the Administration of the Union of Soviet Writers. This profoundly important document of our Party outlines a militant program for the future work of the Administration and of all organizations of writers in the country.

The statement of the Central Committee that the Administration of the Union of Soviet Writers and its president, Comrade N. Tikhonov, had taken no measures to improve the work of the journals of the Union, *Zvezda* and *Leningrad,* is absolutely correct. They not only did not conduct a struggle against the harmful influences of Zoshchenko and Akhmatova and other non-Soviet writers like them, but even encouraged the penetration into the journals of tendencies and morals alien to Soviet literature. The systematic appearance in the pages of the journals — organs of the Union of Writers — of the vulgar and vicious lampoons of Zoshchenko on the Soviet people and the Soviet order, and the printing of the ideologically empty and vacuous verses of Akhmatova, saturated with a spirit of decadence and pessimism, was the direct consequence of the inaction of the Administration of the

Union of Writers and the absence of Bolshevik principles, political alertness, and a sense of responsibility for the work intrusted to them.

The Administration of the Union, the editors of journals, the officials of publishing houses, and literary critics failed to draw the necessary conclusions from the analysis of the literary physiognomy of Zoshchenko which appeared in the journal *Bolshevik*. This analysis showed him to be a man alien to Soviet literature and shamelessly inactive in the cause of the Soviet people, even during the years of the Great Patriotic War.

The essence of the creative work of Akhmatova has long been evident to the Soviet reader. She is a typical representative of the bourgeois-aristocratic poetry of the salon and is an exponent of the supremely injurious bourgeois theory of "art for art's sake," of vulgar estheticism, and of decadent disintegration of poetry.

In spite of this and in spite of the obvious harm of the "creative work" of these non-Soviet writers to the cause of the education of our people and particularly of the youth, their writings have appeared in print. In 1946 the Leningrad branch of the State Publishing House published a book of vulgar stories by Zoshchenko which included "The Adventures of a Monkey," a story full of anti-Soviet attacks (editor S. Spassky). In the "Library of Ogonëk" in Moscow the little book of Zoshchenko was issued in a large edition and contained this very story (editor A. Surkov).

The verses of Akhmatova were printed not only in Leningrad, but also in Moscow journals — *Znamia* and *Ogonëk*.

The organ of the Administration of the Union of Soviet Writers, *Literaturnaia Gazeta,* found it possible to print on November 24, 1945, an interview with Akhmatova and her portrait. And her appearances in Moscow, permitted by the Presidium of the Union of Soviet Writers, took place in an atmosphere of undeserved praise of her creative work.

Obviously, the absence of a struggle on the part of the Presidium of the Union against foreign influences in the journals, publishing houses, and literary media had an adverse effect on the entire life of the Union and the activity of its organs. It was precisely for this reason that vulgar plays, decadent and pessimistic verses, empty and worthless stories appeared in *Zvezda* and *Leningrad*. And it was precisely because the Administration of the Union of Soviet Writers failed to provide genuine leadership and direction that the poetry of Pasternak, neutral in ideology and politics and divorced from the life of the people, was widely disseminated and given publicity by certain critics (A. Tarasenkov in the journal *Znamia*).

Literary people, responsible for leadership in writers' organizations and editorial offices of journals and publishing houses, have forgotten that literature is a mighty weapon in the cause of the education of the Soviet people and especially of youth, and that therefore they must be guided in their work by the fact that the living foundation of the Soviet order is its politics. This leads to gross political errors.

During the quarter of a century of its development Soviet literature has given to us not a few remarkable works, clearly and truthfully expressing our epoch and its people. In the years of the war and the postwar period the best works of Soviet literary writers contributed to the education of the masses of the people in the spirit of Communism and love for the socialist Motherland. But along with such works appeared dishonest works, devoid of content and produced in haste purely for monetary considerations: a play by Alexander Gladkov, *New Year's Night,* a novel by Raitonov, *Exactly at Midnight,* a kino-scenario by Nilin, *Big Life,* second series.

The resolution of the Central Committee of the Party of August 26 on the repertoire points with complete justice to the tremendous errors in the work of dramatists. Lack of political sense, superficiality, trivial treatment of great themes, and ideological vacuity were shown in certain plays: *Forced Landing* by Vodopianov and Laptev, *Extraordinary Law* by the Tur brothers, *The Boat Woman* by Pogodin, *A Window in the Forest* by Rakhmanov and Riss, *The Airplane is Twenty-Four Hours Late* by Rybak and Savchenko.

Ideologically and artistically useless works displaying little knowledge of life and subject-matter have appeared: *At the Capture of Berlin* by V. Ivanov — Journal *Novii Mir, The Sun from the East* by Velednitsky — Journal *Oktiabr*. Also works representing false historical conceptions: *The Brusilov Gap* by Sergeiev-Pensky. Journals print not a few works which are written sloppily and carelessly, works which reveal irresponsibility on the part of their authors with respect to both content and form. At times they even print works which are scarcely literate and befoul the Russian language.

In the creative work of some young poets (for example, in the verses of A. Mezhirov) appears a sickly admiration for suffering and whimpering. The older generation of poets does not oppose these themes. In the works of certain experienced poets may be glimpsed gloomy-pessimistic moods, *Not an Everlasting Memory* by P. Antokol-sky — Journal *Znamia,* or a passion for formalistic experiments which lower the ideological aim of verses, *Alexander Matrosov* by S. Kirsanov — Journal *Oktiabr.*

As a result of the lowering of demands on authors by the editorial boards of journals certain writers cease to labor for the perfection of their works and the improvement of their craftsmanship.

The spirit of servility before the bourgeois culture of the West which is alien to the Soviet people and which was pointed out by the Reso-lution of the Party has been expressed with special clarity in the field of the drama. The shameful conversion by Alexander Gladkov of a novel by a bourgeois writer into a drama of supposedly contemporary Soviet people, *New Year's Night,* is striking proof of this. The pub-lishing house *Iskusstvo* printed a volume of low-grade, vulgar, one-act plays by contemporary English and American dramatists which poi-soned the consciousness of our people with a world view hostile to Soviet society.

Our literary critics, often forgetting the great traditions of Russian criticism, the traditions of Belinsky, Chernyshevsky, Dobroliubov, and Gorky, bear the major share of responsibility for the penetration into our literature of alien influences, of vulgar, politically neutral, ideo-logically and artistically weak works. In their practical endeavors they are altogether insufficiently aware of the brilliant works and directives of Lenin and Stalin in the sphere of literature and art. Up to the present time they have not drawn the necessary conclusions from the speech of A. A. Zhdanov at the First All-Union Congress of Soviet Writers. The theoretical level of many critical articles is low, and scant attention is devoted to an analysis of the ideological tendencies of literary works. Great writers, by not publishing critical articles, violate the noble tradition of Russian literature.

In place of serious discussion of the most important problems of the development of Soviet literature we often have pretentious uproar about secondary questions which distracts writers from the basic prob-lems of contemporary life. A characteristic illustration is the dis-cussion of the drama in the pages of *Literaturnaia Gazeta* and *Sovietskoie Iskusstvo.* The utterances of certain critics (A. Gurvich, for example) are replete with esthetic subjectivism and remoteness from current political problems. Among certain critics and writers formalistic conceptions still prevail.

Critics do not attempt seriously to understand the processes of literary development, to give meaning to and interpret the experience of literature. *Literaturnaia Gazeta* published an unprincipled and vulgar view of L. Rakhmanov concerning a book by Borisov about Green and an esthetic and eulogistic article by Danin about Smeliakov. It prints many articles of little theoretical significance. Also it is remote from the life of the Union, neglects the basic questions involved in the ideological education of writers, is unable to criticize basically and sharply injurious works and foreign influences in literature, and fails to organize criticism and self-criticism in literary organizations.

The damaging theory is propagated that it is wrong to demand of contemporary writers worthy works about our days, that such works can come only in the future. This harmful and confused theory, rudely trampling on the traditions of the great Russian democratic literature which throughout its entire history has been forward-looking and close to life, has not been opposed in the press. Likewise there has been no forthright repudiation of the proposal by I. Selvinsky that socialist realism as a method of artistic expression be replaced by "socialist symbolism." The Ukrainian writer, Petro Panch has expounded the "theory" of the "right of the writer to make mistakes." This "theory" opens the door to the penetration into literature of harmful influences. And it did not receive the necessary qualification on the part of literary critics.

The lagging of theoretical thought on the front of literary writing and criticism is responsible for the fact that up to the present time we have had no textbooks on the theory and history of Soviet literature. We have not even had satisfactory programs for the teaching of the history of Soviet literature in the Literary Institute of the Union of Soviet Writers.

Individual critics, as well as the leaders of the Union of writers and the editors of its organs, are guided in their appraisal of works neither by the interests of the ideological and artistic development of Soviet literature nor by the interests of the state and the people, but by considerations of group and personal friendships. This tendency finds expression particularly in the exaggeration of the merits of writers belonging to one's "own" group, for which the pages of the journals and papers are utilized. The editorial board of *Oktiabr* has been especially at fault here.

The Presidium finds the chief causes for the lagging of criticism in the complete neglect of this area of work in the Union and the lack of concern for the theoretical growth of critics, for the organization of criticism of critics, and for the creation of conditions necessary for their work.

The guidance of the editorial boards of journals and the publishing house of *Sovietskii Pisatel* by the Presidium of the Union of Soviet Writers, which in practice shows many substantial shortcomings, is entirely unsatisfactory. This has led to a weakening of the sense of responsibility on the part of workers in the editorial apparatus of the journals and *Literaturnaia Gazeta* and has facilitated the penetration of harmful influences.

The greatest deficiency in the work of the Presidium of the Union of Soviet Writers and the Administration of the Union as a whole is weak leadership with respect to the literatures of the peoples of the USSR. As a result bourgeois nationalistic tendencies have been revived in different literatures (for example, the sketches of Kiriluk on the history of Ukrainian literature, the glorification of the Khan-feudal epic poetry of Edigei in Tartaria and Bashkiria). Particularly in Union Republics is the theoretical work of critics lagging. Among certain writers of the USSR a tendency to retire from the complex themes of contemporary life into the distant historical past must be noted.

These great shortcomings and gaps in the leadership of the Presidium and Administration of the Union of Soviet Writers as a whole would not have arisen had their work been saturated with a feeling of responsibility before the people and the Party for the education through literature of the masses of people in the spirit of Communism, in Bolshevik principles, in an atmosphere of honest criticism and self-criticism. But the Presidium of the Union of Soviet Writers has not served as a creative and guiding center of literary life. It has given little and only sporadic attention to ideologically creative questions and has failed to insure the development of criticism and self-criticism in literary organizations. In the work of the Presidium collective responsibility has not been established and the broad ranks of the writers have not been drawn into it. In the membership of the Presidium of the Union not a few writers have failed to discharge their responsibilities as leading workers in the field of literature.

Some writers stand aside from the fundamental questions of the present, do not know the life and the problems of the people, and are incapable of expressing the best traits and qualities of Soviet man.

The Administration of the Union of Soviet Writers, instead of directing the creative work of writers to the further development of literature actually withdrew from creative leadership over the writers, did
nothing to raise the ideological-literary level of the works produced,
and failed to combat literary vulgarities and potboilers.

*A radical change in the ideological life and work of the Union of
Writers is necessary.*

The Central Committee of the Party pointed out that the strength
of Soviet literature, the most advanced literature in the world, consists
in the fact that it is a literature which has and can have no interests
except the interests of the people and the interests of the state. The
task of Soviet literature is to aid the state to educate youth correctly, to
meet their needs, to rear a new generation which is hale and hearty,
which has faith in its own cause, which fears no obstacles, which is
prepared to overcome all obstacles.

Consequently any preaching of neutrality in ideas, of neutrality in
politics, of "art for art's sake" is condemned by the Central Committee
of the Party as harmful to Soviet literature and hostile to the interests
of the Soviet people and state. Such preaching can have no place in
our journals, in our books, and in the life of literary organizations.

The Presidium of the Union resolves to make the directives of the
Central Committee of the Party, given in the resolution on the journals
Zvezda and *Leningrad,* the foundation of its further work and to
change decisively the methods of ideological-artistic leadership. The
struggle against harmful influences in literature and against all expressions of neutrality in ideas and politics, the education of the Soviet
writers to express loyally and sensitively the interests of the people and
the Soviet state and to assist the Party in the Communistic education
of the people — all of this must become the chief content of all the
work of the Union of Writers.

The Presidium of the Union sets as its most important task the turning of the attention of the leading organs of the Union, of its journals
and publishing house, as well as all writers, to motifs of contemporary
life, to themes of the heroic work of our people in the restoration and
development of socialist economy, and to the reflection of the best
traits and qualities of Soviet man — those traits and qualities which he
exhibited in the Great Patriotic War and which he manifests with new
strength in the present work of construction for the strengthening of
the power of the socialist Motherland.

It is necessary to propagate systematically among writers the policy of the Party on the fundamental questions of domestic and international affairs, and to inform them broadly on the decisions of the Party and the government.

It is necessary to saturate all this work with the militant spirit of the active and aggressive ideology of Communism.

Soviet writers must lash those works which express any manifestation of servility before the bourgeois West, so foreign to Soviet people. Armed with the teachings of Lenin and Stalin, they must expose in their compositions the nature of capitalist encirclement, struggle against its corrupting influence, and reveal the character of contemporary imperialism which conceals within itself the threat of new bloodletting wars.

The Presidium of the Union of Writers insists that all writers' organizations, journals, and publishing houses demand higher artistic quality in compositions. Publication of works which are careless and sloppy, which bear the mark of flippant and hasty work, or which befoul the language of literature, must not be permitted.

The realization of this decisive shift in the entire work of the Union of Writers as a whole is possible only on the foundation of the development of true and responsible criticism and self-criticism.

Among immediate practical measures the Presidium regards the following as indispensable:

1. To relieve Comrade N. S. Tikhonov of the duties of the Presidency of the Administration of the Union of Soviet Writers.

2. To call in October the Plenum of the Administration of the Union of Soviet Writers for the discussion of the reconstruction of the work of the Union in accordance with the directives of the Central Committee of the All-Union Communist Party.

3. To recommend to the Administration of the republican and oblast divisions of the Union of Soviet Writers the organization at the beginnning of September of conferences of writers for the discussion of the resolution of the Central Committee. To require members of the Administration of the Union of Soviet Writers to participate in the work of the larger organizations for the purpose of rendering practical aid toward the realization of the directives of the Central Committee. To conduct in this same period an all-Moscow conference of writers.

4. To discuss in the nearest future the speeches of the editors of the journals *Octiabr, Znamia* and *Novii Mir,* the editors of *Literaturnaia Gazeta,* and the publishers of *Sovietskii Pisatel* from the angle of the

practical realization of the resolution of the Central Committee. To aid *Zvezda* and the Leningrad section of the Union of Soviet Writers to achieve in the shortest possible time the radical reconstruction of the journal in the light of the directives of the Central Committee.

5. To reconstruct radically the entire system of work of the Union of Writers in the training of young literary people. To aid in the work of the Literary Institute, by creating conditions favorable for the instructional and creative life therein and by insuring the systematic influence of the Presidium of the Union on the activity of the Institute.

6. For the Presidium of the Union to discuss the question and develop measures for assuring the theoretical growth and political maturing of the body of critics and the establishment of conditions suitable for their work.

7. To expel M. Zoshchenko and A. Akhmatova from the Union of Writers for not conforming in their creative works to the demands of Article 2 of the Statutes of the Union, which reads that members of the Union of Soviet Writers must be writers who stand on the platform of Soviet power and participate in socialist construction.

The Presidium of the Union calls upon writers to turn their energies to the achievement of the tasks set by the Central Committee of the Party and assures the Central Committee of the Party and Comrade Stalin that the writers' organization will correct the weaknesses exposed and in Bolshevik fashion fulfill the resolution of the Central Committee of the All-Union Communist Party.

CHAPTER FOUR

DRAMA AS A WEAPON

THE RESOLUTION of the Central Committee of the All-Union Communist Party on the literary journals of Leningrad had a profound impact on Soviet writers. It destroyed some utterly, silenced others at least for a time, made sycophants out of many more, and encouraged the vast majority to find pleasure in the humiliation of a few. Fadeev patently revelled in the degradation of Tikhonov, not to mention Zoshchenko and Akhmatova. But apparently this resolution was only the first move in a carefully conceived general plan to bring the entire Soviet intelligentsia into the active service of the new Party "line." This line contained two great emphases — an unqualified assault on everything "bourgeois" or "Western" and an equally unqualified glorification of everything Russian and Soviet.

2

Long before the reverberations of this first shot had reached their crest, it was followed by a second — a resolution of the Central Committee "On the Repertoire of the Dramatic Theatres and Measures for Its Improvement." This resolution was given to the world on August 26, 1946. Although it was addressed to the general situation in the drama, rather than to one or two particular individuals, productions, or institutions, the usual Party practice, its meaning and implications were altogether clear. A large number of dramatists and plays were judged guilty or defective, according to the standard that had already been applied to literature. The substance of the resolution, as it appeared in *Partiinaia Zhizn*, the journal of the Central Committee, follows: [1]

In discussing the question of the repertoire of the dramatic theatres and measures for its improvement, the Central Committee of the All Union Communist Party recognizes that the condition of the repertoire of the theatres is unsatisfactory.

The chief weakness in the present situation is the fact that plays by Soviet authors on contemporary themes have actually been forced out of the repertoire of the great dramatic theatres of the country. In the Moscow Art Theatre only 3 out of 20 current productions are devoted to questions of contemporary Soviet life, in the Little Theatre only 3 out of 20, in the Theatre in the Name of the Moscow Soviet, only 2 out of 9, in the Theatre in the Name of Vakhtangov only 2 out of 10, in the Kamerni Theatre only 3 out of 11, in the Leningrad Theatre in the Name of Pushkin only 2 out of 10, in the Kiev Dramatic Theatre in the Name of Franko only 3 out of 11, in the Kharkov Theatre in the Name of Shevchenko only 2 out of 11, and in the Sverdlov Dramatic Theatre only 5 performances out of 17 are based on contemporary Soviet themes.

This patently unnatural condition of the repertoire is still further aggravated by the fact that some plays on contemporary themes are feeble and ideologically empty (*Forced Landing* by Vodopianov and Laptev, *Birthday* by the Tur brothers, *The Airplane Is Twenty-four Hours Late* by Rybak and Savchenko, *New Year's Night* by A. Gladkov, *Extraordinary Law* by the Tur brothers, *A Window in the Forest* by Rakhmanov and Riss, *The Boat Woman* by Pogodin, and certain others). As a rule Soviet people are represented in these plays as ugly caricatures, as rude and uncultured persons possessing the tastes and morals of a Philistine, while villains are endowed with brilliant traits of character, with vigor, ingenuity, and strength of will. Such productions often portray events in a false and artificial manner, and thus create an incorrect and distorted view of Soviet life. Many plays on contemporary themes are inartistic and primitive, written very

[1] *Partiinaia Zhizn*, No. 1, 1946, pp. 65–69.

sloppily, in an illiterate fashion, and without sufficient knowledge of the Russian literary and popular language. Moreover, many theatres are irresponsible in presenting works on Soviet life. Frequently managers delegate the staging of these works to second-rate producers who cast weak and inexperienced actors and fail to give proper attention to the mounting of theatrical performances. As a consequence plays on contemporary themes appear colorless and inartistic. Actually therefore many dramatic theatres are not nurseries of culture, of advanced Soviet ideology and morality. Such a condition of affairs in the repertoire of dramatic theatres fails to educate the working people and cannot be tolerated in the Soviet theatre.

A major shortcoming in the activity of the Committee on Artistic Affairs and of the dramatic theatres is their extreme passion for the staging of plays on historical themes. In several plays, having no historical and educational significance now offered in the theatres, the life of tsars, khans, and great lords is idealized. (*Novels of Margarite Navarsky* by Skrib, *Khorezm* by Khadzhi Shukurov, *Takhmos Khodzhentski* by Kasimov, *We Cossacks* by Tazhibaev, *Idukaii* and *Muradym* by Burungulov.)

The Central Committee of the Party holds that the Committee on Artistic Affairs follows an incorrect line by introducing plays of bourgeois foreign dramatists. The publishing house Iskusstvo, in accordance with instructions from the Committee on Artistic Affairs, has published a volume of one-act plays by contemporary English and American dramatists. These plays are a model of base, vulgar, foreign drama, openly preaching bourgeois views and morals. In recent times the Committee on Artistic Affairs has distributed to the dramatic theatres of the country the following plays: *The Murder of Mr. Parker* by Morrison, *The Dangerous Age* by Pinero, *The Circle* and *Penelope* by Maugham, *Le Petit Café* by Bernard, *La Poudre aux Yeux* by Labive and Delacour, *The Man Who Came To Dinner* by Kaufmann and Hart, *Famous Mary* by Durand, *The Corsican's Revenge* or *Uncle's Whimsies* by Augier and Sandeau, and others. Some of these plays have been presented in the dramatic theatres. In essence the production of the plays of bourgeois foreign authors has meant the placing of the Soviet stage at the disposal of the propaganda of reactionary bourgeois ideology and morals. It has constituted an effort to poison the consciousness of the Soviet people with a world-view hostile to Soviet society and to revive the vestiges of capitalism in consciousness and life. The wide distribution of such plays among theatrical workers and the production of these plays on the stage have been the grossest political errors of the Committee on Artistic Affairs.

The Central Committee of the Party notes that the Committee on Artistic Affairs has been a captive of the more backward theatrical workers, has permitted the selection of the repertoire for central and local theatres to slip from its hands, and has left this entire matter to a policy of drift.

The Central Committee of the Party regards the unsatisfactory work of the dramatists as one of the important causes of the large short-comings in the repertoire of dramatic theatres. Many dramatists stand aside from the fundamental questions of the contemporary epoch, do not know the life and problems of the people, are incapable of expressing the best traits and qualities of Soviet man. These dramatists forget that the Soviet theatre can fulfill its important rôle in the education of the working people only if it actively propagates the policy of the Soviet state which is the living foundation of the Soviet order.

In the work of dramatists the necessary creative and co-operative relation with the theatres is lacking. The Administration of the Union of Soviet Writers, whose obligation is to direct the creative work of dramatists to the further development of art and literature, actually withdrew from the task of guiding the activity of dramatists, does nothing to raise the ideological and artistic level of their productions, and fails to carry on the struggle against vulgarity and potboiling in the drama.

The unsatisfactory condition of the repertoire of dramatic theatres is explained also by the absence of responsible Bolshevik theatrical criticism. The number of specially trained people appearing in the rôle of theatrical critics in the Soviet press is insignificant. Newspapers and literary and theatrical journals give little attention to the advancement of new critics who are able to analyze plays and theatrical productions objectively and dispassionately. In their evaluations individual critics are guided, not by the interests of the ideological and artistic development of Soviet drama and theatrical art, that is, not by the interests of the state and the people, but by the interests of group and personal friendship. Often reviews of plays are written by persons of little artistic knowledge. A thorough-going critique of new productions is replaced by subjective and arbitrary appraisals which do not correspond to the actual significance and quality of the plays. Frequently reviews of plays and spectacles are written in language which is meaningless and unintelligible to readers. The newspapers *Pravda, Izvestia, Komsomolskaia Pravda,* and *Trud* underestimate the vast educational significance of theatrical productions and devote very little space to questions of art.

The newspaper, *Sovietskoie Iskusstvo,* and the journal, *Teatr,* are conducted in an entirely unsatisfactory manner. Designed to aid dramatists and theatrical workers to create ideologically and artistically valuable plays and spectacles, these newspapers support good plays faintheartedly and unskillfully. At the same time, they praise mediocre performances without restraint and are silent about the mistakes of the theatre and the Committee on Artistic Affairs. Thus they cultivate tendencies and morals alien to the Soviet press. In the theatrical criticism in the pages of *Sovietskoie Iskusstvo* friendly relations between critics and theatrical workers are in control, and personal interests override the general interests of the state. This paper has been unable to assume a correct and responsible position in the appraisal of dramatic productions and theatrical works. Consequently it has not only not aided but has even hindered the development of Bolshevik theatrical criticism. Theatrical "criticism" of this kind results in the loss on the part of some critics, dramatists, and theatrical workers of their sense of responsibility to the people, in stagnation and failure to aid the further development of Soviet art.

The Central Committee of the All-Union Communist Party resolves:

1. To require the president of the Committee on Artistic Affairs, Comrade Khrapchenko, to eliminate in the shortest possible period the grave shortcomings and mistakes noted in the present resolution.

2. Because of the profound significance of the theatre in the Communist education of the people, to require the Committee on Artistic Affairs and the Union of Soviet Writers to concentrate on the creation of a contemporary Soviet repertoire.

The Central Committee places before dramatists and theatrical workers the task of creating brilliant works about Soviet life and Soviet man of high artistic quality. Dramatists and theatres must reflect in plays and performances the life of Soviet society in its uninterrupted movement forward and must contribute in every way to the further development of the best aspects of the character of Soviet man which were revealed with special force during the Great Patriotic War.

Our dramatists and producers are called upon to participate actively in the education of Soviet youth to be cheerful and joyous, devoted to the Motherland and confident in the victory of our cause, fearing no obstacles, able to overcome all obstacles. At the same time the Soviet theatre is called upon to show that these qualities are characteristic, not of just a few selected persons, heroes, but of many millions of Soviet people.

It is imperative that all writers capable of creating dramatic works enrol actively and creatively in the urgent cause of the development of a theatrical repertoire qualitatively worthy of the contemporary spectator.

3. To place before the Committee on Artistic Affairs, as a basic practical task, the production in every dramatic theatre daily of not less than two or three new spectacles on contemporary Soviet themes of high ideological and artistic quality.

To require theatres to improve radically the quality of works on contemporary Soviet themes, to select for the production of these plays the best producers and artists, and to strive for a high quality of artistic performance.

4. To propose to the Committee on Artistic Affairs to exclude from the repertoire plays of little ideological and artistic value and steadfastly to see to it that faulty, shallow, ideologically empty, and valueless plays do not penetrate the theatre.

5. Recognizing the important rôle of criticism in the development of theatrical art, to require the editorial boards of the newspapers, *Pravda, Izvestia, Komsomolskaia Pravda, Trud, Sovietskoie Iskusstvo,* and *Literaturnaia Gazeta* to attract politically mature and qualified theatrical and literary critics, to publish systematically articles about new plays and spectacles, to wage a decisive struggle against political and ideological neutrality in theatrical criticism.

To require the editorial boards of republican, regional, and provincial newspapers to run systematically articles and reviews on new plays in local theatres.

6. The Central Committee of the Party notes that a serious obstacle to the improvement of Soviet drama is the large number of instances where different individuals are permitted to correct and select plays for publication, and for presentation in the theatre. The reading of plays is put in the hands of workers of local administrations on artistic affairs, of republican committees on artistic affairs, of the Chief Com-

mittee on the Repertoire, of the Chief Theatrical Administration of the Committee on Artistic Affairs, of the Artistic Soviet of the Committee, of leaders of the theatres, of workers in editorial offices and publishing houses. This situation breeds harmful procrastination and irresponsibility and hampers the swift advancement of plays to the stages of the theatres.

To propose to the Committee on Artistic Affairs to remove the obstacles which hamper the publication, distribution, and theatrical production of plays of Soviet dramatists and to reduce to a minimum the number of agencies concerned with the evaluation of plays. To place on Comrade Khrapchenko personal responsibility for the timely and swift examination of plays written by Soviet dramatists.

7. The Central Committee of the Party notes that the Council of Art of the Committee on Artistic Affairs does not fulfill its rôle in the improvement of the quality and the raising of the ideological and artistic level of the repertoire. Since it conducts its work within a limited circle, the results of its activity fail to become the property of the theatrical world as a whole and to profit from the illuminating criticism of the press.

To require the Committee on Artistic Affairs to improve radically the work of the Council of Art. At sessions of the Council of Art to subject new plays and theatrical productions to critical examination. To publish materials on the work of the Council of Art in *Sovietskoie Iskusstvo.*

8. To authorize the Committee on Artistic Affairs and the Administration of the Union of Soviet Writers to organize in 1946–1947 an All-Union Competition for the best contemporary Soviet plays.

9. In view of the extreme poverty of the repertoire of the theatres of both union and autonomous republics and the passion of local dramatists for themes of the distant past, to require the Committee on Artistic Affairs to take measures for the translation into the languages of the peoples of the USSR and the inclusion in the repertoire of the theatres of the republics the best works of Soviet dramatists.

10. To commission the Committee on Artistic Affairs and the Administration of the Union of Soviet Writers to conduct in the autumn of the current year a conference of dramatists and theoretical workers on the question of the repertoire and the problem of the co-operation of dramatists and theatres in creative work.

3

On September 4, 1946, nine days after the publication of the resolution on the repertoire of the dramatic theatres, a third resolution of the Central Committee was made public. This resolution was entitled "On the Moving Picture *Bolshaia Zhizn*." The title of the film means "Big Life" and its author was P. Nilin. In the customary language of the Party and by the standards now become familiar, the dramatist and the picture were condemned and the entire field of cinematography was brought under critical review. Also several directors of world renown were severely censured.[2]

The Central Committee of the All-Union Communist Party notes that the moving picture *Bolshaia Zhizn* (second part, Director, L. Lukov, author of scenario, P. Nilin), prepared by the Ministry of Cinematography of the USSR is ideologically and politically vicious and extremely weak from an artistic point of view.

What are the vices and defects of the film, *Bolshaia Zhizn?*

The film presents but one episode, and an insignificant one at that, in the first stage of the restoration of the Don Basin. This gives an incorrect conception of the actual scope and significance of the restorational work carried on in the region by the Soviet state. Moreover, the restoration of the Don Basin occupies a trifling place in the film, chief attention being devoted to the crude expression of all kinds of personal experiences and life scenes. The content of the picture therefore does not comport with its name. More than this, its name, *Bolshaia Zhizn*, sounds like ridicule of Soviet society.

Two different epochs in the development of our industry are obviously confused. Judged by the level of productive technique and culture represented, the picture seems to portray the period of the restoration of the Don Basin after the conclusion of the civil war and not the modern Don Basin with its advanced technique and culture developed during the years of the Stalinist Five-Year Plans. The

[2] *Partiinaia Zhizn,* No. 1, 1946, pp. 69–72.

authors of the picture create a false impression for the spectator. They suggest that the restoration of the mines and the extraction of coal after liberation from the German robbers are accomplished, not on the foundation of modern advanced technique and mechanization of labor processes, but by means of crude physical strength, long-obsolete technique, and conservative methods of work. Thus the perspective of the postwar restoration of our industry, founded on advanced technique and high productive culture, is distorted.

In the film *Bolshaia Zhizn*, the restoration of the Don Basin is presented as if the initiative of the workers not only received no support, but was even opposed by state organizations. Such a portrayal of the relations between these organizations and the workers is thoroughly false and mistaken. It is known that in our country every sign of enterprise and every success of the workers enjoy the wide support of the state.

In this connection Party workers are falsely represented in the film. The secretary of the Party organization in the restored mine is shown in a deliberately ridiculous position, inasmuch as his support of the initiative of the workers in the restoration of the mine seemingly could place him outside the ranks of the Party. The producers of the picture represent the matter as if the Party would exclude from its ranks people who show concern about the rebuilding of the economy.

The condition of the restoration of the Don Basin is wrongly portrayed in the film so as to create the impression that the Patriotic War was concluded by the liberation of the region from the German robbers. The picture presents the affair as if at the beginning of the restoration the army had been demobilized and all the soldiers and partisans had returned to peaceful pursuits. The film speaks of war, which at that period was at the climax, as of the distant past.

Bolshaia Zhizn preaches backwardness, vulgarity, and ignorance. The mass promotion to leading posts of technically semi-literate workers with backward outlooks and tempers, as shown by the producers, is entirely insincere and incorrect. The director and the scenario writer did not understand that in our country modern cultured people who know their work well, and not backward vulgar people, are highly valued and boldly promoted. They did not understand that now, after the Soviet power has created its own intelligentsia, it is ridiculous and absurd to present in a favorable light the promotion of backward and vulgar people to leading posts.

Bolshaia Zhizn gives a false and perverted picture of Soviet people. The workers and engineers restoring the Don Basin are represented as backward and semi-cultured people possessing very low moral qualities. The heroes of the film spend most of their time loafing, engaging in empty chatter, and drinking. The very best people are portrayed as dead drunks. The chief heroes are people who served in the German police. A character (Usynin), obviously alien to the Soviet order, who remained with the Germans in the Don Basin and whose demoralizing and provocative activity remains unpunished, is presented in the film. Soviet people are endowed with traits entirely strange to our society. Thus Red Army men, wounded in combat for the liberation of the mine, are left without aid on the field of battle, and a miner's wife (Sonia) shows complete indifference and insensibility as she passes by wounded warriors. A heartlessly contemptuous attitude toward young women workers arriving at the mine is expressed in the film. They are lodged in dirty, half-demolished barracks and are placed under the care of an arrant bureaucrat and scoundrel (Usynin). The leaders of the mine fail to show elementary concern for their welfare. Instead of putting in order the damp and leaky building in which they were placed, as if in mockery, entertainers with harmonica and guitar are sent to them.

The film reveals that some workers in art, though living among the Soviet people, fail to observe their high ideological and moral qualities and are incapable of portraying them truly in artistic productions.

The artistic level of the film also does not stand criticism. Individual members of the cast are scattered and are not joined together by a general conception. Many drinking bouts, vulgar ballads, amorous adventures, and nocturnal chatterings in bed serve to link the separate episodes. Songs (composer N. Bogoslovsky, authors of the text, A. Fatianov and V. Agatov), saturated with saloon blues and alien to Soviet people, are introduced into the picture. All these sordid devices, calculated to please the most diverse tastes and especially the tastes of backward people, thrusts into the background the main theme of the film — the restoration of the Don Basin. A company of talented Soviet artists is wrongly used by the producers. Stupid rôles are forced on the artists and their talents are directed toward the portrayal of vulgar people and of life scenes of questionable character.

The Central Committee of the Party ascertains that the Ministry of Cinematography (Comrade Bolshakov) has recently prepared, besides the vicious *Bolshaia Zhizn,* a number of other unsuccessful and faulty films — the second part of *Ivan the Terrible* (director, S. Eisenstein), *Admiral Nakhimov* (director, V. Pudovkin), *Simple People* (*directors,* G. Kozintsev and L. Trauberg).

How is such frequent production of false and mistaken films to be explained? Why have such well-known Soviet directors as Comrades Lukov, Eisenstein, Pudovkin, Kozintsev, and Trauberg failed — directors who in the past have created highly artistic pictures?

The fact is that many masters of cinematography, producers, directors, scenario writers, take their obligations thoughtlessly and irresponsibly and work dishonestly in the creation of moving pictures. Their chief mistake is their failure to study the business which they undertake. Thus, Pudovkin undertook the production of a film on Nakhimov, but he did not study the details of the matter and distorted historical truth. The result was a film, not about Nakhimov, but about balls and dances with episodes from the life of Nakhimov. Consequently the important historical fact that the Russians were in Sinop and that in the battle of Sinop a whole group of Turkish admirals, including the commanding officer, were captured was left out of the film. Eisenstein in the second part of *Ivan the Terrible* exhibited ignorance of historical facts by portraying the progressive army of the Oprichniki as a band of degenerates, similar to the American Ku Klux Klan, and Ivan the Terrible, a man of strong will and character, as weak and spineless, something like Hamlet. The authors of *Bolshaia Zhizn* revealed ignorance of the contemporary Don Basin and its people. Ignorance of their subjects and a thoughtless attitude on the part of specialists and directors toward their work constitute one of the fundamental causes of the release of worthless films.

The Central Committee of the Party ascertains that the Ministry of Cinematography and first of all its head, Comrade Bolshakov, guide badly the work of kino-studios, directors, and scenario writers and are little concerned about the improvement of the quality of the films produced. They expend great sums uselessly. The leaders of the Ministry of Cinematography are irresponsible toward the work entrusted to them and show complacency and carelessness with respect to the ideological and political content and the artistic worth of moving pictures.

The Central Committee of the Party considers that the work of the Council on Art of the Ministry of Cinematography is organized incorrectly and that the Council does not insure an objective and thorough-going criticism of films prepared for release. In its judgments the Council often displays neutrality in politics and pays little attention to the ideological content of pictures. Many of its members are irresponsible in the evaluation of films, making decisions on the basis of relations of personal friendship with the producers. Only thus can the fact be explained that the Council in the discussion of *Bolshaia Zhizn* failed to grasp its ideological content, exhibited a harmful liberalism, and gave an entirely baseless high evaluation of the film. The absence of criticism and the family atmosphere prevailing among creative workers in the field constitute one of the major causes of the production of bad moving pictures.

Workers in art must understand that those among them who hereafter conduct their work irresponsibly and thoughtlessly can easily find themselves over the edge of advanced Soviet art and can pass out of circulation. The Soviet spectator has grown, his cultural needs and demands have increased, and in the future the Party and the state will nurture in the people good tastes and high standards with respect to artistic productions.

The Central Committee of the All-Union Communist Party resolves:

1. In view of the above, to prohibit the release to the screen of the second part of the film *Bolshaia Zhizn.*

2. To propose to the Ministry of Cinematography of the USSR and its Council on Art to draw the necessary lessons and conclusions from the decision of the Central Committee on the moving picture *Bolshaia Zhizn* and to organize the work of artistic cinematography so that in the future there will be no possibility of the release of similar films.

4

During the days and weeks following the promulgation of these two resolutions on the drama, as well as the resolution on literature, conferences of writers and dramatists were held throughout the Soviet Union. These meetings apparently followed a common pattern. A representative of the Party, usually the head of the

Party committee on agitation and propaganda for the city, region, or republic involved, opened the conference with an address interpreting the resolutions and applying them to the local situation. The reader should know that every organizational meeting, whether a collective of farmers or the Supreme Soviet, is always under firm Party control. An account of several of these conferences appeared in the issue of *Literaturnaia Gazeta* for October 5, 1946, under the caption, "Soviet Literature Lives and Must Live in the Interests of the People at Conferences of Literary and Artistic Workers":

ASHKHABAD

At a conference of prose writers and dramatists of Turkmen the resolution of the Central Committee of the All-Union Communist Party "On the Journals *Zvezda* and *Leningrad*" was discussed. After an address by Comrade Zarutsky, head of the Agitation and Propaganda Section of the Central Committee of the Communist Party of Turkmen, lively debates took place.

The speakers sharply criticized the work of the Administration of the Union of Soviet Writers of Turkmen for having given little attention to questions of creative writing and for having done nothing whatsoever to organize political studies for the members of the Union.

The Administration of the Union of Writers and its president, Comrade Kerbabaev, had shown little interest in the creative life of the writers. In fact, they had provided no leadership for the journal, *Soviet Edebiiaty.* The former responsible editor of the journal, M. Kosaev, had failed to perform the duties of his office. Members of the editorial board, as a rule, neither read manuscripts nor discussed plans for the journal. The editors devoted no attention whatsoever to the thematic selection of manuscripts. Contemporary prose, vital essays, and journalism were scarcely present in the magazine.

As a result of the inactivity of the editors and the complete indifference of the Union of Writers, inartistic and ideologically empty works were published. Among such works in the general opinion of the speakers belong an illiterate tale by Berda Soltaniiazov, "Sumbar Flows," a poetical polemic by N. Annaklych and Atakopek Mergenov containing a gross perversion of Soviet woman, and a vulgar pernicious story by Oraz Kadamov, "The Depraved Woman."

The Turkmen State Publishing House made a mistake in publishing a book by Shabend, *Khodzhamberdy-Khan,* with a foreword by K. Karyev. The author of the foreword, by grossly falsifying history, proclaims as a popular hero, Khodzhamberdy-Khan, a man who in actuality was a traitor to his people, served a Persian Shah throughout his life, and betrayed his own country.

The absence of thorough-going concrete criticism has reflected seriously on the ideological growth of the writers. The Administration of the Union has done nothing to revive critical work and to draw into it writers, scholars, and students of literature.

The conference approved a resolution in which it was noted that the writers of Turkmen consider the resolution of the Central Committee of the All-Union Communist Party a program for their future work. Also concrete measures for the radical improvement of the activity of the Administration of the Union in Turkmen and of the editorial board of the journal *Soviet Edebiiaty* were projected.

IRKUTSK

The writers, theatrical workers, artists, and teachers of social science in the educational institutions of Irkutsk met in conference. Comrade Smirnov, Secretary of the Oblast Committee on Propaganda of the All-Union Communist Party, delivered an address on the resolutions of the Central Committee of the Party.

Many of the errors exposed in the historic resolution of the Central Committee of the Party, the speaker noted, are found in the creative work of Irkutsk writers. The leading writers of the oblast, G. Markov, K. Sedikh, and G. Kungurov, are busy with historic themes remote from contemporary Soviet life. During the period of the Patriotic War G. Kungurov wrote a book of stories about the Soviet home front. But then, apparently frightened by the difficulties involved in such work, he abandoned the contemporary theme. G. Markov worked for a long time on a historic subject. Several days ago the second volume of his novel, *Strogovy,* came from the press. It is known that for almost a year now Markov has been writing a story dealing with the Soviet-Japanese war, but just how much progress he is making in his work, we have not heard. K. Sedikh, author of *Daurin,* has limited the range of his writings to the epoch of the civil war. The poet An. Olkhon has published a cycle of verses from his forthcoming book *The Frontiers of the Dear Fatherland.* The author has been successful with pictures of northern nature. But he has not been able to portray Soviet people transforming the Far North. The poems of Elena Zhilkina are primitive and entirely devoid of social interest. The same qualities characterize some of the verses of the youthful poet, Leonid Stekolnikov.

Low ideological level and complete detachment from life explain the fact that the young writer, B. Kostukovsky, chose a deserter as the hero of his last novel on the Patriotic War.

Shortcomings in the activity of Irkutsk writers are explained by the weak ideological-political work among literary people and the absence of genuinely creative conditions in the Section of the Union of Soviet Writers.

An. Olkhon, G. Markov, G. Kungurov, K. Chuiko, director of the Irkutsk oblast publishing house, M. Liashenko, artistic leader of the oblast dramatic theatre, B. Kobelev, Secretary of the Irkutsk City Committee of the Party, and others participated in the discussions of the address.

In a resolution adopted unanimously, the participants in the conference pointed out the tremendous significance of the resolutions of the Central Committee of the Party and outlined concrete measures for the improvement of the creative activity of literary writers. It was decided to open in the Irkutsk oblast at the beginning of the coming year a house for workers in literature and art.

Gorky

A conference of workers in literature and art was held in the Dramatic Theatre in the Name of A. M. Gorky. Comrade Guriev, Secretary of the Oblast Committee on Propaganda of the Party, delivered an address on the state and tasks of ideological work in relation to the resolutions of the Central Committee of the All-Union Communist Party.

The speaker noted that the writers of the Gorky oblast have concentrated their attention for the most part on historical themes. Contemporary life has been reflected very feebly in their works. The theatres in Gorky have rarely produced plays by Soviet dramatists.

Comrade Guriev subjected to criticism the activity of the Gorky Section of the Union of Soviet Writers and the Oblast Bureau on Artistic Affairs.

The conference adopted a resolution on the fulfillment of the resolutions of the Central Committee of the All-Union Communist Party.

STALINABAD

A conference of dramatists and creative theatrical workers of the Tadzhik Republic took place. The conference devoted itself to a discussion of the resolution of the Central Committee of the All-Union Communist Party "On the Repertoire of the Dramatic Theatres and Measures for Its Improvement."

During the current year the five theatres of the republic have presented only one contemporary play. The presentation on the stage of the Stalinabad Theatre of a play by Kasymov, *Takhmos Khodzhentsky,* which has no educational value whatsoever, was a serious mistake. The Leninabad Theatre produced a play by the young dramatist Iskhakov, entitled *Princess Sogdian,* the action of which took place two thousand years ago. The theatre vigorously advertised this play idealizing the lives of tsars and lords. In the Theatre in the Name of Lakhut plays were presented which caricature Soviet people: *Teacher of Love* by the Tadzhik dramatist, Mirshakorov, and *The Five-Ruble Bride* by the Azerbaidzhan dramatist, Ordubad.

The work of the Administration on Artistic Affairs of the Republic was subjected to sharp criticism. The Council on Art had manifested a liberal attitude toward the appraisal of theatrical productions; criticism had been "friendly."

Unanimously approving the resolution of the Central Committee of the All-Union Communist Party, the conference called upon Tadzhik writers, dramatists, and theatrical workers to create artistic productions which will educate working people in the spirit of Communism.

FRUNZE

A two-day conference of writers, artists, and journalists has just been concluded. Comrade Soronbaev, Secretary of the Committee on Propaganda of the Communist Party of Kirghizia, delivered an address on measures for the fulfillment of the resolutions of the Central Committee of the All-Union Communist Party.

The speaker noted that the mistakes pointed out in the resolutions of the Central Committee of the Party are present also in the work of the Union of Soviet Writers of Kirghizia. The Administration of the Union has not guided the creative work of the writers. As a result some ideologically empty productions have appeared. Many books devoted to historic themes and very few reflecting the life of the Soviet people have been published.

Such a situation is explained by the fact that the writers have little contact with the people and give little attention to the raising of their own ideological, political, and cultural level. The absence of serious responsible criticism has had a deleterious effect on the work of writers.

The Committee on Artistic Affairs guides badly the work of the theatres of the Republic. Their repertoire consists for the most part of plays on historical themes. Contemporary plays, particularly *Ekidos* by Shukurbekov, *In School* and *The Bearded Man* by Dzhantoshev, and others, portray people not truly characteristic of Soviet life.

Those participating in the discussions spoke of a complete absence of criticism and an irresponsible attitude toward the work of writers on the part of the Union of Writers and the Committee on Artistic Affairs. They also noted mistakes in the creative work of a number of writers.

The conference adopted a resolution which fully approves the resolutions of the Central Committee of the All-Union Communist Party and points the way for future creative work in the field of literature and art.

KUIBISHEV

Comrade Efremov, Secretary of the City Committee of the Party addressed an all-city conference of writers and literary activists on the resolution of the Central Committee of the All-Union Communist Party "On the Journals *Zvezda* and *Leningrad*" and on the tasks of the writers of the city Kuibishev.

The speaker sharply criticized the work of the Oblast Section of the Union of Soviet Writers and its responsible secretary, A. Savvateev.

In the writers' organization, said Comrade Efremov, an inadmissable indifference toward creative questions and ideological-political work among writers had flowered and responsible criticism had been dulled by relations of friendship. The organization was headed by A. Savvateev — a man without principle who got into literature by accident.

Only complete neglect of the great tasks of Soviet literature can explain the appearance on the pages of the Kuibishev *Literaturnaia Gazeta* and of the almanac *Volga* of the inartistic and vulgar works of Savvateev, Kiziun, Balashov, Kiriushkin, and others.

The writers participating in the discussions, N. Tikhanov, N. Borisov, V. Banykin, E. Shapovalov, and others, acknowledged the justice of the criticism of the work of the Kuibishev section of the Union of Soviet Writers.

The speech of D. Kiziun, a member of the bureau of the writers' organization, was not fully self-critical.

The conference recognized the necessity of removing A. Savvateev from the leadership of the local writers' organization. It was decided to conduct within the next few days new elections to the bureau of the Division of the Union of Soviet Writers. The conference called upon Kuibishev literary workers to devote all their energies to the elimination of the shortcomings existing in their work and to the creation of works of high artistic quality on the Soviet provinces along the Volga.

5

On the eighteenth of November, 1946, a three-day All-Union Conference of Theatrical Leaders and Dramatists was convened for the purpose of getting action on the resolutions of the Central Committee. At this conference, as at other conferences of the same general character, many speeches were delivered, numerous confessions of errors were made, a resolution in conformity with Party directives was formulated and passed, and a memorial addressed to Stalin was composed and approved. The outstanding address, wholly and enthusiastically supporting the Party position, was made by Konstantin Simonov, a noted dramatist who visited the United States immediately following the war and returned to write a popular play, *The Russian Question*, which is a bitter satire on America. The major portion of this address was published in *Sovetskoie Iskusstvo*, November 22, 1948, under the title, "Drama, Theatre, and Life":

The resolutions of the Central Committee of the Party and the address of Comrade Zhdanov are documents which criticize our mistakes and obligate us to examine attentively everything we have done in art and how we have done it. But at the same time they are documents which first of all help us to take a look into the future of our art and literature.

Is it possible to say that no one of us has seen, noted, felt, or even spoken of the shortcomings of the works mentioned in these documents as bad examples? Certainly not. Many of us saw all of this, noted and spoke about it, sometimes even wrote about it; but in the vast majority of cases we did this from incorrect positions, from narrowly literary, narrowly theatrical, narrowly professional positions.

The Central Committee of the Party in its resolutions and Comrade Zhdanov in his address looked upon these phenomena not simply from the point of view of life as a given total of living phenomena, but from the point of view of life understood primarily as a struggle for Communist ideals and for the future of mankind, of life just as we see it and not as our enemies would like to see it.

We say: Soviet literature, Soviet art. And unfortunately we often say this without understanding the meaning of this adjective, without understanding its essence, without understanding that this is not simply an adjective but a definition of art.

From reading some articles, it is possible to infer, let us say, that the words "Soviet art" are a geographical conception and that everything written, presented, or played on the territory from Brest to Vladivostok and from Murmansk to Kushki is automatically Soviet literature and Soviet art. It is ridiculous to talk this way, yet one is obliged to say that Soviet territory and Soviet art are not two concurrent conceptions. The struggle with capitalism, the struggle with alien ideologies, is not only our external struggle. It is also our internal struggle with alien influences, with "native blemishes" of capitalism within our society.

The cause of numerous shortcomings and failures in our literature and art during recent years is found in the fact that many of our artists not only interpret incorrectly the conception of Soviet man as applied to their heroes, but also falsely interpret the conception of Soviet man with respect to themselves.

It is difficult to describe honestly a warrior without being a warrior oneself. It is difficult to describe self-sacrifice, without being able to sacrifice oneself. It is difficult to show honestly that for our hero socialist duty is primary, if for us ourselves socialist duty is not primary.

On the pages of his works, praised and not praised, honored and not honored, and on the pages of his soul the artist must find that by which he has aided and continues to aid the construction of socialist society and he must strike off that by which he has hindered this construction, that which was unworthy of the proud name of a warrior for Communism.

Let us not make too much of laudatory reviews, let us not wave letters from readers, let us not refer to our honors and prizes, let us not rejoice because we are mentioned in a resolution of the Central Committee.

If we approach this question seriously and profoundly we shall see that we are mentioned, even if not called by name.

They mentioned Korneichuk who in his play, *The Front,* was not able to represent the positive heroes of the army even on the same artistic level on which he showed the negative heroes. They mentioned Simonov who in a play, *The Russian People,* was unable to rise above the conception of Russian patriotism and failed to show what Soviet patriotism is. They mentioned Leonov who in his play, *The Invasion,* portrayed the positive hero Kolesnikov weakly and feebly, doing injustice to himself as man and artist.

We must fulfill completely our tasks as artists of socialist society — we have been fulfilling them only in part.

And does the fact not concern us that such a stupid play as *The Airplane Is Twenty-four Hours Late* was presented simultaneously in almost fifty theatres? Should we not take upon ourselves part of the guilt for not having written those five, ten, or fifteen good, high quality comedies which by the very fact of their existence would have prevented even the most undiscriminating producer from presenting this play?

And in the repertoire of the capital cities, where plays may run for years, our plays not infrequently pop out of the repertoire after the first session like corks. Does this not reflect on us, on the quality of our work?

The question of the reconstruction of the repertoire of the theatre, I am deeply convinced, is by no means concluded with the finding of a sufficient number of good Soviet plays for each theatre. This is only one side of the matter. It is still necessary to perform them well.

I do not doubt the purely professional mastery of many of our actors and directors. But I do doubt their knowledge of life, their participation in life, their understanding of those political problems which stand before the Soviet theatre, precisely as they stand before Soviet literature.

In order to strike a spark from a performance, two flints are needed. The drama is only one of these. The other is the theatre.

Moreover, this applies to a performance not only as a phenomenon of art, but also to a performance as a phenomenon of politics. The two must be born from the general effort and the general inspiration of both the dramatist and the theatre.

The dramatist is obliged to be a political leader. But in no less measure are the director and the actor obliged to be political leaders. If we take this position, then we shall understand that the question of the cast to be selected for a Soviet play is a political question for the director and that the question of how the hero of the play is to be portrayed is a political question for the actor. They are participating in the struggle for socialism, in the struggle for our ideals; and an evaluation of their activity is not only an evaluation of the activity of the artist, but also an evaluation of the activity of a soldier of the revolution.

Likewise the question of the period of performance of a Soviet play is not only a question of exigency, but also a question of politics.

I do not understand and I never shall understand why the Art Theatre presented for two or three whole years *The Clocks of the Kremlin* by Pogodin or *The Deep Search* by Kron. By producing these plays the theatre brought into the world and affirmed ideas dear to our society. How then could an artist presenting a spectacle with passion, how could he not strive to plunge into the world with his ideas and passions precisely when they are needed by the spectator, when they are needed by the country, and finally when they are needed by him himself as a political leader?

Conversely it too often happens with us in the theatre that interest in content is sacrificed to form.

Recently I had occasion to see my own play *Under the Chestnuts of Prague* in the Big Dramatic Theatre of Leningrad. With few exceptions it was performed by good actors. But I went away from the play in a state of extreme resentment and even of outrage.

I had written a propagandistic anti-fascist play. With a frankness for which I was even reprimanded, I had expressed my views on the struggle with fascism still unbeaten, on the history of this struggle beginning with Spain and on the future of this struggle. By cutting out part of the text the producer managed to make some pictures from the life of Prague.

I was outraged because I did not want to see how a good actor, supposedly in search of "truth from life," speaks the words "and in my opinion socialism is joy and happiness," while he stands with his back to the spectators.

And this is no detail, but the style of the performance. If you don't like a play, don't produce it. If you are unable to speak with feeling the words written by the author, don't play it. But if you produce and play, be political leaders. The author has no monopoly on being a political leader. Not the author for you, but you yourselves, Comrades actors, must understand the meaning of the word socialism and how it must be pronounced.

I am deeply convinced that something like this goes on in the case of many plays in many theatres. This is not a private matter, but a common problem. It would be possible to conduct a most interesting experiment: to take the producer's copies of several of our contemporary plays, written on sharp political themes, and to note the producer's and actor's adaptations. I categorically assert that these adaptations will testify not only to the immaturity of our drama, which the theatres must correct, but also to the ideological indifference of a whole company of producers and to the absence of elementary political sensitivity on the part of many actors.

The actor or producer is too much concerned about his own ego, about some little truth of life at each step and in each gesture, and often too little concerned about the big truth of life, about fighting for our ideas on the stage.

Too often in contemporary plays producers and actors shy away from any pathos, from any romanticism, from any stirring monologue. They have lost the art of refining these things, they have lost the art of conversing with the audience, not only as actors reproducing life on the stage, but also as actors agitating from the stage.

Often in the theatre there lies beneath the surface of daily truths and little truths an essential untruth about our times and our people, about a romantic time capable of noble deeds and about romantic people capable of noble speeches.

In speaking about the drama and the theatre it would of course be wrong to evade the question of our theatrical criticism and its present condition. The question of criticism in art is indissolubly linked with the question of art itself.

I consider it correct to regard our theatrical critics as participants in and not as critics of our art. We have the same field of activity — our theatre, the same tribune — our press, and the same aim — the building of a socialist society.

But precisely because theatrical critics are participants in our art, I think that they must be held to serious account. Very frequently and very justly, and particularly in recent times, it is said that the writer must know, must study, must see life. About this everybody, and especially our critics, write in all fairness.

But rarely does the very simple thought of a reverse order occur to anyone. Should not the critic who writes about an author and who in his critical article judges how well the author knows life and whether he really does know it, should not this critic also know, see, and study life, life in general and that part of life in particular with which the play deals and which he criticizes?

Dear Comrades critics! The great majority of you have forgotten the tradition of classical Russian criticism — criticism of a work of art from the point of view of life and for life.

Your task is to build a new society working with literature, drama, and the theatre. Your task is to find for art a true place in the ranks of this struggle; to fight deserters from this struggle and to aid the soldiers of this struggle; to study that life which you are able now to see; to study the recent past. You will have occasion to write many military plays because this theme will agitate Soviet literature yet for a long time.

The problems of the restoration of the country expressed in the lives of the people, yesterday's heroes of battle and today's heroes of restoration — this is our theme today. The dramatist, the producer, and the actor cannot and must not depend on the pathos of numbers, the pathos of sums, the pathos of construction, taken in its quantitative grandeur. But pathos of the human soul, pathos of character, taken in its fullness — this is the pathos which is permissible and necessary to our art.

We must write about and we must show on the stage Soviet man, a builder of the future, whose qualities of character and soul will reveal to our audience and to the entire world the ideological and genuinely human superiority of our people, people nurtured by our socialist order.

The dramatist will correctly resolve his international task if he will show in his play the average Soviet man with all his spiritual riches,

with all his will to victory, with all his iron and inflexible character —
one of those millions of people in whose name and with whose support
our delegates at international conferences speak. And the actor in
playing the rôle of such a man will actually speak his own words in
his own language at the international conference.

Such is the general theme into which, as rivulets, many themes flow,
directly and precisely connected with it.

The international theme, the anti-fascist theme, Republican Spain
where on the streets of Madrid Russian boys died by the side of
German anti-fascists from the battalion in the name of Thaelmann, the
Communist armies of China, the Yugoslav partisans and Bulgarian
anti-fascists — all this is also the life of our generation, a part of its
nobility, a part of its romance. This is ours. It enters into the spiritual
interests, into the emotions, into the experience of the rich soul of
Soviet man.

In no other field are there so many seekers after easy gains as in the
field of history. Now they run about and collect their manuscripts
from all quarters with the same haste with which they formerly poked
them everywhere. But is not history with a capital H our theme?
Does it not enter into the interests of our forward-looking man? Does
it not constitute part of our soul?

I see no reason why a dramatist, breathing the air of our epoch,
should write a play about Apolon Grigoriev or about General Skobelev;
but I do see every reason why he should write a play about
Chernyshevsky or Frunze, because they are part of our soul, part of
our experience, part of that which has made our society.

Such as we are, we were not born in a vacuum. The history of the
revolutionary movement, the history of our revolution, the biographies
of the great leaders of revolution — this also is part of our soul. It too
enters into the interests of our man. This is the theme of today. And
the theme of tomorrow.

On the ideological front a tremendous battle is being waged on a
world scale with unparalleled violence.

And in this situation following the war people suddenly appeared
among us who preach the theory of "respite," the theory of the necessity of stopping to catch one's breath, of sitting down for a while, of
telling fortunes by means of coffee grounds — what will happen?

Incidentally, such theorists and practitioners of "restful" art in the vast majority of cases have nothing to rest from — during the war they worked least of all. Then they said that one could not write in time of war, because one must get one's bearings. And now they are saying that they cannot write after the war because they have to take a rest. Just what does this mean? In the last analysis, if they want to rest, we can give them the right to rest. But let them get out and rest beyond the borders of Soviet art.

We shall have to battle on the ideological front and battle not by means of passive resistance, but by means of an active, merciless, and unceasing attack upon our enemies.

This corresponds with the teachings of our Party. It is in keeping with our traditions and with our character, which was nurtured in the days of the Five-Year Plans and hardened in the days of the war.

Our character is rough and unpleasant to our enemies. We shall not change it. We shall not try to seem to be pleasant people. Let our enemies consider us unpleasant people. In the mouth of the enemy this is praise.

In the hearing of everybody and to the whole world we say and will continue to say from the tribune of our art that we struggle for and will continue to struggle for Communism, that we consider Communism as the only correct road for the future of mankind, that our Communist ideals were, are and will remain unchanged, and that no one will shake them.

And if our enemies, wishing to nettle us, say that our art is partisan and tendentious, this is the one thing on which we agree with them.

Yes, our art is partisan and tendentious, and let our enemies dislike it. But above all, let them fear it.

The publication of Simonov's speech was concluded in the next issue of *Sovietskoie Iskusstvo*, the issue of November 23. The following excerpts reveal further the temper of his address:

In all that we have said and written about our art, too often we have failed to realize that we have fought, are fighting, and will continue to fight, and that our art is no museum of historical arms, but an arsenal intended for war.

One can purchase a beautiful gun inlaid with silver and hang it on a rug over the bed in one's home, never checking the precision of its fire, nor even whether it shoots at all. This is entirely logical, if the gun is hung up as an ornament. But would the thought ever enter the head of a man going into battle of not testing his rifle from the point of view of its essential quality — its usefulness in battle? . . .

The battle with capitalism, with an alien ideology is not only an external battle. It is also our internal battle with alien phenomena, with "native blotches" of capitalism within our society. . . .

A most ferocious ideological struggle between two systems, between two world outlooks, between two conceptions of the future of mankind has been, is being, and will be waged in the world.

The people of our Soviet art must be in the foremost rank of the warriors for Communism: we and our *kind of weapon* have our *place* in this foremost rank. . . .

What have we done by the *means* of art to prove and strengthen all of our superiorities over our enemies, by the *methods* of art to set forth these obvious superiorities of our socialist order? In short, do the Party and the people feel the artists at their side in all the grandiose and unprecedented works which they undertake?

And so if we test everything that we have done and are doing from these positions, *from the positions of life and struggle,* it will become clear at once to us that the essence of the Resolution of the Central Committee of the Party on the repertoire of dramatic theatres is not in an inventory of certain feeble and ideologically empty plays, but in the fact that everyone of us must look at himself and at his creative work, and ask himself: Am I in the ranks? Am I in the struggle? And do the people feel me at their side in their struggle? . . .

And to zealots of "pure" art we will say:

There are different views on beauty in art and on beauty in life. There is the view that beauty in life is found outside the limits of struggle, outside the limits of labor, outside the limits of trial, and that, consequently, the beauty of art is also found outside the limits of all of these things. And there is the view that the primary beauty of life is found precisely within the limits of the struggle, within the limits of labor, within the limits of trial, and that within them and precisely within them the beauty of art is confined. Such is our view on life and our view on art. It is profoundly a Party view. This is so. We affirm it. More than that: we are proud of it.

6

The resolution on *Bolshaia Zhizn* brought quick results. The picture of course was never released. Nilin accepted the criticism of the Central Committee in true Bolshevik spirit and turned to the correction of his mistakes by "deeds." The resolution had declared that his "chief mistake" and the "chief mistake" of his companions in disgrace was "their failure to study the business" which they had undertaken. Nilin therefore made an extended trip through the Don Basin, observed the conditions of life, probed into the history of the region, and talked with the people, with men and women, with young and old, with miners, collective farmers, soldiers, and others. He soon discovered that the Party had been entirely correct in its criticisms. He found the "new Soviet man," the man of the "great Stalinist epoch." As an old miner put it, "our man has been so changed that he is unrecognizable." In his account of his enlightening sojourn among the people he informs the "British prosecutor Shawcross" that "the very fact of the existence of our state is the strongest kind of propaganda" and assures Vishinsky that as he "rises in the tribune" of the United Nations "he speaks in the name of our government, in the name of our state and people." And he warns all enemies today that the "halfwits of Berlin, about whom Comrade Stalin spoke in 1941, did not understand in their time the source of our strength and paid bitterly for their malicious ignorance." It is clear that the resolution of the Central Committee transformed Nilin himself overnight into the "new Soviet man" and made him "worthy of the great Stalinist epoch." [3]

Concerning the picture, *Admiral Nakhimov, Sovietskoie Iskusstvo* has this to say on January 1, 1947: "This important historico-biographical film about the Russian naval commander ex-

[3] *Literaturnaia Gazeta,* November 10, 1948.

perienced a unique and instructive fate." Pudovkin responded
positively and creatively to the admonishments of the Central
Committee. He proceeded at once to a "radical revision of the
entire scenario conception of the film," in accordance with the
directives of the resolution. The result is a superb ideological and
artistic achievement. The ball and dance scenes are almost eliminated altogether and Nakhimov shows his complete disdain for
such things. More significantly, the battle of Sinop and the siege
of Sevastopol are brought into the center of the picture. The
Turkish admirals and their commanding officer, Osman-Pasha,
are duly captured and they all testify to the extraordinary valor
and generosity of the Russian admiral and his men. With a fleet of
sailing vessels Nakhimov outfights and vanquishes an enemy
equipped with steamships, as well as sailing vessels, and supported
by powerful land fortifications. Even the British commander at
Sevastopol pays his reluctant tribute: "The Russians are not to my
taste, but they fight better from day to day." The picture seems to
convey the impression that the city did not fall and that the
Russians won the Crimean War. The Admiral has all the modesty
and patriotism becoming a hero. When Prince Menshikov praises
his genius and compares him to Nelson, he replies: "I need no
foreign laurels. It is enough for me to be a Russian admiral." The
English are cast in the rôle of the villain of the story. They
double-cross their allies and appear to be ready to shed the last
drop of French and Turkish blood. Nakhimov gently advises
Osman-Pasha, as if he were addressing the government in Ankara
today, that "we can be friends with Turkey, provided she does not
listen to evil counsel." The Central Committee registered a complete triumph. Pudovkin demonstrated that he can change history, even as Michurin and Lysenko can change nature.[4]

The case of Eisenstein is different. Probably the most famous
of all Soviet moving-picture directors, he had been a pioneer in
cinematography and had directed the production of several films
which received the acclaim of the entire world. A loyal son of the
revolution, he once told one of the authors that his life's ambition

4 See chapter 6 on "Science as a Weapon."

was to produce a picture which would explain to the people the meaning of dialectical materialism. But his independent spirit, a trait which endeared him to his friends, naturally irritated the members of the Central Committee. His *Ivan the Terrible,* at the time of its production, clearly violated the Party "line." He portrayed the *Oprichnina,* the sixteenth century prototype of the Soviet political police, in its true colors as a ruthless band of adventurers thoroughly devoted to Ivan and the establishment of his dictatorship over the people of Muscovy. If shown widely in the Soviet union it would undoubtedly have reminded many of the Cheka — OGPU — NKVD — MVD and perhaps of Stalin. Although Eisenstein died what was reported to be a natural death in the spring of 1948, he seems never to have recovered spiritually from the attack of the Central Committee. He thus followed in the footsteps of his great companions in art: the producer Meyerholdt, the critic Voronsky, the dramatist Tretiakov, the editor Gronsky, the novelist Pilnyak, the theatrical director Tairov, and many others. The circumstances surrounding the disappearance of some of these giants of the pen and the stage are still shrouded in mystery. Eisenstein's confession of error, which may have destroyed his soul, follows: [5]

It is difficult to imagine a sentry who gets so lost in contemplation of the stars that he forgets his post. It is difficult to imagine a genuine tankist engrossed in reading a novel of adventure when going into battle. It is difficult to imagine a foundryman who, instead of concentrating on the mass of molten metal flowing into prepared forms, turns aside to muse on some image of his own fantasy. He would be a bad sentry, a bad tankist, or a bad foundryman. Each would be a bad soldier.

Neither our Soviet Army nor our Socialist production knows such bad soldiers.

It is even more difficult to realize that during the severe tests arising from the demands of our Soviet life such bad and unworthy soldiers were discovered on our front of literature and art.

Reading again and again the resolution of the Central Committee

[5] *Kultura i Zhizn,* October 20, 1946.

of the Party on the film *Bolshaia Zhizn,* I invariably dwell on a question contained therein: "How can the production of so many false and mistaken films be explained? Why have such well-known Soviet directors as Comrades Lukov, Eisenstein, Pudovkin, Kozintsev, and Trauberg, who in the past created excellent films, suffered defeat?"

I must admit first of all that we artists, at a critical moment in our work, forgot for a time those great ideas which our art is summoned to serve. Some of us forgot the incessant struggle against our Soviet ideals and ideology which goes on throughout the world. For a time we lost sight of the honorable, militant, and educational task which rests upon our art during the years of great labor on the part of all the people to build a Communist society.

The Central Committee of the Party justly pointed out to us that the Soviet artist cannot treat his duties in a flippant and irresponsible manner and that workers in the cinema should study deeply whatever they undertake. Our chief mistake is that we failed to meet these demands in our creative work.

Like a bad sentry, we gaped at the unessential and the secondary, thus forgetting the main thing and abandoning our post. We forgot that the main consideration in art is its ideological content and historical truth.

Like a bad foundryman, we flippantly allowed the precious stream of creation to flow over the sand and disperse itself in private and trivial unessentials. This brought us to vices and mistakes in our productions.

The stern and timely warning of the Central Committee stops us, Soviet artists, from moving further along this dangerous and fatal path, a path which leads toward empty and non-ideological "art for art's sake," toward creative degeneration.

The resolution of the Central Committee reminds us with new force that Soviet art has been given one of the most honorable places in the decisive and supreme struggle of our ideology against the depraved ideology of the bourgeois world. Everything we do must be subordinated to the tasks of this struggle.

In the second part of *Ivan the Terrible* we permitted a distortion of historical facts which made the film ideologically worthless and vicious.

We know Ivan the Terrible as a man of strong will and firm character. Does this exclude from the general characterization of the person of the Tsar the possibility of the existence of certain doubts on his part? It is difficult to think that this man, who for his time did such unheard-of and unprecedented things, never meditated over the choice of means or never had doubts about how to act in one instance or another. But could it be that these possible doubts obscured at any time the historical rôle of the historical Ivan, as it was shown in the picture? Could it be thát the essence of this powerful sixteenth-century figure lies in these doubts and not in his uncompromising triumph over them or his inflexible consistency in statesmanship? And must not Ivan the builder hold the center of attention, Ivan the creator of a new, mighty, united Russian power, Ivan the inexorable destroyer of everything opposing his progressive actions?

The sense of historical truth betrayed me in my second part of *Ivan the Terrible*. The private, trivial, secondary, and uncharacteristic obscured the important. The "play of doubts" came into the foreground and the Tsar's strength of character and historically progressive rôle were forced out of the field of attention. As a result a false and mistaken impression of Ivan emerged. The resolution of the Central Committee, justly accusing me of distorting historical truth, says that the film presents Ivan as "weak of character and lacking in will, a kind of Hamlet." This charge is entirely just and well-founded.

The historically wrong impressions of the epoch and reign of Ivan IV, which were widely current in pre-revolutionary literature, were reflected in our film. This was especially true of the film's representation of the *Oprichnina*. The Marxian classics on questions of history have made available and clear to us the historically correct and positive evaluation of Ivan's progressive army. In the light of these works it should not have been difficult to overcome the false impressions of the *Oprichnina* contained in the writings of the Traitor-Prince, Andrei Krubsky. It should have been easy to expose the tendentious descriptions of Ivan's activity which were left us by spies of Western Powers, such as Taube and Kruze, or the adventurer Henry Shtaden. But it proved to be much more difficult to overcome in one's own self the remnants of the former purely imaginary impressions nurtured from childhood on such books as A. Tolstoy's novel, *The Silver Prince*, or the old novel, *Koudeyar*.

As a result, the progressive *Oprichniki* were presented in the film as a gang of degenerates, something like the American Ku Klux Klan. The Central Committee justly condemned this crude perversion of historical facts.

In the light of the resolutions of the Central Committee all workers in art must see the supreme necessity of putting an end to all flippant and irresponsible attitudes toward their obligations. We must fully subordinate our creative work to the interest of the education of the Soviet people, especially the youth. From this aim we must take not one step aside nor deviate a single iota.

We must master the Lenin-Stalin method of perceiving reality and history so completely and profoundly that we shall be able to overcome all remnants and survivals of former ideas which, though long banished from consciousness, strive stubbornly and cunningly to steal into our works whenever our creative vigilance relaxes for a single moment.

This is a guarantee that our cinematography will be able to surmount all the ideological and artistic failures and mistakes which like a heavy load have lain on our art in the first postwar year. It is a guarantee too that in the immediate future our cinematography will again begin to create pictures of high quality, ideologically and artistically worthy of the Stalinist epoch.

All of us, workers in art, must interpret the severe and just criticism of our work contained in the resolutions of the Central Committee as an appeal for the broadest manifestation of ardent and purposeful activity, as an appeal to the masters of art to fulfill their duty before the Soviet people, the state, and the Party by creating ideological and artistic films of high quality.

Some time in the late autumn or early winter of 1946 an All-Union conference of moving-picture workers was held in Moscow for the purpose of responding collectively to the resolution of the Central Committee on *Bolshaia Zhizn*. According to Soviet custom those participating in the conference addressed a memorial to Stalin which in both form and substance constitutes an unusually fine specimen of this particular pattern of thought control. One would have to search long in the literature of self-flagellation to find anything to surpass the concise and comprehensive catalogue of sins contained in the second paragraph of this letter: [6]

Dear Joseph Vissarionovich!

The participants in the All-Union Conference of workers in the

[6] *Iskusstvo Kino*, No. 1, January, 1947.

field of artistic cinematography have discussed the resolution of the Central Committee of the All-Union Communist Party on the film *Bolshaia Zhizn.* This resolution has exposed profoundly the many ideological and creative errors in our work.

Superficial and irresponsible attitude toward their work of many directors and scenario writers, poor leadership on the part of the Ministry of Cinematography, lack of concern for the improvement of the character of films, carelessness and irresponsibility with respect to ideological content and artistic quality, absence of indispensable criticism and self-criticism among creative film workers, failure to study deeply the work undertaken — such are the sources of the extremely grave mistakes which are pointed out in the wise resolution of the Central Committee of the All-Union Communist Party.

We workers in Soviet cinematography are mindful of the attention and concern which the Central Committee of our Party and you personally, Comrade Stalin, have always shown for our work. We are mindful too of the fact that you have always helped and instructed us. This makes it all the harder now for us to bear the mistakes which we have permitted to occur.

In the severe words of the resolution of the Central Committee of the Party about our shortcomings we feel your deep concern for the most advanced and most popular of all the arts.

We assure you, friend and teacher, that this just criticism will assist us — both Party and non-Party Bolsheviks — to correct our work as speedily as possible in order that we may hear again words of encouragement from the people and from you, dear Comrade Stalin.

We will do everything possible to create films worthy of the great Stalinist epoch, films praising the might of our socialist Motherland and glorifying the remarkable Soviet people who victoriously concluded the Great Patriotic War and who now are heroically fulfilling the provisions of the new Stalinist five-year plan.

We assure you, Comrade Stalin, that Soviet artists, leaders and workers in Soviet cinematography, will justify the trust and hopes of our Party and our people.

With firm confidence in the correctness of the paths to the further development of Soviet cinematography, pointed out to us by the Central Committee of the All-Union Communist Party and by you personally, we are launching upon our work in a new way.

7

The three ideological resolutions of the Central Committee on literature, the drama, and the cinema did not pass unnoticed in the Soviet Union. Naturally they were a subject of absorbing, of sometimes terrifying and sometimes triumphant, interest to men and women working in these fields of art. The entire press brought them to the attention of the people, emphasized their importance, and glorified the wisdom of the Party and Comrade Stalin. But their influence went much further. People laboring in other departments of the cultural apparatus sensed almost at once that the resolutions had been directed at them, as well as at writers and dramatists. They consequently proceeded to draw inferences and to take their stand firmly on the side of the Central Committee. Early in October, 1946, the "members of the Third Session of the Academy of Medical Science of the USSR" sent the following letter to "Comrade I. V. Stalin": [7]

Dear Joseph Vissarionovich!
The members of the Third Session of the Academy of Medical Science of the USSR send you, great captain of all victories, their ardent greetings and deep gratitude for your unceasing concern for the growth and development of Soviet science.

Memorable throughout the country are your words at the pre-election meeting of February 9, 1946, to the effect that if necessary assistance is rendered to our scientists "they will be able not only to overtake, but even to surpass in the nearest future the scientific achievements beyond the frontiers of our country."

The Party and the Soviet government, under your leadership, with a generous hand increase the funds for scientific-research institutes, and decisively improve the material living conditions of scientific workers. These tremendously significant acts of the Soviet state are the more impressive because they take place under the difficult conditions

[7] *Pravda,* October 3, 1946.

of the first postwar year, in the period of the resolution of the most complex international problems. People of science are assured the opportunity of devoting themselves entirely to creative work, of directing these labors to the good of the Soviet people and the fulfillment of the grandiose tasks of the Fourth Five-Year Plan.

The resolutions recently adopted by the Central Committee of the All-Union Communist Party on questions of ideological work raise the sense of responsibility of every cultural worker and particularly of every scientific worker to his people, his state, and his Party. They show us the only true direction of scientific-research activity.

No matter how remarkable the achievements of Soviet medical science, no matter how valuable its contribution to the cause of the universal-historic victory in the Great Patriotic War, it still stands in great debt to the Soviet people.

The same shortcomings and mistakes which the Central Committee of the Party opportunely exposed in its resolutions on literature and art are prevalent among scientific workers and hinder the development of medical science.

Your instructions, Joseph Vissarionovich, on the necessity for a genuine movement forward and for the training of personnel by means of responsible, bold, frank, and objective criticism must be transmuted into life in scientific institutes, in medical organizations, in medical journals.

From the resolutions of the Central Committee of the Party we draw the necessary directives for the uninterrupted theoretical growth of our personnel, for the arming of them with knowledge of the advanced science of the development of society, for their ideological maturing to inspire Soviet people to struggle for the victory of Communism.

We assure you that the Third Session of the Academy of Medical Science of the USSR, in summing up its activity for the past two years and in drafting its five-year plan, will examine its work fundamentally, will expose its shortcomings and mistakes, and will think through the question of how to achieve new and better results in the development of Soviet medicine.

We promise you to link medical science even more strongly and intimately with the problems of the restoration and further development of the public economy, with the tasks of the gradual transition of the country from socialism to Communism.

Long live genuine advanced science, revolutionary Soviet medicine!
Long live our great leader and teacher, Comrade Stalin!

About two weeks after this action by the Academy of Medical
Science, an influential body of teachers rallied to the support of
the ideological resolutions. On October 19 a letter addressed "to
the great leader of the peoples of the Soviet Union" was "unanimously approved at a general meeting of professors, instructors,
and leaders of the institutions of higher education of the City of
Moscow": [8]

Dear Joseph Vissarionovich!
We, professors, instructors and directors of the higher educational
institutions of Moscow, the capital of our great Motherland, having
assembled for a discussion of questions pertaining to the further
development of higher education, send you, our dear leader and
teacher, our flaming greetings.

We are infinitely grateful to the Soviet Government, to the great
Bolshevik Party, and to you personally, Comrade Stalin, for exceptional concern for the higher school and science. Even during the very
strenuous time of war we felt your fatherly concern for the student
body and scientific workers, for the strengthening of the Soviet higher
school. We feel this concern particularly now in the days of the
peaceful creative work of our Soviet people.

The past year was the first academic year under the conditions of
the postwar economic and cultural restoration of our socialist Motherland.

We, workers in higher educational institutions, inspired by your
historic speech at the meeting of electors on February 9, 1946, have
achieved substantial successes during the past academic year.

We are glad to inform you that in the present academic year in our
country, 797 higher educational institutions enrolling 632,000 students,
including the 78 institutions of Moscow with 112,000 students, have
begun work.

The 1946 state plan for the admission of new students has been
entirely fulfilled. In the higher educational institutions of the country
200,000 students, the best representatives of our Soviet youth, have
been admitted. Among the new students are 40,000 participants in the

8 *Pravda,* November 25, 1946.

Patriotic War and 7000 graduates of the middle school with gold and silver medals.

For the first time since the war our higher educational institutions began their work under normal conditions of peace.

The progress and discipline of students have been significantly improved. The material base of the higher schools has been increased; laboratories and study rooms have been considerably expanded and furnished with teaching and scientific equipment.

The scientific-research activity of higher educational institutions has been greatly extended.

However, the successes which we have achieved are only a beginning of the vast work involved in the education of the new personnel of the Soviet intelligentsia and in the further development of science in our country.

The Five-Year Plan for the restoration and development of the public economy, which all the Soviet people have begun to fulfill, places before us, workers in the higher school, large and responsible tasks. During the next five years we must prepare 602,000 specialists with higher education for the different branches of public economy and culture.

The first installment in the fulfillment of our Fourth Five-Year Plan has already been made this year. The country has received from the higher educational institutions 71,000 young specialists, including 10,000 graduates from the higher institutions of the city of Moscow.

We are aware of our responsibility to the country, to the people, and to you, Comrade Stalin. Tasks of tremendous importance stand before us: the task of the further raising of the scientific level of the preparation of specialists and particularly now in the first stage of the historical development of our country the task of the ideological and political education of the rising generation of the intelligentsia.

The resolutions of the Central Committee of the Party "On the Journals *Zvezda* and *Leningrad*," "On the Repertoire of the Dramatic Theatres and Measures for Its Improvement," and "On the Moving Picture *Bolshaia Zhizn*," and the speech of Comrade Zhdanov on the journals *Zvezda* and *Leningrad* have historic significance for the whole ideological front and are programmatic documents for the entire vast army of the Soviet intelligentsia. But the meaning of these directives of the Central Committee is peculiarly important for us, workers in the higher school, who are engaged in the education of the younger genera-

tion of the intelligentsia, the new personnel for the building of socialism. These decisions oblige us to strengthen the ideological work,
tirelessly to nurture our youth in the spirit of cheerfulness and of
faith in our cause, in the spirit of devotion to the socialist Motherland,
competent and able to overcome difficulties.

In instructing and educating our youth we do not forget for a moment that every science is a Party science and that its teaching cannot
be separated from the politics of the Party. That politics is the vital
base of the Soviet political order.

We, professors and instructors, obligate ourselves so to conduct our
work that every day spent by a student in a higher educational institution will nurture in him Bolshevik ideology, broaden his political and
cultural horizon, and enrich him with the knowledges of his specialty.

Conscious that the raising of the quality of the preparation of
specialists with higher education is now the decisive task, we assure
you, Joseph Vissarionovich, that in every possible way we will bring
into the teaching process the newest achievements of science and
technique, inculcate in students habits of independent creative work,
and develop science and technique in the spirit of your remarkable
instructions concerning progressive science.

In order to resolve this task successfully, we obligate ourselves unceasingly to perfect our knowledge, unceasingly to raise our scientific
qualifications and our ideological-political understanding, systematically to strive for the mastery of the theoretical riches summed up in
the classical works of Marx, Engels, Lenin, and Stalin.

We will put forth all of our strength to create new textbooks which
are abreast of contemporary achievements in science and technique
and which are appropriate to the task of the education of student
youth.

We obligate ourselves to develop yet more widely our scientific-
research work and concentrate attention especially on the resolution
of the most important and significant problems in the spheres of public
economy and defense.

We assure you, our dear leader and teacher, that we shall put forth
all of our energy and knowledge in order to fulfill with honor your
instruction — not only to overtake, but even to surpass in the nearest
future the scientific achievements of foreign countries.

Our Motherland moves confidently on the road to the completion
of the building of a socialist society and to the gradual transition to

Communism. We, workers in the higher school, will labor so that we may always be in the vanguard of the struggle of the Soviet people for the incorporation into life of the great ideas of Marxism-Leninism.

Long live the great Soviet people!

Long live the Party of Lenin and Stalin, the organizer and inspirer of our victories!

Long live our wise leader and teacher, the greatest scholar of our epoch — Joseph Vissarionovich Stalin!

Toward the latter part of November the august Academy of Science met in session. On November 29 the participants in the session, following in the footsteps of the physicians and the professors, sent a message of loyalty and devotion to the head of the Soviet state [9] and registered their unqualified approval of the resolutions:

Our own dear Joseph Vissarionovich!

The academicians, corresponding members, and scientific contributors of the Academy of Science of the Soviet Union, gathered in regular session, send you, brilliant leader and teacher of the Soviet people, great inspirer and organizer of our victories, their ardent greetings and deep gratitude for unceasing care for the development of Soviet science.

The November session of the Academy of Science of the USSR proceeds in the atmosphere of the heroic struggle of the people of the Soviet Union for the fulfillment of the plan of the first year of the Five-Year-Plan. Soviet scientists occupy a worthy place in the struggle of our people for the further growth of the economic power of the socialist state, for the realization of the transition of the country from socialism to Communism. Before our people in all their grandeur stand the tasks of the restoration and further development of the public economy of the country, suffering from the German occupation. The swiftest achievement of these aims will create the conditions for a new powerful upsurge of socialist industry, transport, rural economy, and culture.

Toward the resolution of the tasks of the postwar Stalinist Five-Year Plan, the plan of scientific research of the Academy of Science of the USSR for 1946–50 is directed.

The Academy of Science of the USSR is living through a new stage

[9] *Pravda*, December 1, 1946.

in its history. Into our family enter eminent Soviet scientists — people who are enriching with their discoveries and researches Soviet and world science.

The resolutions of the Central Committee of the All-Union Communist Party on questions of ideological work set before us a great task — the mastery of the all-conquering theories of Marx, Engels, Lenin, and Stalin — the raising of the sense of responsibility of every scientist to the people, the Party, and the state in his research activity.

We assure you, dear Joseph Vissarionovich, that Soviet scientists will devote all their strength to the fulfillment of your instruction, "to surpass in the shortest period the achievements of science beyond the borders of our country." We are firmly confident that our scientists, attentively studying and utilizing all the achievements of world science and technique, will move science and technique ahead, will enrich science with new investigations and discoveries which will guarantee technical progress in the public economy, will insure the growth of the economic and military power of the Soviet state, and will exalt our Motherland and Soviet science.

Long live our socialist Motherland — the Union of Soviet Socialist Republics!

Long live our great leader and teacher, coryphaeus of science, the Honorary Academician Joseph Vissarionovich Stalin!

CHAPTER FIVE

MUSIC AS A WEAPON

ONTHS PASSED before the Central Committee of the Party struck again. Probably many leaders in the artistic and intellectual life of the Soviet Union, as well as numerous students of Soviet affairs abroad, had begun to think that the purge of the cultural apparatus had been completed with the three resolutions on literature, the drama, and the cinema. It appeared that the resolutions had served their purpose, not only in the specific fields toward which they had been directed, but also throughout the ranks of the intelligentsia. Their meaning had been made abundantly clear. The new policy called in unmistakable terms for an assault on all things Western and the glorification of all things Soviet. And most Soviet citizens knew from experience that the "voice of the Party is the voice of God." Moreover, declarations of abject loyalty had come from the most diverse groups and organizations. It seemed that the new "line" had been fully established.

The purge, however, was not over. As a matter of fact it seems not to be over by any means as these lines are being written. Perhaps the Party feared, in the words of Simonov, that not a few of the "leaders of culture" wanted "to sit down for a while" and "catch their breath." But this was not to be. The Politburo and the Central Committee understand fully the value of the offensive. In fact a basic principle of their strategy is always to hold the initiative in domestic as well as in foreign affairs. Here is one of the secrets of their success from 1917 down to the present moment. Lenin triumphed over his vastly more numerous and seemingly far more powerful adversaries by attacking without surcease and with great energy and resourcefulness. And so it was with Stalin. During the first years of the revolution few observers indeed would have picked him as the successor of Lenin. In the struggle for power with his rivals he always kept the initiative in his own hands.

2

On February 10, 1948, the Central Committee carried the offensive into a new realm. It issued a fourth resolution, and this time on a subject which in other parts of the world is regarded as rather remote from politics — on music. The Committee chose as the immediate object of its attack an opera which had been presented on the most celebrated occasion of the Soviet calendar for 1947 — the Thirtieth Anniversary of the Great October Revolution.

The selection of this composition for unqualified condemnation was an act loaded with drama. It had been lauded in the Soviet press for the "great breadth" of its music, for the "fullness" of its "vocal expression," for the "noble beauty" of its "melodic lines," for its "excellent folk scenes." It was declared to be so "saturated with the mighty optimism of a strong and complete feeling of life" that "it often takes possession of you, carries you away, and conquers you." The critic speaks of the "remarkable assurance and sweep" with which the composer "brings into a single synthesis the legendary grandeur of the old man Dzhemali — the incarnation of the wisdom and conscience of the people — and the profound simplicity of the Bolshevik commissar, the epic tale of Dzhemali about the hero who conquers the dragon and the passionate speech of the commissar about Lenin who brings happiness and light to the people."[1] Moreover, many of the great in Soviet music must have had a hand in the choice of the opera

1 *Sovietskoie Iskusstvo*, November 15, 1947, p. 3.

which was calculated to reveal to the Party and the world the "unprecedented flowering of socialist art." Obviously by no other measure could the Central Committee have struck such a shattering blow at the entire musical fraternity and dramatized so powerfully the new policy which it desired to propagate.

The resolution censured not only the opera and its composer, Vano Muradeli, but also the foremost Soviet composers — Shostakovich, Prokofiev, Khachaturian, Shebalin, Miaskovsky, and Popov. The full shock of the attack can only be sensed if one realizes that these men had been the idols of the musical world right down to the day that the contents of the resolution became known. The issue of *Sovietskoie Iskusstvo* for August 15, 1947, contained an article entitled "Musical Moscow Past and Present." According to this article the "pedagogical faculty" of the Moscow Conservatory, "with such names as Miaskovsky, Shostakovich, Shebalin, Igumanov, Oistrakh, and many others, has no equal in the entire world." [2] An issue of the same authoritative journal for October devoted its leading editorial to "The Concert Season." After announcing that Soviet music is "generally acclaimed as the leading progressive force of universal musical art," the writer boasts that "even the most irreconcilable enemies of the Soviet Union have nothing to compare with the philosophically profound symphonism of Shostakovich and Miaskovsky, the joyous compositions of Prokofiev, and the emotional brilliance of the creations of Khachaturian." [3] In November, Shostakovich, Prokofiev, Khachaturian, and Shebalin were awarded the highly coveted honor of "People's Artist of the RSFSR" and Muradeli and Popov the title of "Honored Leader of Art of the RSFSR." [4] Then on February 10, 1948, the Central Committee issued the following fateful resolution "On the Opera *Velikaia Druzhba* by V. Muradeli": [5]

The Central Committee of the All-Union Communist Party considers the opera *Velikaia Druzhba* (Music by Vano Muradeli, Libretto by G. Mdivani) produced at the Bolshoi Theatre of the USSR on the

[2] *Ibid.*, August 15, 1947, p. 2.   [3] *Ibid.*, October 4, 1947, p. 1.
[4] *Ibid.*, November 15, 1947, p. 1.   [5] *Sovietskaia Muzyka*, No. 1, 1948, pp. 3–8.

Thirtieth Anniversary of the October Revolution to be vicious and inartistic in both its music and its subject matter.

The basic defects of the opera lie first of all in the music. The music is feeble and inexpressive. It contains not a single melody or aria to be remembered. It is confused and disharmonious, built on complicated dissonances, on combinations of sound that grate upon the ear. Some lines and scenes with pretensions to melodiousness are suddenly broken by discordant noises wholly strange to the normal human ear and oppressive to the listener. Between the musical accompaniment and the development of the action on the stage there is no organic connection. The vocal part of the opera — the choral, solo, and ensemble singing — produces a miserable impression. As a result of all this, the potentialities of the orchestra and the singers are not exploited.

The composer has not made use of the wealth of folk melodies, songs, tunes, and dance motifs in which the creative life of the people of the USSR is so rich, and especially the creative life of the peoples of the North Caucasus where the action of the opera is laid.

In the pursuit of a false "originality" in music, the composer, Muradeli, has neglected the best traditions and the experience of the classic opera in general and Russian classic opera in particular, which is distinguished by inner substance, by richness of melody and breadth of diapason, by popularity of appeal, by grace, beauty, and clarity of musical form. These characteristics have made Russian opera the best in the world, a species of music loved by and comprehensible to the wide masses of the people.

The plot of the opera, which pretends to portray the struggle for the establishment of Soviet power and friendship of peoples in the North Caucasus in 1918–21, is historically false and fictitious. The opera creates the erroneous impression that the peoples of the Caucasus, such as the Georgians and the Ossetians, were at that time hostile to the Russian people. This is historically false. It was the Ingushi and Chechen who opposed the establishment of friendship among peoples of the North Caucasus at that time.

The Central Committee of the Party holds that the failure of Muradeli's opera is the result of the formalistic path which he has followed — a path which is false and injurious to the creative work of the Soviet composer.

The conference of Soviet musicians, conducted by the Central Committee of the Party, showed that the failure of Muradeli's opera is not an isolated case. It is closely linked with the unsatisfactory state of contemporary Soviet music, with the spread of a formalistic tendency among Soviet composers.

As far back as 1936, in connection with the appearance of Dmitri Shostakovich's opera *Lady Macbeth of Mtsensk*, *Pravda*, the organ of the Central Committee of the Party, subjected to sharp criticism the anti-popular formalistic perversions in his music and exposed the harm and danger of this tendency to the future of Soviet music. Writing then on instructions from the Central Committee of the Party, *Pravda* formulated clearly the Soviet people's requirements of their composers.

Notwithstanding these warnings, and also in spite of instructions given by the Central Committee of the Party in its decisions on the journals *Zvezda* and *Leningrad*, on the moving picture *Bolshaia Zhizn*, and on the repertoire of the dramatic theatres, no reorganization took place in Soviet music. The individual successes of some Soviet composers in the creation of widely popular songs, in the composition of music for the cinema, and so on, do not alter the general situation.

The state of affairs is particularly bad in the field of symphonic and operatic music. The question at issue concerns composers who adhere to the formalistic anti-popular tendency. The very fullest expression of this tendency is found in the works of such composers as Dmitri Shostakovich, Sergei Prokofiev, Aram Khachaturian, Vissarion Shebalin, G. Popov, N. Miaskovsky, and others whose compositions represent most strikingly the formalistic perversions and anti-democratic tendencies in music which are alien to the Soviet people and their artistic tastes.

The characteristic marks of this music are the negation of the basic principles of classic music: the cult of atonality, the dissonance and discord supposedly expressive of "progress" and "novelty" in the development of musical form; the rejection of such a vital principle of musical composition as melody; and enthusiasm for confused, neuropathological combinations which transform music into cacophony, into a chaotic medley of sounds. This music reeks strongly of the odor of the contemporary, modernistic, bourgeois music of Europe and America which reflects the decay of bourgeois culture, the total negation, the impasse of musical art.

An essential mark of the formalistic tendency is also the rejection of polyphonic music and singing based on the simultaneous arrangement and development of a series of independent melodic lines and an enthusiasm for monotonous unisonic music and singing, often without words. This constitutes a violation of the many-voiced system of music and singing native to our people, and leads to the impoverishment and decadence of music.

Many Soviet composers despise the best traditions of Russian and Western classical music, reject these traditions as supposedly "obsolete," "old-fashioned," and "conservative," and contemptuously regard composers who strive conscientiously to master and develop the methods of classical music as advocates of "primitive traditionalism" and of "epigonism." In the pursuit of mistakenly understood innovations, they have lost contact in their music with the needs and artistic tastes of the Soviet people, formed a narrow circle of specialists and musical gourmands, lowered the high social rôle and narrowed the significance of music, confining it to the satisfaction of the perverted tastes of esthetic individualists.

The formalistic tendency in Soviet music has bred in a section of Soviet composers a one-sided enthusiasm for complex forms of instrumental symphonic textless music and a disdainful attitude toward such musical forms as opera, choral music, popular music for small orchestras, for national instruments, vocal ensembles, and so on. The inevitable result of all of this is that the foundations of vocal culture and dramatic artistry will be lost and that composers will forget how to write for the people. Evidence of this is the fact that not a single Soviet opera on the level of the Russian classical operas has been written in recent times.

The loss of contact with the people by some Soviet composers has resulted in the propagation of the putrid "theory" that the failure of the people to understand the music of many Soviet composers is due to the fact that the people are not yet sufficiently "mature" to understand their complex music, that they will understand it centuries to come, and that the lack of popular appeal of certain musical works is nothing to worry about. This thoroughly individualistic and fundamentally anti-popular theory has still further encouraged some composers and musical critics to draw off from the people, from the criticism of the Soviet public, and to retire into their shells.

The cultivation of these and similar views brings the greatest harm to Soviet musical art. A tolerant attitude toward such views indicates the presence among representatives of Soviet musical culture of alien tendencies which lead to a blind alley in the development of music, to the liquidation of musical art.

The vicious anti-popular formalistic tendency in Soviet music also has a baleful influence on the preparation and education of young composers in our conservatories and, first of all, in the Moscow Conservatory (the Director of which is V. Shebalin) where the formalistic tendency is dominant. Respect for the best traditions of Russian and Western classical music is not inculcated in the students, and love for popular creative art and democratic musical forms is not nurtured in them. The work of many students in the conservatories is a blind imitation of the music of Shostakovich, Prokofiev, and others.

The Central Committee of the Party finds the state of Soviet musical criticism utterly intolerable. The opponents of Russian realistic music, the partisans of decadent and formalistic music, hold a leading position among the critics. They interpret every new composition by Prokofiev, Shostakovich, Miaskovsky, or Shebalin as a "new conquest of Soviet music." They glorify the subjectivism, the constructivism, the extreme individualism, and the technical complexity of the language of this music, that is, precisely everything that should be subjected to criticism. Instead of smashing views and theories harmful and alien to the principles of socialist realism, musical criticism assists in the spread of these views by praising and proclaiming "advanced" those composers who in their work share erroneous creative purposes.

Musical criticism has ceased to express the judgment of Soviet society, the judgment of the people, and has been converted into a speaking trumpet for individual composers. Some music critics, instead of giving objective criticism based on principle, have taken to humoring and fawning on these or those leaders and praising their creative genius to the skies, for reasons of personal friendship.

All of this means that some Soviet composers, nourished on the influence of contemporary decadent West European and American music, have not yet shaken off the vestiges of bourgeois ideology.

The Central Committee of the Party considers this unfavorable situation on the front of Soviet music to be the result of the incorrect line which has been pursued by the Committee on the Arts of the Council of Ministers of the USSR and the Organizational Committee of the Union of Soviet Composers.

The Committee on the Arts of the Council of Ministers of the USSR (of which Khrapchenko is chairman) and the Organizational Committee of the Union of Soviet Composers (headed by Khachaturian), instead of developing the realistic tendency in Soviet music which is founded on a recognition of the tremendous progressive rôle of the classical heritage, and particularly the traditions of the Russian musical school, actually encouraged the formalistic tendency which is alien to the Soviet people. They failed to utilize and develop this heritage with its emphasis on union of high content with artistic perfections of musical form, on honesty and realism, on deep organic connection with the people and their musical and vocal art, on high level of professional artistry combined with simplicity and comprehensibility of musical works.

The Organizational Committee of the Union of Soviet Composers has become the tool of a group of composers of the formalistic school and the main nursery of formalistic perversions. In this committee a stale atmosphere has been created; creative discussions are lacking. The heads of this committee and the musicians grouped around them sing the praises of anti-realistic, modernistic compositions undeserving of support, while works which are distinguished by their realistic character and by an effort to continue and to develop the classical heritage are declared to be second-rate, remain unnoticed, and are treated in a supercilious manner. Composers who pride themselves on being "innovators" and "arch revolutionaries" in music conduct their activities in the Organizational Committee like champions of the most backward and mouldy conservatism, showing a contemptuous intolerance toward the slightest suggestion of criticism.

The Central Committee of the Party considers that the situation and the attitude toward the tasks of Soviet music which are found in the Committee on the Arts of the Council of Ministers of the USSR and in the Organizational Committee of the Union of Soviet Composers can no longer be tolerated because they do immeasurable harm to the development of Soviet music. During recent years the cultural needs and the level of artistic taste of the Soviet people have advanced greatly. They expect from composers works of high quality and ideological content in all categories — in operas, in symphonic music, in song writing, in choral and dance music. In our country composers enjoy unlimited opportunities for creative work and all the conditions essential for the genuine flowering of musical culture. They have an audience such as no composer of the past has ever known. For them to fail to make use of all these rich possibilities and to direct their creative efforts along the correct realistic path should be inexcusable.

The Central Committee of the All-Union Communist Party resolves:

1. To condemn the formalistic tendency in Soviet music as against the people and as leading actually to the liquidation of music.

2. To propose to the Administration of Propaganda and Agitation of the Central Committee and the Committee on the Arts that they endeavor to correct the situation in Soviet music, liquidate the shortcomings set forth in the present resolution of the Central Committee, and ensure the development of Soviet music in the direction of realism.

3. To call upon Soviet composers to become aware of the lofty demands made on musical art by the Soviet people, to clear away everything that weakens our music and hampers its development, to ensure that upsurge of creative work which will advance Soviet musical culture rapidly and lead to the creation of finished works of high quality, worthy of the Soviet people, in every branch of music.

4. To approve organizational measures of the appropriate Party and Soviet organs directed toward the improvement of musical affairs.

3

The response of the musicians was immediate and overwhelming. For the purpose of "discussing the historic resolution of the Central Committee" a conference of local composers and students of music was held in Moscow from the seventeenth to the twenty-sixth of February, 1948. The tone of the meeting was set by N. N. Danilov, Secretary of the City Committee of the Party. "With great power" he "sounded a call to the composers to raise their ideological standards and conquer the heights of Marxist-Leninist teachings. Without this condition we cannot create genuine people's music, the most advanced and most perfect music in the world." Since this conference was attended by practically all of the composers mentioned in the resolution and since it established the pattern of response, it was probably more important for purposes of understanding than the First All-Union Congress of Composers held later.

At the conference the major address seems to have been delivered by T. Khrennikov, General Secretary of the Union of Soviet composers, under the title, "For Creative Work Worthy of the Soviet People." The general temper of his remarks is revealed in his concluding words: [6]

Soviet composers must sweep away, as useless and pernicious rubbish, the vestiges of bourgeois formalism in musical art. They must understand that the creation of ideological compositions of high quality in all branches of music — in operatic and symphonic music, in song music, in choral and dance music — is possible only by following the principles of socialist realism.

Composers must remember the words of the great Russian Gorky, that "socialist realism affirms existence as work, as creation, whose aim is the unceasing development of the valuable individual talents of man for the sake of his victory over the forces of nature, for the sake of his health and long life, for the sake of the great happiness of living on the land . . . "

The historic task of Soviet composers, as Comrade Zhdanov has said, consists not only in carefully guarding Soviet music from baneful Western influences, but also in taking the offensive against decadent bourgeois art, raising high the banner of Soviet music — the art of profoundly progressive ideas and genuine humanism. The Central Committee of the Party, by conducting a three-day conference on questions of music and by the resolution of February 10, has given extraordinary attention and aid to the cause of the development of Soviet musical art and to us — Soviet composers. It is our duty to conserve the vital force of these historic documents for years to come, making them our militant creative program.

The resolution of the Central Committee calls us "to become aware of the lofty demands made on musical art by the Soviet people, to clear away everything that weakens our music and hampers its development, to ensure that upsurge of creative work which will advance Soviet musical culture rapidly and lead to the creation of finished works of high quality, worthy of the Soviet people, in every branch of music."

[6] *Ibid.*, p. 62.

It is our duty to mobilize all of our creative energies in order to answer worthily and in the very shortest period this call of our Party, this call of our great leader, Comrade Stalin.

The Moscow conference concluded its deliberations with the following letter addressed to "the Great Leader of the Soviet People, Comrade Stalin": [7]

Dear Joseph Vissarionovich!

The composers and musicians of the Soviet capital, assembled for the discussion of the historic resolution of the Central Committee of the All-Union Communist Party of February 10, 1948, on the opera by Muradeli, *Velikaia Druzhba,* send you, our dear leader and teacher, ardent greetings and wishes for your good health.

We experience a feeling of tremendous gratitude to the Central Committee of the Party and to you personally, dear Comrade Stalin, for the stern but profoundly just appraisal of the present condition of Soviet musical art, and for the attention which you and the Central Committee of our Party have manifested toward the cause of the development of Soviet music and toward us, Soviet musicians.

The conference of the leaders of Soviet music in the Central Committee of the Party, and particularly the address of Comrade Zhdanov and the resolution of the Central Committee of January 10 are events of historic significance. The extraordinarily forceful, profound, and precise analysis of the present state of Soviet musical art and the indication of clear ways for freeing it from these defects — all of this is an invaluable aid to us, testimony to the great power and sagacity of the Communist Party.

We, composers and musicians of the city of Moscow, acknowledge the full justice of the Party's criticism of Soviet music, which henceforth liberates us from the deadening effect of bourgeois-formalistic routine, from decadent influences.

It is clear to us that representatives of the tendency discussed in the resolution of the Central Committee of the Party, proceeding along the road of formalistic pseudo-innovations, have lost contact with the songs of the people, have forgotten the musical speech of their own people, have humiliated themselves by subjugating their talent to models and dogmas of West-European and American modernism. In the presence of the Soviet people whose voice sounds in every line of

7 *Ibid.,* pp. 27–28.

the resolution of the Central Committee of the Party we confess that many of us had forgotten the great traditions of Russian musical realism. The words of the brilliant Glinka, who proclaimed "the people create music, and we, artists, only arrange it," did not find full expression in the creative work of Soviet composers. Consequently the popular element in our operatic and symphonic art was ignored and the fundamentally vicious subjective-idealistic theory was disseminated — the theory that the broad mass of auditors, supposedly, is not "mature enough" to understand modern music.

For us, Soviet musicians, yet more grievous is the consciousness that we have been unable to draw true and logical conclusions from those warnings, which our Party has made not infrequently, whenever Soviet musical art has strayed from the true realistic path. The articles, "Confusion Instead of Music" and "The Deception of the Ballet," published in *Pravda* twelve years ago, the resolutions of the Central Committee of the All-Union Communist Party "On the Journals *Zvezda* and *Leningrad*," "On the Moving Picture *Bolshaia Zhizn*," "On the Repertoire of Dramatic Theatres and Measures for Its Improvement" did not call forth, as the resolution of the Central Committee of the Party states with profound truth, any reform of Soviet music. Soviet composers and critics were unable to evaluate in the necessary way the current and precise instructions of the Central Committee of the Party and thus brought most grievous harm to Soviet musical culture. Only loss of contact with the life of the people can explain the fact that our composers were unable to evaluate according to merit the colossal, the unprecedented growth of the artistic tastes and interests of the broad masses of the people and were therefore unable to respond to these tastes and demands of the great Soviet people.

Your personal instructions, dear Joseph Vissarionovich, concerning the creation of a Soviet operatic classic, which you gave in a conversation with the composer Dzerzhinsky concerning his opera *Quiet Don* remain for us a militant program of creative work. We shall apply all our knowledge and artistic craftsmanship to the composition of brilliant realistic productions which will reflect the life and struggle of the Soviet people.

With the creative reticence of composers we must have done forever. Petit bourgeois individualism has no place in the musical compositions of a country where the artist enjoys all the conditions necessary for the full development of his creative individuality, where he is surrounded with care and attention about which the artists of bourgeois countries do not even dare to dream. In no other land does the composer have such an audience as in ours.

The Soviet artist is a servant of the people. Here is the first conclusion which must be drawn by all Soviet composers and musicians. To this high democratic principle the creative genius of every Soviet musician must be wholly subjected. Not for snobs must music sound, but for all of our great people.

We assure you, our dear leader and teacher, that the appeals of the Central Committee of the All-Union Communist Party, addressed to us Soviet musicians, will become the militant program of our creative work. We shall devote all of our strength to the cause of a new and unprecedentedly high upsurge of Soviet musical art.

We swear to you and to the entire Soviet people to direct our art along the road of socialist realism, to labor untiringly for the creation in all branches of music of models worthy of our great epoch, to strive to make our music loved by all of the great Soviet people, and to find in our art a vivid and imaginative expression of the great ideas which will inspire our people to their universal-historic deeds.

Long live the Leninist-Stalinist people, the people industrious, the people victorious, conquering a truly socialist art, the most advanced in the world!

Long live the Leninist-Stalinist Central Committee of the All-Union Communist Party!

Long live our leader and teacher, father of the people, the great S T A L I N!

4

Muradeli was given several opportunities to make his peace with the Central Committee of the Party. The first occasion apparently was at a conference of Soviet musicians in Moscow in the middle of January, some time before the resolution was given to the press. At this conference, called by the Central Committee, Andrei Zhdanov presented the views of the Party. In his response Muradeli accepted fully, one might almost say gratefully and enthusiastically, the strictures on his work contained in the resolution. He said that the criticism of his opera was "just and severe," that he had "pondered the question soberly, humanly, and deeply," and that "as a man, as a citizen, and as a Communist" he "agreed with the evaluation." After exploring the sources of his errors he concluded as follows:

Comrades, today is the most important day of my life, of my life as an artist as well as of my life as a man. I cannot tell you how very painful it is for me to know that I was so severely mistaken. I worked over my compositions sincerely; I wanted to give to the Thirtieth Anniversary of the Soviet Power everything I could. I wanted to live so as not to be ashamed to die.

I assure Andrei Alexandrovich [Zhdanov], the Central Committee of the Party, and all my friends that I shall strive to understand my errors and to do whatsoever the Central Committee of our Party asks of us." [8]

At the later conference in Moscow from the seventeenth to the twenty-sixth of February Muradeli repeated his confession. According to the account of his remarks published in the official organ of Soviet composers, he subjected his "grave errors" to "thorough criticism," admitting that his work revealed "artificiality," "lack of skill," "snobbishness," "formalistic pretentiousness," "detachment from the spiritual needs of the people," and "inability to grasp the genuine significance of the traditions of Russian classical opera." He also admitted that he had been a party to the use of the Musical Fund to finance "the creative work of a small group of formalists" and to the pursuit of "undemocratic methods of work" in the Organizational Committee. Having repeated his confession, he then proceeded to repeat his assurance of good behavior for the future:

I have set before myself the clear aim of comprehending without ambiguities the full seriousness of my creative mistakes and to correct them honestly and fundamentally in my new compositions. The resolution of the Central Committee is one more clear demonstration of

8 *Conference of Musicians and Composers in the Central Committee of the Communist Party* (Moscow, 1948), pp. 17–21. (In Russian.)

the concern of our Party for the fate of Soviet socialist culture. This
historic resolution is a clear creative program for Soviet composers
which will lead to a mighty upsurge of Soviet musical art. I shall
strive with all my heart to earn the right to serve devotedly native
Soviet music.[9]

This confession would seem to be complete. Yet Muradeli
failed to reply, except by indirection, to one very important criticism of *Velikaia Druzhba* contained in the resolution of the Central Committee. Since the issue involved illuminates a fundamental feature of Communist mentality, methods, and morals, a
word should be said about it. Reference is here made to the charge
of historical inaccuracy. On this point the resolution reads:

The plot of the opera, which pretends to portray the struggle for
the establishment of Soviet power and friendship of peoples in the
North Caucasus in 1918–21, is historically false and fictitious. The
opera creates the erroneous impression that the peoples of the Caucasus, such as the Georgians and Ossetians, were at that time hostile
to the Russian people. This is historically false. It was the Ingushi
and Chechen who opposed the establishment of friendship among
peoples of the North Caucasus at that time.

As a matter of fact the Bolsheviks had a great deal of trouble
with the Georgians during the period of the Civil War following
the revolution. Georgia was one of the few really strong centers of
Menshevism at the time. But to recognize this fact today would
mean to follow "bourgeois objectivism" in historical writing. The
Soviet historian, whenever he deals with a subject with political
implications, whether it has to do with the collectivization of agriculture or the life of Stalin, is expected to show "discretion" and
respect the "line" of the Party. History is a "weapon" of politics,
quite as much as literature or drama or music. So the ancient
struggle in Georgia must be forgotten and erased from the record.
But the Ingushi and Chechen, two small nationalities of the North
Caucasus, were disloyal to the Soviet Government in the Great
Patriotic War when Hitler's armies marched into the region and,

9 *Sovietskaia Muzyka*, op. cit., p. 65.

as a consequence, "were resettled in other regions of the USSR." Muradeli failed to realize that the severe punishment visited upon them should be justified in his opera which dealt with the earlier period.

With few reservations Dmitri Shostakovich admitted his mistakes, promised to alter his ways, and called upon all other composers to do likewise: [10]

When we look back on the road over which our art has travelled, it is entirely clear to us that every time the Party has corrected the mistakes of this or that artist, pointed to deviations in his creative work, or condemned severely certain tendencies in Soviet art, it has always benefited all Soviet art as well as the work of individual artists.

The instructions of the Central Committee of the Party are permeated with concern for the raising of the role and significance of art in the development of our Soviet society.

When in 1936 *Pravda,* the central organ of our Party, severely condemned my opera, *Lady Macbeth of Mtsensk,* and pointed to my serious errors, to my formalism, I felt deeply my creative failure. I pondered over the matter a great deal and endeavored to extract all necessary lessons. And it seemed to me that in subsequent years my creative work began to develop in a different direction. I endeavored to respond to the large and important questions which confronted the entire Soviet land and the entire Soviet people. It seemed to me that to a certain extent I overcame those vicious traits to which *Pravda* had pointed: the complexity of musical language, the complexity of musical thinking, the anti-esthetic tendency, and so on.

The severe but just criticism of the Party forced me to study Russian classics and Russian folk music even more thoroughly. Thus in part I envisaged my work on Mussorgsky's *Boris Godunov,* when I labored on the revision of its orchestration. I regret that this composition has remained unknown.

Now, when I look back in spirit on everything I have written since *Lady Macbeth,* it seems to me that in my symphonic and chamber compositions new creative qualities have appeared which, if it were possible for me to develop them, would give me the opportunity of finding the way to the heart of the Soviet people. But this has not

[10] *Ibid.,* pp. 78–79.

happened. And now I see clearly that I have exaggerated the depth of my creative reconstruction and that several negative factors inherent in my musical thinking have prevented me from making the intended break in a whole series of recent compositions. Again I swerved to the side of formalism and began to speak in a language incomprehensible to the people.

When today the Party and our entire country, in the words of the resolution of the Central Committee, criticize this direction of my work, I know that the Party is right and I know that the Party is showing concern for Soviet art and for me, a Soviet composer.

All resolutions of the Central Committee of the Party on art in recent years and particularly the resolution of February 10, 1948, on the opera, *Velikaia Druzhba,* point out to the Soviet artist that tremendous national exaltation by which our country and our great Soviet people live at present.

Certain Soviet artists, myself included, have endeavored to express this great national exaltation in their works. But between my subjective intentions and the objective results a crying chasm has appeared.

With complete clarity and precision the Central Committee of the Party has pointed to the absence in my compositions of the transformation of the character of the people, of that great spirit by which our people live.

I am deeply grateful for this and for every criticism contained in the resolution.

All of the instructions of the Central Committee and particularly those which touch me personally I accept as evidence of a severe but fatherly concern about us, Soviet artists.

Only work, stubborn, creative, and joyous work, in writing new compositions which will find their way to the heart of the Soviet people, which will be understood and loved by them, which will be linked organically with folk art, developed and enriched by the great Russian classical traditions — here is the worthy answer to the resolution of the Central Committee of the Party.

In my *Poem of the Motherland* I attempted to create a symphonic composition laden with song and melody. It proved to be unsuccessful.

On the foundation of those principles which are outlined so clearly in the resolution of the Central Committee, I shall attempt again and again to create symphonic compositions that are comprehensible and close to the people in ideological content, in musical language, and in form.

I shall labor still more stubbornly on the musical incarnation of models of heroic Soviet people.

At present I am working on music for a moving picture, *The Young Guard,* and I have begun a work on an opera of the same title. I hope that in these works I shall fulfill in part those wishes of mine about which I have just spoken.

Several of my songs have gained a certain popularity with the people. Now, armed with the instructions of the Central Committee of the Party, I shall try again and again to create Soviet songs for the masses.

I have no doubt that Soviet music faces a tremendous creative upsurge. This upsurge will develop through the transmutation of the wise and just instructions of the Central Committee of the Party into the creative work of composers.

I call upon all composers to devote all their strength to the fulfillment of this remarkable resolution.

By a letter addressed to the chairman of the conference Sergei Prokofiev agreed to correct his errors through deeds rather than words and promised to create a new opera "worthy of our people and our great land": [11]

Since the condition of my health deprives me of the opportunity of attending and speaking at the general conference of composers, I desire to express my thoughts concerning the resolution of the Central Committee of the All-Union Communist Party of February 10, 1948, by this letter which I ask you to present at the conference, if you find it needful.

The resolution has separated the decayed from the healthy cells in the creative work of composers. No matter how painful it is for a number of composers, myself included, I hail this resolution which creates conditions for the restoration of the health of the entire organism of Soviet music. The resolution is especially valuable because it points out that the formalistic tendency is alien to the Soviet people and leads to the impoverishment and the ruin of music. With boundless clarity it outlines for us the aims toward which we must strive in order to serve best the Soviet people.

11 *Ibid.,* pp. 66–67.

Speaking of myself: elements of formalism characterized my music fifteen to twenty years ago. The contagion resulted, apparently, from contact with a number of Western currents. After the exposure in *Pravda* (in 1936), in accordance with the instructions of the Central Committee of the Party, of the formalistic mistakes in an opera by Shostakovich, I pondered much over my own creative methods and concluded such a course to be incorrect. I consequently searched for a clearer and more satisfying form of expression. In a number of my subsequent works, such as *Alexander Nevsky, Zdravitsa, Romeo and Juliet, The Fifth Symphony,* I endeavored to free myself from formalism and, it seems to me, I succeeded to some extent. Its presence in some of my compositions is explained, undoubtedly, by a certain complacency and an insufficiently clear realization of the fact that this is not needed by our people at all. But after the resolution, which has shaken profoundly our entire body of composers, just what kind of music our people need and the course to follow to root out the formalistic disease became clear.

On the question of the importance of melody I never have entertained any doubts. I love melody very much, consider it to be the most important element in music, and have been working for many years on the improvement of its quality in my compositions. To find a melody at once comprehensible, even to an untutored listener, which is original at the same time, is a most difficult task for a composer. Here he must be on guard against countless dangers: one may fall into triviality and vulgarity, or into repetition of some earlier work. From this standpoint the composition of more complex melodies is much easier. Also in working for a long time over his melody and improving it, the composer may without noticing it himself, make the melody extremely exquisite and complex, and abandon simplicity. Obviously in the course of my work I fell into this trap. Great vigilance is needed in composing in order to retain simplicity of melody, without at the same time making it cheap, saccharine, or imitative. This is easier said than done, and I shall direct all my efforts to the end that these words may be realized in my subsequent works and not remain merely a prescription.

Of atonality, which frequently is closely related to formalism, I am also guilty. Yet I must cheerfully confess that my yearning for tonal music dates from a time long ago when I clearly felt that the construction of a musical composition on tones is comparable to building a house on a sound foundation, and construction without tones like building on the sand. Moreover, tonal and diatonic music offers many more possibilities than atonal and chromatic music. This is especially obvious in the impasse at which Schoenberg and his followers have arrived. In some of my compositions of recent years there are certain atonal elements. Half-heartedly I have nevertheless employed this method chiefly for purposes of contrast, and in order to emphasize the tonal portions. In the future I hope to abandon this method.

In my operatic composition I have often been accused of making recitative dominant over cantilena. I am very fond of the stage and think that a person who comes to hear an opera has a right to demand not only auditory but visual impressions as well. (Otherwise he would go not to an opera, but to a concert.) But every movement on the stage is more readily related to recitative, whereas cantilena calls to a certain extent for immobility on the stage. I recall how painful it was for me to watch the stage in some of the Wagnerian operas when not a single person would move during a whole act, lasting almost an hour. And it was this fear of immobility which prevented me from devoting too much time to cantilena. In connection with the resolution I carefully pondered this question also and came to the conclusion that every operatic libretto contains portions which call absolutely for recitative, while other portions demand arias. But there are portions, and very important portions, perhaps in their total one-half of the entire opera, which the composer can interpret according to his own wish by means of either recitative or arias. Let us take as an illustration the letter of Tatiana from *Eugene Onegin:* it would not be at all difficult to use recitative here, but Tchaikovsky directed his musical language toward cantilena and converted the entire letter into a tremendous aria. This method has another advantage in that it is executed simultaneously with action on the stage, thus supplying food not only to the ear, but also to the eye. And it is precisely in this direction that I want to move in my work on a new opera on a contemporary Soviet subject — *The Story of a Genuine Man* by Boris Polevoy.

I was much rejoiced by the instruction in the resolution on the desirability of polyphony, especially in chorus and ensemble singing. This is truly an interesting task for the composer and a great satisfaction for the listener. In the above-mentioned opera I contemplate introducing a trio, duets, and choruses developed contrapuntally, for which I shall utilize exceedingly interesting notes on northern Russian folk songs. Clear melodies and language as simple and harmonic as possible — such are the other elements toward which I will strive in this opera.

In conclusion I wish to express my thanks to our Party for the clear instructions in the resolution which will help me in my search for a musical language comprehensible and near to our people, worthy of our people and our great land.

True to his promise Prokofiev threw himself into the task of writing the new opera on a "contemporary Soviet subject" and before the end of the year completed *The Story of a Genuine Man*. But again he was doomed to disappointment. The opera was condemned without qualification as a "typical relapse into formalism." The judgment then went on to say that "obviously the composer did not apply to himself the conclusions from the historic resolution of the Party." [12] Prokofiev promised to try again.

The confession of Aram Khachaturian, so recently praised for the "emotional brilliance" of his creations, follows: [13]

The resolution of the Central Committee of the All-Union Communist Party expresses the will of our people and reflects in full the opinion of the Soviet people about our music.

The decree sets us musicians free. In actuality it casts off certain chains which for many years have shackled us. In spite of my grievous moral state, whose cause you understand, I have a feeling of great gladness and satisfaction.

Life has become easier and freer, and the way is clearly marked, the road is marked, along which Soviet music must move impetuously. I see that way clearly and I have but one wish — to correct as quickly as possible and above all through my creative work all of my mistakes.

How did it happen that I arrived at formalism in my creative work? I have made use of not a few native songs and, in the first instance, of my own native Armenian songs. Also I have made wide use of popular melodies — Russian, Ukrainian, Georgian, Uzbekian, Turkmenian, and Tatar. I have written a number of songs based on these melodies.

---

[12] *Literaturnaia Gazeta*, January 8, 1949.
[13] *Sovietskaia Muzyka*, op. cit., p. 69.

I have always said that I do not recognize music without melody, that melody is the foundation of musical composition. But in spite of the fact that in my time I have stood on such apparently correct creative positions, I have nevertheless arrived at formalistic mistakes.

I see two causes of these mistakes of mine. The first was enthusiasm for technical perfection. I was often charged with insufficient technical mastery in my compositions. This was reflected in my consciousness. The effort to master technique fully passed imperceptibly into an enthusiasm for technique which manifested itself with particular clarity in *Simfonia-Poema*.

Thus, fascinated by abstract technique, I arrived at formalism.

The other chief cause and chief mistake was loss of contact with the national soil. All great composers of the past became universal geniuses by being at the same time national geniuses. This is particularly clear in the case of Russian music. Russian composers created the classical school of Russian national music. Being clearly national, Russian music became a world phenomenon, became a possession of all progressive mankind. More than this, Russian music, in the person of Mussorgsky, Tchaikovsky and others, began to influence Western music.

I lost contact with the national soil; I lost contact with that earth on which apparently I had firmly stood. When critics and students of music suggested that it was time for me in my creative work to advance beyond national boundaries, to repudiate the so-called narrow stylistic trend of my music, I listened to this advice. I was unable in time to repudiate these harmful creative tendencies. Recently I have moved farther and farther away from my native Armenian verses; I wanted to become a cosmopolitan.

Andrei Alexandrovich Zhdanov in his address at the conference of the Central Committee of the Party said that internationalism in music can develop only on the foundation of the enrichment, the flowering, and the growth of national music and not on the foundation of the obliteration of national elements.

Creative errors and sympathy for formalistic patterns in our music could not help being reflected in my work in the Organizational Committee. The committee became a nursery of formalism. And how could it combat formalism when the people who composed it embraced in full or in part the positions of formalism or were sympathetic toward it. As head of the Organizational Committee I had every opportunity to initiate and lead the struggle against these tendencies in music; but I did nothing.

I proved to be a bad leader and my methods of work in the Organizational Committee were undemocratic. In recent years I fenced myself off from our public of composers. The members of the committee became lords who plumed themselves on their "creative merits," and as a result became generals without an army. Criticism and self-criticism in the committee were silenced.

The resolution of the Central Committee said that a stagnant atmosphere was created and that creative discussions were lacking. One of the chief factors blighting the work of the Organizational Committee was the absence of unity among its members. We were occupied with petty squabbles and the clarification of personal relationships. We forgot that we were supposed to lead the Union of Soviet Composers and that we should carry with us the entire mass of composers. Hypocritically flattering each other, we, members of the Organizational Committee, found ourselves in extremely antagonistic relations.

For the unhappy state of Soviet music, created as a result of the incorrect line which the Organizational Committee pursued under my leadership, I bear full responsibility.

I want to speak here about one more very grave peril. I want to warn those comrades who, like me, hoped that, if their music is not understood today by the people, then it will be understood tomorrow by coming generations. This is a destructive theory. At present in our country the judges of music are millions of persons, the entire Soviet people. What tasks can be higher and more honorable than those of writing music intelligible to our people, of giving gladness to millions by our creative work?

I call on all Soviet composers and, first of all, on Shostakovich, Prokofiev, Shebalin, Popov, Miaskovsky, and Muradeli to respond to the severe and just resolution of the Central Committee of the Party with a decisive reconstruction of their views on music and to prove by their creative work the depth and sincerity of this reconstruction.

Our chief task now is for all of us to rally around the decision of the Central Committee, to work ever harder and better, to show by deed that Soviet composers march in the front rank of the all-conquering Soviet culture.

A fifth distinguished Soviet composer, who was criticized in the resolution of the Central Committee, also spoke at the Moscow conference — V. J. Shebalin. A brief and severe account of his remarks, which undoubtedly failed to restore his peace of mind, appeared in the official record: [14]

V. J. Shebalin's address was entirely unsatisfactory; he limited himself to a formal declarative and in no way a binding admission of his errors. Applying the charge of formalism to his earlier compositions, condemned long ago and deservedly forgotten, Shebalin evaded an evaluation of his later works in the light of the resolution of the Central Committee — works which are saturated to a large degree with the spirit of artisanship and cold stylization. Likewise, by attributing the guilt of the leadership of the Moscow conservatory to lack of persistence and fear of impairing good relationships with professors and others, Shebalin endeavored to conceal from the body of composers the perverted course which he had followed consistently in the conservatory. This course was designed to divorce the professional training from the ideological and esthetic training of students and to replace valuable mastery with narrow technical skills.

5

On April 19 the First All-Union Congress of the Union of Soviet Composers opened in Moscow. It was a grand affair. Delegates were present from all sixteen union republics and included the greatest composers, music critics, and leading workers in philharmonic orchestras and musical theatres. Present as guests were distinguished public figures, writers, artists, and scientists of the capital. With tumultuous applause the members of the Politburo were elected to the honorary presidium. The "name of the great friend and guide of Soviet art, Comrade Stalin" evoked a "prolonged and thunderous ovation" from delegates and guests. Naturally not one of the great composers attacked in the resolution of the Central Committee was elected to the presidium.

14 *Ibid.*, 79–80.

The General Secretary of the Union of Composers, T. Khrennikov, delivered the major address at the Congress. Twelve thousand words in length, it was devoted to the announced theme of
the meeting, "Thirty Years of Soviet Music and the Tasks of Soviet
Composers." Running through the address from beginning to end
is this thought: "Never and nowhere have questions of musical
art called forth such broad and general public interest as in our
country." He closes his speech with a tribute and an expression
of gratitude to the Party and Stalin: [15]

The Party has rendered us, composers, the greatest aid by condemning
on foundations of principle formalistic perversions in Soviet music.

Armed with the clear directives of the Party we shall be able to
shatter to bits every manifestation of anti-people's formalism and
decadence by whatever protective coloration it may be disguised.

We shall no longer permit the destruction of the magnificent temple
of music created by composers of genius in the past.

With the same irreconcilability we will struggle in music against
pernicious vulgarization and soulless workmanship and for complete
unity of ideological content with beauty and perfection of form.

In the name of the entire company of multi-national composers of
the Soviet Union I want to assure the Party and the government, and
the entire Soviet people, that our music will justify the hopes reposed
in it. We will sweep from our path everything that for many years has
prevented our music from becoming genuinely democratic and we
shall make our magnificent people proud of our artistic genius. We
are guaranteed unprecedented opportunities for creative work. We
have a magnificent audience, sensitive and appreciative, which has
grown immeasurably in cultural stature. We are led and inspired
ideologically by the most advanced Party in the world, the Bolshevik
Party of Lenin and Stalin. We are rich in highly gifted people. No
other country on earth today possesses a body of composers equal in
power and diversity of talent to that of our Soviet Union. We are
the only successors in the world of the finest aspirations of the advanced classical composers. On us falls the historic mission of saving
musical art from decadent ruin, of setting the new powerful Soviet
classical art over against the depraved art of the bourgeois world.

[15] *Sovietskaia Muzyka*, No. 2, 1948, pp. 45–46.

We have a body of highly promising youthful composers, reared in the Soviet epoch, vital and talented. To them belongs the beautiful future of our music.

Let us study more boldly and more profoundly our wonderful Soviet reality. Nearer to life, Comrade Composers! For us the richest fantasy is no substitute for vital study of contemporary life, for direct contacts with people, for visits to mills, collective farms, and army units, for intercourse with our own natural surroundings, with the life of our people.

"Not just to become acquainted with the people, but to crave brotherly communion with them" — let these passionate words of Mussorgsky serve as a bold watchword for all Soviet musicians. We have faith that Soviet music stands on the threshold of a new and unprecedented flowering. All of our creative ardor and enthusiasm, all of our knowledge and talents, we dedicate to the achievement of this honorable task.

Long live the great and glorious Party of Bolsheviks, leading our country to Communism!

Long live the powerful multi-national Soviet people!

May Soviet music, the most democratic, the most advanced in the world, flower and grow stronger!

May the best friend of Soviet art, the great and wise Stalin, live and prosper many years!

The official record of the Congress, as published in *Sovietskaia Muzyka,* contains an account of the behavior before the delegates of the great composers criticized in the resolution of the Central Committee. Prokofiev and Miaskovsky apparently refused to take the floor and Shebalin and Popov failed to attend, making their confessions of error by letter. In courage these men must be ranked high in the history of the struggle for the freedom of the mind. Here is the account of this aspect of the proceedings of the Congress: [16]

The delegates of the Congress rightfully expected speeches from the formalistic composers whose creative work had received such severe appraisal in the resolution of the Central Committee of the All-Union Communist Party, in the speech of Comrade Zhdanov at the con-

16 *Ibid.,* pp. 71–72.

ference of musical leaders, and in innumerable comments of ordinary Soviet citizens in the pages of the Soviet press. However, the majority of the leaders of the formalistic tendency spoke from the tribune of the Congress only under the pressure of numerous declarations and demands from the delegates. On the first day of the discussions only Comrade Muradeli spoke. He acknowledged the justice of the criticism of his opera and promised in his future work to discover the way to realism and popular approval. But his speech did not satisfy the delegates. They expected from him a much more profoundly critical analysis both of his own creative work and of the formalistic tendency as a whole to which he had adhered in his compositions. The speech of Comrade Muradeli contained no such analysis.

In the course of the first and at the beginning of the second session many delegates to the Congress expressed their indignation toward the anti-social position occupied by the formalistic composers.

Right up to the end these just voices were not even listened to by composers S. Prokofiev and N. Miaskovsky. Composers V. Shebalin and G. Popov sent to the Congress written declarations repudiating their former positions. However, the Leningrad delegation in its appeal to the Congress justly branded the letter of V. Shebalin as an unworthy bureaucratic effort to meet the criticism of the people "by correspondence."

The addresses of A. Khachaturian and D. Shostakovich bore a significantly more serious character.

Comrade Khachaturian spoke vehemently about the tremendous ideological and artistic mistakes in his former creative work and promised, in answer to the just demands of the Central Committee of the Party, to direct all of his energies to the creation of compositions close and comprehensible to the millions of Soviet people.

The Congress took into account the statement of Comrade Khachaturian about his immediate creative plans.

However, Comrade Khachaturian should have told the Congress not only about his musical activity. In the resolution of the Central Committee of the Party he is mentioned twice: as a composer and as a leader of the Union of Soviet Composers. Comrade Khachaturian bears full responsibility for all those serious mistakes which were allowed in the work of the Union. It is a pity that he chose to evade this question in his speech.

Comrade D. Shostakovich told the delegates to the Congress of the beneficial influence which the resolution of the Central Committee of the Party on the opera by Muradeli, *Velikaia Druzhba,* had on his new artistic ideas. "No matter how grievous it is for me to hear the condemnation of my music," he said, "I know that the Party is right, that the Party wishes me well, and that I must search for and find concrete creative ways which will lead me to Soviet realistic people's art. It is impossible for me not to search for these new ways, because I am a Soviet artist, reared in the Soviet land; I must and I want to find the way to the heart of the people."

The speech of Comrade Shostakovich contained also criticism of the mistakes which are characteristic of his former creative work.

The speeches of composers Comrades M. Ashrafi, V. Trambitsky, and D. Kabalevsky at the congress revealed superficial understanding of the Party criticism of formalism. These talks confirmed the justice of the speeches of Comrades M. Chulaki, K. Dankevich, and S. Vasilenko, warning against the tendency of certain comrades "to put on the brakes" gradually in the struggle against formalism. It was precisely for this reason apparently that Comrade Ashrafi, in telling the Congress about the Uzbek composers, said not one word concerning the formalistic tendencies which showed themselves grievously in the creative work of individual comrades. With incomprehensible indifference and apathy Comrade Trambitsky spoke of the modernistic zigzags characteristic of the works of certain Sverdlovsk composers.

Also the speech of Comrade Kabalevsky was not free of serious defects. At the beginning he rightly emphasized that the resolution of the Central Committee of the Party leads to an enrichment and widening of the creative opportunities of Soviet art. The ideal of Soviet music formulated by the Party is the deepest and noblest ideal ever known in the history of the development of world esthetic thought, and Soviet composers should devote all of their creative powers to the embodiment of this ideal in their artistic practice.

However, in the second half of his speech, having made a number of true observations directed toward the raising of professional culture in the creative work of a number of composers, Comrade Kabalevsky made several confused statements. He attempted to subject to doubt the thesis disseminated in our press about two tendencies struggling in Soviet music, mistakenly calling for the repudiation of the division of composers into "saints" and "sinners." "False and correct tendencies," Comrade Kabalevsky affirmed, "are characteristic of almost all composers." It is clear that such reasoning merely confuses the musical profession and prevents it from understanding the chief meaning of the criticism given to us by the Party. The pernicious reasoning of Comrade Kabalevsky can only distract attention from the criticism of formalistic composers.

6

One of the most interesting and characteristic features of the Soviet system of thought control is the mobilization of "public opinion" in support of Party action. Following an important decision, resolution, or pronouncement the pages of the press are filled with "letters from the people," every last one of which supports without qualification and often with hysterical exaggeration the position of the Party. In so far as the communications are genuine, they are probably the result of the activity of the well-organized and disciplined network of Party cells and rank-and-file Party members which embraces the entire country and all institutions. Anyone who has had experience with the American Communist Party is familiar with this pattern of operation. Possibly some letters, critical of the official line, come to the Soviet press. If they do, they are not published and their authors may get into difficulties. But whatever the mechanism of this distinctive and powerful form of control, it must have a devastating and demoralizing effect on all who suffer the displeasure of the Party. They read the newspapers and listen to the radio in vain for a friendly voice. However sturdy their character, they must soon begin to feel terribly lonely and forsaken.

This system of beating the individual into submission was fully utilized in the Party assault on Shostakovich, Prokofiev, Khachaturian, Muradeli, and other composers, as well as on all other objects of Party wrath reported in the dismal chapters of this book. Already by February 15 *Pravda* could say, under the caption "The Voice of the People," that "the resolution of the Central

Committee of the All-Union Communist Party on the opera *Velikaia Druzhba* was received by all strata of the Soviet people with exceptional interest and deep satisfaction." Other newspapers and journals joined in this fictitious representation of public opinion. Here are a few samples of "letters from the people" taken from the section of the January-February, 1948, issue of *Sovietskaia Muzyka,* entitled "From the Pages of the Press": [17]

The entire press of the Soviet Union publishes numerous responses to the resolution of the Central Committee of the All-Union Communist Party on the opera *Velikaia Druzhba.*

These responses coming from people of diverse professions and diverse cultural levels are unanimous in their evaluation of the historic document of the Bolshevik Party on questions of music. The Soviet people passionately approve the resolution and regard it as most timely and wise, answering the spiritual inquiries and needs of many millions of people.

Citizens of Leningrad step forward excitedly. They note the unsatisfactory condition of Soviet music today and speak with conviction of its future flowering: "With profound satisfaction I re-read the resolution of the Central Committee of the All-Union Communist Party which indicates the future flowering of such an important branch of Soviet culture," writes an engineer, A. Lebedev, in *Vechernii Leningrad.* . . .

A nurse, O. Kamenetskaia, and a student of the historical faculty, L. Tarasuk, write in *Leningradskaia Pravda:* "Listening to some contemporary musical productions, one feels disappointed and cheated. What do the authors of these compositions think of the Russian people? . . .

"It has been impossible to understand why 'the critics' have gone into such raptures over a chaos of sounds, possessing no melody, and praised music which only irritates and fatigues the listener." . . .

The workers of Soviet Ukraine and Soviet Belorussia unanimously and passionately greet the resolution of the Central Committee of the All-Union Communist Party. . . .

The newspaper *Sovietskaia Belorussia* of Minsk publishes the words of Comrade Tryfimovich, chief of the assembly room of a Minsk radio factory: "The Soviet people demand from composers works which will

[17] Pp. 111–121.

reveal the grandeur of Soviet man and aid our people to resolve successfully the majestic tasks of Communist society." . . .

Comrade T. Paperite, a worker in a sewing-machine factory, says that the music of Glinka, Tchaikovsky, and Rimsky-Korsakov "arouses the desire to work still better for the glory of the beloved fatherland."

She appeals to Soviet composers with a call to follow these glorious traditions and closes with the passionate words: "To creative successes, Comrade Composers!"

The workers of the Trans-Caucasian republics are unanimous in their responses to the resolution of the Central Committee of the Party. A section foreman in Azneft, G. Azhotkin, writes in *Bakinskii Rabochii* of Baku: "We love music, but music that is genuine, close to and intelligible to the people. . . . We are infinitely grateful to the Central Committee of the Communist Party because in the resolution on the opera, *Velikaia Druzhba,* it expressed with clarity and brilliance the opinion of the Soviet people." . . .

The desire of the toilers of Trans-Caucasia is excellently expressed in a note in *Bakinskii Rabochii* by a skilled oil-worker. . . . B. Bagirov: "I am confident that if the creative work of our composers were organically connected with the interests of the people, our musical culture would achieve a remarkable flowering. Then more often than now, I, an ordinary Soviet man, would be able to obtain deep spiritual satisfaction from attending concerts or operas."

In the republics of Central Asia the discussion of the resolution of the Central Committee of the All-Union Communist Party also proceeds actively and passionately.

"Music must serve the people," say the workers of the Central Asiatic Republic, as they call upon composers to listen to the voice of the masses. . . .

One must agree with the conclusion of the newspaper *Komsomolets Uzbekistana:* "Time marches on. The toilers of Uzbekistan are writing new pages in the glorious annals of the Stalinist epoch. And up to the present time the musical workers are in debt to the people, to our heroic youth."

And one must also agree with the profound thought of a people's artist of the Uzbek Republic, M. Turgunbaeva: "Let the composers not fear to create complex productions. If the productions are musical and are built on the riches of melody of folk art, the listener will understand them."

"A great event in our life," so say the toilers of Moldavsky SSR of the resolution of the Central Committee of the All-Union Communist Party. The newspaper *Sovietskaia Moldavia* publishes numerous responses to the resolution: "We are building Communism in our country," said Comrade Letloit, a factory Stakhanovite. "Daily we are fulfilling the norm by 170–180 per cent. Yet not a few difficulties stand on our path. And we want music to aid us to overcome these difficulties." . . .

Comrade Efremov, a turner Stakhanovite in Moldavia, gives strong and convincing advice to composers: "Formalistic composers are gravely mistaken when they babble that we, the workers, have not 'grown up' to music. This is a gross slander against the Soviet working class. We will love and understand Soviet composers when they abandon formalistic tricks and create music near and dear to the Soviet people."

In the Karelo-Finnish Republic questions of music are discussed in all ranks of the population.

In the newspaper *Leninskoe Znamia* of Petrozavodsk, V. Gurevich and R. Eilentukh, workers in the Administration of Communications, write: "We had occasion to hear in the Leningrad Maly Opera Theatre, the opera by Shostakovich, *Lady Macbeth of Mtsensk*. At that time, twelve years ago, the Central Committee of the Party had already judged quite correctly the musical grimaces of Shostakovich. However, during the subsequent period he did very little to make his music actually accessible and comprehensible to the people." . . .

Kabardinskaia Pravda of Nalchik, in expressing itself on the resolution of the Central Committee of the Party, notes that: "together with the well-known decisions of the Party on questions of Soviet literature, cinema, and theatre, this historic document is the most important landmark in the development of Soviet art. It expresses the vast concern of the Party for the spiritual needs of the people and for the protection and development of the best traditions of Russian folk music."

The newspaper publishes the comment of a skilled foundry worker in a machine-construction factory, Comrade A. Zagoruiko: "The decree is correct. It brings music closer to the people. Some Soviet composers, for whom the people have created all the conditions desirable for creative work, write music to which one must turn a deaf ear. Neither rhyme nor reason — a wild whirlwind of sounds." . . .

Buriat-Mongolskaia Pravda expresses the hope that the resolution of the Central Committee of the Party "will help composers to understand clearly their mistakes and to create music worthy of the Great Stalinist epoch."

Udmurtskaia Pravda of Izhevsk publishes various expressions of the toilers of Udmurtia. G. Shemiakin and A. Chugunov, workers in an Izhevsky factory, ask: "Can our people reconcile themselves with formalism in music?" and answer: "Certainly not! We love the compositions of the great Russian composers, Tchaikovsky, Glinka, and Mussorgsky, because they evoke in us lofty feelings and reach the heart of every listener. But when they broadcast over the radio certain compositions of Shostakovich, Prokofiev, and Khachaturian, one does not feel like listening. It is almost impossible to discern any melody in them whatsoever; and as for sense, you get nothing at all." . . .

M. Semenov, N. Deriagin, I. Gumov, and N. Moiseev, presidents of collective farms, write: "We, workers in agriculture, have long been expecting from our composers a good opera about the Soviet peasantry, about the heroes of collective farm production who grow the rich Stalinist crops. We are expecting musical compositions worthy of our times and intelligible to the broad masses of the people."

An old mechanic of the Uduguchinsky Machine Tractor Station, F. Tokarev, expresses faith in the great creative possibilities of Soviet composers: "Music must be understood by the people, must express the grandeur of our Stalinist epoch. Such music the people will always understand and love. And we are confident that it will be created." . . .

The toilers of Chuvashia say: "Our Soviet people have grown spiritually; the demand for good music is a necessity in their lives; they love it just as they love to work well for the glory of our Motherland." . . .

The *Groznenskii Rabochii* of Grozny has devoted much attention to music. Here is a comment by a physician, N. I. Zavadskaia: "I love music very much and have always thought that I could comprehend the beauty of a musical composition and evaluate it correctly. But recently with bitterness I have begun to think that apparently I am a complete ignoramus in music, because the compositions of many famous composers do not reach me. I did not even cherish the hope of 'growing up' to this music, because it nauseated me. The resolution of the Central Committee of the All-Union Communist Party brought me great joy and a feeling of relief: I understood that not I alone, but millions of Soviet people were 'rehabilitated' by it."

It is impossible to disagree with the candidate of medical science, V. A. Popel, who declares: "This is an event of the greatest importance not only in the world of composers and musicians; it touches the fundamental interests of all Soviet people."

Groznenskii Rabochii publishes materials from a conference on questions of musical art. At this conference a very old local composer, A. Alexandrov, spoke: "The resolution of the Central Committee of the All-Union Communist Party forces each of us, working in this sector of the ideological front, to re-examine his entire practice and to ponder his mistakes. I write music for plays in our theatres. Now, as I look through my music for the past several years, I discover here at times formalistic dislocations, nonsensical sound combinations, rhythmic leaps, and a complete absence of melody. For a long time I was a captive of the authority of the so-called 'leading' group of composers, now dethroned by the resolution of the Central Committee of the Party."

The newspaper *Znamia Kommuny* of Novocherkassk, *Armavirskaia Kommuna,* and *Novorossiiskii Rabochii* make passionate appeals for true music, for a musical art marked by a lofty ideology and devotion to the people.

E. Breibardt and A. Snesovskaia, mill workers in Novorossiisk, express themselves in the following words:

"The composers Shostakovich, Prokofiev, Khachaturian, and others, while offering to the Soviet people under the guise of music earsplitting noise and racket, aggravated their mistakes still more by arrogant statements slandering the Soviet people, to the effect that the people have 'not grown up' yet to an understanding of their complex music, that they will understand it in a hundred years, and that the failure of some musical compositions to find listeners is nothing to worry about.

"Our people are deeply musical. We sing not only when we are happy, but also when we are grieved and sad. The boatmen sang 'Dubinushka.' During the Great Patriotic War, during years of most grievous ordeals for the Motherland and the people, song called to victory and gave birth to confidence in the righteousness of our great cause.

"We love, we understand, and we are proud of the great Russian classics of musical culture — Glinka, Tchaikovsky, Rimsky-Korsakov. We are proud of them for the Russian breadth, for the tunefulness and melody of their music.

"Music and song help us to build, to create, and to rest joyously. Good music awakens in us deep human feelings and makes them purer and higher. . . ."

In the newspaper *Volzhskaia Kommuna* of Kuibishev workers in textile factories, Comrades T. Kuznetsova, N. Kozlovskaia, and A. Maslina, address themselves to the composers: "We are fulfilling the Five-Year Plan in four years. Give us a song about our remarkable work, a song about Stakhanovites! We are young and happy in our land — give us a song about happiness and youth!" . . .

In the newspaper *Prizyv* of Vladimir teachers of piano, O. Selivanova and V. Konstantinova, speak of music for children: "Prokofiev and Vainberg have special albums for children. But the works given in them under the caption of children's music are entirely incomprehensible not only to children, but even to teachers." . . .

A student in Molotov University, Comrade Perminov, speaks of the opera *Velikaia Druzhbai* "From the beginning I was struck by the fact that the hall was almost empty. The harsh music, difficult to comprehend and abounding in dissonances, repelled the audience. They refused to accept the opera from the very first performances."

CHAPTER SIX

SCIENCE AS A WEAPON

THE POSITION OF SCIENCE in the Soviet state has attracted the attention of students since the first days of the Great October Socialist Revolution. Being good Marxists, the Party leaders repudiated religion in all its forms as superstition and pinned their hopes on science as the source of knowledge and control over nature. Consequently they took pride from the first in their devotion to science and proceeded to support it with a generosity that, in terms of their resources, surpassed the practice of any other state in the world. In the course of the years and particularly after the launching of the First Five-Year Plan in 1928, they organized a vast network of scientific institutes, stations, bases, and laboratories for the conduct of a comprehensive program of research. All this, like everything else in the Soviet Union, was done according to a grandiose plan formulated and elaborated with great care. Agriculture alone boasts of 965 scientific research institutes, stations, and experimental farms.[1] Crowning the system is the Academy of Science of the USSR.

The development of science in the Soviet Union, however, is not free. It is regarded as a weapon of politics, much as education, literature, and art. This means first of all that it is an instrument through which the Party conquers nature, vanquishes enemies, and builds socialist society. But it also means much more. The Soviet order is founded on a world outlook known as dialectical

[1] Eric Ashby, *Scientist in Russia* (New York, 1947), p. 212. This is one of the most valuable books on Soviet Russia.

materialism and on a conception of history called historical materialism. As the years have passed, this body of doctrine has congealed into dogma whose authority cannot be questioned, even by the most gifted scientist. Yet no investigator can be sure that his findings and conclusions are in harmony with the teachings of Marx, Engels, Lenin and Stalin, until the Party has spoken. Its word of course is final, unless it changes its mind and places its stamp of infallibility on some new interpretation. All this has led to the return to the world of science of the appeal to political authority and the eradication of "harmful teachings" and heretical views.

Since the war, as the resolutions printed in this chapter demonstrate, the Central Committee of the Party is being driven by one of its dogmas to the repudiation of bourgeois science. According to the teachings of Marx and Lenin, as understood and applied by Stalin, all divisions of the culture, including science, are reflections of the basic modes of production and exchange. This can only mean that science developed in bourgeois states must reflect the interests of the bourgeoisie as they exploit the toiling masses and seek to maintain their rule. This outlook explains in some measure the current attack on bourgeois science and the demand to develop socialist science on the foundation of dialectical materialism and in the interests of the people. But it does not wholly explain the costly and systematic efforts made by the Soviet leaders to get hold of the results of research carried on in the laboratories of the various bourgeois states of the world.

The story unfolded in these pages deals primarily with one branch of Soviet science — biology in general and genetics in particular. For many years a controversy had been gathering momentum in this field. Until the nineteen-thirties this branch of Soviet science was developing in relation to the course of world science. The leading Russian scientists were familiar with and influenced by the researches conducted in the West, especially the researches of such outstanding figures as Mendel, Weismann, Morgan, and their followers and successors. The tendency in this school of biology was toward the separation of the germ plasm

from the body plasm and the repudiation of the ancient doctrine
of the inheritance of acquired characters. Their recognized leader
in Soviet genetics was the distinguished biologist N. I. Vavilov,
first president of the All-Union Academy of Agricultural Science
founded in 1929.

In 1932, under the influence of the Party, the All-Union Conference on genetics passed a resolution demanding that this branch
of science develop thenceforth in conformity with the principles
of dialectical materialism. The action was destined to have far-
reaching consequences. A young man trained as a plant breeder,
thirty-four years of age at the time, stepped into the situation,
associated himself with the teachings of I. V. Michurin, a Russian
Luther Burbank, repudiated the basic positions of Western
genetics, and espoused the doctrine of the transmission from generation to generation of traits acquired by the individual organism
in the course of its life. He defended his thesis with something approaching religious zeal, appealing to considerations of evidence,
necessity, desirability, orthodoxy, and authority. He argued that
the inheritance of acquired characters was proved by his own experience, was necessary to explain the evolutionary process, was
desirable in order to improve Soviet agriculture, was in accord
with the ideas of dialectical materialism, and was supported by the
greatest leaders of mankind — Marx, Engels, Lenin, and Stalin —
and the greatest biologists — Darwin, Timiriazev, and Michurin.
With a tendency toward mysticism, he ridicules experimental
methods and speaks of "the 'soul of plants' and their 'love mar-
riages' when fertilized by mixtures of pollen, happily referred to
as 'the lads.' " [2] The name of this young zealot was T. D. Lysenko.

Lysenko quickly won the favor of the Party. His projects received generous financial support and his achievements were
hailed in the Soviet press. As the inspired apostle of dialectical
materialism to the biologists, he took the offensive against all
deviationists and students of Western "bourgeois genetics." He
speedily vanquished his most severe critic and vigorous opponent,
N. I. Vavilov, and displaced him as President of the All-Union

[2] *Ibid.*, p. 106.

Academy of Agricultural Science. He saw his adversary dismissed from the directorship of the Institute of Plant Industry, arrested and imprisoned on various charges, and die in disgrace, some time during the war. Honors were showered upon him. He was elected to the Presidium of the Academy of Science, made Director of the Institute of Genetics, placed in charge of a number of important research institutions, and received the award of Hero of Socialist Labor. He also became a distinguished public figure attaining the coveted office of Vice-President of the Supreme Soviet.

In 1945 the Australian Government sent one of their scientists, an Englishman by birth and training, on a one-year mission to Moscow. Being a botanist, he soon found himself deep in the mysteries of the "new genetics," made the acquaintance of Lysenko, and studied his work. Though intrigued by the mind and personality of the man, he was somewhat shocked by his methods and had little confidence in his findings. "In a country as great as Russia," he wrote, "with such an impressive body of first-class scientists, who are familiar with science in the rest of the world and are contributing substantially to it, the 'new genetics' is a strange anomaly." But this "strange anomaly" did not disturb him because he apparently could not believe that it would actually triumph: "It is well past its zenith but it still flourishes in uneasy truce beside the 'old genetics.' Lysenko and his school are clearly a deep embarrassment to *bona-fide* biologists." [3] The story, showing how mistaken Professor Ashby was, is contained in the record of the momentous session of the Academy of Agricultural Science which opened in Moscow on August 4, 1948.

2

The 1948 session of the Academy marked the complete triumph of Lysenko and his ideas. Apparently, however, this was not definitely known when the session opened. Although the Party

[3] *Ibid.*, p. 114.

had clearly taken him under its protection, it had never un-equivocally and officially placed the stamp of its approval on his doctrines. But as the work of the conference proceeded from day to day the average Soviet citizen must have sensed that matters of the greatest importance were unfolding. As President of the Academy, Lysenko opened the session with a twelve-thousand-word address "On the Situation in Biological Science." This address was printed in full in *Pravda,* as well as fifty-two additional speeches by other members of the Academy in attendance. For eight days, from August 4 to August 11 inclusive, each issue of *Pravda* devoted one fourth or more of its entire space to the pro-ceedings of the session. It was obvious that the Party regarded this discussion of biology as one of the outstanding events of the year.

In his address Lysenko identified the two tendencies in biology with two historical currents, the reactionary and the progressive; with two ideologies, the idealistic and the materialistic; with two social systems, the capitalist and the socialist; with two worlds, the West and the Soviet. In the temper of a bitter political or theological controversy, he attacked his enemies with ridicule and venom, directing his shafts particularly at Academician L. A. Orbeli, Director of the Pavlov Physiological Institute, Academician I. I. Schmalhausen, Director of the Institute of Evolutionary Morphology, Professor N. P. Dubinin, Director of the Laboratory of Cytogenetics, Professor A. R. Zhebrak of the Timiriazev Agricultural Academy, and at the biological faculties of the uni-versities of Moscow and Leningrad. The scientists involved were all labelled reactionaries and enemies of the people, grovelling before the West. The substance of his theoretical position is set forth in the following brief excerpts from his address: [4]

We, representatives of the Michurinist tendency, affirm that the in-heritance of characters, acquired by plants and animals in the process of their development, is possible and necessary. Ivan Vladimirovich Michurin through his experimental and practical labors took ad-vantage of these possibilities. The most important consideration is

[4] *Pravda,* August 4 and 5, 1948.

that the teachings of Michurin, as expounded in his works, open to every biologist the way to the control of the nature of plant and animal organisms, the way to the modification of nature in accordance with practical needs by controlling the conditions of life, that is, through physiology.

The sharply aggravated struggle, which divides biologists into two irreconcilable camps, has become inflamed over the old question: *Is the inheritance of traits and characters acquired by plant and animal organisms in the course of their lives possible?* In other words, does a qualitative change in the nature of plant and animal organisms depend on the quality of the conditions of life which act on the living body, on the organism?

The Michurinist teachings, materialistic-dialectical in their essence, prove this dependence by facts. . . .

The Mendel-Morganist teachings, metaphysical-idealistic in their essence, reject such dependence as unproved. . . .

I conclude my address. So, Comrades, as to the theoretical situation in biology, Soviet biologists consider that the Michurinist positions alone are scientific. The Weismanites and their followers, denying the inheritance of acquired characters, do not deserve mention. The future belongs to Michurin. [*Applause.*]

V. I. Lenin and I. V. Stalin discovered I. V. Michurin and made his ideas the property of the Soviet people. Through their great fatherly attention to his work they saved for biology his remarkable teachings. The Party and the Government, and *I. V. Stalin* personally, are concerned increasingly for the further development of these teachings. For us, Soviet biologists, no task is more honorable than the creative development of the teachings of Michurin and the instilling into all of our activity of the Michurinist method of investigating the nature of the development of life.

Our Academy must feel concern for the development of the teachings of Michurin, just as we are taught by the personal example of concern for the work of I. V. Michurin on the part of our great teachers — V. I. Lenin and I. V. Stalin. [*Tumultuous applause.*]

The four-day session of the Academy, according to *Pravda*, was devoted to a "discussion" of the address by Lysenko. As a matter of fact, it would appear from the record that those present were for the most part taking advantage of the opportunity to declare themselves to be firmly and enthusiastically on the side of the President of the Academy. The fifty-two speeches reported in *Pravda* may be divided into two categories: those that received applause and those that did not. Of the former there were forty-nine, of the latter, three. These three were made by three scientists who had been attacked as Weismann-Morganites in Lysenko's address: Schmalhausen and Zhebrak, already mentioned, and Professor I. M. Poliakov of the University of Leningrad. The following concluding remarks of ten of the forty-nine who were applauded would seem to convey a fairly accurate impression of the atmosphere of the session: [5]

Thousands of Michurinites in the most distant corners of our Motherland are working to bring forth better varieties, worthy of the fields and gardens of the great land of socialism. Every one of us knows that in all of our selectionist achievements we are indebted to the creative force of the Michurinist teachings. Every one of us remembers the words of Michurin cut on the pedestal of his monument in Michurinsk: "Man can and must create new forms of life better than those of nature." [*Applause.*] — S. I. ISAEV, Saratov Agricultural Institute.

It seems to me that the time has come to put an end to the unrestrained propaganda of essentially reactionary teachings. The time has come when the doors of all Soviet universities and technical schools must be opened wide to Michurinist genetics. [*Applause.*] — Academician N. G. BELENKY.

Before Soviet scientists stands a noble task: to be indefatigable warriors in the construction of the grandiose building of Communism. Soviet biologists can fulfill this task if they will stand firmly on the advanced positions of Michurinist theory. [*Applause.*] — Professor N. I. NUZHDIN, Institute of Genetics of the Academy of Science.

In surmounting the theoretical mistakes of Mendelism-Morganism in biology, the correct training of personnel is a most important task. Existing textbooks on genetics are not suitable; they are full of formalistic, anti-scientific rubbish. The creation of new textbooks constructed on the foundation of Michurinist genetics is imperative. [*Ap-*

[5] *Ibid.* Issues of August 5 to 11, 1948.

plause.] — Professor S. G. PETROV, Scientific Research Institute of Poultry-farming.

The leadership of the biological faculty actively corrupts the views of Michurin and Lysenko not only in the consciousness of students but also in the consciousness of professors.

From things said, one can see how actively the leaders of the biological faculty of the Moscow State University fight against the teachings of I. V. Michurin and T. D. Lysenko. Why Iudintsev, Alekhanian, and others are silent now is incomprehensible. For one of two reasons — either they have nothing to say or they think that what takes place now is just another discussion which does not concern them. They apparently believe that by remaining silent now they will gain an opportunity in the Moscow State University to create their own conference and get revenge.

But it is clear that their hopes will not be fulfilled. The strength of our Party resides in the fact that it knows what it is fighting for, and knows under the banner of what ideas and what theory it will conquer. The teachings of V. I. Michurin and T. D. Lysenko have been proved true in the practice of socialist construction. The theoretical foundation of these teachings is dialectical materialism. To it and to these teachings the future belongs. [*Applause.*] — Professor Z. Y. BELETSKY, Moscow State University.

Collective farms and state farms constitute the only possible base for the transmuting into life of all the magnificent thought and audacity of science and technology. Fertilized by the great teachings of Marx, Engels, Lenin, and Stalin, Soviet biological science will win grandiose victories. [*Applause.*] — Academician V. P. BUSHINSKY.

I think that I express the opinion of all attending the session if I say that we wish the Academy of Agricultural Science and particularly its new academicians to develop Soviet agronomic science further so that it will assist yet more effectively the creation of that abundance of products which is necessary for the transition from socialism to Communism. To develop agronomic science in accordance with the demand of the great coryphaeus of science, wise teacher and leader of the Soviet people, Comrade Stalin. [*Applause.*] — V. S. DMITRIEV, Head of the Administration of Agricultural Planning of the Gosplan of the USSR.

Academician T. D. Lysenko, the Michurin of our time, has brought a tremendous endowment to the development of biological science and to the practice of socialist rural economy. I think that I express the opinion of the overwhelming majority of those present if I say that, thanks to his bold and fearless struggle with the conservatives of science, the further development of the Michurinist tendency in biology and impressive successes in our agrobiological science are assured. [*Prolonged applause.*]

Under the leadership of the Bolshevik Party the grandiose process of the building of Communism proceeds in our country. Communism — that bright, joyous, and not distant future! Already now we can measure approximately the distance in years to Communism. In this battle on the road to the construction of a Communist society a most honorable place belongs to our scientists and to innovators in the field of theory and practice.

Under the leadership of the greatest genius of the contemporary epoch, our beloved and dear teacher, Comrade *Stalin,* Soviet science and our scientists-innovators will achieve yet greater successes. [*Prolonged applause.*] — Academician M. B. MITIN.

We, Michurinites, place before our native Morganites the question: How long will you, professors of pseudo-science, how long will you, popularizers and henchmen of pseudo-science, fail to understand that the way of Soviet scientists and the way of foreign bearers and preachers of idealism in biology are entirely contradictory? [*Applause*] — Doctor I. E. GLUSHCHENKO, Institute of Genetics of the Academy of Science of the USSR.

One can say that just as in Gorky our working class has seen itself raised to the heights of culture, so in Lysenko millions of collective farmers see their own creative passion for the transformation of nature, the revelation of their talents in the struggle for Communist abundance. [*Prolonged applause.*]

The truth of the matter is that for a long time Lysenko has not been alone, that with the aid of the Party he has raised a whole galaxy of scientific Michurinites. They are all people of action. We have heard them at this session, we know their deeds. They are not bookworms, they are conscious of their responsibility to the public. And the truth of the matter, I think, is that all Soviet people are grateful to Comrade Stalin, to the Party, and to the government for the bold re-enforcement of the Academy with new Michurinist academicians.

Finally, the truth of the matter is that the creative genius of the

progressive tendency in biology in this session will show its influence
on the scientific front as a whole, so tenderly nurtured by Comrade
Stalin, and will aid the entire front of science to fulfill its honorable
task in the struggle for the building of Communism. [*Prolonged applause.*] — A. V. MIKHALEVICH, Acting Editor of *Pravda Ukrainy*.

The three scientists who received no applause at the session of
the Academy, according to *Pravda*, were Schmalhausen, Zhebrak,
and Poliakov. Orbeli and Dubinin presumably either were not
present or remained silent. At any rate, no speech by either was
reported in the newspaper. Zhebrak confined himself to a report
of the results of certain of his researches. And since he returns to
the story later, his remarks will not be included here. Poliakov,
in the body of his speech, came out one hundred per cent against
"bourgeois biologists" and one hundred per cent for Timiriazev,
Michurin, and Lysenko. But before he had finished he got into
trouble. His past caught up with him in the form of an interruption by Lysenko who was presiding. Here is an account of the incident: [6]

Our science, united around the advanced ideas of Michurin which
Academician Lysenko has raised on his shield, will achieve yet greater
successes.

Academician LYSENKO: You speak of the Michurinist tendency. But
in your laudatory review of a book by Schmalhausen, *Factors of Evolution,* you did not point out that Schmalhausen did not say a word
about Michurin or about Timiriazev, either in the text or in the list
of references. Do you regard this as correct?

I see no reason for opposing to the Michurin tendency everything
that is positive in the works of Schmalhausen. In the books of Schmalhausen the achievements of patriotic science are widely utilized, and
in his *Problems of Darwinism* a number of pages are devoted to Michurin. A series of important and practically effective methods of changing organic nature, proposed by geneticists working in other tendencies, cannot be passed by.

Both Darwinism and genetics should develop in our country on a
wide front.

6 *Pravda*, August 10, 1948.

Professor I. I. Schmalhausen must be regarded as one of the brave men of our time. He stood up in the presence of a hostile audience, behind which was ranged the absolutism of the Soviet state, and endeavored to defend himself and his position. Whether under pressure he will send in his confession of error, as Professor Zhebrak did later, remains to be seen. But here is the speech of a courageous man: [7]

In my address I want to reply to the charges which have been made against me.

The first charge is the charge of autogenesis. I have always endeavored to stand on the materialistic interpretation of evolution and have consistently fought against idealism of all shades. An attempt was made here to place me in the camp of geneticists and of formal geneticists at that. For the benefit of those who are not informed, I must say that, as a matter of fact, I am not a geneticist, but a morphologist, an embryologist, and a phylogenist. My only relation to genetics is my work on the phenogenetics of race traits in chickens. My works do not and never have had any relation to genetics, far less to formal genetics.

I have endeavored to be a consistent materialist; and it seems to me that this is expressed with sufficient clarity in all of my works. It is precisely from this position that I have criticized all those idealistic views which have been attributed to me here. In my *Problems of Darwinism* you will find criticism of Weismann and de Vries, of formal genetics, of the views of Lotze, and of the theory of pre-adaptation. Many of these theories, the theory of pre-adaptation, for example, were subjected to fundamental criticism in the Soviet Union for the first time precisely by me.

Upon what then do the charges of autogenesis and consequently of idealism rest?

Apparently this concerns the question of the sources of variability.

I believe that the source of variability resides in the external environment, but that this variability is realized in the interaction of the organism and the environment. And the specifics of variability are determined more by the organism than by the environment because of the complexity of the structure of the organism.

I am considered guilty of emphasizing the indefiniteness of the varia-

[7] *Pravda,* August 8, 1948.

bility of the organism. But I speak of the indefiniteness only of the new variations and not of the indefiniteness of variations in general.

In the process of evolution under the creative influence of natural selection they are transformed into adaptive changes.

These changes, as a rule, are hereditary. It is clear that in the main these are the changes which we now call mutations. However, their combinations and the unfit changes linked with them in part enter here. In the material of nature we practically always have to deal with indefinite individual differences.

The idea of evolution proceeding along a declining curve, according to the notion of Daniel Rose and other bourgeois scientists, has been imputed to me.

It seems to me that I was the first of the Darwinians to note precisely the acceleration of the process of evolution, and not its extinction.

Here, too, the theory of the stabilization of selection has been mentioned, but in essence nothing has been said. Only the conception of a "reserve" of inherited variability, which has no necessary connection with the theory, has been appraised. I introduced this conception as different from the conception of the "genofund" of genetics for the designation of the entire stock of inherited changes of whole populations.

In this "reserve," of course, there is no stock of adaptive mutations ready for any circumstance, as Academician Prezent imputes this view to me.

Never and nowhere have I spoken or could I speak about this. On the contrary, I have steadfastly disputed the question with geneticists, since I consider all mutations injurious. This means that I could not speak of adaptive mutations and their accumulation in a reserve.

I have introduced the conception of a reserve of inherited changes precisely as a counterpoise to the idea of *genofund* of formal genetics. If *genofund* is a statistical conception, then reserve is a dynamic conception. Hereditary material is not only diverted into a reserve, but goes also into an uninterrupted accumulation of hereditary changes. In *Factors of Evolution* I speak of the accumulation of a reserve to the account of mutability, of the diffusion of mutations, of their combination, and of their transformation into complex hereditary changes. The accumulation of hereditary changes proceeds particularly freely under conditions of domestication. This means in the case of domestic animals and cultivated plants that we have the maximal accumulation of hereditary changes.

I have never given a positive evaluation to separate mutations. A special book of mine is devoted to the question of the evolution of the organism as a whole. In it I prove that only changes in the entire organism as a whole can be useful for the possessor of these changes. Separate and partial changes cannot be useful. Therefore any mutation is harmful. Never and nowhere have I spoken of the utilization of separate mutations, and further I have not recommended this to selectionists. I have always spoken of complex hereditary and non-hereditary changes.

Finally, the last important charge is the charge of disarming practice. Already from the preceding, it is apparent that this charge is without foundation. It is imputed to me that I say that "the tempestuous formation of species at the dawn of culture gradually moves toward extinction." This is in not one of my books, not one of my articles, not one of my addresses. Never have I asserted this.

Recall the selection of the sugar beet for sugar content which was begun only in the last century, and not at all at the dawn of culture. It very quickly reached a limit. To struggle with a limit, if it is physiological, is possible; and I definitely indicate this by raising variability through hybridization and through action of external factors.

The last charge — why don't I speak of Michurin, why don't I speak of other achievements of our selectionists? Because the book *Factors of Evolution* is not devoted to this question.

Incidentally, I make almost no reference to works prior to 1920. And to the classics there are no references. I take material which I need for the basis of the theory of the stabilization of selection, and nothing more.

Simultaneously with this book, another book was published — *Problems of Darwinism*. Really must I repeat in one book what is written in another? In *Problems of Darwinism* there is a history of the question of the factors of evolution and an exposition of the practical conclusions of Darwinism. In this book much attention is devoted to the classics of Darwinism, particularly to Timiriazev, and also actually to the remarkable achievements of Michurin. Here also I give a sufficient place to Academician Lysenko, Academician Tsitsin, and other Soviet selectionists.

It seems to me that I have noted the fundamental reproaches against me. Perhaps there is only one more remark.

Prezent reproached me for attaching excessive significance to hybridization. It would seem strange. Michurin too attached large significance to hybridization. But, it turns out as if I had placed this as a necessary condition of the existence of evolution.

I am not so illiterate that I do not know that bacteria, for example, have no sexual process. Yet they evolve. I note the tremendous significance of the sexual process and crossing in the evolution of organisms, particularly higher organisms. But this certainly does not mean that this is an indispensable condition of every kind of evolution. Hereditary changes appear independently of hybridization. Moreover, Prezent draws the conclusion that I attach to hybridization the same significance as Weismann in his theory of amphimixis. The theory of amphimixis of Weismann proposes that crossing is the source of variability. I deny this categorically. I speak of external factors as the source of variability, and I regard crossing as a means of permitting a more rapid combining and synthesizing of the expressions of separate mutations. It is clear that my ideas have nothing in common with the long rejected theory of amphimixis.

With this I conclude my response to the remarks expressed here on my address.

3

The Academy met in final session on August 7. As Lysenko rose to deliver his concluding address the atmosphere was electric. Those present sensed that a pronouncement of most profound and far-reaching consequence for Soviet biology and biologists was about to be made. Perhaps there had been rumors. "Before beginning the concluding address," said the speaker, "I must respond to a note which has reached the Presidium. I am asked: What is the attitude of the Central Committee of the All-Union Communist Party to the address which I delivered at this session? My answer is: The Central Committee of the All-Union Communist Party examined and approved my address, 'On the Situation in

Biological Science.' " [8] The response of the audience to this announcement and the essence of Lysenko's concluding address are thus reported in *Pravda:*

This announcement by the President evoked the general enthusiasm of the members of the session. With one impulse all those present rose from their seats and engaged in a stormy and prolonged ovation in honor of the Central Committee of the Party of Lenin and Stalin, in honor of the wise leader and teacher of the Soviet people, the greatest scholar of our epoch, Comrade Stalin. . . .

In clear and profoundly thoughtful theses Academician T. D. Lysenko exposed the hopeless attempts of various representatives of the reactionary and decadent school of Mendel and Morgan to defend their positions in science. At the same time he outlined the militant tasks of biological science in the immediate future.

"In science," says Academician T. D. Lysenko, "there is no place for chance. Physics and chemistry achieved stupendous successes in their development because they repudiated the explanation of natural phenomena in terms of chance. Biological science must profit from this experience.

"The entire idealistic chromosome theory of inheritance is based on chance. The process of fertilization is subject to pure chance. The splitting of hybrids is subject to chance. The causes of hereditary changes are unknown and are also due to chance. Chance reigns everywhere. Such a theory cannot serve as the foundation of biological science.

"Only the Michurin teaching can serve as a foundation for the development of biological science. It studies the natural laws of the development of plant and animal forms, the laws of inheritance and its variability, and opens practical ways for the direction of living nature."

In his closing remarks Academician T. D. Lysenko proposed a toast in honor of the teachings of the great moulder of nature, I. V. Michurin, in honor of the Party of Lenin and Stalin which discovered Michurin for the world, in honor of the great friend and coryphaeus of science, Comrade Stalin. The last words of the orator were greeted with a tempest of applause.

8 *Ibid.*

Lysenko's concluding address was published in full in the issue of *Pravda* for August 10. The words with which he closed this address deserve a place in this account:

I think that I am not mistaken when I say that this session is a great holiday for all workers in biological and agricultural science. [*Applause.*]

Fatherly care is shown by the Party and the government for the strengthening and development of the Michurinist tendency in our science, for the removal of all obstacles on the way to its fullest flowering. This obligates us to develop the work yet more widely and deeply for the fulfillment of the command of the Soviet people on arming the state and collective farms with advanced scientific theory.

We must earnestly put science and theory at the service of the people in order to raise ever more swiftly the harvest of the fields and the productivity of livestock, to raise the productivity of labor on state and collective farms.

I call on all academicians, scientific workers, agronomists, and animal breeders in close union with the progressive workers of the socialist rural economy to direct all their energies to the fulfillment of these great and noble tasks. [*Applause.*]

Progressive biological science is indebted to the geniuses of mankind — *Lenin and Stalin — for this: the teachings of Michurin entered into the treasure-house of our knowledge, into science as a golden fund.* [*Applause.*]

Long live the teachings of Michurin, the teachings on the transformation of organic nature for the welfare of the Soviet people! [*Applause.*]

Long live the Party of Lenin and Stalin for revealing Michurin to the world and for the creation in our country of all conditions necessary for the flowering of advanced materialistic biology. [*Applause.*]

Glory to our great friend and coryphaeus of science — our leader and teacher, Comrade Stalin!

(All stand and applaud for a long time.)

The session of the Academy, however, did not adjourn until it had "approved unanimously" a letter to Stalin thanking him, according to Soviet custom, for everything. Here is the letter: [9]

9 *Pravda,* August 10, 1948.

Dear Joseph Vissarionovich:

Members of the session of the All-Union Academy of Agricultural Science in the Name of V. I. Lenin: academicians, agronomists, animal breeders, biologists, mechanicians, and organizers of socialist agricultural production send you their warm Bolshevik greetings and very best wishes.

Every day and hour scientists and practical workers in the rural economy feel the manifold concern of the Communist Party and the Soviet state for agricultural science and for constant personal sharing in its further development and flowering.

To you, the great creator of Communism, the science of the fatherland is indebted. By your brilliant works you enrich and exalt it before the entire world. You guard it from the peril of estrangement from the needs of the people. You assist it in achieving victory over reactionary teachings hostile to the people. You watch over the continuous growth of scientists.

Carrying on the work of V. I. Lenin, you have saved for progressive materialistic biology the teachings of the great remolder of nature, I. V. Michurin, and, in the presence of the entire world of science, you have raised the Michurinist tendency in biology to the position of the only correct and progressive tendency in all the branches of biological science. Thus you have strengthened yet further the natural-scientific foundations of the Marxist-Leninist world view whose invincible might is confirmed by the entire experience of history.

You, our dear leader and teacher, daily assist Soviet scientists in the development of our progressive materialistic science which serves the people in all of their labors and exploits, a science which expresses the world view and the noble purposes of the man of the new socialist society.

The system of collective farming, created under your wise leadership, has opened up unlimited opportunities for the vigorous raising of the productive forces of all branches of rural economy and has showed its invincible power. The Party of Lenin and Stalin has nurtured among collective farmers remarkable warriors for a high harvest of crops and for a high productivity in animal husbandry. Michurinist agricultural science, called by you to develop boldly and decisively scientific researches in the active transformation of the nature of plants and animals, arms practical workers in their struggle for a high culture in socialist rural economy. In their turn, the forward-looking people of the collective farms, innovators in agricultural production founded on an all-people's socialist competition, enrich our science with new methods and new achievements.

We assure you, dear Joseph Vissarionovich, that we shall put forth all our energies in order to assist collective and state farms to achieve a yet higher harvest in the socialist fields and a yet higher productivity in animal breeding. This will insure the abundance of goods in our country which is one of the most important conditions of the transition from socialism to Communism. We see opportunities for the achievement of this great purpose in a science closely linked with the people and with the forward-looking personnel of the collective farm. You have always taught and you continue to teach this to us, both Party and non-Party Bolsheviks. Science, separated from the people and practical life, is not science.

Our agro-biological science, developed in the works of Timiriazev, Michurin, Williams, and Lysenko, is the most advanced agricultural science in the world. It is not only the lawful successor of the progressive ideas of the forward-looking scientists of the whole history of mankind, but is also a new and much higher stage of the development of human knowledge concerning agriculture. The Michurinist teachings also constitute a new and higher stage in the development of materialistic biology. And in the future Michurinist biological science will develop Darwinism creatively, expose unwaveringly and decisively the reactionary-idealistic Weismann-Morganist scholasticism divorced from practice, fight against slavishness before bourgeois science unworthy of the Soviet scientist, and liberate investigators from the vestiges of idealistic and metaphysical ideas. Forward-looking biological science repudiates and unmasks the vicious idea of the impossibility of shaping the nature of organisms through the control by man of the conditions of life of plants, animals, and microorganisms.

Science must teach investigators to be bold in searches for ways and means of shaping nature to the needs of men.

The victorious teachings of Marx, Engels, Lenin, and Stalin in science and practice inspire us on this road.

Your teachings on forward-looking science, which serves the people, values traditions, but does not fear to raise the hand against everything decadent, inspire us on this road.

Long live the forward-looking biological Michurinist science!

Glory to the great Stalin, leader of the people and coryphaeus of forward-looking science!

4

The impact on Soviet biologists of Lysenko's statement that the Central Committee of the Party had approved his address and its basic theses must have been tremendous. To Lysenko and his followers the action of the Party meant complete and final victory. To the survivors of the school of Vavilov it meant, under the most favorable circumstances, demotion and a measure of disgrace. And every one of these scientists was confronted with the profound personal and ethical problem: to retract or not to retract. If he buried his scientific scruples and retracted, he might hope after a period of probation to be accepted again in the ranks of Soviet scientists. But if he remained loyal to the ideal of truth and refused to retract, he could at best only contemplate a fate somewhat kinder than that which overtook Vavilov. As Professor Zhebrak faced this issue in the hours following the session of the Academy, he must have been torn by the very same emotions that Galileo experienced three centuries before. And he decided as Galileo did, to confess, and recant, or at least to recant and promise to sin no more. On August 9, two days after Lysenko's triumphant announcement, he sent his letter of capitulation to *Pravda*. Published in the issue of August 15, it was a pathetic appeal to be permitted to live and work in the ranks of Soviet science:

To the Editors of the Newspaper *Pravda*:
   I request the publication of the following text of my declaration.
   As long as our Party recognized both tendencies in Soviet genetics and as long as debates between them were regarded as a creative discussion of theoretical questions of contemporary science facilitating the discovery of truth, I persistently defended my views which at some points differed from the views of Academician Lysenko. But now, since it has become clear to me that the basic theses of the Michurin school

in Soviet genetics are approved by the Central Committee of the All-Union Communist Party, I, as a member of the Party, cannot defend positions which have been declared mistaken by the Central Committee of our Party.

I regard as absolutely correct Lysenko's criticism of Weismannism as an idealistic current in biology. His criticism of Weismann's conception of body-plasm and germ-plasm is in accord with my criticism which appeared in various publications in the years 1936 and 1937 and which is derived from my experimental work in the measurement of cross-fertilization. . . . [10] Permit me a few citations from my old articles: " . . . the very condition of the experiments [of Weismann] was so primitive that his theoretical conclusions could not possibly be based on them."

" . . . from the point of view of dialectical materialism the Weismannite conception was dualistic. It divided the organism into two substances and excluded the reciprocal movement between these substances of one and the same organism. Yet more astonishing is the fact that this conception was maintained for a very long time in genetics and that even some contemporary geneticists stand fundamentally on the very methodological positions on which the supporters of Weismann stood several decades ago . . . " Further I showed the falsity of the theory of Weismann and a number of other theories which logically flow from it, and in particular the theory of the phenotype and the genotype.

On the question of the influence of the external environment on the organism my views also do not contradict the Michurinist tendency. In 1936 I formulated my views as follows:

" . . . we think that phenotypical changes (acquired characters), whether evoked by growth or by environmental change, are inherited. They are inherited in the sense that germ cells are formed in a concrete phenotype, in a concrete modification, and since the phenotype of an organism is different, then different also are those processes which take place in a changed organism. It follows that these differences must be reflected in some measure in the germ cells which subsequently can be the beginning of a changed organism."

The point of view expressed in my works on methodology is opposed to that of Weismann and Morgan. My conception was based on a great number of experiments. Incidentally, permit me to note that

[10] Here Zhebrak refers to specific articles.

my works were given to the press by Academician V. R. Williams.

My experiments in obtaining new *amphidiploid* varieties of wheat by the method of distant hybridization and by the action of chemical elements are in accord with the recognition of the dependence of the hereditary element on the external environment. In 1944 this thought was expressed as follows: "In all of our works it is particularly important that results obtained through the creation of new amphidiploid types of wheat are achieved through the action on the hereditary element of such an external factor as colchicine. This completely shatters the view of the earlier autogeneticists who considered the germ-plasm to be isolated from external conditions and capable of resisting external influences. . . . "

I have cited these references for the purpose of showing that I was not implicated in the idealism of Weismann or the idealism of the autogeneticists. In the discussion of 1936 I spoke from my own point of view which differed as much from the one as from the other side in the dispute.

In my scientific work I have endeavored and I am endeavoring to live up to the motto of Michurin: "Not to expect favors from nature, but to wrest them from her is our task"; and the motto of Marx: "not merely to understand the world, but even to transform it." Unquestionably man can create better forms of plants than nature.

That I used effective methods for the transformation of plants and the obtaining of amphidiploid kinds of wheat and other cultivated plants is demonstrated by the practical achievements of our laboratory, which give precedence to our country. In my scientific work I use Michurin's method of distant hybridization, of the hybridization of geographic species, of the action of chemical and physical factors, etc.

Since it is the sacred duty of the scientists of our country to march in step with the entire people for the purpose of satisfying their needs and vitally essential demands of their state, of struggling with the vestiges of capitalism, of aiding the Communist education of the toilers, and of moving science ahead without interruption, then, as a member of the Party and as a scientist from the ranks of the people, I do not want to be regarded as a renegade, I do not want to be barred from assisting in the achievement of the noble tasks of the scientists of our Motherland. I want to work within the framework of that tendency which is recognized as forward-looking in our country and with the methods which are propounded by Timiriazev and Michurin. Henceforth I shall strive with all my powers to make my works of maximum use to my country, to develop creatively the heritage of Timiriazev and Michurin, to assist the building of Communism in our Motherland.

I think that my experimental works in the transformation of culti-vated plants, based on the theory of Timiriazev and Michurin, will contribute their mite to the development of Soviet biological science.

In the same issue of *Pravda* and on the same page, directly below Zhebrak's letter, appeared a response from the editors which defi-nitely placed him on probation for an unspecified period. They charge him with falsifying the record as follows:

From the Editors:

In publishing the letter of Professor A. R. Zhebrak the editors of *Pravda* cannot accept a number of his mistaken assertions:

1. His assertion is incorrect that "our Party recognized both tend-encies in Soviet genetics," i.e., the progressive materialistic Michurin-ist teaching and the reactionary idealistic Weismannist tendency in biology. Dialectical materialism being the foundation of our world view has always conducted an irreconcilable and decisive struggle with every kind of idealism in the field of the natural sciences, as in the field of the social sciences. The Party therefore supports the Michurinist teachings which are based on the unshakable theses of dialectical materialism and which truthfully reflect objective truth.

2. False and pretentious is the assertion of Prof. A. R. Zhebrak that the criticism of Weismannism in a speech by Academician Lysenko "On the Situation in Biological Science" coincides with the criticism which he gave in references cited in his letter. In actuality, A. R. Zhebrak in his works on the fundamental questions of biology stands on the positions of Weismann, Mendel, and Morgan. In these works he praises and glorifies the Mendel-Morgan doctrines. "The school of Morgan," he writes, "enriched genetics with new insights and raised it to a higher theoretical stage. . . . " [11]

On the fundamental questions of biology the author of the letter stands in the works cited on the positions of Weismann. He affirms that "the development of biology and particularly that part of it which is concerned with the study of heredity and mutability — genetics — has accumulated a tremendous mass of experimental data

[11] Here the editors refer specifically to an article by Zhebrak.

against the inheritance of acquired characters. . . . The germ cells participated in the historical establishment of species as well as those historical influences which were experienced by organisms in the process of their individual lives. It is fully understood that the leading and fundamental rôle in this process belonged to the inherited elements."

It is clear that in the light of such assertions the declaration of A. R. Zhebrak that he was not implicated in the Weismann-Morgan doctrines is incorrect and false.

3. In his letter Professor Zhebrak attempts to prove the unprovable, namely, that in his works he made use of the methods and the motto of Michurin. However, in order to reveal the entire falsity of Professor Zhebrak's statement, it suffices to cite just one of his characteristic assertions which contains a contemptuous evaluation of the works of I. V. Michurin. Thus, for example, in the article, "Categories of Genetics in the Light of Dialectical Materialism," Professor Zhebrak writes: "No matter how great may be the merits of some of our great selectionists, among them even Ivan Vladimirovich Michurin, we cannot rely completely on their authority."

At the same time, as was pointed out, A. R. Zhebrak praised in every way the founders of Mendelism-Morganism. Thus it appears that A. R. Zhebrak, while declaring that he could not continue to hold positions condemned by our Party, simultaneously endeavors to show that he has not held those positions. Such inconsistency is not becoming to a man who wishes honestly and openly to condemn his own mistakes.

4. Professor A. R. Zhebrak tends to oppose the teachings of I. V. Michurin to the works of Academician T. D. Lysenko and other Michurinites. Comrade Zhebrak is silent on the basic questions of the struggle with the Mendel-Morgan school, above all the question of the inheritance by plants and animals of qualities and characters acquired under the action of the conditions of life. He endeavors to prove that the Mendel-Morgan views do not contradict the teachings of Michurin. One must recognize these maneuvers of Comrade Zhebrak as improper.

5. As for the boastful declaration of Professor Zhebrak concerning his imaginary "practical achievements" in the field of the transformation of plants, it is now generally known that in point of fact Zhebrak has produced not a single valuable variety; he has made not a single suggestion of any practical worth for our agricultural economy. Like

other representatives of the Weismann-Morgan tendency, Professor
Zhebrak resembles a barren fig tree.

6. The editorial board takes note of the declaration of A. R.
Zhebrak that he does not wish to be regarded as a renegade and promises to develop creatively the heritage of Timiriazev and Michurin and
aid in the building of Communism. The subsequent work of Professor
A. R. Zhebrak will show whether this declaration is sincere.

5

This struggle to eradicate the "reactionary idealistic" tendency in
biology did not terminate with the triumph of Lysenko in the
Academy of Agricultural Science. As a matter of fact this was only
the beginning, and according to all portents the end is by no
means in sight. The battleground was broadened immediately to
include the Academy of Science itself in whose personnel and institutions the "bourgeois" heresy was most deeply rooted. On
August 26, 1948, the Presidium of the Academy issued a resolution
"On the Question of the Condition and Tasks of Biological
Science in the Institutes and Institutions of the Academy of
Science of the USSR." This resolution was in complete harmony
with the spirit of Lysenko's address which had been approved by
the Central Committee of the Party. At the same time it constituted an abject confession of error and incompetence on the part
of the Academy. It was published in full in the issue of *Pravda* for
August 27:

The Session of the All-Union Academy of Agricultural Science in
the Name of V. I. Lenin placed before Soviet biological science a
series of most important tasks. The resolution of these tasks must
contribute to the great cause of socialist construction. The Session
exposed the reactionary anti-people's essence of the Weismann-
Morgan-Mendel tendency in biological science and unmasked its
special exponents. The defeat of the anti-Michurinist tendency

opened up new possibilities for the creative development of all branches of progressive biological science.

The materials of the Session showed with complete clarity that in biological science a struggle has been going on between two tendencies which are diametrically opposed in their ideological and theoretical positions: the struggle of the progressive materialistic Michurinist tendency against the reactionary idealistic Weismann-Morganist tendency.

The Michurinist tendency, which has creatively enriched the theory of evolution and revealed the laws of development of organic nature, has made an outstanding contribution to the practice of socialist rural economy through its methods of directed change of the nature of plants and animals. The Weismann-Morganist tendency, asserting changes in the heredity of an organism to be independent of the special ways and conditions of its existence, defends idealistic and metaphysical positions. Being divorced from life, it engages in fruitless experiments and disarms practical workers in the rural economy who are engaged in the improvement of existing and the creation of new varieties of plants and breeds of animals.

The Academy of Science not only has taken no interest in the struggle against the reactionary bourgeois tendency in biological science, but in fact has supported representatives of the pseudo-science of formalistic genetics in the Institute of Cytology, Histology, and Embryology, in the Institute of Evolutionary Morphology, in the Institute of the Physiology of Plants, in the Chief Botanical Garden, and in other biological institutions of the Academy of Science.

The Presidium of the Academy of Science of the USSR admits that its work in guiding the biological institutes of the Academy is unsatisfactory.

In its work the Presidium of the Academy of Science and of the Biological Division, under the flag of an objective attitude toward the two contradictory tendencies in biological science, has in fact encouraged the reactionary Weismannist tendency and in every way slighted and restrained the only correct, the Michurinist, tendency.

The Presidium of the Academy of Science has permitted the organizational strengthening of the supporters of the pseudo-scientific Weismannist tendency of formalistic genetics. In 1946 it tolerated the mistake of raising the question of the creation of a special Institute of Genetics and Cytology as a counterpoise to the existing Institute of

Genetics headed by Academician Lysenko. The Presidium has supported the concentration of representatives of Morganist genetics in a number of the biological institutions of the Academy of Science.

The Bureau of the Division of Biological Science and its leader, Academician L. A. Orbeli, have not been able to put the theoretical work of the biologists of the Academy of Science at the service of the urgent tasks of socialist construction in the field of plant and animal breeding.

The struggle against bourgeois reactionary currents in biology in the institutes of the Division of History and Philosophy has been conducted in an entirely inadequate manner. Thus the Institute of Philosophy of the Academy of Science of the USSR, when called upon to conduct a persistent struggle against every kind of manifestation of idealism in science and to defend the materialistic world outlook, did not offer the needed support to the Michurinist materialistic tendency in biology and did not engage in the scientific refinement of the methodological problems of biological science.

The Council of Editors and Publishers and the editorial boards of the journals of the Division of Biological Science in fact converted their publications into organs of the anti-Michurinist tendency.

The address of Academician Lysenko, approved by the Central Committee of the All-Union Communist Party, places before the scientists of the Soviet Union and, first of all, before biologists and representatives of other branches of natural history a series of new theoretical questions. It demands of scientific institutions a complete and profound reorganization of research work in the field of biology and a genuine transformation of biological science into a mighty weapon for changing organic nature in the interests of building a Communist society.

The address of Academician Lysenko correctly exposed and condemned the scientific bankruptcy of the idealistic-reactionary theories of the followers of Weismannism — Schmalhausen, Dubinin, Zhebrak, Navashin, and others.

Through the works of such leading scientists as I. M. Sechenov, I. I. Mechnikov, K. A. Timiriazev, and A. N. Severtsov, our country has developed and defended Darwinism from the reactionary attacks of a number of West-European biological-idealists — Weismann, Morgan, Lotze, Bateson, and others.

V. V. Dokuchaev and V. R. Williams, leading scientists of our country, created a progressive theory of the formation and development of soils. The latter, one of the greatest Soviet scientists, originated the fruitful doctrine of the unity of the organism and the soil conditions of its life, and formulated the theory of the continuous improvement of the fertility of soils.

The highly gifted moulder of nature, I. V. Michurin, created through his work a new epoch in the development of Darwinism. His teachings are based on the great creative force of Marxist-Leninist philosophy. They set as their chief task the control of organic nature and the creation of new forms of plants and animals needed by socialist society.

Tsarist Russia was unable to appreciate the significance and transforming power of the scientific creative genius of I. V. Michurin.

Michurin was discovered for our people and for progressive science by the genius of Lenin and Stalin. In the epoch of socialism his teachings have proved to be a powerful lever in the cause of the transformation of nature. They have received wide opportunities for development and public recognition.

If Darwinism in its old form set itself the task of merely explaining the evolutionary process, then the teachings of Michurin, which have received further development in the works of Academician Lysenko, pose and resolve the task of the controlled change of the inherited characters of plants and animals. They pose and resolve the task of directing the evolutionary process.

T. D. Lysenko, his adherents, and pupils have made a substantial contribution to Michurinist biological science, to the cause of the development of socialist rural economy, to the cause of the struggle for a high harvest of farm crops and a high productivity in animal breeding.

The Presidium of the Academy of Science of the USSR binds the Division of Biological Science, biologists, and all investigators who work in the Academy of Science to reorganize their work fundamentally, to assume a leading position in the struggle against idealistic-reactionary teachings in science, against servility and slavishness toward foreign pseudo-science. The scientific institutes of the Academy of Science must struggle actively for the further flowering of patriotic biological science and, first of all, for the further development of the teachings of I. V. Michurin, V. V. Dokuchaev, and V. R. Williams which have been continued and developed by T. D. Lysenko.

The Presidium of the Academy of Science of the USSR decrees:

1.   To relieve Academician L. A. Orbeli of the duties of Secretary of the Division of biological science. Temporarily (until the election of the general assembly) to assign the duties of secretary to Academician A. I. Oparin. To appoint to the staff of the Bureau of the Division of Biological Science Academician T. D. Lysenko.

2.   To relieve Academician I. I. Schmalhausen of the duties of director of the Institute of Evolutionary Morphology in the Name of A. N. Severtsov.

3.   To abolish in the Institute of Cytology, Histology and Embryology the Laboratory of Cytogenetics, headed by the corresponding member, N. P. Dubinin, since it has held anti-scientific positions and has demonstrated its sterility in the course of a number of years. To close in the same institute the Laboratory of Botanical Cytology, since it has the same incorrect and anti-scientific direction. To liquidate in the Institute of Evolutionary Morphology in the name of A. N. Severtsov the Laboratory of Phenogenesis.

4.   To require the Bureau of the Division of Biological Science to revise the plans of scientific-research for 1948–50 with a view to refining and developing the Michurinist teachings and subjecting the scientific-research work of the institutions of the biological division to the needs of the public economy of the country.

5.   To require the Council of Editors and Publishers and the Division of Biological Science during 1948–49 to prepare for publication in the series, *Classics of Science,* a scientific biography of Michurin.

6.   To revise the staffs of the scientific councils of biological institutes and the editorial boards of biological journals, to remove advocates of the Weismann-Morgan tendency in genetics, and to appoint representatives of progressive Michurinist biological science.

7.   To commission the Division of History and Philosophy to provide in the plan of the division for works on the theoretical summation of the achievements of the Michurinist tendency in biology and of the criticism of the pseudo-scientific Weismann-Morganist tendency.

8.   To commission the Bureau of the Division of Biological Science to revise the structure, the administration, and the professional staffs of the scientific institutions of the division. To submit within one month a project for the reorganization of the Institute of Evolutionary

Morphology in the Name of A. N. Severtsov and the Institute of Cytology, Histology, and Embryology.

9. To commission the Council of Editors and Publishers within one month to revise publishing plans for the purpose of insuring the publication of scientific works in the field of Michurinist biology.

10. To commission the Division of Biological Science to organize in October, 1948, a broad session, devoted to the problems of the development of Michurinist biological science. To conduct the session with the cooperation of the All-Union Academy of Agricultural Science in the Name of V. I. Lenin, the biological institutions of the republican academies and their affiliates, and the bases of the Academy of Science of the USSR.

11. To commission the Bureau of the Division of Biological Science to revise the plan for the preparation of aspirants in its institutes, being guided in the matter of preparation of scientific personnel by the interests of the development of Michurinist biological science.

12. To publish the materials of the enlarged conference of the Presidium in the current issue of *Vestnik Academii Nauk.*

This definitive, inflexible, and powerful resolution passed a death sentence on several important institutions of Soviet science and cast into outer darkness fifteen or more distinguished scientists. Also it constituted a clear mandate from the Party to conduct a heresy hunt throughout the ranks of biologists and workers in the related sciences. Against this onslaught the individual is helpless, being protected neither by constitutional guarantees nor by opportunities for employment under other auspices. In a monolithic state, holding absolute power over all branches of the economy and the cultural apparatus, there are no pockets or crevices in which the individual may hide or find sanctuary. And the hope of flight beyond the borders of the country to some happier realm is silenced by harsh laws and a harsher police. This unprecedented effort to still the voice and stifle the thought of the scientist in the name of science and human liberty can be understood only as a terrifying nightmare troubling the sleep of modern man.

The members of the Presidium of the Academy, in order to

make complete their desecration of the altar of science, sent a memorial to Stalin in which they swore that they really meant everything they had said in the resolution. The history of science knows no parallel to this action of men who presumably live and work in the great tradition of freedom of the mind from Socrates and Lucretius down through Copernicus and Galileo to Darwin and Einstein. The letter reads as follows: [12]

Dear Joseph Vissarionovich:

The enlarged conference of the Presidium of the Academy of Science of the USSR, devoted to the discussion of the question of the condition and tasks of biological science in the Academy of Science of the USSR, turns to you, our beloved leader and teacher, with warm Bolshevik greetings and gratitude for the attention and aid which you have extended daily to Soviet science and Soviet scientists. Soviet science is indebted to you for its finest achievements. You have always directed the development of science in the interests of the people. You have always aided and you continue to aid us in vanquishing reactionary and harmful teachings and in defending forward-looking Soviet science from the danger of loss of contact with the people and with practical life.

The recent session of the All-Union Academy of Agricultural Science in the Name of V. I. Lenin and the address of Academician T. D. Lysenko, "On the Situation in Biological Science," which has been approved by the Central Committee of the All-Union Communist Party, have decisive significance for the further development of biological science.

Before us stands a task of exceptional importance — the task of developing Michurinist biological science and of exterminating the anti-people's idealistic Weismann-Morgan tendency in biology.

The best representatives of biological science in our country, Sechenov, Pavlov, Mechnikov, Timiriazev, Michurin, Dokuchaev, and Williams, have fought for a forward-looking biological science and have defended the materialistic theory of the development of the organic world. Our great compatriot and academician, I. V. Michurin, created a new epoch in the development of materialistic biology. The official science of old Russia was incapable of appreciating this great

[12] *Pravda*, August 27, 1948.

reformer and his teachings. Michurin was discovered for our people and for progressive science by the genius of Lenin and Stalin. In the Soviet land, under the conditions of the victory of the socialist order, the teachings of Michurin have borne remarkable fruits and have received wide opportunities of development.

The reactionary current of Weismann-Morgan in biology has been enlisted as a counterpoise to the revolutionary teachings of Michurin. This idealistic tendency, dominant in capitalist countries, unfortunately has found advocates among Soviet biologists, and particularly among scientists in the Division of Biological Science of the Academy of Science of the USSR.

The Presidium of the Academy of Science of the USSR and the Bureau of the Division of Biological Science have permitted a most serious mistake by giving support to the Mendel-Morgan tendency to the detriment of the progressive Michurin teachings. The Presidium of the Academy of Science has directed the biological institutions of the Academy of Science unsatisfactorily. Opponents of the teachings of Michurin have held leading posts in some biological institutions of the Academy. As a result the scientific institutions of the Division of Biological Science have co-operated feebly in the resolution of the practical tasks of socialist construction.

The Presidium of the Academy of Science promises you, dear Joseph Vissarionovich, and, in your person, our Party and government to correct resolutely the mistakes permitted by us, to reorganize the work of the Division of Biological Science and its institutes, and to develop biological science in a genuinely materialistic Michurinist direction.

The Academy of Science will take all necessary measures to insure the full development of Michurinist biological science in biological institutes, journals, and publishing operations. The biological institutes of the Academy of Science are revising their programs of scientific research for the purpose of bringing the work of the institutes into close contact with the needs of the public economy of the country. In the programs of biological institutions work on the theoretical summation of the achievements of Michurinist biology and on the unmasking of the reactionary "theories" of the Weismann-Morganites will be given proper attention.

We promise you, Comrade Stalin, to take a leading position in the struggle against idealistic, reactionary teachings and to clear all ways for the unhampered development of Soviet science in the name of the great purposes of our people, in the name of the victory of Communism.

In this humiliating spectacle the degradation of the All-Union Academy of Agricultural Science in the Name of Lenin is followed by the degradation of the Academy of Science of the USSR. In the struggle for favor and perhaps survival, involving all the arts and sciences, each organization endeavors to surpass its predecessor in prostrating itself before the gods of power. So the participants in a session of the Division of Biological Science of the Academy of Science of the USSR agree to send a letter to the "leader of the Soviet People" in which they promise to be good in all things: [13]

Dear Joseph Vissarionovich:

Participants in the session of the Division of Biological Science of the Academy of Science of the USSR: academicians, corresponding members and scientific workers in the biological institutions of the Academy of Science of the USSR, of its branches and stations, of the All-Union Academy of Agricultural Science in the Name of Lenin, of the Academies of Science of the Union Republics and Academies of Medical Science send you, coryphaeus of Soviet science and friend of Soviet scientists, their cordial Bolshevist greetings.

We have met in these historic days for our science in order to discuss the theoretical foundations and programs of research in biology during the years immediately ahead.

We, Soviet biologists, are deeply indebted to the Party of Bolsheviks and to you personally, dear Joseph Vissarionovich, for the complete victory of the revolutionary, dialectical-materialistic Michurinist teachings over the reactionary, idealistic tendency in biology — Weismann-Morganism.

The ideas of our brilliant scientist, Ivan Vladimirovich Michurin, were suppressed and could not be appreciated in pre-revolutionary Russia.

Advanced biological science is indebted to the great Lenin and to you, our dear leader and teacher, for the preservation of the teachings of Michurin for progressive Soviet science and for the entire Soviet people.

[13] *Pravda,* November 9, 1948.

The rout of the foreign anti-people's Weismann-Morganism has opened before us the widest range for further work in the active transformation of living nature.

Armed with the teachings of Michurin, developed creatively by T. D. Lysenko, Soviet biology will leave bourgeois biological science far behind.

From a science devoted merely to the elucidation of the laws of nature, biology in the Soviet Union will become a science directed toward the transformation of living nature in the interests of socialist society.

Our guiding conception, as Soviet biologists, is the recognition of the possibility and the necessity of the inheritance of traits acquired by organisms. Soviet biologists place before themselves the profoundly complex task of elaborating this central problem of biology in the interests of the development of theory and the resolution of the supreme tasks of socialist agriculture and animal-breeding.

Our plans for 1948–50 reflect the fundamentally new tasks standing before Soviet biology today of the further creative development of the teachings of Michurin.

We are actively included in the great campaign of the Soviet people against drought and for the creation of an abundance of products, as one of the most important conditions of the transition of our country from socialism to Communism.

Questions pertaining to the development of animal-breeding and to the achievement of stable and high harvests through the introduction of superior varieties of plants and the infusion into agriculture of the methods of Dokuchaev, Kostychev, and Williams, occupy a central place in our scientific work.

We are obligated steadfastly and decisively to unmask reactionary, idealistic perversions in biology and to conduct an active struggle against servility toward bourgeois science, unworthy of a Soviet scientist.

Soviet biologists will give an account of themselves in the discharge of this heavy responsibility which they bear before the country.

We are fully confident that we will resolve successfully the tasks standing before us. Our confidence rests on the fact that in our work we lean on the most advanced theory — the teachings of Marx, Engels, Lenin and Stalin — and constantly feel your wise leadership, attention, and care.

Long live advanced Michurinist biological science!

May our leader, teacher, and friend of scientists, the great Stalin, live and prosper many years as the coryphaeus of advanced science!

6

It would seem now that the cup of bitterness of Orbeli, Schmalhausen, Dubinin, Zhebrak, and their many students, admirers, and associates in biological science had been filled to overflowing. But the members of the Central Committee, following a pattern established long ago, add a final touch. They turn to the people and incite them in their blindness to wring from the victims the last drop of anguish. This side of the story is told very fittingly in the pages of the official organ of Soviet writers, perhaps because they would still their own consciences disturbed over the fate of Zoshchenko and Akhmatova. As the reader reads this article entitled "The People Are For Michurin," he should realize that, if the Party had so decreed, the heading would have been "The People Are For Vavilov": [14]

From the tribune of the session of the All-Union Academy of Agricultural Science in the Name of V. I. Lenin rang out the passionate speeches of Michurinist scientists and practical workers, discussing the address of Academician T. D. Lysenko. In those days it seemed as if the walls of the auditorium moved and as if the entire (Soviet) people not only were present invisibly during the disputes of the materialistic with the idealistic biologists, but also expressed themselves most precisely and explicitly in support of the science which leads to abundance and the improvement of life. It is not by chance that many Soviet people experienced a heightened holiday mood.

No sooner was the address published than an endless torrent of telegrams, letters, and responses poured in. Some comrades, as if participating in the discussions, responded to this or that speech and sent telegrams to the All-Union Academy of Agricultural Science in the Name of V. I. Lenin. Excited by the speech and the discussions,

[14] *Literaturnaia Gazeta,* September 8, 1948.

scientists and collective farmers, teachers and engineers, at the end of the working day seized the pen. For the question involved a subject nearest and dearest to them — the subject of the victory of Soviet thought, the victory of Soviet science over alien and hostile pseudo-science.

They sent letters to the editors of *Pravda* and to the editors of *Sotsialisticheskoe Zemledelie,* to the Ministry of Rural Economy, to comrades who participated in the discussion, and personally to Trofim Denisovich Lysenko. Thousands of letters on questions of biology were received in less than ten days. Of what tremendous spiritual growth of our Soviet man do they speak! The most diverse strata of the people respond with lively interest to such seemingly specialized questions as biological theory. To Morganites, having lost contact with life, this concern of the people is an accusation and a condemnation of the "science" in which they labored so long and so fruitlessly.

Letters came from everywhere! The envelopes were stamped with the postmarks of Kalinin and Osipovichey (Belorussia), Podolsk and Piatigorsk, Moscow and Grozny. Letters from Leningrad and Petro-zavodsk, from the Crimea and Tashkent, from Dniepropetrovsk, Rostov, Kirov, Kuibishev, Frunze, and Kharkov, from Kizliar, from Latvia, from tens of collective farms and villages of the divers oblasts of our vast land. Everybody writes to Academician Lysenko: Professor Kovarsky from Kishenev, and the honored leader of science Professor M. Revo, and a woman student of the University of Central Asia, M. Korzhavina, and I. Priakhin from "Tulsky Preserve," and officers G. Zelen from Belorussia and G. Maximov from Kandalaksh, and an economist S. Afanasiev, and a worker N. Doronin, and an agronomist Y. Aksinin. Here we have the teacher Genfilov and the engineer Tolmazov; here too the rural Party worker of Smolenshchin, I. Litvinov. . . . But the mere enumeration of names and professions would occupy a whole page of a newspaper. And no matter who wrote, or whence the letters came, they were all born out of an ardent interest in the flowering of Michurinist science for the good of the people and united by the keen thought and passionate patriotic feeling prompting them and the diverse suggestions which they contained.

In their letters and telegrams the Soviet people express great joy over the triumph of the Michurinist tendency.

The collective farmers of the artel "Podmoskovnyi Khleborob," having read the issue of *Pravda* containing the speech of T. D. Lysenko, at once wrote an animated letter:

"Comrade Lysenko! Please permit us to express our own feelings and the feelings of many collective farmers in this neighborhood. We congratulate you on the great victory of our Michurinist teachings! They have proved themselves by high harvests. Soviet science educates our people in the Communist spirit, forms stalwart and cheerful people, fearing no difficulties or obstacles.

"Long live our leader Comrade Stalin!

"Long live our Soviet science!

"We wish you success!"

Professor V. Sukharev sent T. D. Lysenko a telegram:

"Your statement that the lever for raising productivity and perfecting varieties consists of food plus living conditions fundamentally and correctly reflects life. My experiments with radio-active food have not infrequently confirmed this position. I rejoice in your victory. I bow before the wisdom of the government for increasing the number of Michurinites in the Academy."

Not only did individual scientists respond to the work of the session. Letters from scientific bodies, from institutes and academies, and from all parts of the country began to arrive at the address of Academician Lysenko.

From Riga, the capital of a young Soviet Republic, they telegraphed:

"We, the Michurinites of the Latvian Agricultural Academy, congratulate you on the brilliant victory over the reactionary tendency in biology. Your profound address at the session inspires us to a yet more stubborn struggle against local Mendelites. Your address will soon be published in the Latvian language." — Professor Doctor Peive, Professor Berzin, and Candidate of Science Avotyn-Pavlov.

The letter of Professor V. Pisarev, a selectionist, is noteworthy. For him the realization of a mistake means, not the "wrecking of a life" (as for many sterile scholastics), but a step toward the mastery of new creative heights in the service of the people. . . .

"During the forty years of my practical work as a selectionist," writes V. Pisarev, "I first and foremost set myself the task of giving our rural economy more productive varieties and particularly more productive varieties of spring wheat for the north of the Union. For a theoretical base I studied neither genetics nor selection in any higher institution to secure a theoretical foundation for my work, because such subjects were not taught then. But under the influence of the literature the so-called chromosome theory, which was then in high repute, gradually took possession of me.

"However, I must honestly confess that this theory did not relieve the difficulties of my work. Perhaps it is more inexcusable for me, an old selectionist, than for anyone else to have remained silent up to the present time about a whole series of data from my selectionist work, data for which the mechanical system of chromosomes had no room.

" . . . My fault was that, hypnotized by the chromosome theory, I ignored these facts which are explained so simply and clearly by the teachings of Michurin on inheritance which has been developed by you and your students.

"The development of a variety of spring wheat, 'Moskovka,' was due, not to the successful combination of traits according to Mendel, but to those special conditions around Moscow in which the young hybrid variety was formed.

"All this I pondered and examined carefully after your address at the session of the Academy.

" . . . And now I see clearly that my stubbornness in defending the essentially reactionary views on heredity of the bourgeois scientists of the West and our own so-called 'formal geneticists' was based on nothing.

"Now when a ferocious ideological struggle goes on between two worlds, there can be no middle road. And I want to be in the ranks of the Michurinist movement in order to work for the good of our socialist rural economy.

"True is the proverb: 'Moscow does not believe in tears.' Consequently the obligation rests with me to prove by word and deed my devotion to the Michurinist movement in our Soviet biology."

Hundreds of ordinary Soviet people are filled with pride over the victory of their scientists, of their Bolshevik science.

"I, an ordinary man, read your address at the session. It should be read by everybody. I understood what a tremendous, difficult, and important task stands before you. How sorry I was after hearing the addresses of your opponents that I am neither a biologist nor an agronomist, and that I cannot help you to vanquish them. But you, a man of the common people, managed them yourself. I am proud of you! What a brilliant application of dialectical materialism to biology.

Your speech was like rain in a spring drought. A shattering blow was struck against dried-up reactionary theories both outside and within our country. I applaud and congratulate you on the victory!" writes Comrade Kostromin.

Comrade A. Zemtsov of Minsk, a man having no direct relation to biology, on reading Lysenko's address wrote to him immediately:

"I simply do not know how to express the feeling that beats in my breast. It is as if you had arranged a holiday for me. Having read the address, I read it once again, and then I could not hold myself. In spite of the lateness of the hour I began to telephone my friends. And they were engaged just as I was, and their feeling and joy were the same as mine.

"Your cause will conquer, Trofim Denisovich. The people have faith in you. The people support you. You are close to them and understood by them. Permit me, not a scientist, but an ordinary man, to proclaim: may our own, patriotic, revolutionary, bold, Stalinist, Soviet science be triumphant! May it serve better the cause of our great people, the interests of the common man of labor, the demands of practical work, the needs of life."

The oldest collective farmer and experimenter of the Kurgan district, Terentii Maltsev, who conducts a large research work in a cottage-laboratory and in the fields of a collective farm, sent a letter to his teacher, T. D. Lysenko:

"With all my heart and soul I rejoice in the historic victory over the forces of reaction which for so long had enjoyed the opportunity of entangling the minds of the students of our country with a pseudo-scientific outpouring of words in the lecture rooms of our educational institutions, singing in different tunes the teachings of bourgeois biologists and preaching an ideology alien to the spirit of our ideology.

"A great future belongs to our own glorious Michurinist teachings, which are wholly and fully appropriate to the progress of biological science in our country building Communism.

"From now on Michurinist science, founded on Marxist-Leninist teachings, will serve as a starting point for the further discovery of new and ever new depths of biological science, new and ever new truth about the life and the development of organisms. You have literally liberated science, by giving to it unlimited possibilities to move forward."

With true love and concern for genuine science sound the voices of our people.

"We, members of the agricultural artel 'Put k Socialismu' (Ramensk region, Moscow district) demand the banishment from the universities of the parasites of bourgeois science, slaves of foreign influences. For them there is no place among the scientists of our Motherland! What have they given to a people marching with firm step toward Communism?

"We are sorry that Comrade Lysenko was unable earlier to create a healthy condition in the Academy and to man its staff with Michurinites. But it is not too late. Act, Comrade Lysenko, act more boldly, because these pseudo-scientists are enemies of forward-looking socialist science. We wish success for the session." — At the request of the collective farmers, Andrei Ivanov.

Along with the letter from the collective farmers of the Moscow region came numerous communications from teachers demanding changes in the school programs in biology.

Also the address of Lysenko could not help exciting students who had been forced against their wills to study Mendelian-Morganist "science." "Is it not tragic to discover in the fourth year of your study that for three years you had been studying 'pseudo-science'?" writes a woman student of the biological faculty of the State University of Central Asia, Marina Korzhavina.

It is not by chance that in the discussions at the session Academician E. Ushakova, yes, and other speakers, said that the majority of specialists, on graduating from the biological divisions of higher institutions, on coming into contact with practice, are compelled to re-learn what they had been taught.

An agricultural economist, N. Simonov, head of the department of political economy of a Moscow institute declares: "I consider that the Ministry of Higher Education of the USSR is politically responsible for having maintained 'neutrality' in the struggle between the two tendencies in science, instead of introducing your ideas decisively into practice."

And as if by agreement, tens of people from the most diverse localities write that the materials of the work of the session, books popularizing the Michurinist tendency, classics of materialistic biology, and new textbooks must be published as quickly as possible. They write about this from Moscow, from Dagestan, from Tambov . . .

In a great many letters people speak of their experiments which confirm the truth of the Michurinites about the successful application of Michurinist methods to animal breeding. These letters bring suggestions of value to science and practice, and reveal the inexhaustible initiative and the keen creative thought of the people.

Reading these human documents, one thinks of the great spiritual unity of our Soviet people, and of the fact that the Soviet government is bound by thousands of threads with the people, with their thoughts and with their hopes.

Reading these letters, one sees that by supporting the Michurinites and aiding them in the struggle against reactionary theories in biology Comrade Stalin and the Party expressed the will of the entire people.

As if in answer to these letters, the government decided to strengthen and enlarge the staff of Michurinites of the All-Union Academy of Agricultural Science and to man it with a new glorious troop of academicians — companions-in-arms of Lysenko.

And as if in answer to the letters from students, collective farmers, agronomists, and teachers, and to the wishes of many thousands of Soviet people, the programs in biology in all educational institutions of the country are being changed. The works of I. V. Michurin, the works of T. D. Lysenko, and the proceedings of the session of the Academy are being published in enormous editions of two hundred thousand copies.

Reading these letters, one sees how the wall separating mental from physical work falls to the ground, how with each day the shoots of Communism develop in our land.

"Science must descend from its pedestal and speak the language of the people," so dreamed Timiriazev.

And now by reading the letters of collective farmers and agronomists, of common Soviet people, one thinks of a dream come true. In these letters there is faith in the triumph of Communism, in the power of human labor to change the world. Also that genuine creative optimism which flows from our entire mode of life and which has become an inalienable part of the character of Soviet man.

7

The assault on biology was apparently but the first major skirmish in a far-flung campaign to rid Soviet science of the last vestige of "reactionary idealistic bourgeois influences." At any rate the signal triumph of Lysenko and his cohorts was quickly followed by the launching of attacks in the name of the "science of the sciences" and under the banners of the "Party of Lenin and Stalin" along other sectors of the "scientific front." Mention will be made here of certain developments in the spheres of architecture, mathematics, and physics.

On September 25 an inspired article on "Questions Brewing in Soviet Architecture" appeared in *Pravda*. Following the line laid down by the Central Committee of the Party in all of the ideological resolutions, the author subjected to severe criticism the work of the Academy of Architecture of the USSR, of subordinate institutes and institutions, and of practically the entire fraternity of architects. He charged that the "Academy had not produced a single Marxist work on Soviet architecture," that the "baneful and putrescent influence of bourgeois formalism is found in the creations of some of our architects," and that certain leaders in the field "have forgotten that in architecture socialist realism is engaged in a struggle with bourgeois formalism." He inveighed against the neglect of "questions of ideology" and declared that the formalistic tendency "is nourished on the putrid reactionary ideology of the bourgeois West and is saturated with a spirit of grovelling before foreign architecture which is unworthy of a Soviet architect." The article aroused the officers of the Academy to call a special and broadened session of the members of the Presidium. Those present praised the critical wisdom of the article, agreed that its strictures were absolutely correct, and engaged in a general and rapturous confession of guilt and irresponsibility toward the Party and the Soviet people. They concluded

their conference with a resolution in which they formally acknowledged "most grievous shortcomings in the work of the Academy"
and promised thereafter to build things of beauty worthy of the
"great Stalinist epoch!" [15]

The naïve mind probably assumes that mathematics at least is
beyond the reach of the Central Committee and that two and two
make four in any language and under any social system. But of
course such an assumption is without foundation. The Soviet
leaders have long had difficulties with their statisticians and mathe-
maticians, charging them with failure to master the "greatest conquest of mankind — the Marxist-Leninist World-view" and to grasp
fully the conception of "mathematics as a weapon" in the struggle
against the "bourgeoisie." The issue is brought out sharply in an
editorial in the May–June, 1948, issue of *Planovoie Khoziastvo,*
organ of the State Planning Commission. Here three statisticians
are singled out for rebuke — Professors A. Boyarski, B. S. Yastrem-
ski, and P. P. Maslov. They are advised that "Soviet statistics is
the most advanced statistics in the world," that "the strength of
Soviet statistics resides in the fact that it is founded on the great
teachings of Lenin and Stalin," and that "models of scientific
statistical analysis are contained in the works of Comrade Stalin."
Instead of "grovelling before bourgeois statisticians," they should
engage in a "genuinely militant criticism of contemporary bourgeois theories and statistical methods" and a "systematic exposure
of the falsification of facts by bourgeois statistics."

The view has long been held by Western students of Soviet life
and institutions that politics impinges on scientific inquiry and
thought only at the upper levels of the hierarchy of the sciences.
According to this view, the physicist works in a realm so remote
from questions of Communist ideology that he enjoys a condition
of complete freedom of operation. But as the realm of investigation shifts from the physical to the biological, from the biological to the psychological and social sciences, and from all of
them to their practical applications to life, it has been assumed
that the rôle of politics increases until in these topmost regions its

[15] *Pravda,* November 10, 1948.

dominion becomes complete. This position rests in part on sound observation and inference, but only in part, and then only superficially. As a matter of fact, for reasons to be developed in the following pages, it seems quite probable that the Central Committee will conduct its most ruthless struggle against heresy in the field of physics.

The opening gun in the current battle to eradicate the influence of "bourgeois" thought in the physical sciences was fired in the official organ of the Union of Soviet Writers. This fact itself is revelatory of a fundamental Communist position respecting the co-ordination of the several branches or divisions of the intellectual life. Every organ, newspaper, journal, or publication must have on its staff a theoretician, trained in Marxism-Leninism in the Party schools, to guide the theoretical education of the reader along the path of orthodoxy. When the Soviet leaders speak of this body of doctrine as the "science of the sciences," they mean precisely what they say. They mean that it holds sway over all the sciences, directs the course of their development, and brings them all into a single mighty synthesis. Consequently anyone familiar with Soviet literature is never surprised if he finds an important article or resolution in a journal in which, according to Western "bourgeois" notions, it could appear only by the strangest sort of accident.

The article appeared as an editorial on November 20 under the title "Science and Socialism." Its author was M. Mitin, a member of the Academy of Science. The first and major part of the article is devoted to the course of biology during the nineteenth and twentieth centuries and the triumph of the teachings of Michurin. The academician then turns to the problems confronting Soviet physics. The essence of his analysis and position is contained in the following passages: [16]

Recently Comrade V. M. Molotov noted the vast significance of the discussion of questions of biology and the victory of Michurinist biology.

[16] *Literaturnaia Gazeta*, November 20, 1948.

The creative significance of materialistic principles for all branches of science is tremendous. They are capable of giving remarkable results in every field of knowledge. . . .

Soviet physics has large achievements to its credit. During recent years our physicists have enriched science with discoveries of first-rate significance.

However, very large tasks still confront them. There is no doubt that the struggle on the basis of high principle against idealism, against every manifestation of servility before bourgeois idealistic science, will contribute to the further flowering of our physics and make it the most advanced in the world.

In the field of theoretical physics, particularly since the end of the nineteenth and the beginning of the twentieth century, as is well known, the sharpest kind of struggle has been waged between materialism and idealism. For a logical exposition of these two tendencies in science the brilliant work of V. I. Lenin, *Materialism and Empiriocriticism,* is a mighty weapon. Now, when the reactionary flunkies of Anglo-American imperialism in the field of science draw the most obscurantist conclusions from the newest achievements of physical science, this struggle has acquired a peculiarly irreconcilable character.

One of the foundational theoretical positions of contemporary quantum mechanics is the so-called "principle of indeterminacy," formulated by Heisenberg in 1927.

The content of this "indeterminacy" is linked with the circumstance that quantum mechanics is not fully developed and finds itself in a condition of interrupted growth. However, idealistic physicists call this indeterminacy the "principle of indeterminacy," thus drawing philosophical conclusions from the data to the advantage of mysticism and agnosticism.

In its development contemporary physics has approached the study of the interaction between the physical phenomena of the micro-world and the apparatus of our observation. The raising of this question is an achievement of science and bears witness to its forward movement. However, under the conditions of imperialist reaction the living tree of knowledge yields poisonous flowers of idealism and mysticism: from the new rôle of an instrument in the investigation of micro-particles idealistic conclusions are drawn about the unreality of the micro-world.

Only materialistic physics can wrench contemporary physics from the road of idealism. Only consistent materialism can *purge physics of idealistic tendencies and open up before it in the field of theory and practice* new creative perspectives.

By enriching physical science with their new researches and by utilizing all genuine achievements of bourgeois physics, Soviet scientists will be able to resolve the general theoretical and methodological questions on an ideological plane so high that it is beyond the limited reach of bourgeois scientists.

Dialectical materialism is a remarkable weapon for the resolution of the theoretical questions of contemporary physics. It teaches that science recognizes no boundaries to knowledge of nature, that the most complex processes of the micro-world are entirely within the range of human knowledge.

The time has come for our scientists to confront bourgeois science with their own treatment of the newest achievements in physics, with their own theoretical conclusions based on dialectical materialism. Is such a task not capable of raising spiritually and giving wings to people of science?

Comrade Stalin has set before our scientists the task: "not only to overtake but to surpass in the shortest time the achievements of science beyond the borders of our country."

Inspired with the ideas of our great leader, Soviet scientists will achieve this task and attain further significant successes in the general upsurge of our Soviet science and culture.

The offensive against "bourgeois idealistic" physics was continued somewhat more sharply in a special article in the same issue of the journal with the fitting title of "Troubadours of Idealism in Physics." Here the author launches a rather savage attack on certain Western physicists. The extracts below reveal the political and ideological tendency of the article: [17]

The exposure of reactionary-idealistic forces, operating in Soviet biology, force us to examine the state of affairs on other sectors of the scientific front.

We refer to physics and to the theory of the atom.

Today Soviet physical science, armed with the advanced and mighty method of dialectical materialism, is confronted with the question:

17 *Ibid.*

Will it travel the shortest road toward the great goals set before it? Will Soviet physicists assume a firm position in the warfare which is being waged now between two irreconcilable movements in science on the structure of matter? Will they take the lead in shattering reactionary, pseudo-scientific views in atomic physics? Or will these views, which flow from the West and are obligingly taken over by some of our professors, spread and confuse Soviet theoretical workers, thus retarding the progress of materialistic science?

The twenties of our century were marked by events of vast importance in the history of physics. During these years the foundations of the so-called quantum or wave theory of matter were laid. It follows from this theory that with each atomic particle interrupted in its motions, that is, with the atomic particle isolated in space, is linked an undulating material process which embraces the entire uninterrupted space.

This discovery was a significant contribution to the materialistic dialectic of nature. It brought physics closer to the establishment of unity of interruption and continuity in matter.

Having assumed by 1927–28 more or less clear outlines, the quantum theory was able to enrich practice with a number of large achievements. But the successful elaboration of dialectical synthesis, begun so auspiciously, which lies at the base of the atom, subsequently failed to develop. This synthesis has remained unfinished and incomplete. From the discoveries of contemporary atomic physics, idealistic and mystical deductions have been drawn. The profound crisis of theoretical physics, which sprang up in the soil of the general decay of bourgeois culture, is just as far from solution in our day as it was a quarter of a century ago.

How did this crisis arise?

The basic equation of atomic physics is established by the wave character of the movement of atomic particles. With the aid of this equation a simultaneous and entirely precise definition of co-ordinates and speeds of microparticles is impossible. The origin of this "inaccuracy" or "indeterminacy" remains thus far the subject of discussions and disputes. But regardless of the outcome of these disputes, one thing is clear: the fog of "indeterminacy" enveloping atomic mechanics is explained by the *incompleteness and imperfection* of the quantum theory in its present form. To dispel this fog is the task of materialistic physics. . . .

In the years 1942–44 V. Heisenberg invents the "characteristic matrix of dispersion S," "liquidating" at the same time the basic index of the reality of physical matter — the quantity of *energy*. . . . Messrs. Jordan and Figner tell us, further, of their "perfecting" of the "method of indeterminacy." The "principle of indeterminacy," you see, becomes now not only the speeds and co-ordinates of particles, but also the tensions of the electrical and magnetic field. Eddington (he died in 1944), juggling with the "mystical number 137," constructs in his turn a "world equation," permitting the calculation of the total number of electrons in the entire universe. With Eddington competes G. Lemaître, professor of theoretical physics and Catholic priest. Lemaître computes with the aid of his own "equations" the date of the "first day of creation." For this "research" he is elected an honorary member of the Washington Academy of Science.

- Such is the "result" of certain recent "achievements" of bourgeois theoretical physics. Before us now are not only attempts to *interpret* in idealistic terms the new theories and discoveries in physics. Before us are not only harmless literary exercises on physical themes. No! The fact is that we are now confronted with the direct *falsification* and unconcealed "mathematical" mystification of atomic physics.

"All the forces of obscurantism and reaction are now established in the service of the struggle against Marxism. . . . The subterfuges of contemporary bourgeois atomic physicists lead them to conclusions about the 'freedom of the will' of electrons. Who then, if not we — the land of victorious Marxism and her philosophers — are to stand at the head of the struggle against depraved and infamous bourgeois ideology! Who then, if not we, are to deliver the shattering blows!"

These words of Comrade Zhdanov must become the militant program of action for Soviet physicists. But is all well today on the front of Soviet theoretical physics?

The article closes with the question: But is all well today on the front of Soviet theoretical physics? The question is of course rhetorical and doubtless more than one physicist began to ponder his future. The initial answer is given four days later on November 24, in words which no one can misunderstand in an editorial in the same journal, *Literaturnaia Gazeta*. Three Soviet physicists, Y. I. Frankel, M. Markov, and V. Sviderski, are warned that they have been pursuing a course in their work which is "alien to Soviet ideology." Obviously, if they are not to find themselves outside the ranks of Soviet scientists they must speedily renounce

their past and promise to do everything possible to drive "bourgeois tendencies" out of Soviet physics. Also they will probably
proceed at once to master Marxism-Leninism so that they may
never again grovel before the West.

The reader is perhaps somewhat startled by the intensity and
savagery of this whole attack on certain European physicists. To
be sure, the reader who has read this far in the present volume
is accustomed to the swing of the Soviet pendulum of literary expression from one extreme to the other, from hysteria on the left
to hysteria on the right. All "Party literature," whenever it deals
with opponents or "enemies," assumes a highly vituperative character, regardless of subject matter. On the other hand, whenever
it touches friends and the objects of worship, Marx, Engels, Lenin,
and Stalin, the Party of Bolsheviks, the Soviet Motherland, and
even the "new people's democracies," it attains a level of flattery
and adoration which can only be matched in the literature of
hagiology. But still it must probably seem to the uninitiated that
the display of such passion in the sphere of theoretical physics is a
bit incongruous. It would appear that the Russians are carrying
the political struggle into realms beyond politics.

Such a conclusion, however, is not warranted. There are solid
grounds for the passionate denunciation of "idealistic physicists"
found in *Literaturnaia Gazeta* which have little to do with the
application of physics to either the public economy or military defense. As a matter of fact the Soviet spokesmen are engaged in
defending the very citadel of their faith, the ultimate foundations
of their beliefs. Their devotion to a materialistic interpretation
of the universe is not an academic question. On the contrary it is
the emblem by which they hope to conquer both at home and
abroad. The following quotation from their *Brief History of the
All-Union Communist Party,* a book that is published and sold by
millions of copies every year, is the heart of their "world view":

The philosophical materialism of Marx holds that the world in its
very nature is *material,* that the manifold phenomena of the world
represent different forms of matter in motion, that interrelationship
and interdependence of phenomena . . . constitute a law of the development of matter in motion, that the world evolves according to the

laws of the movement of matter and stands in need of no "world spirit." [18]

These words are sacred words. Even though they express a position developed by Marx and Engels in the middle of the nineteenth century and reflect the thought of the extreme rebels of the period, rebels who were revolting against both theology and classical philosophy, they stand beyond revision or even critical examination today. The ultimate reality is matter and matter in the nineteenth-century sense. To resolve matter into energy or spirit, or to accept an element of indeterminacy in nature would mean the dissolution of the very foundations of their faith and of their claim to infallibility. An appropriate parallel can only be found in a religious sect whose conception of the universe rests in the final analysis on a belief in God. Everyone knows how the Christian Church down through the centuries feared and opposed the development of science lest it "expel God from the universe." The struggle in Soviet physics will be carried on more ruthlessly than in any other field. Nothing less than everything is at stake. In the ideological struggle physics is the "commanding height" which must be held at all costs. The reader should note that the priesthood of the "science of the sciences" is implacably hostile not only to "idealism and mysticism," which is easily understood, but also to "agnosticism." In this materialistic religion there is no place for doubt or scepticism. All must believe!

8

The action of the Central Committee of the Party and the resolutions of the academies brought responses from beyond the borders of the Soviet Union. On September 23, 1948, Professor H. J.

[18] *Brief History of the All-Union Communist Party* (Moscow, 1945), p. 106. (In Russian.)

Muller of Indiana University sent to the officers of the Academy of Science of the USSR a letter of resignation as "Corresponding Member" of the Academy. A biologist of great distinction and a winner of the Nobel Prize for Medicine, he had worked as senior geneticist in the Institute of Genetics of Moscow from 1933 to 1937. The following paragraph from his letter of resignation conveys the essence of his thought on the intervention of the Party in the work of the scientist:

The deep esteem in which I have held your organization in the past makes it the more painful to me to inform you that I now find it necessary to sever completely my connection with you. The occasion for my doing so is the recently reported series of actions of your Presidium in dropping, presumably for their adherence to genetics, such notable scientists as your most eminent physiologist, Orbeli, and your most eminent student of morphogenesis, Schmalhausen, in abolishing the Laboratory of Cytogenetics of your most eminent remaining geneticist, Dubinin, in announcing your support of the charlatan Lysenko, whom some years ago you had stooped to take into your membership, and in repudiating, at his insistence, the principles of genetics. These disgraceful actions show clearly that the leaders of your Academy are no longer conducting themselves as scientists, but are misusing their positions to destroy science for narrow political purposes, even as did many of those who posed as scientists in Germany under the domination of the Nazis. In both cases the attempt was made to set up a politically directed "science," separated from that of the world in general, in contravention of the fact that true science can know no national boundaries but, as emphasized at the recent meeting of the American Association for the Advancement of Science, is built up by the combined efforts of conscientiously and objectively working investigators the world over. [19]

On November 25 Sir Henry Dale, a leading British scientist and also a winner of the Nobel Prize for Medicine, resigned his honorary membership in the Academy. He took this action as a "protest against the subjugation of science in the Soviet Union to political dogma" and the "disappearance of N. I. Vavilov" who had been a "great contributor to science for the whole world." [20]

---

[19] Copy of original letter.   [20] *New York Times*, November 26, 1948.

On December 14 the Presidium of the Academy of Science of the USSR responded to Professor Muller's letter of resignation. The communication closed with the following words:

> Professor Muller at one time was reputed to be a progressive scientist. This is not a very comfortable position in present-day America. In attacking the Soviet Union and Soviet science, Muller has gained the favor and recognition of all reactionary forces in the United States. Without any feeling of regret the Academy of Science of the USSR parts company with its former member, who has betrayed the interests of genuine science and openly passed over to the camp of the enemies of progress and science, of peace and democracy.[21]

This is doubtless the judgment which would have been passed on Orbeli, Dubinin, Schmalhausen, Zhebrak, and other Soviet scientists, if they had resisted the Central Committee of the Party of Lenin and Stalin. They held no passports to a free country.

Twelve days later the Presidium considered the case of Sir Henry Dale. In resolving to "deprive him of honorary membership in the Academy" the Presidium observed that "Professor Dale's consent to become an obedient tool of anti-democratic forces can arouse only a feeling of sorrow among all honest scientists of the world." [22] This action was approved at a plenary meeting of the Academy early in January. The meeting also provided an opportunity for at least one of the Soviet scientists who had been humbled by the Party to begin his long journey back to favor and respectability. Professor L. A. Orbeli, in whose interests the resignations of Muller and Dale had in part been tendered, "called attention to the fact that Professor Dale under the flag of the neutrality of science in reality defends the interests of certain political groups acting against genuine science and democracy." [23] For those scientists who capitulate the process of rehabilitation will doubtless continue over a period of years.

[21] *Pravda*, December 14, 1948.   [22] *Pravda*, December 26, 1948.
[23] *Pravda*, January 13, 1949.

CHAPTER SEVEN

EDUCATION AS A WEAPON

T HE PRESENT CHAPTER may be regarded as a capstone of nearly all that has gone before in the volume. The fact is difficult to conceive in the West that in the Soviet Union the term "education" is made to embrace all the processes and agencies involved in the moulding of the mind of both young and old. This means that the ways of life and all institutions have a recognized educational function and are under perpetual scrutiny from the standpoint of current Party policy. But it means more especially that certain branches of the culture which in other countries are supposed to enjoy a measure of independence are judged in the Soviet Union first of all in terms of their bearing on political education and propaganda. The resolutions of the Central Committee stress this point over and over again.

This vast educational enterprise includes the school system as one of its important branches. But it also includes as major divisions the press in all of its aspects, other media of mass communication such as the radio and television, all agencies of entertainment such as the theatre and the moving picture, literature and art in all of their forms, libraries, museums, and "parks of culture and rest," and all basic institutions of family and community. The trade union, the co-operative, the Red Army, and all organizations of the people are expected to perform educational functions. The Party, of course, with its societies for children and youth, falls under this category. Indeed, the Society of Young Pioneers and the League of Young Communists, the one enrolling about twelve

million boys and girls from ten to sixteen years of age and the
other with approximately seven million youth from fourteen to
twenty-three, are powerful and faithful arms of the Party. The
Soviet educational system constitutes the most gigantic and comprehensive marshalling of forces to shape the human mind in the
whole history of mankind. It is under the close supervision of the
central organs of the Party and is directed toward the achievement
of Party purposes. It is, indeed, as the Soviet leaders never tire of
repeating, a "weapon of Communism."

The way in which the Party exercises control is revealed in the
"ideological resolutions" on literature, the drama, the cinema,
music, and science. These resolutions were aimed directly at certain branches of the cultural apparatus and at certain specified
works, institutions, and persons in each branch. But their influence extended almost immediately to the farthest corners of the
system of thought control. People working in science, medicine,
and university teaching, for example, recognized that the Party
criticism of two literary journals in Leningrad had meaning for
them. Sometimes they sought to forestall expressions of displeasure on the part of the Central Committee by anticipating the
action of the Party and making the changes implicit in the expressed policy of the Party.

2

The impact of the resolutions on the system of public schools
was swift and far-reaching. But before this aspect of the matter is
considered, attention will be directed briefly to five closely related
developments: the founding of a special society for the waging of
ideological warfare, the critical appraisal of the work of the daily,
periodical, and book presses, the conversion of humor into a
"weapon of politics," the use of the official calendar for political
ends, and the reorganization and expansion of the Party schools.
Each of these moves will be reported briefly.

One of the most significant consequences of the ideological resolutions was the launching in June, 1947, of the All-Union Society for the Dissemination of Political and Scientific Knowledge. The purpose of the society was to carry on a vigorous and aggressive campaign to propagate throughout the Soviet Union the ideological positions contained in the resolutions. The organizers addressed the following appeal to "all leaders of Soviet science, literature, and art, and to the scientific, social, and other organizations and institutions of the Soviet Union":

We call upon all leaders of Soviet science and culture to work yet more actively in order to raise the socialist consciousness of the working people. Members of the Society must interpret through public lectures the foreign policy of the Soviet state, resolutely expose provocateurs of a new war and aggression, reveal the falsity and limitations of bourgeois democracy, and unmask the reactionary essence of the ideology of the contemporary imperialistic bourgeoisie and its reformist lackeys. It is necessary to show in the lectures the advantages of the Soviet social and state order over capitalism, the successes of economic construction in the USSR, the achievements of Soviet science, literature, and art, and the tasks confronting the Soviet people. We must show the grandeur of our socialist Motherland and cultivate in the Soviet people a feeling of pride in the Soviet land, in our heroic Soviet people. At the same time we must conduct a decisive battle against the tendency of some citizens of the USSR to grovel before the contemporary bourgeois culture. The duty of the members of the Society is to explain the most important questions of Marxist-Leninist ideology, to propagandize a materialistic world outlook, and to struggle against all kinds of unscientific views and all vestiges of foreign ideology persisting in the consciousness of the people.[1]

Apparently the Society has been well-financed. Certainly it has been very active and has devoted itself to the purposes outlined in the appeal. It has organized many lectures and issued a veritable flood of propaganda pamphlets. These pamphlets are from ten to fifteen thousand words in length and are published in first editions

1 *Bolshevik,* No. 11, June 15, 1947, pp. 4–5.

ranging from sixty-five thousand to one hundred and fifty thousand copies. They sell for sixty or seventy-five kopecks, five or six cents, per copy. The following titles convey a fairly good idea of the range and emphasis in the pamphlets: *The Party of Lenin and Stalin — the Guiding and Directing Force of Soviet Society, The Soviet Union — the Leading Force in the Democratic Camp, The Soviet Union in the Struggle for the Freedom and Independence of Peoples, The Marxist-Leninist World View — the Greatest Conquest of Mankind, The Great October Revolution and the Formation of the New Man, On Soviet Patriotism, On Soviet Patriotism in Literature, On the Patriotic Duty of the Soviet Intelligentsia, The Crisis of Bourgeois Democracy, The Philosophizing Henchmen of American Reaction,* and *Race "Theories" and Discrimination in Anglo-American Countries.* These pamphlets of the Society are supplemented by a great volume of publications on similar themes under other auspices.

In the ideological struggle the daily press could not long be overlooked, for Stalin once said that "it is the sharpest and most powerful weapon of our Party." So in the spring of 1948 the entire Soviet press was haled before the bar of Party criticism and asked to render an account of its stewardship. Very fittingly this movement was launched on May 5, the day of the year long celebrated in the Soviet Union as "Bolshevik Press Day," commemorating the first issue of *Pravda* on May 5, 1912. An All-Moscow Conference of Workers of the Press was held in the famous Hall of Columns.[2] From Moscow the conference spread during the following month to other great centers of the country.

The Moscow conference was called by the Department of Propaganda and Agitation of the Central Committee of the All-Union Communist Party and was addressed, according to Party custom, by the Acting Director of the Department, L. F. Ilichev. The following brief account of the conference appeared in *Pravda*, May 6:

In his address Comrade Ilichev pointed to the great rôle which the Bolshevik press, created by V. I. Lenin and I. V. Stalin, has played in the revolutionary struggle of the peoples of our Motherland. "The press," so teaches Stalin, "is the most powerful weapon with which the Party speaks daily and hourly to the working class in its own language. No other comparable instrument, no other comparable apparatus, exists in nature for strengthening the spiritual ties between Party and class."

The entire road of our press is illuminated with the light of scientific socialism. It is precisely for this reason that it fulfills successfully its rôle of collective propagandist, agitator, and organizer. The fundamental characteristics of our press are inherent in its very nature; its mass character, its truthfulness, its closeness to the people.

The Soviet press confronts the great tasks of educating the working people in Communism and of struggling with the vestiges of capitalism in the consciousness of the people.

Comrade Ilichev emphasized that the Bolshevik Party attaches tremendous significance to the improvement of ideological work among the wide masses of the working people. Soviet journalists must remember that propagation of the great ideas of Communism is the noblest task of our press. . . .

"The Party has entrusted to the workers of the Bolshevik press," said L. F. Ilichev in conclusion, "one of the most responsible and militant tasks in the universal struggle for the building of Communism. Let us therefore give all our strength, knowledge, and experience to the cause of serving the great Party of Lenin and Stalin, to our heroic Soviet people!"

With tremendous enthusiasm those participating in the conference agreed to send a letter of greetings to Comrade Stalin.

On May 19 and 20 another conference was held in Moscow under the auspices of the Division of Propaganda of the Central Committee of the Party. The meeting was directed primarily to the book press and was attended by directors of publishing houses, editors of central newspapers and journals, representatives of ministries and administrative organs, and various Party workers. This conference, which was followed by similar meetings in the capitals of the Union Republics, devoted itself primarily to questions of ideology and Party loyalty in the work of the publishing houses.[3]

At the conference in Moscow the discussion was led again by

[3] *Kultura i Zhizn*, May 21, 1948.

L. F. Ilichev, Acting Director of the Division of Propaganda and Agitation. He declared that the resolutions of the Central Committee on literature, the drama, the cinema, and music "raise the level of all the means of socialist culture and mark a new stage in the ideological work of our Party." He also called upon "all workers on the ideological front to be guided in all their activities by the principles of Bolshevik Party loyalty." The May 21 issue of *Kultura i Zhizn* reports the conference in a leading article entitled "For Bolshevik Party Loyalty and High Ideology in the Work of Publishing Houses." The following excerpts give the substance of the article:

An examination of the activity of certain central publishing houses and the discussion of the question of publishing at the conference revealed serious shortcomings and mistakes in . . . this important field of ideological work. . . . In 1947 the Publishing House of the State Planning Commission published a number of injurious books in which the contemporary problems of bourgeois economics are treated objectively. Most publications suffer from a non-political approach in analyzing the economics of imperialistic countries. The books fail to expose the organic relation between economics and the policy of imperialism and to analyze the basic differences between socialist and bourgeois economics. Such mistakes are the result of the dulling of Bolshevik vigilance among some workers in publishing houses. . . .

A care-free and complacent spirit is intolerable everywhere and is especially intolerable on the ideological front. Workers in publishing houses must raise their revolutionary vigilance and strengthen their warfare against bourgeois ideology. . . . Publishers must realize fully their responsibility before the Party and the Soviet people and take all necessary steps to improve the ideological and scientific level of books published.

A Soviet publishing house [said Comrade Ilichev], regardless of its literary specialty, cannot be merely a mailbox which accepts everything sent to it. It must be an ideological fortress against which each and all attempts to drag in an ideology alien to our Party and our people are shattered to bits.

Soviet publishing houses must abandon once and for all their care-free and complacent mood and raise their Bolshevik vigilance. Party members commissioned to supervise publishing work must assume a more active rôle in the struggle against the depraved and infamous ideology of capitalism and against bourgeois objectivity. They must battle for purity of Communist ideology. . . .

The speaker mentioned several books which contain ideological errors and in which Marxist-Leninist theory is perverted. He referred particularly to the works of M. Bokishizky, *Technological and Economic Changes in the Industry of the USA during the Second World War* and *Changes in the Economy of Raw Materials and Fuel during the Second World War,* which give an objective analysis of the economy of capitalist countries . . .

An analysis of the errors in these books, said Comrade Ilichev, leads to the conclusion that we are confronted with an attempt on the part of some writers to disparage socialist ideology in some measure. And every "disparagement, every repudiation of socialist ideology means the strengthening of bourgeois ideology." (V. Lenin.) . . .

Some publishers [said Comrade Ilichev] regard scientific and technical literature as unrelated to ideology. They think that such literature is ideologically and politically unconditioned and presumably stands outside of politics and ideology. They assume that it is to be judged only by scientific and technical standards. That such a view is evil is entirely obvious.

In speaking of translations of foreign literature, the speaker emphasized particularly that books written by bourgeois authors require qualifying introductions which explain to the readers the basic content of the book and subject its shortcomings to Marxian criticism. . . .

Party organizations and directors of publishing houses are not insisting sufficiently that editors master Marxian theory and acquaint themselves fully with questions of the domestic and foreign policy of the USSR. Workers in publishing houses must constantly improve their Marxist-Leninist education in order to carry the principle of Party loyalty into literature and wage successful warfare against all signs of bourgeois ideology.

Publishers and particularly their directing personnel, said the speaker, are assigned by the Party of Lenin and Stalin to one of the most important positions on the ideological front, to its advanced line. The abundance of the spiritual culture of our Soviet people, creator and builder of Communist society, depends in large measure on the work of publishers. And it is our task to launch with Bolshevik passion and enthusiasm an immediate campaign for the correction of errors. We must fulfill those lofty and honorable demands which Comrade Stalin makes on workers on the ideological front. . . .

One of the most extraordinary resolutions ever issued by the Central Committee of the Party appeared on September 11, 1948. It is directed toward the "politicalization" of humor! In the West and in almost all other parts of the world there is a time-honored notion that laughter is good in itself and that the creator of laughter, if he does nobody harm through his jokes, is a public benefactor and worthy of honor. But the members of the Central Committee are wiser. They maintain that humor, like artillery, is a "weapon whose effect depends on who holds it in his hands and at whom it is aimed." And they seem to maintain further that laughter is not to be wasted but rather is a valuable form of energy which should be harnessed to some useful purpose.

The resolution was heralded by certain statements appearing in the Soviet press at the time of the conference of publishers in May. On the twenty-first of that month *Kultura i Zhizn,* organ of the Administration of Propaganda and Agitation of the Central Committee, warned a certain humorist, Arkadii Paikin by name, that "recently his humor over the radio is nothing more than laughter for laughter's sake." The journal went on to remark that the practice of building a newspaper column on anecdotes "is a trick of bourgeois columnists and brings nothing but vulgar trivial mockery and caricature of Soviet life and institutions." It also objects to any article "built on a most humorous incident," if it fails to "benefit our general cause, if it fails to educate anyone, if it teaches nothing." One can only imagine how a Soviet version of the Gridiron Club, lampooning the great and the near-great, including Stalin himself, socialist construction, and the "great Soviet people," would be received. But one would not have to imagine long. Here are the relevant parts of the resolution of the Central Committee which was directed at the famous humorous journal, *Krokodil.*[4]

The Central Committee of the Party pointed out that the journal *Krokodil* is conducted in an entirely unsatisfactory manner and is not a militant organ of Soviet satire and humor.

The editors of the journal are divorced from life, work without a plan, and fail to maintain the necessary ideological and artistic level

[4] *Kultura i Zhizn,* September 11, 1948.

in articles, stories, verses, and drawings. Undistinguished and inartistic material predominates. The appearance of the journal is unattractive, is printed on poor paper, and uses colors of inferior quality. Its make-up lacks taste, originality, and artistic imagination. . . .

The Central Committee of the Party has relieved Comrade G. E. Riklin of the duties of editor and has appointed in his place Comrade D. G. Beliaev. . . .

The resolution of the Central Committee of the Party points out that the chief task of the journal is the struggle against remnants of capitalism in the consciousness of people. By means of satire the journal must expose thieves of public property, grafters, bureaucrats, and every manifestation of boastfulness, servility, or vulgarity. It must respond quickly to burning international events and subject the bourgeois culture of the West to criticism, revealing its ideological insignificance and degeneracy.

The Central Committee of the Party has called upon the editorial board of the journal . . . to acquaint readers with the best materials printed in local humorous journals and in journals of the countries of the people's democracy, and with the satirical writings of progressive foreign writers. The journal should publish documentary photographs from foreign papers and journals with sharp political comments.

An interesting organ of Soviet propaganda is the official and only Soviet calendar. Indeed, it is one of the most revealing documents in the whole field of education. Addressed to the entire Russian people and containing more than one thousand political items, it is prepared with great care and is regarded as an ideological weapon in the struggle for Communist objectives and against enemies at home and abroad. Through pictures of persons and scenes, homiletic verses and sayings, quotations from speeches and writings of the great, commemorations of important events and achievements, it strives to mould the popular mind according to the desired pattern. Each of its pages and each item on a page is devoted to teaching a lesson, arousing an interest, conveying an idea, propagating a value, or inculcating a loyalty. Each instance of commemoration in the Soviet calendar has some political purpose. The Central Committee would be as hostile toward "commemoration for commemoration's sake" as toward "art for art's sake," or "science for science's sake," or "laughter for laughter's sake." Everything is for the sake of politics. Consequently the direction of Soviet policy can be gauged in some measure by the subjects chosen for recognition in the calendar.

The calendar for 1949 is a remarkable document. It is published in a huge Russian edition of five million copies. From January 1 to December 31 it reflects and supports the policies developed in the ideological resolutions. By means of quotations and pictures it tells in brilliant colors the story of Russian and Soviet greatness. No one can read through its pages without feeling proud that he is or sorry that he is not a Russian. It provides a purified and glorified record of achievement and pre-eminence in almost everything. Beginning with the visit to India in 1469 of Athanasius Nikitin and continuing down to the last day of the present "great Stalinist epoch," it leaves one almost breathless with the thought that one people could have accomplished so much in all the arts and sciences of life. The calendar is filled to overflowing with patriotic sentiments and unqualified praise of Russia and the Russians. "Firm in enterprise, tireless in execution — such are the distinguishing qualities of the Russian people," Radishchev tells the reader, and then adds: "Oh, people, born to greatness and glory." The paean is continued by Dobroliubov: "Our own Russia possesses us above all else. For her we labor tirelessly, unselfishly, and passionately." Along with many others, the great Tolstoy exclaims: "How can one not rejoice living in the midst of such a people? How can one not expect everything beautiful of such a people?" The heroic episodes and creative minds of the Russian past are all identified with the appropriate days of the year.

For the Soviet epoch emphasis is placed on scenes from the revolution, the civil war, and the Great Patriotic War, from socialist construction, collective agriculture, and industrial technique, from Soviet dances, sports, and cultural activities, and from the life and labor of the "new people's democracies." In these select pages appear the pictures of the great, from both the dead and the living. To be placed in this hallowed company is undoubtedly one of the most highly coveted honors. Lenin and Stalin of course

top the list with fifteen appearances each. Then the birth of each
of the other members of the Politburo is commemorated. In addition three scientists and five artists and writers among the living,
as well as several representatives from the heroes of socialist labor,
culture, and sport, are included. Strangely enough, although
Russian valor runs through the calendar as a vital theme, not a
single living commander is found in the gallery of pictures.
Suvorov is there, to be sure, with his modest boast: "Nothing will
stand against Russian arms — we are strong and confident." Also
a number of other great soldiers of the past. The Party view seems
to be that a general, unless he is a member of the Politburo, can
be safely honored only after he is dead.

The contribution of the rest of the world to the company of
Soviet heroes includes of course Marx and Engels and a number
of other revolutionary leaders such as Garibaldi and Thaelmann.
Tito, by the way, is gone. The calendar also commemorates the
birth or the death of some twenty giants in the arts and sciences
of the West, from Dante, Leonardo, Galileo, and Shakespeare to
Diderot, Beethoven, Darwin, Pasteur, and Anatole France. Among
contemporary figures only avowed friends of the Soviet Union are
included, and then scarcely at all. Presumably capitalism, though
fertile in its days of youth and vigor, is incapable of nurturing
creative genius in its declining and "decadent" years. The only
reference in the calendar which might be construed as favorable
to the United States is the commemoration of the discovery of
America by Columbus in 1492.

A great change has come over the Soviet calendar since 1945.
The issue of that year breathed a friendly spirit toward the West.
It commemorated with pictures the Anglo-Soviet alliance formed
in May, 1942, the visit of Molotov to the White House in the
same year, the Teheran conference in November, 1943, a dinner
in the Kremlin in honor of Winston Churchill in October, 1944.
The calendar spoke with warmth of the "unanimity of opinion
and co-ordination of action among the three Great Powers" and
of the principle of "mutual aid in the prosecution of the war
against aggression." It printed Stalin's tribute to the Allies on the

landing on the shores of Normandy. And it included pictures of Churchill, Eden, Roosevelt, Harriman, and other English and American leaders. By 1949 the good will of the war years is gone. Instead there are three bitter cartoons directed first of all toward the United States, one on the Marshall Plan, a second on "freedom" of the bourgeois press, and a third on the state under capitalism. The calendar for 1949 contains not a single friendly reference to the collaboration of the war years. The "forcing of the Channel" is forgotten and the tribute of Stalin erased from the record.

Each issue of the Soviet calendar designates certain days for the intensive propagation of desired ideas and loyalties. On these days the press is filled with special articles and items dealing with the subject being celebrated. The radio and other agencies of mass communication add their voices in a powerful and harmonious chorus of propaganda. Below is given the list of special days for 1949. The strong military emphasis is readily apparent.

JANUARY	22	DAY IN MEMORY OF V. I. LENIN
FEBRUARY	23	DAY OF THE SOVIET ARMY
MARCH	8	INTERNATIONAL WOMAN'S DAY
MARCH	18	DAY OF THE PARIS COMMUNE
MAY	1	INTERNATIONAL HOLIDAY OF THE TOILERS
MAY	5	DAY OF THE BOLSHEVIK PRESS
MAY	7	DAY OF THE RADIO
MAY	9	HOLIDAY OF VICTORY
JULY	17	ALL-UNION DAY OF PHYSICAL CULTURE
JULY	24	DAY OF THE SOVIET NAVY
AUGUST	7	DAY OF THE SOVIET RAILROAD MAN
AUGUST	18	DAY OF THE SOVIET AIR FLEET
AUGUST	28	DAY OF THE MINER
SEPTEMBER	3	HOLIDAY OF THE VICTORY OVER JAPAN
SEPTEMBER	11	DAY OF THE TANKISTS
NOVEMBER	7	THIRTY-SECOND YEAR OF THE GREAT OCTOBER SOCIALIST REVOLUTION
NOVEMBER	19	DAY OF ARTILLERY
DECEMBER	5	DAY OF THE STALINIST CONSTITUTION

The adoption after the war of a militant and aggressive policy toward the West and the revival of the revolutionary mood and hopes of 1917 placed before the Party the urgent task of training and retraining its personnel. The condition itself and the measures undertaken by the Central Committee to meet it are set forth frankly in an address given by George M. Malenkov in September, 1947, at the famous meeting of representatives of European Communist Parties. Speaking as a member of the Politburo and Secretary of the Central Committee, he reported on the activity of the Central Committee of the All-Union Communist Party. Toward the end of his address he emphasized the great importance of "assisting the millions of workers in the Party and the state apparatus to master Marxist-Leninist science and to arm themselves with knowledge of the laws of social development, with knowledge of the economy of the country and the economic policy of the Soviet government, and also with an understanding of questions pertaining to the international situation and Soviet foreign policy — a task of supreme importance over which the Party is working now." [5] He then told of the plan already well under way to reconstruct, expand, and improve the Party's own system of schools.

Few Americans realize that in addition to the regular system of schools open to the people generally there is in the Soviet Union a second system at the youth and adult level designed to provide that special kind of preparation necessary for Party members and particularly for Party functionaries and leaders. Since its central function is the training of the Communist priesthood, it may be likened to the theological schools which have been maintained by religious sects and theocratic states from time immemorial. Moreover, wherever the Party may be found in strength in other countries, it endeavors to establish schools after the Russian model. There are several such schools in the United States which are to be distinguished primarily from their prototypes in the Soviet Union, not by their doctrinal emphasis, but by their names. After some years of experience American Communists sought the pro-

5 G. Malenkov, *Informational Report on the Activity of the Central Committee of the All-Union Communist Party* (Moscow, 1947), pp. 24–25. (In Russian.)

tective coloration of such glorious democratic names as Benjamin Franklin, Thomas Jefferson, and Abraham Lincoln.

The Soviet system in its postwar structure, according to Malenkov, is organized on three levels. At the first level, as of September, 1947, there were 177 "two-year Party Schools and nine-month courses" enrolling "about 30,000 Party, Soviet, Komsomol, and newspaper workers." These institutions prepare for the lower posts in Party and state. At the second level is a three-year Higher Party School which prepares a smaller number for positions in the upper ranges of the Party and state apparatus. In 1947 approximately one thousand students were enrolled. At the third and highest level is the Academy of Social Sciences. This institution is "called upon to prepare theoretical workers for central Party institutions, Central Committees of the Communist Parties of the Union Republics, regional and provisional committees of the Party, and also qualified teachers for higher technical schools and universities and theoretical workers for scientific-research institutions and scientific journals." That the Academy, though only recently organized, is destined to play a central rôle in the entire cultural life of the country in the years to come is indicated by the nature and breadth of its program. It is supposed to prepare "workers in the following special fields: political economy, the economics and politics of foreign states, political and legal theory, international law, history of the USSR, general history, international relations, history of the All-Union Communist Party, dialectical and historical materialism, history of Russian and West European philosophy, logic and psychology, science of literature, and science of art." [6] This system of Party schools rests upon a comprehensive network of "polit-schools" or "political schools" which are supposed to carry Party doctrine to the rank-and-file membership in factories, in shops and mines, and on collective farms.

The attention given to this system of Party schools and the founding of the Academy of Social Science demonstrate the utter seriousness of the postwar domestic and foreign policy on which

[6] *Ibid.*, pp. 25–26.

this action of the Party rests. The power of the ideological drive is also suggested by the unprecedented scale of the publication and distribution of the sacred scriptures of Communism. Thus, according to Malenkov, during the first two postwar years "the various classical works of Marxism-Leninism were published to the number of more than ninety million copies." There were printed in the same period also ten million copies of the *Short History of the All-Union Communist Party*. And a *Short Biography of Stalin* which presents the "Great Leader" in a purified and glorified version, is being published and sold in millions of copies.[7] The Party is throwing the entire weight of its propaganda behind a campaign to arouse the people to read and study all the books of the Soviet Bible. The emphasis throughout is on the authenticity of the Communist apocalypse and the authority of the Communist prophets. By way of contrast one should know that approximately twenty-five million copies of the Christian Bible, published in over one thousand languages and dialects, are distributed throughout the world annually.

3

The Soviet system of public schools embraces a vast network of institutions from the nursery school and kindergarten through the primary and secondary schools and the various vocational, technical, and professional schools of different grades to the universities and scientific institutes and academies. By 1939, according to Stalin's report to the Eighteenth Congress of the Party, the total number of pupils and students of all ages attending these schools and classes part time or full time reached the tremendous figure of 47,422,100. After generous allowance is made for the "use of statistics as a political weapon," the material growth of the Soviet school system is extremely impressive.

The school of course is also a weapon. The Central Committee therefore has shaped and guided its development with great care.

[7] *Ibid.*, p. 27.

It has devoted time and energy not only to broad matters of philosophy, ideology, and program, but also to details of textbook preparation, teaching methods, and classroom organization. Nothing is too small or insignificant to engage its attention. On one occasion it issued a resolution fixing the number and length of the recess periods for the primary school.

The ideological resolutions of the Central Committee of August and September, 1946, calling for an assault on Western "bourgeois" culture and for the glorification of Soviet life and institutions, had an immediate impact on the schools and on all references to the educational practices of other countries and particularly of the United States. The first issue thereafter of *Sovietskaia Pedagogika*, official organ of the Academy of Pedagogical Science of the RSFSR, devoted its leading editorial to the resolutions under the title, "For Bolshevik Ideology in Soviet Pedagogical Science." [8] The editorial proclaimed that "the serious shortcomings exposed recently by the Central Committee on the ideological front are unquestionably present in our pedagogical sciences," that "the ideological training of our youth is above all political," that "we must not forget for a moment that every science is Party science," that "teaching cannot be divorced from the politics of Party and state," that "workers in pedagogical science must first of all study stubbornly, persistently, and consistently the science of sciences — the Marxist-Leninist theory," and that they "must become bold and militant propagandists of the great Communist ideas of educating the new man." The editorial reported also that the resolutions "stirred profoundly the whole of Soviet society." It is entirely appropriate to note here that in the Middle Ages under the dominion of the Church theology was called the "queen of the sciences." The parallel would appear to be quite close.

During the next twelve months meetings and conferences of teachers and educators were held throughout the country to consider the work of the schools in the light of the resolutions of the Central Committee. At a meeting of the members of the Academy of Pedagogical Science on October 11, 1946, the President of the

[8] *Sovietskaia Pedagogika*, No. 10–11, October–November, 1946, pp. 3–8.

Academy, I. A. Kairov, delivered an address in which he drew the obvious conclusions. "The Central Committee of the Party," he said, "demands that all workers on the ideological front, and consequently workers in pedagogical science, understand that they are placed in the advanced line of fire." [9] On April 17 and 18, 1947, the Ministry of Education of the RSFSR held a conference with teachers and educational workers from Moscow and Leningrad. The addresses and reports given at the meeting revealed that the resolutions of the Central Committee had "shaken the Moscow and Leningrad teaching body and aroused a great creative upsurge in their work," and had stimulated the majority to study "independently the history of the All-Union Communist Party and the writings of Comrade Stalin." [10] An All-Russian conference of heads of departments of pedagogy, psychology, and methods of teaching in pedagogical institutes and teacher training schools met in conference from July 1 to 8, 1947, in Moscow. The leading speaker warned that conditions in the institutions represented were far from satisfactory, that "many faculties have not as yet understood their tasks," and that their work had not improved "in the light of the resolutions of the Central Committee." He declared further that "some faculties and their leaders" had "failed to draw the necessary inferences" and had "not grasped as yet the fact that the resolutions on literature and art have significance in principle for all ideological work." [11]

The attention of teachers was quickly directed to the application of the resolutions to the various subjects of study in the public schools. The teachers of natural science are told that their "chief aim" is "to arm the students with knowledge" so that they may "achieve a conscious mastery of the natural-scientific foundations of the Communist world outlook." [12] A reviewer of a volume on the history of the Middle Ages says that "the very greatest fault of the textbook is its insufficiently high Bolshevik ideology." [13]

9 Ibid., No. 12, December, 1946, p. 3.
10 Ibid., No. 6, June, 1947, p. 120.
11 Ibid., No. 9, September, 1947, p. 116.
12 Ibid., No. 1, January, 1947, p. 27.   13 Ibid., No. 8, August, 1947, p. 23.

Geography of course has its obvious uses. Thus, "in comparing the USSR with capitalist countries" the teacher should "show the superiority of socialist over capitalist economy" and point out "that the USSR is certain to develop much more rapidly than any capitalist country, including the United States of America." [14] Literature should reveal to the young that "love for the socialist Motherland in Soviet people is joined with burning hatred toward her enemies." The writer then quotes from Stalin: "You cannot defeat an enemy without learning to hate him with all your soul." [15]

The program of teacher training was sharply criticized at many points. Instruction in psychology was subjected to careful review. A writer on this question opens with the observation that "psychology is first of all a world-view subject." He then asserts that the "correct formation of the Communist world-view demands a knowledge of scientific psychology" and that "this thesis acquires peculiar significance because of the necessity for a decisive and irreconcilable struggle against foreign idealistic and decadent teachings." [16] In the teaching of the history of education it is necessary to present a "much clearer picture of the *latest contemporary bourgeois pedagogy*." The instructor should point out "that the majority of the representatives of *contemporary* West-European and American educational theory actually serve reactionary political purposes under a mask of 'objectivity,' 'scientific approach,' and 'love for the child.' " The writer notes that the "rôle of Dewey is very significant in this connection." [17] Soviet educational journals overflow with materials of this general character.

14 *Ibid.*, No. 9, September, 1947, p. 30.   15 *Ibid.*, No. 2, February, 1948, p. 10.
16 *Ibid.*, No. 7, July, 1947, p. 73.   17 *Ibid.*, No. 10, October, 1947, p. 84.

4

The discussion of the impact of the ideological resolutions on the Soviet public schools will be closed with excerpts from an address delivered under the auspices of the All-Union Society for the Dissemination of Political and Scientific Knowledge on October 24, 1947. The subject was "Thirty Years of Soviet Education" and the speaker A. G. Kalashnikov, Minister of Education of the RSFSR. The entire address of more than twelve thousand words would be of great interest to American teachers, but only those portions which deal with the subject of the present volume are included in this account. In his opening paragraphs the speaker, one of the foremost Russian educational leaders, summarizes briefly the current Soviet orientation: [18]

The thirty years of the existence of the Soviet state are thirty years of struggle — thirty years of victories which the Soviet people have conquered under the banner of Lenin, under the leadership of Stalin. During these years a new and most progressive social and governmental system has been created in our country. A socialist industry has been established and the collectivisation of rural economy has been carried through successfully. Under the leadership of the Communist Party a genuine cultural revolution has been achieved, resulting in the extension of education to the widest masses of the people.

The Soviet Union has become the center of a progressive socialist culture, a light to illuminate the road for other peoples and states. The prophetic words of the great Russian critic Belinsky have been fulfilled. Looking into the future of Russia (in 1840), he wrote: "We envy our grandchildren and great-grandchildren who are destined to see Russia in 1940 standing at the head of the civilized world, giving laws to science and art and receiving reverent tribute from all enlightened humanity."

For the first time in the history of mankind education has become

[18] A. G. Kalashnikov, *Thirty Years of Soviet Education* (Moscow, 1947), 31 pages. (In Russian.)

actually popular, that is, accessible to all the people and directed to the satisfaction of the interests of the people.

In questions of public education the Bolshevik Party has been led by the Lenin-Stalin teaching of the intimate relation of the school to politics.

" . . . Education," as Comrade Stalin pointed out in his conversation with H. G. Wells, "is a weapon, whose effect depends on who holds it in his hands and at whom it is aimed." [19] In capitalist society the school is a weapon in the hands of the bourgeoisie for the ideological enslavement of the workers, a weapon for the strengthening of their ruling position. The bourgeoisie in fact deprive the working masses of education, doling it out to the people only in the measure that satisfies their interests.

The class character of education in pre-revolutionary Russia was often exposed in the writings of Lenin and Stalin. In the words of V. I. Lenin, the popular masses in Russia, "from the point of view of education, were robbed of light and knowledge." The class or caste school of tsarist Russia nurtured, on the one hand, gentlemen, and, on the other, servile slaves and efficient workers capable only of giving profits without being troublesome to their masters.

In 1913 in exposing the anti-people's character of the activity of the Ministry of Public Education under the leadership of the vicious reactionary, Kasso, V. I. Lenin wrote: "The working class . . . will know how to prove . . . its ability in the revolutionary struggle for genuine freedom and for a genuinely classless and casteless public education." [20]

The bourgeois theoreticians and politicians always strove to conceal the class character and political direction of the school, to cloak it with long discourses about the "neutrality" and the "universal quality" of education, expressing hypocritical indignation toward the Marxist-Leninist position about the relation of the school to politics. Through the voice of V. I. Lenin the Communist Party sharply and clearly declared to the whole world that "a school outside of life, outside of politics is a lie and an hypocrisy." Also Marx wrote: "The most enlightened part of the working class fully recognizes that the future of its class and consequently the future of mankind as a whole depend on the education of the rising generation."

And by bringing the great masses of workers and peasants in contact

[19] I. Stalin, Talk with the English Writer, H. G. Wells, p. 17. *Partisdat*, 1935.
[20] V. I. Lenin, *Works*, vol. XVI, p. 416.

with culture, by educating the young in the spirit of Communism, our Soviet school has become the instrument of a cultural revolution, a weapon for the Communist rebirth of society.

Throughout the entire course of its history Soviet education, both in its ideological content and in its methods and organization, has been determined by the politics of the Communist Party.

After giving a brief account of the development of Soviet education during the early years of the Revolution, Kalashnikov returns to the question of purposes and controlling philosophy:

The aims and tasks of the Soviet school, which determined the content and the organization of its work, were formulated in a program of the Party, adopted at the Eighth Congress in 1919. The Party set as its goal the completion of the task begun by the October Revolution of converting the school from a weapon of the class state of the bourgeoisie into a weapon for the complete annihilation of the division of society into classes, into a weapon for the Communist rebirth of society.

For the first time a great reformative function was imposed on the school. It was confronted with the task of the nurture of a new man, free from the slavish psychology of capitalist society. In achieving the tasks of Communist education the school had to provide an all-round development of its pupils, to make of them rational and cultured people, to form in them a scientific-materialistic point of view, to instill in them a Communist morality.

The task was imposed on the school of becoming an exponent of the principles of Communism through the widest masses of the toilers, of becoming the organizer of the educative influence of the proletariat and its vanguard — the Communist Party — on the semi-proletarian and non-proletarian toiling masses. The Party regarded the school, not as a self-inclosed educational institution, but as an educational center, disseminating Communist ideology and Communist morality outside the school, and above all in the family.

As the Soviet state grew and developed, the principles governing the education of the rising generation, which formed the basis of the work of the Soviet school from the beginning of the Great October Socialist Revolution, were clarified, broadened, and made concrete. The classical works of Lenin and Stalin laid the theoretical foundation of Soviet pedagogy — a new Soviet science of the education of children.

Kalashnikov proceeds at this point to draw in broad outlines an impressive picture of the material growth of the Soviet educational system down to the close of the war. He then pauses to report an ideological struggle which developed in connection with Stalin's rise to power and which has some bearing on present tendencies:

However, during the years 1925–30 deviations from the instructions of Lenin were observed in school practice. The obsequiousness and genuflection on the part of some Soviet educators before the educational theory and practice of Western Europe and America led to the uncritical introduction into the Soviet school of methods of education evolved by reactionary bourgeois pedagogy. This found its expression in the so-called complex programs, the project method, the Dalton Plan, and the laboratory brigade method, which were imposed on Soviet schools. These injurious methods of teaching hampered the work of our schools and prevented them from carrying on the serious general educational preparation of pupils demanded by the Party and the country.

The struggle of the Trotskyist and right-opportunist elements against the general line of the Party during the period found its counterpart in the field of pedagogy. The Party was obliged to conduct a decisive warfare, on the one hand, with the leftist, anti-Leninist "theory of the withering away of the school," and, on the other hand, with the right-opportunist elements who strove to preserve the remnants of the old scholastic school and disregard the socialist nature of the Soviet school.

The Party exposed all of these anti-Leninist tendencies and straightened out the line of development of the Soviet school. Of historic significance in this respect was the resolution of the Central Committee of the Communist Party of September 5, 1931, "On the Primary and Secondary School."

While recognizing great strides in the field of school work, the Central Committee stated that the Soviet school is far from complying with the demands made upon it by the contemporary stage of socialist construction. The school had failed to give the necessary body of basic knowledge and consequently had failed to prepare for entrance into technicums and higher schools fully literate people who had mastered well the foundations of science.

The Central Committee pointed out that teaching in schools must rest on the basis of definite, carefully prepared courses of study and teaching plans organized within the framework of a firm schedule of studies. As a guide for all further work of the school the Central Committee proposed the use of the instructions of Lenin given as early as 1920 in his comments on the theses of N. K. Krupskaia "On Polytechnical Education" at the Third Congress of the League of Young Communists.

Having condemned all anti-Leninist tendencies in educational theory and practice, the Party suggested that the school employ those methods of teaching which contribute to the education of active and energetic participants in socialist construction. It also pointed to the necessity of strengthening the struggle against all attempts to indoctrinate children in the Soviet school with the elements of a non-proletarian ideology.

This resolution played an outstanding rôle in the life of the Soviet school and served as the most important theoretical and practical weapon in the struggle for the improvement of the quality of instruction.

In subsequent years the Party adopted a number of significant resolutions, directed toward the further improvement of school work and the development of Soviet pedagogy. Especially noteworthy was the resolution of the Central Committee of the Communist Party of August 25, 1932, "On Courses of Study and the Regimen of Primary and Secondary Schools." The resolution stated that the basic form of the organization of instruction in primary and secondary schools must be the recitation with a careful classification of all pupils and a systematic schedule of studies. Thus the time-tested class-recitation system was restored to its rightful place in the schools. The same resolution outlined a series of concrete instructions on methods of teaching and the strengthening of the leading rôle of the teacher in the organization of educational work and the struggle for conscious discipline in the school.

The remarks of Comrades I. V. Stalin, A. A. Zhdanov, and S. M. Kirov on outlines for textbooks in the History of the USSR and the New History constituted a document of large ideological and theoretical value, played an important rôle in developing a correct conception of the work of the school, and gave a genuinely scientific Marxist direction to the teaching of history.

During the succeeding years Soviet pedagogy achieved new successes.

The rout of the so-called pedology, which had been introduced into our school by worshippers of foreign, chiefly American, bourgeois pedagogy, was completed. The Central Committee of the Party in its resolution of July 4, 1936, "On Pedological Perversions in the System of Narkompros," exposed this pseudo-science which was founded on false premises concerning the nature of the child, unmasked its reactionary-bourgeois essence, and demanded the full restoration of the rights of pedagogy and teachers. The resolution played a fruitful rôle in the activity of the Soviet school and in the development of pedagogical science.

The same rôle was played by the instructions of the Eighteenth Congress of the Party on the significance of Communist education and the overcoming of the remnants of capitalism in the consciousness of the people — builders of Communism. In this Congress Comrade Molotov said: "On the success of Communist education in the broad meaning of the word, of Communist education embracing the entire mass of workers and the entire Soviet intelligentsia — first of all, on our successes in this sphere depends the resolution of all other problems." [21]

The decisions of the Eighteenth Congress of the Party demanded that the school improve decisively the Communist education of pupils and insure that general educational, ideological, and cultural preparation of the younger generation which would meet the growing demands of the Soviet people. The Congress set itself the task of achieving universal secondary education in the city and universal seven-year education in the village.

This account reveals clearly the rôle which the Central Committee of the Party has played in the development of Soviet education in the past. A little further on the speaker returns to the question of doctrine and introduces the ideological resolutions of the Central Committee:

And now when our country is achieving the grandiose plan for the restoration and development of the public economy, questions of the instruction and ideological education of the young continue to stand in the center of the attention of the Party and the entire people.

[21] Address by Comrade Molotov on the Third Five-Year Plan of Development of the Public Economy. Stenographic record of the 18th Congress of the All-Union Party of Bolsheviks, p. 312. 1939.

The historic resolutions of the Central Committee of the Party on the question of ideological work, approved in 1946, were particularly significant in the life of the school. In the postwar period, when the reactionary bourgeoisie passed over to attack on the ideological front, employing the weapon of the lie and slander in order to revile the Soviet social order and to discredit socialist culture, the struggle with reactionary ideology and decaying bourgeois culture took on a peculiarly sharp character. The Party demanded of all workers on the educational front, including the Soviet teaching body, the strengthening of political vigilance and Bolshevik Party loyalty. The Party set before the school the task of educating our youth to become cultured people, ideologically mature, with high moral standards, firm, energetic, able to overcome obstacles.

The Party declared that the most important task of the school is the cultivation in the Soviet people of patriotism, national pride, and self-respect, the overcoming of the remnants of humility before the reactionary culture of the imperialistic bourgeoisie. The school was obligated to cultivate in pupils conscious pride in the great conquests of Soviet society, supreme loyalty to the Motherland, and readiness under the most difficult conditions to defend the interests and the honor of the Soviet state. These tasks demanded from the school and from the teaching profession the strengthening of the ideological and political direction of classroom studies, and also of the extracurricular and out-of-school education of pupils.

After comparing the new Soviet school with the old Russian school in terms of curriculum and instruction, Kalashnikov gives an account of the activity of non-school agencies. This brings him to a brief report on the rôle of the Young Communist and Pioneer organizations:

In the achievement of the task of Communist education, first among the assistants of the school are the League of Young Communists and the Pioneer organization which it guides.

The Young Communist and Pioneer organizations in the school aid the teachers in training future active builders of Communist society. By drawing the pupils into participation in social life, they contribute to their ideological-political and moral education and develop in them an earnest attitude toward their studies.

The results of the Soviet system of education are seen in the remarkable traits which our youth revealed in the years of the Stalinist Five-Year Plan when, trained in the realization that labor in our country is a matter of honor, valor, and heroism, they achieved genuine labor victories. Thus also in the years of the Great Patriotic War against fascism when the high understanding, deep patriotism, and lofty moral qualities of Soviet youth were a powerful factor in our victory over the enemy.

The high ideals of our school children are not infrequently revealed in school compositions. Already from the school benches Soviet children dream of serving their Fatherland, of heroic deeds which they will achieve in its name in the future. They are proud of their Motherland, of its heroic past, of its socialist present. Here, for example, is what Sasha S., a pupil of the fourth grade, writes in a class composition: "I was born and grew up in Smolensk, but my Motherland is the entire Soviet country. I am proud of the Soviet Motherland. I am proud that I am a Russian. There is no other such country as ours. All of our people have equal rights, and there is no oppression of nationalities. We are rich in everything and we need no assistance from foreigners."

The love of children for the Motherland is linked indissolubly with their love for Comrade Stalin. "There is one man," writes a pupil in the fourth grade, Vera F., "who has made our life happy and joyous. The entire country knows and loves him. His name is Stalin. This name lives in our hearts." [22]

And there is no doubt that under the leadership of the Party of Lenin and Stalin the Soviet school will achieve new successes in the achievement of lofty and responsible tasks in the education of the younger generation, builders of Communism.

Except for the final section, the remainder of the address is devoted to the Soviet teacher, special schools for adults and for urban and rural youth, the care of homeless children, pre-school education, and the perspectives of the development of the Soviet school and pedagogical science. These sections are extremely interesting to the American educator and tend to develop in the reader an attitude of good will. Then one turns the page to

[22] *Sovietskaia Pedagogika*, No. 8, 1947.

Kalashnikov's concluding remarks on "The Degradation of the School and Pedagogy in Bourgeois Countries." Here is the bitter fruit of the ideological resolutions of the Central Committee as they affected an important part of Soviet educational thought:

While in the Soviet Union genuine democratic and humanistic principles of education are being realized, in the schools of a number of countries, of so-called "bourgeois democracy," hypocrisy is being nurtured, hatred toward freedom-loving peoples and contempt for peoples not belonging to the white race are being inculcated. Science is falsified or altogether eliminated from the educational institutions of these countries.

Moral education, which should aim at the formation of noble qualities of human personality, is converted into the cultivation of the traits of the petty-huckster, the self-centered egoist, who sees the source and goal of human activity in money, in personal enrichment.

In an American journal, *The Baltimore Bulletin of Education* (No. 4, 1942), there appears a very characteristic article by Anne C. Phillips, "The Little Child's America," dedicated to questions of moral education. "At opening exercises," it is recommended in this article, "the class can be told that in some countries people are not allowed to read the bible. How fortunate are we in America to be able to read the word of god and pray to him. The lunch period is a time to give thanks to god for our food."

And this is how a teacher in a recitation explains the meaning of "freedom."

"For one thing freedom means that we in America are free to worship god and to pray to him in our homes and schools and churches. In America men and women are free to work and earn money. Aren't you glad that you live in America? Do you pray every day and thank god that you are an American, and ask him to bless America?"

Thus the thought is instilled in children that freedom is the right to earn money and to thank god for success in "business." Thus is inculcated the unconditional bowing-down before the dollar which is represented to them as a measure of the moral conduct of man.

The anti-democratic and anti-humanistic practice of American schools is in full accord with those pedagogical "theories" which are widely disseminated in contemporary America and are an expression of the class interests of American imperialists.

The famous American philosopher and educator, Dewey, in his book, *The Problems of Men,* attempts to prove that the purpose of education is to cultivate in the child those mental and moral tendencies and habits which would enable him to occupy the most comfortable and profitable position in society, that is, to become a shrewd "businessman."

The task of the school, "preaches" Dewey, is to nurture in the younger generation "an intelligent understanding of social life necessary for the strengthening of the new social orientation," that is, that warlike reaction which is propagated by American imperialists.

The depths to which bourgeois science has sunk is shown in a questionnaire, recently prepared and circulated by the famous American psychologist, Thorndike. The purpose of the "investigation" was to "measure the extent to which this or that pain or moral shock differs from another."

For a unit of measurement the dollar of course was selected. Students, teachers, and unemployed were the subjects of the "Research." The questionnaire asked, for example: "For how many dollars would you agree to eat a quarter of a pound of human flesh?" Certain students and teachers expressed the willingness to do this on the average for one million dollars, but certain unemployed — for a hundred thousand dollars. Students and teachers agreed to spit on the portrait of their mother for ten thousand dollars, whereas the unemployed asked for this twenty-five thousand dollars, etc.

Aside from the fact that the very circulation of such a questionnaire calls forth a feeling of most extreme loathing on the part of every person who has not lost all humane feelings, the content of the answers bears witness to those "fruits of education," which American pedagogy is reaping. Everything is for sale and everything is to be bought. Whatever brings profit is moral. Such is the code of morality cultivated in the American school. Such is the true content of bourgeois education.

If in the Soviet Union from year to year the network of educational institutions and the number of pupils increase, in the countries of capitalistic Europe and America public education is on the decline.

The educational department of the *New York Times* conducted for six months an investigation of the schools of the United States. Here are some of the findings presented by the editor of the department, Fine.

Since 1940, 350,000 teachers have left the schools of the United States. Two million children receive instruction of poor quality because of the inadequate preparation of the teacher: 125,000 teachers, or every seventh teacher, are inadequately prepared for their work, do not have the appropriate training, and are employed on the basis of a temporary certificate. Sixty thousand teachers have received no more than secondary-school training, and thirty thousand teaching posts are vacant.

The rural school in America is in a particularly impoverished position. In rural communities twenty per cent of the children leave school without completing the course, fifty-nine per cent drop out of secondary school, and up to ninety per cent do not reach higher schools. The cause of such a phenomenon is very simple: children of workers do not have the means for the completion of education.

Approximately the same situation exists in the public schools of other countries of so-called "bourgeois democracy." In 1944 in England a new law was passed concerning public education which presupposed, it would seem, an extension of the system of schooling. However, in reality the law remains law and life remains life.

In an English journal, *The Times Education Supplement of* February 23, 1946, the results of a study of the knowledge and skills acquired by children in the elementary school are presented. "School studies," writes the journal, "show also that there is still a vast amount of illiteracy and low literacy among pupils who have completed the school at the age of 14 years.

"Moreover, data obtained from youth clubs, or army educational centers on adolescents from 14 to 18 years of age show that among those completing the elementary school may be observed a marked tendency to lose with age the little that they acquired in the sphere of reading, spelling, and writing."

A severe crisis in public education is also experienced by postwar France. Since 1939 not a single secondary school building has been constructed, even though during the war a great number of old buildings were destroyed or severely damaged.

Particularly grave is the material position of teachers in the capitalistic countries of Europe and America. To this condition the wave of teachers' strikes in America bears witness. From September, 1946, to February, 1947, twelve great strikes of teachers occurred. The wages of teachers have been reduced. According to the testimony of the journal, *The School Executive,* No. 10, for 1947, the wages of public-school teachers in the United States at the present time are on the average twenty per cent lower than they were eight years ago.

But yet more grave is the moral position of the teacher in the West. He is compelled to teach a falsified science and to cripple the souls of children to please the reactionary policy of the bourgeoisie. Widely known are the "oaths of allegiance" of American teachers who are compelled to swear that they will not "teach Communism to children."

Only in the Soviet Union is the school genuinely democratic and truly humanistic.

The thirty-year road of development of Soviet education is the road of uninterrupted improvement in accordance with those tasks which are placed before the school by Lenin, Stalin, the Party of Bolsheviks, and the Soviet state.

The truly grandiose work in the field of public enlightenment which during the thirty years of Soviet power has been conducted in our country under the leadership of the Party of Lenin and Stalin is one of the decisive factors in the victories and achievements of socialism. Our schools, children's homes, higher educational institutions, and numerous schools and courses for adults have prepared people for industry and agriculture, science and technique, art and literature. They have introduced vast multitudes of people to the cultural heritage, they have assisted in the flowering of Soviet culture, socialist in content and national in form. They have reared a new man — the man of the Stalinist epoch.

And into this magnificent house of socialism which is constructed in our country went not a little labor of the workers of public education. With full right they can repeat the stirring words of Vladimir Mayakovsky:

> I rejoice
> that
> my labor
> is poured
> into the labor
> of my republic.

In celebrating with the entire Soviet land thirty years of the Great October Socialist Revolution, the workers of public education realize with pride that their labor in the education of the rising generation brings nearer the realization of Communism and contributes to the final victory of the cause of Lenin and Stalin.

5

Here is a highly instructive document for the free world. This report to the Russian people by their minister of education on education in the "bourgeois countries" should be read by every American and by every citizen of every free society on the earth. It should not be read of course for the purpose of learning about the condition of education in the United States or any other country mentioned. For such a purpose it is utterly worthless. Indeed it is much less than worthless, because it is profoundly false. But it should be of great value to all who wish to see the face of Soviet morality without masks, without veils, and without embellishments, to use the words of Stalin.

In the course of these pages the reader has seen frequent reference to "Party literature" or "Party science" or "Party journalism" or "Party something else." He has probably wondered over the meaning of the qualifying term and may have been led by the context to assume that it means genuine. Kalashnikov has completely resolved all difficulties, queries, and doubts. No longer need anyone live in a state of ignorance or obfuscation regarding this matter. The word "Party," when used as an adjective, gives notice that the thing, institution, or person qualified is committed to do the bidding of the All-Union Communist Party of Bolsheviks without asking questions. The minister of education knew that his references were false, but as a good "Party man" he "lashed out boldly" at bourgeois education in obedience to the command of Zhdanov and the Central Committee. As the analysis to follow will show, his report on education in America is a perfect exhibit of "Party literature." Whether the "Party writer" selects truth or falsehood depends on which he thinks is the "sharper weapon" at the moment.

Kalashnikov begins by asserting without qualifications, among other things, that "science is falsified or altogether eliminated from the educational institutions of these countries." It is certainly to be hoped that "Party science" is not being taught in American schools. But since a democracy is founded on the principle that individuals and even groups "have the right to make mistakes," no one can be sure about this. In the nature of the case no free society can have any "official science" to be imposed on all by the power of the police. Neither can it have any "science of the sciences" based on authority that everyone must master. The Russians should know, however, that there are many science teachers and investigators who believe that the old "question of the transmission of acquired characters," if broadly conceived, has by no means been settled. Lysenko, if he were ever to abandon his tendency toward mysticism and show more respect for experimental method, would find not a few friends among them. At least he would find minds ready to listen to the evidence. With regard to the status of science in the educational system of the United States the record is clear and unequivocal. Both quantitatively and qualitatively it stands at a higher level than ever before in the history of the country.

Kalashnikov's use of the article in the *Baltimore Bulletin of Education* by Anne C. Phillips reveals the Communist technique of deliberately perverting truth. One may be sure that he searched long for this relatively obscure report on American education in order to find the particular words he was looking for. He probably had in his office statements on educational purposes in the United States which carry far more authority. But that was not what he wanted. He was engaged in the serious business of writing "Party" literature and he had to meet rather severe and exacting specifications.

In the article Miss Phillips gives a verbatim report of the conduct of a kindergarten lesson devoted to the development of the concept of liberty. By failing to give any indication whatsoever, by means of elliptical markings, that he has omitted parts of the account, the Soviet educator succeeds in reducing the American idea of freedom to "the right to earn money and to thank god for success in business." This generalization of course is in complete accord with the view of "bourgeois" liberty developed in the "science of the sciences" and therefore must be true. The section of Miss Phillips' article from which the Russian minister of education makes his selections and fabricates his story, in obedience to the recognized canons of "Party literature," reads as follows, with the parts selected in italics:

Teacher: . . . "Does anybody know what we mean by freedom?" After a moment, "I'll tell you one thing freedom means, and then you tell me some others. *For one thing freedom means that we in America are free to worship God and to pray to him in our homes and schools and churches.* Do you know that in some countries people are put into prison or killed for praying to God and reading the Bible? Wouldn't that be terrible? (Pause) Can you think of another thing Americans are free to do that many other people can't do?"

Child: "Listen to the radio."

Teacher: "Yes. In a great many countries in the world people are killed for listening to the truth over their radios. The Nazis want their people to believe their lies, and so they punish any one who tells the truth. Children, that is why we are fighting the Nazis, the Italians, and the Japanese. Can you imagine how awful it would be to live in a world where no one told the truth? God tells us in the Bible not to lie. (Pause) Can you think of another freedom?"

Child: "We are free to walk around any place we want to go. Those other countries can't do that."

Teacher: "You are right! Millions of people are forced to stay in one place or are sent to horrible concentration camps or to other countries where they don't want to go. We in America may go anywhere we want. What else does freedom mean? (Pause) *In America men and women are free to work and earn money* to buy food, clothes, homes, and coal to heat their homes. Children, many, many people in the world are made to work hard and are paid no money. Many have no warm clothing, food, or heat. *Aren't you glad that you live in America? Do you pray every day and thank God that you are an American, and ask Him to bless America?*" [23]

[23] Anne C. Phillips, "The Little Child's America," *Baltimore Bulletin of Education*, vol. XIX, No. 4 (April, May, June, 1942), p. 169.

The complete distortion of the educational philosophy of John Dewey reveals a disregard for truth that confounds the imagination. Kalashnikov represents the great philosopher as standing precisely for those things against which he has always fought. He says that, according to Dewey, the purpose of education is to nurture in the young the qualities of the "shrewd 'businessman.' " To anyone who knows the man or ever read anything he ever wrote on education this assertion is so false that it is ridiculous. But the most extraordinary piece of fiction is the Soviet educator's attempt to link Dewey with postwar "American imperialists." He turns to *The Problems of Men* and takes from it one half of one sentence which ends with the words "the new social orientation." Then he proceeds to put into these words the meaning that is required by the foreign policy of the Politburo — a meaning that is not even suggested by a single sentence in the entire book. With a disregard for truth that is utterly frightening he states that "the new social orientation" is "that warlike reaction which is propagated by American imperialists."

To obtain a measure of the mendacity of this statement the inquirer must go to *The Problems of Men,* see what the book is about, and find the passage on which Kalashnikov builds his case. Though published in book form in 1946, it was in reality a collection of articles and essays written over a period of many years. The chapter from which the Soviet minister took his half-sentence is entitled "The Teacher and His World," appeared originally as a magazine piece in 1935, was reprinted without change in 1946, and so could have no relevance for the postwar period when according to Soviet mythology "American imperialists" donned the mantle of Hitler. In the article Dewey discussed an issue which was a subject of considerable controversy at the time — the issue of indoctrination. Because of the great changes in the foundations of society, he recognized the need for a new social orientation on the part of the American people. But he argued that this orientation should come not from a process of indoctrination, but from a scientific study of the facts of social life. The paragraph and the sentence from which Kalashnikov apparently obtained his half-sentence follows, the sentence being italicized:

My other remark is to the effect that one great business of the schools at present is to develop immunity against the propaganda influence of press and radio. Julian Huxley in his book on *Scientific Research and Social Needs* (a book which every teacher should read) says that, "one aim of education should be to teach people to discount the unconscious prejudices that their social environments impress upon them." The press and the radio are two of the most powerful means of inculcating mass prejudice. War propaganda and the situation in Hitlerized Germany have proved that unless the schools create a popular intelligence that is critically discriminating, there is no limit to the prejudices and inflamed emotion that will result. An intelligent understanding of social forces given by schools is our chief protection. *Intelligent understanding of conditions and forces cannot fail, in my judgment, to support a new general social orientation.* There are difficulties enough in the way of the schools obtaining the power to promote this understanding. Concentration on this task is directly in line with the professed function of public education, and it alone will give the educators concerned with a new social orientation a herculean task to perform.[24]

Kalashnikov's reference to Thorndike rests on a body of fact. The great psychologist did make a study in the nineteen-thirties of the "attitudes of people toward prospective 'disutilities' in the form of pains, discomforts, deprivations, frustrations, restrictions, and other undesired conditions." [25] He presented to two groups, one consisting of sixty teachers and students of psychology and the other of thirty-nine unemployed men and women under thirty years of age working on a government project, a series of fifty-one hypothetical instances of "pain, deprivation, or frustration" and asked them "for how much money" they would perform the act or suffer the condition indicated. The report of the investigation received so little attention in America that the present authors had difficulty locating it. It was not one of Thorndike's impor-

24 John Dewey, *The Problems of Men* (New York, 1946), p. 82.
25 Edward L. Thorndike, "Valuations of Certain Pains, Deprivations, and Frustrations," *Journal of Genetic Psychology*, vol. 51, December, 1937, p. 227.

tant studies, nor did it represent in any way his system of values, except in a negative sense. By definition his list embraced only undesirable, offensive, and revolting situations, including the most repulsive he could imagine. It involved every kind of deprivation from the extraction of "one upper front tooth" to loss of "all hope of life after death." It seems possible that question twenty-six and the response offended Kalashnikov more than those he mentioned. It asked the subject: "For how much money" would you undertake "to live all the rest of your life in Russia?" The median compensation demanded by the students and teachers was one million dollars, while that asked by the unemployed was only one hundred fifty thousand. Yet the Russian educator should have been comforted by the fact that these same people regarded with almost equal aversion spending the rest of their lives "on a farm in Kansas, ten miles from any town."

The reference of the Russian minister to the condition of public education in the United States following the war also had a factual basis. At a time of rising costs of living, persons and classes on fixed salaries and especially teachers unfortunately always suffer for a time. They suffer until public sentiment is aroused in their favor and a redress of grievance is achieved. On this occasion many teachers left the profession, something that would not be permitted in the Soviet Union. Also they made a lot of noise and even organized strikes in some communities. At any rate they made themselves heard and succeeded quickly in improving their condition, although they are by no means entirely satisfied. It is to be hoped that they will continue their agitation for the improvement of both their lot and the standards of education. It seems quite probable that some Soviet teachers would like to protest or even strike, if under the prevailing condition of thought control the idea should ever occur to them. The authors know of no instance of an American teacher jumping out of a third-story window of an American consulate in a foreign land to keep from returning to her native country.

Kalashnikov dwells on the sad state of affairs in secondary and higher education in the United States. American liberals agree that the situation is far from satisfactory in many respects and applaud the report of the President's Commission on Higher Education entitled, *Higher Education for American Democracy,* which calls for a doubling of the enrollment in institutions above the secondary level by 1960. The "grandiose" character of this proposal, to employ one of the most common Soviet expressions, is evident when the reader realizes that at the time the Russian minister was speaking the number of American youth attending higher schools of all types was 2,354,000, about four times the corresponding figure for the entire Soviet Union with a population exceeding that of the United States by approximately sixty million and with a college age-group proportionately far larger. It should be recalled too that the Soviet higher school rests on a ten-year program of general education, elementary and secondary combined, rather than on a twelve-year program as in America. Kalashnikov's declaration therefore that public education in America "is on the decline" is patently false. The truth lies in precisely the opposite direction. The reader can only wonder whether the Russian minister's account of Soviet education is any more trustworthy than his report on "The Degradation of the School and Pedagogy in Bourgeois Countries."

CHAPTER EIGHT

INTELLECTUALS AS SOLDIERS— AT HOME

PERHAPS the reader need not be told again that Stalin said to H. G. Wells: "Education is a weapon whose effect depends on who holds it in his hands and at whom it is aimed." Also perhaps he need not be told that all the arts and sciences, and all the agencies through which they are nurtured and practiced, are recognized as educational processes and institutions subject to state control. And finally perhaps he need not be told that the guiding of this vast apparatus for influencing and moulding the mind of the Soviet people is a jealously guarded monopoly of the central organs or high command of the All-Union Communist Party of Bolsheviks. Yet he who would understand the Soviet Union must ever keep these obvious and oft-repeated propositions clearly in mind.

If the arts and sciences are weapons, if education in each and all of its manifold organized forms is a weapon, then it follows that those who practice these arts and sciences and thus participate in the education of the Soviet people, and particularly in the education of the youth, are soldiers of Communism. They are reminded of this condition daily in almost every issue of *Pravda* or *Izvestia*, over every radio station, in books and pamphlets and journals, at the theatre and the cinema and on the athletic field. They are told without ceasing that they occupy a forward position in the current battle for the world, that they are fighting on the "ideological front" in the first "line of fire." If they believe what they hear, read, and behold, they must see themselves marching

in the serried ranks of an invincible army toward the bright apocalypse of Communism. They must see themselves too under the
command of the most brilliant captain of the ages, the coryphaeus
of all branches of human learning and endeavor, their own beloved father and teacher, the great Stalin. One would think that
the human spirit would rebel against this barrage of adoration.
Perhaps it does, but remains silent under duress.

The "patriotic" rôle of the intellectual in the Soviet Union, of
the journalist, the writer, the dramatist, the artist, the scientist,
and the teacher, is emphasized in nearly all the documents presented in this volume — in the responses of the individuals and
organizations directly involved no less than in the resolutions and
pronouncements of the Central Committee of the Party. But the
most comprehensive statement of the Soviet outlook was made by
S. V. Kaftanov, Minister of Higher Education of the USSR, in an
address delivered on July 10, 1947, under the auspices of the All-
Union Society for the Dissemination of Political and Scientific
Knowledge. The subject of the address, printed under the auspices of the Society in a first edition of 115,000 copies and sold
for sixty kopecks (about five cents), was "On the Patriotic Duty of
the Soviet Intelligentsia." Kaftanov is a man of great personal
power and of considerable political influence at the level of the
partly initiated. In his outlook he has been comparatively friendly
toward the West and at one time would have welcomed the exchange of students and professors. His statement is consequently
marked by a degree of tolerance not often found after the war in
the utterances of Russian leaders. It is at the same time a comparatively persuasive presentation of the Soviet position. It
retains much of the idealism of the early years of the Revolution.
Yet, in so far as the rest of the world is concerned he is at least
purblind, to use the term of H. G. Wells.

2

Kaftanov's address [1] was approximately ten thousand words in length. Except for a section devoted to recent technological advances and their significance for the development of the Soviet economy, it is published in full below.

The Triumph of the Soviet Political and Social Order and the Flowering of Soviet Patriotism. During the thirty years of its existence the Soviet state has achieved tremendous successes in all branches of political, economic, and cultural life. History records nothing comparable to the successes which we have achieved in such a short period.

As a result of the victory of the socialist revolution in our country radical changes have taken place. Through the will of the Party of Lenin and Stalin and through the strenuous efforts of the entire people the most democratic and progressive social and political order in the world has been created and a state of a new type has been built — a socialist state.

The fundamental characteristics which distinguish the Soviet order from any other social order and which define its democratic and progressive character are found in the absence of antagonistic classes, of private property in the means of production, of the exploitation of man by man, and of class and national oppression. The establishment of the socialist mode of production, of socialist relations among citizens of the USSR, and the high consciousness of state and social interests on the part of our citizens constitute the great moving force of Soviet society and a powerful lever for raising the economy and the culture of the country.

From a backward agrarian country in the not distant past our land has been transformed into one of the leading industrial empires of the world in a comparatively short historic period. In the USSR a powerful socialist industry has been created, new branches of manufacture have been established — machine construction, airplane and motor construction, shipbuilding, automobile and tractor construc-

[1] S. V. Kaftanov, *On the Patriotic Duty of the Soviet Intelligentsia* (Moscow, 1947). (In Russian.)

tion. There has been created in the east a new metallurgical and coal base; there has grown a tremendous net of electro-stations and hydro-stations.

For centuries the Russian village lived in poverty and ignorance and was subjected to cruel exploitations by kulaks, landlords, and capitalists. It must have seemed before the revolution that there was no escape from this harsh position of the village. But the Bolsheviks, and our great leaders Lenin and Stalin, found the way.

Under the leadership of the Party of Bolsheviks the Soviet people freed the peasants from the exploitation of kulaks, landlords, and capitalists. On the foundation of the collective farm the most advanced rural economy in the world was created in our country. This system opened up unlimited opportunities for the introduction into the rural economy of the most productive machine labor and for the utilization of all the achievements of agronomic and zootechnical science. All of this formed the basis for the economic and cultural flowering of the collective farm village.

The new social and political order enabled the Soviet people to attain vast successes in the sphere of cultural development. These successes are the direct result of the fact that in our country all achievements of science, art, and technique become the property of the people. "Formerly," said V. I. Lenin, "the entire human mind, all of its genius created only in order to give to one all the benefits of technique and culture and deprive others of the thing most essential for enlightenment and development. And henceforth all the miracles of technique, all the conquests of culture will become the possession of the people and the human mind and genius will not be converted into an instrument of violence, into an instrument of exploitation." [2]

Under the leadership of the Party of Bolsheviks the Soviet people fulfilled a great program for the raising of the culture of the people of the USSR and achieved a cultural revolution. On the foundation of the great ideas of Marxism and Leninism they created a new culture, national in form and socialist in content. Thus Soviet socialist culture marks a new epoch in the development of a universal culture, for it is a culture of a higher type, a culture which is the possession of millions of workers, which reflects the interests and multiform spiritual life of our people, which nurtures genuinely human qualities and which leads to the bright future of a Communist society.

[2] V. I. Lenin, *Works*, vol. XXII, p. 225.

In its very nature and content Soviet culture differs radically from bourgeois culture. If the latter, particularly in the epoch of imperialism, rests and develops on the principles of the rule of private property, of the exploitation of man by man, of the struggle for personal enrichment at the expense of others, Soviet culture rests and develops on new principles, on the foundation of public property in the tools of production, on the Leninist and Stalinist ideas of friendship of peoples and mutual aid, on the principles of struggle against oppression and exploitation, of struggle against egoism and individualism, on the ideas of Communism.

In fulfilling the great program of cultural construction our country during a brief historical period has been transformed into a country of complete literacy. In all the Union republics, in autonomous provinces, and national districts, the people have created their own schools, institutes, theatres, and intelligentsia.

Remarkable successes have been achieved in the Soviet Union in the development of science and higher education. More than 800 higher institutions have been created in which more than 600,000 students receive instruction. Annually the country receives about 100,000 specialists with higher education and almost 250,000 with secondary education.

Along with the broadening and strengthening of the staff of Soviet science and of the Academy of Science of the USSR, during the Soviet period academies of science have sprung up and are developing successfully in union republics (Ukraine, Belorussia, Georgia, Azerbaidzan, Armenia, Uzbekistan, Kazakistan, Latvia, Lithuania, and Estonia). The academies of the Kazak, Aberbaidzhan and Armenian republics appeared and began to develop during the hard years of the Patriotic War. In the days when our country carried on the bloody battle with fascism, defending its freedom and independence and rescuing entire civilized mankind from the deathly peril of fascism, the Soviet people created new institutes, schools, academies of science, new works of art and literature.

Thus did the Soviet people demonstrate their unshakable faith in victory, their greatness and strength of spirit, their boundless love of their Motherland, their devotion to the Party of Lenin and Stalin.

The Soviet power, having freed the people of tsarist Russia from material and spiritual dependence, from economic and spiritual slavery, transformed our country into a genuinely free and self-governing state, a dependable bulwark of world civilization and progress.

In the furious process of socialist transformation carried on in our country, the people themselves, as the active force of this transformation and the creator of socialist life, were changed.

The very nature of the Soviet order which awakened the energies of the people and cleared the way for their unlimited creative work, the policy and all the varied activities of the Communist Party nurtured a new generation of Soviet people with a new countenance and with new moral qualities.

Boundless love of the Motherland, heroism, steadfastness and courage in all situations, the will to overcome difficulties, a lofty sense of political and social duty, purposefulness, boiling energy, nobility, indignation toward everything destructive of human dignity, freedom from the prejudices of the old society, and above all from class and national prejudices — such are the basic traits which characterize the people of the new generation, educated by the Soviet power and the Bolshevik party. "Where will you find such people and such a country as ours," said Comrade Zhdanov. "Where will you find the magnificent qualities which our Soviet people displayed in the Great Patriotic War and which they display in their daily work as they pass to the peaceful restoration and development of economy and culture! Every day our people rise higher and ever higher. Today we are not what we were yesterday, and tomorrow we shall not be what we are today. Already, we are not the same Russians we were before 1917, our Russia is different, our character is not the same. We have changed and grown along with those great reforms which have profoundly changed the face of our country." [3]

Only a colossus of the strength and spirit of our great Soviet people could strike with a shattering blow the black forces of fascism which attempted to conquer and enslave the entire world, to turn mankind back to the dark times of the middle ages.

The greatness of soul of the Soviet people, their boundless devotion to their Motherland and to their patriotic duty was clearly revealed in the Patriotic War where it expressed itself in mass manifestations of heroism and sacrifice at the front and in the rear. This greatness of soul and the invincible strength of the Soviet people are nourished by the powerful source of vital Soviet patriotism, patriotism of a higher type. Victory over fascist Germany disclosed to the entire world the

[3] Speech of Comrade Zhdanov on the journals *Zvezda* and *Leningrad*, p. 36. Gospolitizdat, 1946.

impregnable fortress of the Soviet state and the greatness of spirit of the Soviet people. In the course of the war the Soviet people became ever more convinced of the superiority of our socialist economic and social order, of our science and culture.

"Patriotism," as Lenin used to say, "is one of the deepest feelings, formed by centuries and thousands of years of existence of separate societies." [4]

As the conditions of social life undergo transformation with the development of society, patriotism naturally cannot remain unchanged. Being historically and class conditioned, it is influenced in its manifestations by the social order and the class status of people.

In bourgeois society, where the exploitation of man by man and national oppression and social injustice exist, the feeling of patriotism cannot be as deep as under the conditions of socialist society where love for the Motherland is not darkened by the vices of bourgeois society.

They say that patriotism is love for one's own people, for their language and culture, for their historical past, for the monuments of this past, for their traditions and national traits, and so on. All of this is so. But is it possible to assert that the Russian nobleman of the eighteenth and nineteenth centuries, who exchanged his language for French and who mercilessly flogged his own people for the slightest offenses, loved his people and his fatherland as much as the peasants who with their pitchforks and axes opposed the invasion of Napoleon in 1812 in order to teach him not to covet foreign soil and foreign property, who drove from the native land the ravishers and usurpers whose language and culture the exploiting classes of Russia adopted so enthusiastically?

Clearly the attitudes of oppressed and oppressors toward an existing social and political order cannot be identical.

In a society marked by contending classes, naturally the basic elements out of which the feeling of patriotism is formed come into conflict, into collision with one another.

The entire history of the development of human society is a history of class struggle, of struggle between oppressors and oppressed. One cannot speak therefore of a fully rounded feeling of patriotism, of love for one's own fatherland on the part of the toilers of capitalist countries. To them this feeling cannot be as complete as under the

[4] V. I. Lenin, *Works*, vol. XXIII, p. 290.

conditions of the Soviet state, for it is darkened and depressed by the social conditions of life.

The patriotism of ruling and exploiting classes is confined by their selfish class interests. If their class interests come into conflict with the interests of the motherland, they easily proceed to treason. This is confirmed by numerous facts of history.

It is known, for example, that in 1871 the French bourgeoisie entered into a treaty with Prussian reaction, in order to suppress with the aid of Prussian cannon the Paris Commune which was actually defending the national interests of the French people.

After the Great October Socialist Revolution the Russian landlords and bourgeoisie incited against Russia the armies of foreign interventionists and not only betrayed but also wanted to sell the freedom and independence of their Motherland.

In the period of the second world war "the 200 families" of France and their representatives, the Lavals and the Petains, in the name of their own selfish interests sold France to German fascism. Various quislings in Norway, Belgium, Holland, Hungary, Austria, Czechoslovakia, and the Balkans did the same thing. Only the toiling masses and their representatives consistently and to the end defended the interests of their people.

Even under the very dark conditions of the old order, as in tsarist Russia, the true patriots were always the toilers and those representatives of the intelligentsia who went along with the people and defended their interests.

The great Russian revolutionary democrats, Hertzen, Belinsky, Chernyshevsky, Dobroliubov, Nekrasov, and others were the genuine patriots of their Motherland. Their love for the Russian people, for their own soil, was boundless. They threw themselves passionately against servility toward Western bourgeois culture.

Chernyshevsky, defining patriotism, said that one could not help loving one's own people. That is precisely why the revolutionary democrats loved their Motherland and their own people so ardently, and why they hated passionately the social and political order of feudal Russia.

This double feeling of genuine patriots of the Motherland under the conditions of tsarist Russia was expressed by Nekrasov in beautiful words which sounded the call to struggle: "He who lives without grief and anger does not love his fatherland."

In his article "On the National Pride of the Great Russians," V. I. Lenin, the greatest patriot of his Motherland, wrote: "It grieves us to see and to feel to what violence, oppression, and ridicule the tsarist executioners, the noblemen and capitalists, subject our beautiful motherland." [5]

The Party of Bolsheviks, embracing the best of the Russian proletariat and other toilers, is linked by all of its roots to the peoples of the Soviet Union. Many of the finest sons of the Bolshevik Party, supreme patriots of their people, gave their lives in the struggle for the welfare of the people, for their deliverance from the yoke of tsar, landlords, and capitalists. And they did not die in vain. The cause of the Party triumphed. Under the leadership of the Party of Lenin and Stalin the Great October Socialist Revolution achieved victory, brought to the peoples of Russia complete deliverance from class and national oppression, and united them in one family of brotherly republics — the powerful Soviet Union.

The Great October Socialist Revolution struck a shattering blow at the assiduously propagandized theory that everything forward-looking and progressive is born in the West and that the fate of Russia is blind imitation. Long before the October Revolution Comrade Stalin said:

"The possibility is not excluded that Russia is just the country which will show the road to socialism. . . . We must throw off the outlived conception that only Europe can show us the way." [6]

With Great October Soviet patriotism was born, a patriotism of new, advanced, and profound ideas and feelings which could not exist or which were suppressed under the rule of tsar landlords, and capitalists. Under the conditions of the Soviet state the love of toilers for their Motherland, their natural surroundings, their language, and their national traditions is supplemented by the feeling of love of and devotion to the new political and social order which guarantees an historically unprecedented flowering of the material and spiritual energies of the people. The Soviet man feels himself master of his country, master of the fruits of his labor, master of all material and spiritual values. This lifts the Soviet man above the people of capitalist countries, instills in him a feeling of lofty dignity, breeds and develops in him the noble feeling of boundless love for his Motherland,

[5] V. I. Lenin, *Works*, vol. XVII, p. 81.   [6] I. V. Stalin, *Works*, vol II, pp. 186–187.

for the people, for the Soviet social and political order. As a result of the construction of a socialist society in our country, a brotherly comradeship of nations in one socialist state has been created, has grown immeasurably, and has strengthened that Soviet patriotism which was born in the socialist revolution.

Soviet patriotism is the great vital force of our victorious march toward Communism. In the brilliant words of Comrade Stalin, "the strength of Soviet patriotism consists in the fact that it is founded on neither race nor national prejudices, but on deep devotion and loyalty to the people of the Soviet Motherland, on brotherly comradeship of the toilers of all the nations of our country. In Soviet patriotism the national traditions of peoples and the common life interests of all the toilers of the Soviet Union are harmoniously blended." [7]

That is why we say that Soviet patriotism is a new and higher stage of patriotism, an all-conquering power which can be fully revealed on such a mass scale only in a socialist society.

The Rôle of the Soviet Intelligentsia in the Further Development of Science and Technology. During the years of Soviet power the Party of Bolsheviks and the Soviet state have directed their efforts toward the solution of the problem of the creation from the ranks of toilers of a Soviet intelligentsia. The Party and the state have realized fully that without a numerous intelligentsia of their own, which would serve faithfully and truly the people, the swift advance of our country on the road to socialism would be impossible. This task of the creation of a genuine people's socialist intelligentsia has been brilliantly accomplished.

In his speech at the Eighteenth Congress of the Party, Comrade Stalin said that we had given birth to a "numerous new Soviet intelligentsia, derived from the ranks of the working class, the peasantry, and Soviet employees, bone of the bone and blood of the blood of our people — an intelligentsia, not knowing the yoke of exploitation, despising exploiters, and ready to serve the people of the USSR truly and faithfully.

"I think that the birth of this new people's socialist intelligentsia is one of the most important results of the cultural revolution in our country." [8]

---

[7] I. Stalin, *On the Great Patriotic War of the Soviet Union,* pp. 160–161, Gospolitizdat, 1946.

[8] I. Stalin, *Problems of Leninism,* eleventh edition, p. 589.

The creation of a numerous Soviet intelligentsia insures the successful achievement of the grandiose tasks which stand before the Soviet state in all fields of socialist construction. The time has long since passed when the Soviet state was compelled to turn for scientific-technical aid to specialists of foreign countries. Now there is no field of science and technique in which we could not get along with the forces of our own Soviet scientists, our own engineering-technical intelligentsia. More than this: the honor for many scientific discoveries and very significant technical inventions of recent years belongs to the scientific and technical intelligentsia of our land.

In the intensive creative work of the years of the pre-war Stalinist five-year plans and subsequently of the period of the Great Patriotic War our intelligentsia acquired a colossal political and technical experience, grew immeasurably and matured. Exhibiting along with their people the noble feeling of Soviet patriotism, our intelligentsia built a new society in the years of peaceful labor and defended their Motherland in the years of war.

In the period of the Great Patriotic War the Soviet intelligentsia gave all their strength, experience, and knowledge to the cause of the swift defeat of the enemy. They aided our workers and peasants to convert industry and agriculture to a war basis and to supply the army with all things necessary for the achievement of victory.

Even under the difficult conditions of war time our intelligentsia enriched Soviet science with new achievements, equipped industry with new methods for raising the productivity of labor, and invented new kinds of machines, instruments, and weapons for the army. Through their creative labor the Soviet intelligentsia made an invaluable contribution to the cause of the defeat of the enemy. Their heroic labor in the years of war earned the high esteem of the leader and teacher of the Soviet people, Comrade Stalin.

During the postwar years the Soviet intelligentsia, inspired by the historic victory and by the majestic program for the further reconstruction of the country outlined by Comrade Stalin, joined in the resolution of new tasks — tasks involving the restoration and further development of the public economy, of Soviet science and technique, literature and art, public education.

The great vital force in the creative work of the Soviet intelligentsia is their patriotism, their love for their Motherland, for their people, their love and devotion to the Soviet state, the Soviet social order. In no other country of the world can the intelligentsia possess such a sublime sense of patriotic duty.

In the course of many centuries the best representatives of mankind have dreamed of creating for the people, for their Motherland. But this dream could not be realized in bourgeois states, because " . . . the bourgeoisie," wrote K. Marx and F. Engels in the *Manifesto of the Communist Party*, "stripped the halo of sanctity from all kinds of activity which previously had been regarded as honorable and had been looked upon with a sense of awe. They converted the doctor, the jurist, the priest, the poet, the man of science into their own hired men." [9] Many cultural workers have sacrificed their lives in their effort to serve the people and to develop genuine science and culture in the name of humanity.

Under the conditions of capitalist society the intelligentsia work and produce, not for the people, but for the enrichment of capitalists and imperialists. Only in the Soviet state do the intelligentsia receive for the first time in history the opportunity to produce, not for the enrichment of capitalists, but for the people, for their own Motherland, for the universal cause of the building of a new and socially just society. This condition creates unlimited opportunities for the utilization of the creative labor and creative growth of the intelligentsia. At the same time the unprecedented and ever-increasing rôle of the intelligentsia in the life of the people and of the entire state is emphasized.

To the intelligentsia, who under the conditions of the Soviet state constitute an equal member of society, belong the grand rôle of the transformation of our country, of the construction of a Communist society, of the education of the masses of toilers in the ideas of Communism. The further our country develops along the road to Communism the greater is the significance attached to the work of the intelligentsia. They must find new ways of development in industry, transport, and economy and create new works of art and literature marked by high idealism to challenge us to go ahead and to train the will and character of the people. To them belongs the exceptionally important and prominent rôle of educating the masses and of overcoming the vestiges of the old society in the consciousness of the people. That is why in our country the intelligentsia enjoy the universal love and support of the entire Soviet people and the Soviet state. Never in any other country of the world have the intelligentsia enjoyed and

9 K. Marx and F. Engels, *The Communist Manifesto*, p. 24.

continued to enjoy such support by the state and the people as in our country where all the conditions essential for their creative work have been established. The workers in science, art and literature, the vast army of engineers, doctors, teachers, economists, jurists, agronomists and others are surrounded by universal love and regard. Many representatives of the Soviet intelligentsia are deputies of the Supreme Soviet of the USSR, the Supreme Soviets of Union Republics, and deputies of local organs of government. Numerous representatives of the people's intelligentsia are awarded the Orders of the Soviet Union and are honored with the high title of Hero of Socialist Labor and laureate of the Stalin prize. This condition proves the exceptional attention shown the intelligentsia by our government and at the same time imposes upon the intelligentsia a responsible and noble task — to serve the people supremely, to give the people and the state all their strength and knowledge, to make their contribution to the cause of building a Communist society. Herein lies the patriotic duty of scientists, engineers, technicians, writers, teachers, economists, jurists, workers in the Soviet apparatus, and other representatives of the vast army of the Soviet intelligentsia.

Particularly great and honorable is the task of the intelligentsia in the fulfillment of the Five-Year Plan for the restoration and development of the public economy and in the realization of the majestic program for the further flowering of our Motherland as outlined by Comrade Stalin in his speech of February 9, 1946.

Comrade Stalin placed before our country the task in the coming ten to fifteen years of doubling or tripling the prewar level of production in the most important branches of industry, of achieving a vast program of cultural construction, of surpassing the level of science beyond the borders of our country.

The fulfillment of this grandiose program for the further development of our country will demand the concentrated energies of all the Soviet people. But a particularly large rôle in the achievement of these tasks belongs to the intelligentsia, to scientists, engineers, technicians, inventors, and leading Stakhanovites. This is due to the fact that the attainment of a twofold or threefold increase of industrial output requires not only the use of known methods, but also the introduction into the public economy of all the newest achievements of science and technique and the guaranteeing in this way of a substantial raising of the productivity of labor and growth of industrial production.

The achievement of this great program, as outlined by Comrade Stalin, calls urgently for the further advance of the scientific studies and creative exploits of the Soviet intelligentsia, for new achievements in all branches of science and technique, and for the application of these achievements to the practical work of socialist construction. In the broad introduction of scientific advances into the public economy reside inexhaustible resources for the creation of an abundance of material and spiritual values.

The activity of our scientists, inventors, engineers and technicians must be directed to the resolution of the actual tasks of science and technique, which flow from the plan for the restoration and development of the public economy. The awarding of Stalin prizes, especially during the year 1946, showed that many of our engineers and technicians are working successfully on the solution of the practical problems of science and technique and are assisting our industry in the discovery of new sources of raw materials. Many engineers are awarded Stalin prizes for the invention of automatic conveyer lines and the introduction of new methods into production, for the creation of new airplanes, locomotives, and other mechnical improvements in the sphere of technique, for the selection of new and more productive kinds of wheat and new breeds of productive cattle, for remarkable investigations in the fields of law, history, philology, and other sciences.

However, not all scientific workers have linked their scientific activity sufficiently with the tasks of socialist construction and the life of our country. We still have scientists who work on themes of little significance, often of no real worth to either the science or the public economy of the Union. And scientific problems which have great significance are at times developed very slowly because of the dissipation of the scientific forces of this or that research group. Consequently the needed results are often gained after they have lost their importance and are becoming obsolescent. And at times the results gained are introduced very slowly into the practice of socialist construction. In such an event the country fails to receive proper results from the material expenditures for the conduct of scientific studies.

In some scientific institutes themes of little actual value and even pseudo-scientific in character are elaborated. Thus, in one of the great scientific institutions of our country such "a scientific problem" as the breeding of spiders for the purpose of obtaining silk from their webs was studied for many years. On this problem the institute expended state funds and fitted out expeditions to the regions of Central Asia. At the same time the institute did not complete satisfactorily important scientific researches which were linked with the real tasks of the development of the public economy.

Many worthless themes may be found also in other scientific institutions. For example, some of our scientific workers are occupied with the study of the positive influence of the culture of the Mongol-nomads on Russian culture, although it is known to all that Russian culture was significantly higher than that of the Mongol-nomads.

It is important to declare a decisive struggle against scholasticism and pseudo-scientific themes in science and to direct the activity of every scientist and scientific body toward the solution of the actual problems which are linked with the tasks of the further strengthening of the economic and defensive power of our country and with the further development of socialist culture.

Only the linking of the activity of scientists and science with the life interests of the people and the policy of the Party and the Soviet state defines the progressive character of science and its socialist content. The union of science and practice, as the entire history of science shows, is a powerful source of strength for science itself. All great discoveries are made by scientists in the solution of important practical problems.

The activity of Lomonosov, Mendeleev, Michurin, Pavlov, and many other outstanding scientists of the past is a remarkable example of the relation of science and practice. Here, for example, is how Mendeleev understood his rôle as a scientist. "As long as I can," he said, "I will strive to give fruitful, industrious, tangible work to my country, with the assurance that politics, construction, education, and even the defense of the country today are impossible without the development of industry. The crowning glory of the reforms which I desire and all the freedom we need, are concentrated here. Science and industry — such are my dreams."

There is no task more honorable for the Soviet scientist than the task of service without stint for his people, for his Motherland. In this is the duty of the Soviet intelligentsia, in this must be made manifest the patriotism of Soviet scientists, their love for their people, for their fatherland, for their state.

Against Slavishness and Servility Toward Bourgeois Science and

Culture. Several other very substantial weaknesses in the scientific work of certain Soviet scientists must be noted. The survival even to this day of elements of slavishness and servility toward bourgeois science and culture constitutes their great vice. This slavishness was cultivated for centuries among the intelligentsia by the ruling classes of tsarist Russia who opposed everything original and progressive in the Russian people and worshipped everything from abroad. The nobility of Russia even exchanged their own rich Russian language for the French and German languages. Ideas of servility before everything foreign were always actively supported by the ruling classes of other lands who strove to enslave tsarist Russia spiritually and economically. Elements of servility toward bourgeois science and culture are found also in a certain section of the Soviet intelligentsia who as yet have not fully renounced the cursed heritage of the past. Manifesting a lack of ideological stability, this section of the intelligentsia is susceptible to the baneful influence of bourgeois culture and the capitalist environment. This leads above all to an over-evaluation of the significance of the decaying bourgeois culture, to an under-evaluation of the great significance and progressive character of Soviet culture and science, and to an incorrect attitude on the part of certain of our scientists toward their own scientific achievements.

Soviet science has tremendous successes to its credit. It has all the foundations for surpassing in the very near future the achievements of science abroad. The contemporary imperialistic bourgeoisie are attempting to revive the former legends about the backwardness of Russia in order, as before, to rob Russian scientists, to appropriate their discoveries, to obtain for their imperialistic masters that superiority in science which is needed as a weapon of exploitation, as a means of personal enrichment.

Some of our scientists yield to these solicitations, manifest servility toward bourgeois science, and in pursuit of personal glory are motivated by pseudo-humanistic aims or individual interests. They ignore the interests of their own state and endeavor to announce their scientific achievements abroad as soon as possible.

As a result of such anti-patriotic and anti-state actions the achievements and discoveries of our scientists not infrequently become known and are put to use abroad before they are known or put to use in our country. Leading to a loss of prestige for our scientists and a loss of the rights of the Soviet government to new discoveries, this brings serious damage to our country. The anti-patriotic and anti-state character of such actions is entirely obvious.

Some scientists calculate that by acting in this fashion they exhibit humanist qualities and aid all mankind to make use of the new discovery. This of course is a mistaken view.

First of all, as soon as scientific discoveries reach capitalist countries, they become the property, neither of the workers nor of the people, but of capitalists and imperialists. One should not forget that only in our country do all scientific achievements and discoveries serve the people and become the property of the people. Abroad the achievements of scientists become the property of firms, corporations, and great capitalists who, moved by their own selfish interests, apply these achievements to the strengthening of the exploitation of the workers, to the making of huge profits, or to imperialistic expansion.

The utilization of the discovery of atomic energy may serve as a brilliant illustration. Nuclear energy could provide the greatest impulse for the development of productive forces. The achievements of science in this field signify a tremendous victory in man's conquest of the forces of nature. However, contemporary monopoly capital strives to utilize nuclear energy only as a weapon of destruction.

The German fascists exhibited glaring examples of the use of the achievements of science and technique against humanity. They encouraged only those researches which perfected their weapon in the struggle against progressive mankind. The invention of "soul destroyers," the construction of mechanized "factories of death," and the utilization of human corpses for industrial purposes show to what barbarism the reactionary forces of imperialism can go in the use of new technics against mankind.

Thus, science in the hands of exploiting classes is used against the people, against progressive forces, and against the true purposes of science itself.

The concurrence of the interests of science with the interests of the people became possible only under the conditions of the Soviet state, where there is no private property in the means of production, where there is no exploitation of man by man, where science has become an achievement of the people and is called upon to serve the people.

From this it is clear that the most important patriotic duty of workers in Soviet science and technique is the protection of the priority rights of our country in the scientific discoveries and inventions made in the Soviet Union.

Every patriot of our Motherland strives to enrich his country and his culture with new achievements and new discoveries and thus to raise still higher the power, the prestige, the greatness and the glory of his country.

Only to people without family and race is the feeling of national pride for their land and their people alien. The foremost leaders in science and culture of the past were great patriots. In this connection it is appropriate to introduce the remarkable words of the distinguished Russian scientist Popov, whom many countries endeavored to claim as their own after his discovery of the wireless telegraph. Popov renounced all these proposals, declaring: "I am a Russian and all of my knowledge, all of my labor, all of my achievements I may rightfully give only to my Motherland. I am proud that I was born a Russian and, if not my contemporaries, then perhaps our descendants will understand how great is my devotion to our Motherland and how happy I am that this new means of communication is discovered, not abroad, but in Russia."

If under the conditions of tsarist Russia the great Russian scientists valued the priority of Russian science and were concerned about the advance of Russian science and culture in world science, how much more intense must be the feeling of pride in the science of the fatherland on the part of Soviet people and Soviet scientists, who enjoy unlimited opportunities for creative work and who conduct their scientific investigations at state and public expense in scientific institutions created by the Soviet people.

Therefore it is entirely inadmissable and deserving of severe condemnation for individual scientists on making a discovery or an invention to be unconcerned about guarding the priority of our country, to fail to observe indispensable secrecy in work, and often to strive for immediate publication, and in the foreign press rather than in our own. This brings great loss to the Soviet state.

It is unnecessary to prove that the scornful attitude of individual scientists toward the question of where their scientific discovery will be put to use, whether at home or abroad, has nothing in common with Soviet ideology, with Soviet patriotism.

The experience of recent years shows that, sometimes as a result of the non-observance of secrecy respecting scientific discoveries, the Soviet state, having expended vast sums for the conduct of scientific studies, has failed to profit from them. Having become the property of other states, the results of these studies have been developed and sometimes patented abroad.

Thus, for example, the methods of extracting synthetic organic acids from natural oil were discovered by Soviet scientists. These acids can take the place of vegetable and animal fats and other deficit products in a number of branches of industry. The scientists of other countries, who began to work in this sphere later, utilized our work to a large extent, appropriated the achievements of Soviet scientists, and thus created for themselves an industry for the extraction of synthetic oil acids.

The methods for aromatic cyclization of carbohydrates, which have great value for the public economy, were elaborated by Soviet scientists. These studies were widely published. As a result during recent years a large number of works making use of the discoveries of Soviet scientists in this field have appeared abroad and a number of factories have been built according to a method based on these discoveries.

In the field of radio-physics and radio-technics our scientists have produced a number of great theoretical works which in significant measure have served as a foundation for the creation of contemporary radio-technique throughout the world.

It is known also that in the field of medicine, as a result of failure to maintain state secrecy, knowledge about new preparations penetrated abroad before they were tested and utilized in our country. This has resulted in great damage to the Soviet state.

Can we continue this attitude toward the results of our scientific discoveries? Certainly not. An indispensable secrecy must be observed in relation to all new discoveries made by our scientists. They must be handed over to the Soviet state and Soviet industry for practical development.

Why should we expend public money for every invention or discovery made abroad and be entirely indifferent to the utilization of our own inventions and discoveries? To maintain the priority of our scientists and our country, to maintain an indispensable secrecy in work is the sacred duty of Soviet scientists.

In this connection the question of the order of publication of scientific works must be considered. Some of our scientists publish their works abroad before they do so at home. To prove that such actions are anti-patriotic is not necessary. They happen because of the undervaluation of the significance and rôle of Soviet science, and sometimes because certain people, in whom a strong feeling of slavishness and servility toward everything foreign persists, love constantly to look beyond the border and ingratiate themselves with bourgeois scientists and bourgeois science. To such people a note about their work in some remote foreign journal or a review by an obscure scientist, often half-baked or a simple ignoramus, seems much higher praise than the appraisal of our Soviet scientists, of our Soviet journals and scientific bodies. For Soviet scientists this is obviously dishonorable.

"Is such servility becoming to us, Soviet patriots, to us who are building a Soviet order which is a hundred times higher and better than any bourgeois order?" said Comrade Zhdanov, speaking to the writers of Leningrad.[10]

This same question should be asked of that contingent of Soviet scientists who as yet have been unable to overcome the psychology of slavishness and servility toward bourgeois science.

Soviet science has numerous institutes and academies, a vast body of scientists, and outstanding achievements in all branches of human knowledge. It is not necessary for us to seek recognition in the lobbies of bourgeois science. The highest recognition of the works of Soviet scientists is the recognition of the Soviet people, the recognition of the Soviet scientific world, and the receiving of Stalin prizes.

Therefore the practice of certain scientists of publishing their studies and monographs abroad prior to publication in our country is inadmissible from the point of view of both the honor and the patriotic duty of the Soviet scientist.

Our state is very attentive and sensitive to the interests of the Soviet people and in every way protects those interests in the material as well as in the spiritual domain of life. The Soviet state denies personal fame to no individual. On the contrary it honors people publicly for service to the general welfare. We have fully recognized the principle: the country must know its heroes. But our people resolutely condemn those persons who strive to separate their personal fame from the fame of the whole people, from the fame of the socialist Motherland.

It is the patriotic duty of our Soviet intelligentsia to conduct an irreconcilable struggle against manifestation of slavishness and servility toward bourgeois science and culture and to defend in every way the interests of Soviet science and culture, the interests of the Soviet state.

[10] Speech by Comrade Zhdanov on the journals *Zvezda* and *Leningrad*, p. 18.

Does this mean that we repudiate the achievements and significance of foreign science? Certainly not. Our patriotism has nothing in common with that reactionary nationalism which for example came to full bloom in German science in the time of fascism and which is being cultivated now in certain other bourgeois countries. We study carefully and evaluate according to merit all achievements of foreign science. At the same time we consider it a matter of honor for every Soviet scientist to struggle in every way for the priority of Soviet scientists in new discoveries and inventions, for the protection of the interests of our state in the field of science. And the regard of the Soviet people for the achievements of science abroad is revealed in the fact that in many universities, agricultural institutes, and other higher institutions of our country a course in Darwinism is studied, while no such course is offered in the universities of Darwin's motherland.

The slavishness and servility toward Western culture and science of certain scientists also appear sometimes in the evaluation of the achievements of the science and culture of the past and the present. Some scientists are inclined to regard the best achievements of science and culture of the Russian and other peoples of the USSR in the past as reflection in our Russian life of the accomplishments of Western culture. This tendency appears also in the evaluation of eminent representatives of Russian literature and the greatest Russian scientists.

The remarkable evaluation of Russian literature, given by one of its great representatives, M. Gorky, is well known. "In the history of the development of European literature," wrote Gorky, "our youthful literature presents itself as a stupendous phenomenon. I do not exaggerate when I say that there is no literature of the West which came to life with such force and swiftness, with such powerful blinding brilliance of talent. No one in Europe has created such great books, recognized throughout the world, no one has created such marvellous beauties, under such indescribably harsh conditions. This fact is indisputably established through a comparison of the history of Western literature with the history of our own; nowhere in the course of less than a hundred years has there appeared such a luminous galaxy of great names as in Russia."

This statement by Gorky refers in the first place to our classical literature which has given to the world such giants of human thought and literature as Pushkin, Dostoievsky, Leo Tolstoy, Chekov, Gorky, and many other remarkable literary figures.

The Russian literature of the nineteenth century, one of the most original national literatures, has exercised and continues to exercise the most colossal influence on the development of Western literature. The fact of the systematic and fruitful influence of Russian literature on Western literature necessarily places before our literary people the task of analyzing and appraising this influence. Unfortunately, up to the present this task has not only not been resolved; it has not even been comprehended in its full stature. If our literary scholars have ever attempted to resolve the question of the interaction of Russian literature with Western literature, they have undertaken it in terms of the influence of Western literature on the Russian. They have scarcely broached the reverse process.

It is sufficient to point out that even the creative work of Pushkin has sometimes been regarded as a product of the influence on him at different times of Voltaire, Molière, Byron, Goethe, Shakespeare, and other writers. If we were to believe certain literary scholars and their "generalizations," the deeply national creative life of Pushkin appears to be only a talented reflection of foreign influence, beginning with ancient writers and ending with his contemporaries.

An example of the incorrect appraisal of the creative life of Pushkin is a book by Professor Nusinov which has been justly criticized in the pages of our press.

The same sins are to be found in the treatment of questions in the history of imitative art, music, and the theatre.

Frequently the greatness of the creations of Tchaikovsky, Glinka, Repin, Surikov, and others has been insufficiently illuminated in lectures and in scholarly and popular literature. And often in courses of instruction on the history of music and art their names have been mentioned at the end of the course following numerous names of less significant composers and artists of the West.

Analogous defects may be encountered also in the treatment of certain questions in the history of science. Here it is impossible to enumerate even briefly the great discoveries of Russian scientists of the past, but it is not impossible to direct attention to such historical facts as the discovery by Lomonosov of the law of the conservation of matter and the law of conservation of energy many years before Western scientists made these discoveries, the creation by Polzunov of the first steam engine twenty-two years before Watt, the invention by Kulibin of the first steamboat in the world, the prototype of the modern steamship, several decades before Fulton. Yet in our Soviet educational institutions, in a number of textbooks, in the lectures of scholars, and in scientific works, these facts are often passed over in silence.

The great creative work of Pushkin, Gogol, Turgenev, Belinsky, Tolstoy, Gorky, Repin, Surikov, Tchaikovsky, and many other figures in literature and art, the pre-eminent scientific discoveries of the brilliant Russian scientist Lomonosov, of the world-renowned physiologists Sechenov and Pavlov, of Mendeleev, the creator of the periodic system of chemical elements which determined the future course of the development of chemistry, of Popov, the inventor of the wireless telegraph, of the famous geographer Przhevalsky, and many other figures in the science and culture of the past must be treated fully in lectures, textbooks, and scientific works. We are obligated to do this by our patriotic duty to our Motherland.

We must do justice to many of our scientific and cultural leaders of the past who could not be recognized under the conditions of tsarist Russia. During many centuries the ruling classes, imbued with slavishness and servility toward the West, not only failed to foster the development of national culture; they strangled everything progressive and original in our people.

It suffices merely to recall the fate of Lomonosov and his struggle against foreign, against German domination of the Academy of Science, which was dedicated to the elevation and development of Russian science and literature: or the fate of the great Russian scientist Mendeleev, who first was defeated in the election to the Academy of Science in favor of the German Belshtein and later was dismissed from the university. It suffices to recall "the universities" of Gorky or the lot of the brilliant troubadour of the Ukrainian people, Taras Shevchenko, and many other great and talented sons of the Russian and other peoples of the USSR, in order to reveal the onerous conditions surrounding the creative work of the foremost cultural leaders and the reactionary character of the policy of tsarist Russia.

Only under the conditions of the Soviet state are the achievements of past leaders in science and culture evaluated according to merit and unlimited opportunities for the development of the culture of the people of the USSR provided.

Scientific and cultural workers must produce literary and scientific works and monographs which will reveal the greatness of the creative exploits of our people and evaluate those exploits according to merit. This constitutes their urgent task and patriotic duty.

The Patriotic Duty of Workers in Soviet Social Science, Literature, and Art. In the fulfillment of the task of strengthening the Communist education of workers, of liquidating the vestiges of the old society in the consciousness of individuals, of raising further the cultural level of the Soviet people — in the fulfillment of this task as a decisive condition for the successful building of Communism in our country, a special rôle belongs to workers on the ideological and cultural front, to leaders in social science, literature, and art.

Soviet social science must sum up and illuminate the tremendous experience of socialist construction in our country. It must reveal in all of its fullness the progressive character of the Soviet state, the superiority of the Soviet order over the bourgeois, of the Soviet system of economy over the capitalist, and of the Soviet culture over the culture of the bourgeoisie.

We live in days of sharp struggle between progressive social forces and forces of reaction. In the historic fight with fascism the forces of progress achieved victory and our country achieved victory. Our country bore the chief burden of the war, demonstrated to all peoples its superiority over the capitalist world, and stood rightfully at the head of all the progressive forces of mankind.

Fascism is defeated, but its reactionary ideas are not yet completely rooted out. The war with fascist Germany was concluded only recently, yet reactionary circles in the United States, England, and other capitalist countries have again begun to spread mistrust and seeds of discord between peoples.

The Soviet government and our diplomacy consistently pursue a policy directed toward the establishment of lasting peace and co-operation among nations. This policy reflects in full the strivings and the hopes of the Soviet people.

Active workers in social science must make their contribution to the cause of the struggle for the establishment of a lasting peace. They must arm our people with scholarly studies which disclose the true meaning of current events in international life, and they must carry on an irreconcilable ideological struggle with the reactionary forces of society. Such is the historic duty of workers in social science.

During the thirty-year period of its existence the socialist state has shown to all peoples the strength and vitality of the Soviet order. The Soviet Union saved world civilization from the deadly peril which fascism, conceived in the capitalist world, brought upon it. Our country has created material and spiritual values of vast universal historical significance. All this must be scientifically summed up and widely illuminated in the works of historians, philosophers, and economists, and in the compositions of leaders in literature and art.

For the successful accomplishment of this task we possess the vast experience of the Bolshevik Party and the Soviet government, guided by the ideas and the living example of the development of Marxist-Leninist theory under new historic conditions in the works of V. I. Lenin and I. V. Stalin.

However, there are still many defects in the theoretical studies of scholars in social science. Illustrative is the absence of significant works on dialectical and historical materialism which generalize the vast experience of socialist construction. Significant works are also lacking on the newest achievements of natural science — works which expose the attempts of West-European and American philosophers to illuminate the contemporary problems of social life from bourgeois reactionary positions and to interpret the developments in natural science from the standpoint of idealism.

In the USSR the most progressive political and social structure in the world, insuring the wholly unprecedented flowering of all the forces of our Motherland, is being constructed. As a result of the unparalleled successes of socialist construction there is being built in the Soviet Union a socialist society in which relations between people are being created anew: among citizens and between the workers and the state. The most democratic state in the world has been established. For the first time in the history of mankind the exploitation of man by man and the oppression of classes and nations have been abolished and a great friendship among peoples has been formed and strengthened. The sublime rights of the citizens of the USSR with regard to work, rest, and education are outlined in the pages of the Stalinist Constitution. These conquests of the Soviet people ring out with peculiar clarity and majesty in our days when the wolfish law of exploitation exists in bourgeois countries, when the whip of unemployment in the first postwar year threw out upon the street millions of people in the countries of Western Europe and particularly in America, when in certain bourgeois countries racial discrimination persists, and millions of people are destined to poverty, illiteracy, and political injustice.

The task of our theoretical workers on the basis of the great experience of the Soviet state is to create scientific works in the field of law worthy of our epoch. In these works the greatness of our achievements, the progressive character of the Soviet political and social order, and the triumph of a genuinely popular Soviet democracy must be presented. The reactionary essence of bourgeois systems and laws must be shown to our youth and the superiority of the Soviet order over the bourgeois disclosed. However, as yet workers in the science of law have done little in this field. They have prepared and published few works on the actual themes of the contemporary world. More than this: our higher educational institutions do not have textbooks for the most important divisions of law. There are almost no studies which unmask the anti-scientific, reactionary, anti-peoples' character of many bourgeois laws, and the "scientific works" of bourgeois scholars who defend the foundations of capitalist society, of capitalist modes of production, of bourgeois morality.

During the period of the second world war a new type of democracy, a people's democracy, arose and continues to develop successfully in Yugoslavia, Albania, Bulgaria, Poland, Rumania, and other countries. The substance of this people's democracy and the possible ways of its development concern deeply the people of our country and all progressive mankind. But this development in the East and Southeast of Europe is scarcely illuminated at all in our literature.

It is the patriotic duty of social-science workers to liquidate the intolerable backwardness of theoretical work, to produce monographs, scientific works, and textbooks in all branches of social science, appropriate to our great epoch and responsive to the actual tasks of the ideological education of the popular masses and of the younger generation.

The supreme example of the integration of science and life, of theory and practice, is found in the activity of the coryphaei of science of the contemporary world, V. I. Lenin and I. V. Stalin. In creating the Party of Bolsheviks and leading the first socialist state in the world, they enriched Marxist-Leninist science with new generalizations and achievements of universal historical significance. Through the development of Marxist-Leninist science V. I. Lenin and I. V. Stalin have always helped our country to move forward — toward Communism.

Through these brilliant examples we must learn to link scientific-theoretical activity with the practical work of socialist construction.

In the fulfillment of the tasks indicated above, and particularly in the cultivation of the feeling of Soviet patriotism, an exceptional rôle belongs to Soviet writers whom Comrade Stalin has called engineers of the human soul.

During the years since the revolution Soviet literature has grown and matured immeasurably. It has a number of great names. First of all, there is the great Russian writer, Gorky, the founder of socialist literature, who has enriched Soviet and world literature with productions of vast significance and artistic power. Then there is the finest and most talented poet of our Soviet epoch, Vladimir Mayakovsky, whose poems even today sound the call to battle.

Universal recognition has been accorded to such highly artistic and ideologically sound works of Soviet literature as *Chapaev* by Furmanov, *Quiet Don* by Sholokhov, *How Steel Was Forged* by Ostrovsky, *The Young Guard* by Fadeev, and many other compositions which reflect the struggle of the Soviet nation and the richness of the spiritual world of our people. These works are worthy of the great Stalinist epoch.

At the present time Soviet literature, the most advanced literature in the world, is in the ascendant. It is the duty of Soviet writers to show by means of the inspired artistic word the greatness of Soviet man and to reveal his traits of character, his spiritual beauty, his advanced ideas.

These same tasks stand before the workers of Soviet art. Having absorbed the finest traditions of the past, leaders in this sphere must continue to develop successfully Soviet music, painting, and the theatre. The names of the composers Shostakovich, Prokofiev, Miaskovsky, and Khachaturian,[11] of the artists Gerasimov and Konchalovsky, of the sculptors Mukhina and Merkurov, and of many outstanding leaders of the Soviet theatre are known not only to the Soviet people, but also beyond the borders of our country.

It is the patriotic duty of workers in the field of Soviet art to convey to the ages the glory of the first socialist state in the world, the glory of our people who achieved the Great October Socialist Revolution,

---

[11] In the light of the resolution of the Central Committee on *Velikaia Druzhba* this reference to the "big four" among composers suggests the well-known Soviet maxim or recipe for good health and long life:

> If you think, don't speak!
> If you speak, don't write!
> If you write, don't publish!
> If you publish, recant immediately!

the glory of the people who conquered the forces of fascism and saved world civilization from ruin and catastrophe.

Today the literature and art of bourgeois countries, particularly the literature and art which have been devoted wholly to the service of the imperialistic purposes of contemporary reaction, are experiencing a period of deep ideological, moral, and artistic decline.

It is our duty to protect the Soviet people and Soviet youth from the degenerative influence of bourgeois culture and bourgeois ideology, to reveal to youth the greatness and superiority of Soviet socialist culture over bourgeois culture, to cultivate in the broad masses the spirit of the great friendship of peoples — a friendship which can rise and develop successfully only on the foundations of the Soviet state of many nationalities.

The Friendship of Peoples is a Powerful Source of the Strength of Soviet Patriotism. The friendship of peoples which has risen in our country is a mighty source of the strength of the Soviet state and an inexhaustible fountain of the great feelings of Soviet patriotism. There is and there can be no true love for the Motherland in a country where national antagonism and national discrimination exist. No people enslaving another can be free. Even less can the enslaved be free.

It is known that in capitalist countries of many nations one particular nation always occupies a privileged position in relation to the others. It places in political and economic subjection the more backward nations. It holds in its hands all the means for the creation of material and spiritual values. And the ruling nation is the possessor of these values. The falsehood of the apologists of imperialism, who assert that the advanced bourgeois countries perform a civilizing function in colonial and quasi-colonial countries, is evident from the fact that more than ninety per cent of the population of India, Indonesia, and Australia, of African and South American countries, are illiterate.

In justification of such a condition the ideologists of the bourgeoisie, philosophers, economists, and historians, formulate "teachings" in which they develop the idea that peoples are divided by their nature into two categories, one of which must rule and the other must submit. German fascism carried these reactionary ideas to racial fanaticism and hatred of mankind.

After the defeat of fascism these very same ideas were resurrected by the reactionary elements of England and America, with this one difference that now it is not the Germans but the English-speaking peoples who assume the rôle of ruling the nations of the world.

The Soviet socialist state of many nations and our socialist culture are built on entirely different principles. The national program of the Bolshevik Party from the moment of its conception provided for equal rights to every nation.

The Bolshevik Party has conducted a struggle against imperialistic chauvinism which seeks to deny the necessity of the development of the national cultures of the peoples inhabiting our country. Also it has conducted a merciless struggle against the intrigues of local nationalisms which reflect the interest of the declining exploiting classes and which strive to divide one people from another, to tear a national culture away from the general Soviet socialist culture, and to direct the development of national culture along the bourgeois road.

At the foundation of the development of our culture lies the struggle for the building of a Communist society. Cultural construction in our country therefore is inseparable from the politics of the socialist state. The separation of culture from the policy of the Bolshevik Party and the Soviet government opens the door to the penetration of bourgeois ideology and nationalism.

All efforts to divide and divorce national culture from the general Soviet culture signify a tendency to separate the national form of culture from its socialist content, from Leninism.

The further strengthening of the great friendship of the peoples of the USSR, which is a powerful source of the economic and cultural strength of the Soviet Union, is the patriotic duty of the intelligentsia. The irreconcilable struggle against bourgeois ideology and bourgeois nationalistic elements is the sacred duty of the Soviet intelligentsia.

At times individual workers in history, literature, and art permit mistakes of a bourgeois-nationalistic character to enter their productions. Turning to the historic past, for example, they emphasize those periods, moments, and events which tell of the antagonisms of the peoples of our state and of their struggles with one another.

Even if, as a result of the activity of reactionary and chauvinistic elements, these moments and events actually are authentic, they are not important. The great striving of our people for unity and friendship was the decisive and unconquerable force of their historical development.

People who commit the errors of bourgeois nationalistic interpretation forget the advice of V. I. Lenin and I. V. Stalin. They pointed out that under the conditions of the bourgeois state every nation contains two nations and that the ruling minority of tsarist Russia, though in power, did not represent the entire Russian people. The Russian people were represented by those men and women who expressed its hopes, its struggle against tsarism and oppression. And if one approaches the facts of the past from this point of view, which is the only correct one, it is not difficult to see that the friendship between the peoples of our country and her outstanding representatives was historically determined.

The great Ukrainian poet, Taras Shevchenko, was a like-minded and an ideologically close friend of Chernyshevsky and Dobroliubov. The outstanding leader of Georgian culture, Ilia Chavchavadze, was an ardent admirer and disciple of Belinsky, Dobroliubov, and Chernyshevsky. The founder of the literature of Azerbaidjhan, Mirza Akhundov, loved passionately and publicized in his motherland the brilliant Russian poet, Pushkin.

During the darkest period of oppression and exploitation and the struggle with tsarism and imperialism the Russian people created a supremely great national culture which was imbued with respect for the culture of the other peoples of our country. Out of the midst of the advanced contingent of the Russian and other peoples of Russia, V. I. Lenin and I. V. Stalin created the great Party of Bolsheviks which brought our people to victory in the revolution of 1917 and to the world-wide historic successes of the years of socialist construction.

Decisive struggle with errors and perversions of every kind on the national question is a most important task and a patriotic duty of the Soviet intelligentsia and particularly of the workers on the ideological front.

Irreconcilable Struggle with Bourgeois Reactionary Ideology is the Patriotic Duty of the Soviet Intelligentsia. The second world war brought a change in the relations of the forces of reaction and the forces of democracy. In a significant number of European states, where formerly the forces of reaction had ruled, new popular democratic orders were established. The peoples of the entire world see in the visage of the Soviet state a firm and consistent warrior for a just and enduring peace.

This does not mean, however, that the forces of international reaction, which suffered defeat in the war, have laid down their arms. In the course of the Great Patriotic War fascism, the most violent expression of imperialism, was destroyed in a military sense, but the struggle on the ideological front is far from finished. The reactionary forces of the United States of America and Great Britain are attempting to restore fascist and semi-fascist orders in a number of European states. The ideologists of imperialism and reaction slander the Soviet Union and the democratic countries of Southeastern Europe. They set as their task the disparagement of the importance of our country in the war victoriously concluded, the sowing of distrust toward the people of the Soviet Union, the intimidation of world public opinion with the ghost of aggression on the part of the USSR.

It is entirely obvious that reactionary forces are attempting with the aid of the radio, the press, and other media to disseminate their reactionary ideas even among our people.

"Our successes within our country as well as in the international arena do not please the bourgeois world," said Comrade Zhdanov. "As a result of the second world war the positions of socialism have been strengthened. The question of socialism has been placed on the order of the day in many countries of Europe. This is unpleasant to imperialists of all colors. They fear socialism, and our socialist country, which is a model for all progressive mankind. Imperialists and their ideological servants, their writers and journalists, their politicians and diplomats, strive in every way to defame our country, to represent it in a wrong light, to slander socialism. Under these conditions the task of Soviet literature is not only to reply blow for blow, to all this base calumny and to the assaults on our Soviet culture and on socialism, but also to lash out boldly and attack bourgeois culture which is in a state of emaciation and depravity." [12]

The ideological intrigues of reactionary forces, no matter in what forms and shapes and from what source they may attempt to penetrate into our midst, must be most decisively repulsed. To this end it is necessary to give to all of our educational, propagandist, pedagogical, and scientific work a more politically sharp and aggressive character.

There is no doubt that our Soviet intelligentsia will put forth all of their strength to achieve new successes in the discharge of their patriotic duty to their great people, to our beloved Motherland.

[12] Address by Comrade Zhdanov on the journals *Zvezda* and *Leningrad*, pp. 34–35.

3

Three weeks after Kaftanov delivered his powerful address *Kultura i Zhizn* devoted its leading editorial [13] to the "Bolshevik Education of the Soviet Intelligentsia." This editorial, appearing in the official organ of the Central Committee on propaganda and agitation, seemed to possess the authority of a Party resolution. At any rate it quickly became a guide for the reconstruction and strengthening of the political education of the professional and intellectual classes. Its closing paragraphs constitute a kind of practical application of the substance of Kaftanov's address:

Hatred on the part of the Soviet people of every form of oppression, being intimately associated with the passionate love of the Socialist Motherland, cannot exist by the side of servility toward bourgeois culture. Such servility signifies a recognition of spiritual dependence on capitalism, on the world of exploiters. This is the more inadmissible because the contemporary capitalist order is an order that is declining to its doom. The bourgeois culture is degenerate; it serves reaction.

A profound understanding by the entire Soviet intelligentsia of the grandeur of our Motherland and her superiority over the bourgeois state raises to a still loftier plane the feeling of vital Soviet patriotism — the mighty moving force in the struggle for Communism.

The drive to persuade the Soviet intelligentsia, in the words of Kaftanov, to "put forth all of their strength to achieve new successes in the discharge of their patriotic duty to their great people" bore bitter fruit in the months to follow. Much of this story in the realms of science, music, and education has already been told in the preceding pages of the present volume. It remains to mention briefly three developments in the first half of 1949 — the assault on "cosmopolitans," the campaign of hate against America, and the authorization of the preparation of a

[13] *Kultura i Zhizn,* July 31, 1947.

new edition of the *Large Soviet Encyclopedia,* "worthy of the great Stalinist epoch."

The assault on "cosmopolitans" was apparently launched at a meeting of the Plenum of the Administration of the Union of Soviet Writers early in January, 1949. According to an editorial in *Pravda* at the end of that month, the offensive was opened with an attack on a "certain anti-patriotic group of theatre critics" who had "lost their sense of responsibility to the people — bearers of a homeless cosmopolitanism, profoundly repugnant and alien to Soviet man." They were warned that "resolutely and once for all a stop must be put to liberal toleration of all this aesthetic trash which is devoid of the healthy feeling of love for the Motherland and for the people and which has nothing to recommend it but malice and inflated conceit." They were told that "the atmosphere of art must be cleansed of anti-patriotic Philistines" and that "Party Soviet criticism will demolish the bearers of views foreign to the people." [14] This editorial seemed to be the signal for a torrent of savage articles and pronouncements in *Literaturnaia Gazeta, Sovietskoie Iskusstvo, Kultura i Zhizn,* and other journals during succeeding months under such captions as "Homeless Cosmopolitans," "Down with Anti-Patriotic Critics," "The Living Dead," "Raise Higher the Banner of Soviet Patriotism," "Expose to a Finish Cosmopolitan Critics," and "Love for the Motherland, Hatred for Cosmopolitans."

The campaign to eradicate "cosmopolitans," of course, did not stop with the theatre critics. It moved swiftly through the entire cultural apparatus, through literature, the drama, scholarship, science, and even into the realm of amusements. On March 5 an article entitled "Apologists of the Bourgeois Circus" appeared in *Sovietskoie Iskusstvo.* A noted student of the circus and two directors were singled out for harsh reprimand for imposing "foreign bourgeois tendencies on the Soviet circus," for having "led the Soviet circus away from those basic tasks with which life confronts them." Only by fully exposing these "cosmopolitan theorists and formalistic directors," the article concludes, "can Soviet circus

14 *Pravda,* January 28, 1949.

art flower anew and become a genuine medium of the spiritual might of the people inhabiting our great Motherland." Under the tsar the famous clown Durov often directed the barbs of his wit at the government and the army!

Even a superficial examination of this assult on "cosmopolitans" reveals that it is essentially an assault on the Jewish intellectuals. Those attacked are overwhelmingly from this cultural group. And the methods employed were obviously designed to identify "cosmopolitans" as Jews. Thus where a Jew had adopted a Russian name, a common practice in the Soviet Union, the Jewish name followed in parentheses — Gan (Kogan), Sanov (Smulson), Steben (Katznelson), Yasny (Finkelstein) and Zhadanov (Lifshits). The author of a glossary for the second edition of the *Large Soviet Encyclopedia* was rebuked for giving as much space to "contemporary Jewish literature" as to "Uzbek, Kazakh, and Georgian literatures together." His unpardonable sin probably lay in the fact that he "listed Soviet writers alongside the contemporary hucksters of America, Palestine, and other countries." The Jewish Anti-Fascist Committee was dissolved and the only remaining Soviet Jewish language newspaper, the Moscow *Einigkeit,* was closed. Although the ideological base for this attack on the Jews is political rather than "racial," as in the case of the Nazis, the victims probably are not impressed by the difference.

In his powerful address on August 21, 1946, at the First All-Union Congress of Soviet Writers, Andrei Zhdanov called upon the Soviet intelligentsia to "lash out boldly and attack bourgeois culture which is in a state of emaciation and depravity." As the months passed the attack was directed more and more toward the United States. By the spring of 1949, at the very time when many Americans were looking hopefully to the Paris Conference for signs of a softening of Soviet policy, the attack assumed the aspect of a campaign of hate against America. Without the slightest regard for facts and in the spirit of "Party literature," the pages of periodicals were turned to the task of erasing from the minds of the Soviet people, and particularly the youth, the last vestige of friendly feeling toward their wartime ally. The spirit of this campaign is reflected in two articles in the April 2 issue of *Literaturnaia Gazeta:* one entitled "Poverty and Deprivation Are the Lot of Millions in the USA," and the other, "The Morals of American 'Golden Youth.' " The former concludes with these words: "Unrestrained enrichment of the highest capitalist ranks and uninterrupted lowering of the standard of living of the working people who plunge ever deeper into the abyss of poverty and hunger — such is contemporary America." The latter informs the reader: "An overgrown hooligan, an ignoramus in a purple jacket — such is the worthy ideal of bourgeois youth in the USA."

It is to be hoped that the campaign reached its climax in the publication of a volume by the publishing house of the Young Communist League under the title, *Here She is — America!* This book is a compilation of "travel impressions about America" by a number of Russian authors, including Gorky and Maiakovsky. According to a review in *Komsomolskaia Pravda,* "this truthful book repudiates convincingly the deceitful propaganda, daily polluting the ether, of all those 'voices of America' which strive to present the USA as a land of prosperity, democracy, and freedom." The writers quoted, though observing "America independently and at different times," were in complete agreement. Moreover, "they set down their impressions, while their hearts bled for the millions of plain Americans, whose muscles and brains are exhausted by slave labor and whose conscience, feeling of self-respect, and class consciousness are corrupted and stupefied by the dreadful capitalist reality." The "sketches" of certain of the authors "tell of the poverty and hunger of the unemployed, of marching throngs of people having no roof over their heads, clad in rags, and craving but one thing: bread, bread, bread, even at the price of the heaviest and meanest labor." [15] At the same time all Soviet writers are moved by a "genuine human love for the plain people of America."

The tendency of the "ideological resolutions" of the Central Committee is to be given lasting expression in a new edition of the *Large Soviet Encyclopedia.* Here all the intellectual resources

15 *Komsomolskaia Pravda,* May 17, 1949.

of the country, "scientists, publicists, writers, artists, and other workers on the cultural front," are being mobilized for the "purpose of illuminating the decisive victories of socialism in our country, the achievements of the USSR in the fields of economics, culture, science, and art." The Encyclopedia "must show with conviction and in full the superiority of socialist culture over the decadent culture of the capitalist world" and, "proceeding from the Marxist-Leninist theory . . . must expose imperialist aggression and apply Party criticism to contemporary bourgeois movements in the realms of science, technology, and culture." The Encyclopedia "must be saturated with Bolshevik Party spirit." [16] Clearly, the line set by the All-Union Communist Party in the closing months of the war is expected to continue through many years.

[16] *Pravda*, March 26, 1949.

CHAPTER NINE

INTELLECTUALS AS SOLDIERS—ABROAD

THE ALL-UNION COMMUNIST PARTY recognizes the value to their cause of foreign intellectuals — of teachers, journalists, writers, artists, scientists, and even clergymen. They cultivate these people partly because of their prestige value and partly because of their active rôle in the shaping of public opinion in free societies. All of this is peculiarly in the Russian revolutionary tradition. The point was emphasized in an earlier chapter that the men and women who conducted the century-long struggle to overthrow the autocracy of the tsar were neither workers nor peasants nor traders. They belonged or thought of themselves as belonging to the intelligentsia as Kaftanov uses the term — a particular species of the intelligentsia, to be sure, but of the intelligentsia nevertheless.

In the Soviet Union the Party rules the intelligentsia without masks and with an iron hand. As the documents of this volume demonstrate, the Central Committee makes no pretense of valuing or guarding the creative independence of the members of this class. Thy have no "right to make mistakes." Their "freedom" is limited to doing precisely what they are told to do by the Party of Lenin and Stalin in the spirit of the good soldier. They are expected to accept correction with a smile, a salute to the Central Committee, and an expression of undying faith and loyalty to Stalin. In case of a severe reprimand they can reinstate themselves in grace only by figuratively getting down on their knees and kissing the feet of the Party, while placing the right hand reverently on the collected works of Lenin and Stalin. If they refuse thus to humiliate and degrade themselves, they may be treated with the utmost severity, brutality, and cruelty, all in the name of "our great Soviet people." An intellectual who values personal integrity above loyalty to the Party is regarded as worse than useless — as positively dangerous and a threat to the Soviet state. Indeed he may be regarded as a traitor to his Motherland, an enemy of the people, and an agent of the "bourgeoisie." But intellectuals who obey without question are showered with honors, emoluments, and expressions of solicitude.

The Party places an equally high value on the intellectuals of foreign countries lying beyond the "iron curtain." But the approach is profoundly different. Here the All-Union Communist Party of Bolsheviks works through its various national branches. Each of these branches, while on occasion professing patriotic sentiments, is loyal first of all to the Soviet state. Generally concealing this loyalty in words, it approaches the intellectuals of the given country in the spirit of the Catechism of a Revolutionist. With "liberals of various shades" it "conspires in accordance with their program, making them believe one follows them blindly and at the same time one should take hold of them, get possession of all their secrets, compromise them to the utmost, so that no avenue of escape may be left to them, and use them as instruments for stirring up disturbances in the State." The instrument through which these liberals, usually intellectuals, are brought into the service of the Party is the "front organization." The history of the Communist movement in the world, since the launching of the Third International in 1919, and particularly since the propagation of the idea of the "united front of all progressive and democratic elements" beginning in 1935, is strewn with the wreckage of countless such organizations and of the lives of thousands of "liberals" and "idealists." The Party has not even hesitated to enroll clergymen in the ranks of its fellow travellers abroad while at home it has degraded their brothers in religion to the level of outcast or untouchable.

2

On August 25, 1948, there opened in Vroslav, Poland, a "World Congress of Leaders of Culture for the Defense of Peace." Though organized by agents of the revived Third International under the direction of the Kremlin, the call for the Congress was calculated to convey the impression that the intellectuals of all nations, representing the great common heritage of human culture and independent of the policies of their governments, would meet to strive to build the foundations of peace and understanding among the peoples of the earth. To minds untutored in Communist methods and morals, the announced purposes seemed admirable and entirely unexceptionable. But the Congress soon revealed itself to be an effort to form the most ambitious and comprehensive "front" in the whole history of the Communist movement — a "front" which would include leading figures in the arts and sciences from all countries. A number of innocents from the West returned home disillusioned. Yet this fact did not prevent others from being drawn into meetings organized under the same auspices in New York and Paris in March and April of 1949.

The Congress received considerable space in *Pravda*. According to the TASS account "delegates" from forty-five countries, including the United States, attended. Mr. Henry Wallace sent a message of good will which was read at the meeting and reported with satisfaction several times in the Soviet press. "Your Congress," he wrote, "has profound symbolic significance. It is a confirmation of the fact that human thought facilitates mutual understanding and destroys all barricades which divide peace-loving people." [1] In an editorial after the Congress adjourned *Pravda* said the benediction. "The Congress in Vroslav," it declared, "is an event of international significance. It is clear evidence of the growing solidarity of the democratic forces of the entire world, of

1 *Pravda*, August 28, 1948.

the will of the peoples toward peace and toward the struggle for peace." [2]

The general tone and direction of the Congress were set on the first day by an address by the head of the Soviet delegation, A. Fadeev, General Secretary of the Union of Soviet Writers — the man who because of his record of unswerving loyalty to the Party stepped into the position of leadership following the resolution of the Central Committee on the Leningrad journals. The subject of his address was "Science and Culture in the Struggle for Peace, Progress, and Democracy." According to the report in *Pravda*, the speaker was "frequently interrupted by the tumultuous applause of the delegates." The address by the most important political figure in the field of Soviet letters is a most revealing document. The full text, as published in *Pravda*, follows: [3]

Permit me first of all to use this tribune to transmit in the name of the delegation of the USSR brotherly greetings to the forward-looking Polish intelligentsia — writers and artists, scientists and engineers, teachers and doctors — to all those who with their people are successfully creating the new democratic Poland. Permit me also to thank the government and people of Poland for their hospitality.

Only three years ago here in this ancient Polish city where we have gathered today, the Soviet army, together with the Polish forces, raised forever the banner of liberty.

Breslau, a fortress of fascist aggression which resisted to the last the fall of Hitler's Germany, again assumes its ancient Slavic name and becomes Vroslav — a city of free democratic Poland. This fact cannot be regarded as a figure of speech. For us Soviet people this victory and our friendship will always be a source of national pride, the most unselfish and pure that the history of nations has ever known. The memory of these days cannot be erased even by those who often strive to this end.

Only yesterday the large and small countries of Europe lay under the heel of Hitler. And no matter how courageous the forces of popular resistance, whose heroic representatives from various countries we can greet here as delegates to the Congress, their native lands would be enslaved to this day by the German fascists, had there not come to the

[2] *Ibid.*, August 30, 1948.   [3] *Ibid.*, August 29, 1948.

aid of millions of common people — the greatest liberating force in the world — the socialist state of the Soviet Union.

I have taken the liberty to recall this fact because it is not merely a word, it is the blood of millions of Soviet soldiers.

The Camp of Democracy Against the Camp of Reaction. What human agony beyond words, what numberless victims and ruins whose traces have been preserved even to this day, did Hitler's monstrous plan for the conquest of the world cost the people!

And now only three years after the defeat of Hitler's Germany, we, scientists, writers, and artists, are obliged to gather here again, troubled by the provocative activity of warmongers. The imperialists of that country, whose façade by the irony of fate is adorned by the Statue of Liberty, have taken upon themselves in great haste the rôle of conspirators and organizers of a new war.

What is the matter? Why do they rush to unloose a new world war? "War," said I. V. Stalin, "pitilessly snatched away all the covers and veils which concealed the actual face of the state, the government and the Party, exhibited them on the stage without masks, without embellishments, with all their faults and merits."

After the war the common people of all countries began to understand better what goes on in the world. What are the Mr. Monopolists to do when the hope for a worthy human existence — not in an abstract future, but now — stirs to aspiration and action millions of common people throughout the world? I. V. Stalin said that victory over fascism is "a great landmark in the progressive development of mankind." And actually, in spite of the great sacrifices, the forces of the people grew immeasurably after the war. To this the powerful growth of the democratic movement throughout the world bears witness. To this the tremendous successes of the countries of the new democracy bear witness. The new democratic rule in Poland, Bulgaria, Rumania, Czechoslovakia, Hungary, and Albania, supported by the masses of the people, has been able to carry through in the shortest time progressive democratic reforms of which bourgeois democracies are incapable. And the most brilliant expression of the process of the advance of mankind is the unprecedented swiftness of the restoration and development of public economy and culture, of the growth of the well-being of the masses in the Soviet Union.

After the war peoples, as never before in history, perceived in the example of the Soviet Union the great advantages of a socialist order. With especial clarity they saw in their fullness the might, the nobility, and the moral greatness of a socialist power, the decisive significance of Stalinist policy for the fate of mankind, craving peace, security, and liberty. And from this the common people draw their own conclusions.

And so the Mr. Imperialists have plenty to worry about!

After the second world war the entire world was divided into two camps: the democratic, anti-fascist, anti-imperialist camp led by the Soviet Union and the anti-democratic, reactionary, imperialist camp led by the ruling circles of the United States of America.

The geographic map gives no semblance of a correct conception of these two camps, because the line of division passes through the interior of each of the capitalist countries, through every city and village — through New York as well as through London, through Paris as well as through Rome, through Brussels as well as through Rio de Janeiro. Each camp has its own program, its own aims and tasks.

The democratic camp led by the USSR sees as its chief task the securing of a just and lasting peace for mankind. It strives to strengthen the victory over fascism, achieved at the cost of great sacrifices, to make possible the free development of democracy, to protect the independence and sovereign rights of great and small nations.

The imperialist camp seeks to preserve and strengthen the tottering building of the capitalist system, to suppress the people's movement, to crush socialism, to establish the rule of reaction in the image and likeness of Hitlerism. So the preparation of a new war is the most important part of the program of this camp.

More assured, however, sound the voices of those who call upon progressive mankind not to overestimate the forces of reaction, to have more faith in their own strength, to struggle firmly and unceasingly for peace and security, for democracy, for equality of rights between large and small nations. More assured sound the voices of those who call upon peoples to defend national sovereignty and to struggle against the aggressive plans of the new pretenders to world domination — the American expansionists and their European agents.

Small wonder then that the Mr. American Exploiters first of all strive to become the gendarmes of the peoples!

The American press speaks of this with extraordinary cynicism and frankness. The journal, *United States News,* in an article entitled

"The U.S.A. in the Role of World Policeman" declares that "circumstances force the United States to take upon itself chief responsibility for the establishment of police supervision over the world . . . The new role of policeman demands a kind of vigorous action to which the United States has been unaccustomed in the past." It was pointed out in the article that the United States of America has the opportunity to furnish this police supervision of the world "without the aid of any other power."

The rôle of world gendarme demands the establishment of a corresponding régime in the country pretending to such capacity. And not without reason even during the years of war, did De Witt,[4] an editor of the reactionary American journal, *Reader's Digest,* loudly declare "We need fascism in the United States to hold in check the radicals with their system and philosophy, to prevent them from raising their heads."

And so to put handcuffs on mankind, to convert the entire planet into one great police station and its population into silent slaves of capitalism — such is the aim of the American monopolists and their allies, the imperialists of England, France, and Italy, the great and small Beneluxites.

The American gendarmes hold in their arsenal no small means for the realization of their schemes. We have in view the plan for the enslavement of the countries of Europe under the flag of "economic aid," the punitive expeditions in the manner of the intervention in Greece, the grasping of military bases and the enactment of anti-Communist laws, the splitting of trade unions and the bullets of Scelba and Jules Moch, the hypocritical speeches of labor leaders and the policy of the ruin of the toilers, the slanderous anti-Soviet campaign and the ignoble attempts on the lives of leaders of the working class by hired thugs.

Among these many methods and measures the campaign of reaction against progressive ideology occupies a prominent place.

Appearing on the stage first of all is direct force. Progressive leaders in science, literature, and art are being persecuted. Irène Joliot-Curie was subjected to arrest the moment she showed herself in the immediate vicinity of the Statue of Liberty. Leading American writers, such as Howard Fast, John Howard Lawson, Dalton Trumbo, and others have already been sentenced to imprisonment. The American

4 Presumably De Witt Wallace.

radio, publishing houses, and moving picture studios in Hollywood have been "purged" of progressive commentators, scenario writers, and actors.

By bribery and intimidation scientific and technical thought is placed in the service of atomic armament.

"People whom we call 'the staff of big business,' " writes one of the prominent leaders of American culture who is obliged to conceal his name, "have thrown all their forces against us, and after two years of savage propaganda unequalled as yet in any other country of the world the American intelligentsia finds itself facing the threat of 'cold terror' . . . Henceforth in the United States the expression of any thought which might be regarded as 'dangerous' will be punished with ten years in prison, a fine of ten thousand dollars, and deprivation of American citizenship. . . . A writer who writes anything dissenting from the official policy of the government of the United States is also threatened with ten years in prison. This rude violence, this mad effort to impose fascism on America by legal means is the answer of reaction to the growing strength of the people's movement in our country."

Those who continue the policy of Hitler are found not only in the United States. The younger partners of the American capitalists follow the example of their masters: the labor government of Attlee, Bevin, and Morrison in England passes the same anti-Communist laws and organizes just such "purges."

The Ideological Expansion of American Imperialism. Attempts at the violent extirpation of progressive culture, recalling so vividly the practices of Hitler, represent one side of the matter. They are accompanied by an unrestrained ideological expansion of American business.

Vulgar American films which demoralize the spectator crowd the screens of English, French, Italian, and Swedish moving-picture theatres. Constituting 65 per cent of the entire world output of moving pictures they strangle the national cinematography of European countries dependent on the United States.

American publications, cheap mystery novels and similar concoctions, pour their muddy stream into the European book markets. Reactionary wastepaper, like such journals as *Reader's Digest, Life,* and *Time,* is forced upon European readers in millions of copies. These publications are published in many languages and supplement national journals. The ether is jammed with impudent advertisements of American expansionism under the brand of the "Voice of America."

"Patented religions, standardized literary ideals, theatre, moving pictures, sport jargon, endless novels, lively street songs, all beginning with Christian doctrine and ending with shivering American swing — this modern convulsive St. Vitus dance is all, absolutely all, we get now from America. Soon we will be Americanized more than the Americans themselves." Here you have the expression of a Swedish journalist. This can be acknowledged as entirely just.

What then is the content of all this that the contemporary American "enlighteners" are driving into the heads of people in the name of art, science, and literature?

First of all, it is the propaganda of world domination by American monopolists, the propaganda of militarism, the propaganda of a new imperialistic war which is directed in the first instance against the Soviet Union.

An American geopolitics, inherited from fascist ideologists of the type of Haushofer, is flowering in the United States. Such "works" as *Bases Overseas* by George Weller, which proclaims the necessity of creating American military bases, encircling Europe and embracing the Atlantic, the Mediterranean, and the Adriatic, the approaches to Africa, the Near and the Far East, are being published and advertised. This book, if you will permit me to say so, is concluded with a "prayer" composed by the author in which he promises the Lord God to achieve throughout the world the expansionist plans of American usurpers.

Geographical atlases, such as the one by Harrison, with original projects "Americanizing" the map of the world, are published in the United States. It is shameful that various scientific institutions and universities appear in the rôle of propagandists for a new war. "Scientists" of Yale University in a pseudo-scientific volume entitled *The Absolute Weapon* advocate the launching of an atomic war against the USSR. These people, a disgrace to science, are ranged beside the English clergyman, Davis, who in a book, *Theology and the Atomic Age,* published last year in London, praises the atomic bomb as "something bigger" than a simple invention — as a "new form." This "peaceful" pastor declares that the atomic bomb "has destroyed hope in a fabricated utopia," that is, in a better social order. The promoters of the atomic bomb and the preachers of "the western bloc," associated with Malraux and united with American generals of politics and politicians of the barracks, engage in saber-rattling and kindle a new war in the interests of the world domination of Wall Street.

The propaganda for a new war is combined with the preaching of racism and race discrimination. Thus is laid bare the imperialist and fascist character of all this so-called "ideology."

Reactionaries fear, like fire, the movement of the people, fighting for a better future. Their literature therefore preaches the repudiation of the social nature of man, develops egoistic tendencies, and strives to strip man of his will.

To the motley literary crew of reaction belong a number of American writers — O'Neil, the dramatist, Miller, the author of pornographic novels, and Dos Passos, the renegade. Spiritual lechery is inspired by the "existentialist philosophy" of the type of Sartre which attempts to put man on all fours. The base desecration of human life by these authors is mingled with mysticism, with a malicious struggle against reason and praise of the irrational. The leader of the English decadents is the mystic and esthete Eliot. Known for his pro-fascist sympathies he recommends himself as follows: "We are hollow people, people stuffed with rubbish."

These degenerates attempt to rob man of the possibility of rational thought. They fulfill the law of their masters who only dream of converting working people into robots.

But what does the representation of man as an unsocial creature mean, a creature whose action is devoid of rational motive? It means that the beast is put in the place of man. Contemporary bourgeois literature and art are precisely the apologetics of the beast.

A certain French "poet" proclaims: "Man imagines that he is civilized . . . but he always remains a cannibal." Such a declaration is nothing but a plagiarism from Hitler who wanted German youth to be like "young wild beasts."

German fascism needed beasts. American monopolists find beasts indispensable for the realization of their plans of world domination. Reactionary writers, scenarists, philosophers, and artists are ready to serve their masters. They place on a pedestal schizophrenics and drug addicts, sadists and pimps, provocateurs and monsters, spies and gangsters. These beastlike creatures fill the pages of novels, volumes of poetry, casts of moving pictures. They are presented as "heroes" to be emulated, as examples to be followed.

If jackals could learn to use the typewriter and hyenas could master the fountain pen, they no doubt would write just like Henry Miller, Eliot, Malraux, and other Sartrists.

The propaganda of crime, of lechery, of beastly instincts is indispensable to reaction for the conversion of the masses of the people into their obedient tools.

It is no accident that at the very time when American reactionaries spare no means for such propaganda, they are not disposed to devote money to schools, and particularly to higher educational institutions for the people. It suffices to say that the total expenditure on public education in the United States is only one and one-half per cent of the national income. But the filth which is purveyed on the pages of reactionary newspapers and journals and which is put in books and scenarios receives large sums from its masters.

The great Lenin said that American imperialists pillaged hundreds of billions of dollars. And on each dollar there are traces of filth. When one becomes acquainted with the writings of contemporary reactionary authors, then one sees the distinct mark of this loathsome filth on the dollar.

A quarter of a century ago V. I. Lenin said that the so-called American "modern democracy" represents nothing but the freedom to preach whatever it is profitable to the bourgeoisie to preach. And it is profitable to the bourgeoisie to preach the most reactionary ideas, obscurantism, defense of the exploiters, and so on.

Reactionary scholars, writers, and artists are particularly unmasked by their zoological hatred for the country of socialism, for the Soviet Union. All these people hate the USSR doubly, so to speak. In the first place, they hate it because they are the chained dogs of their masters, the capitalists. In the second place, they hate it because it is a state where high cultural and moral values have been and are being created, where science, literature, and art serve the people and therefore develop and flower freely.

In the writings, in the pictures, in the films, in the music of the bearers of the "culture" of imperialism are reflected, as in a mirror, the fall and the collapse of the entire reactionary camp. But is this all? By no means!

The anti-human propaganda of militarism and fascism, of pornography, of mysticism, of the brutalization of man — these are the poisonous substances and suffocating gases which reaction directs against progressive mankind.

It is for this reason that all forward looking creators of the true and genuine culture of democracy, inspired by the example of the country of socialism, must draw together and conduct an irreconcilable, vigorous, and active struggle against those whom I. V. Stalin has branded as the tyrants of our species.

Masters of Culture — to the Defense of Peace and Democracy. Millions of people throughout the world do not want the horrors of a new war; they do not want fascist tyranny and caprice. Intellectuals and creative people do not want and have no right to subjugate their thoughts to the dictatorship of the dollar or to serve as a weapon in the criminal hands of the propagandists of a new war.

But it is not enough "not to want" — one must act!

The fate of mankind depends on mankind itself. The future of culture depends on how intimately the masters of culture are linked with the people who carry on the struggle for liberty and independence. Active and courageous resistance of vital progressive thought to all forms of reaction — such now is the task of all intellectuals, friends of peace and progress.

Profoundly alien to the true intellectual, son of his people, is the cult of mysticism, the preaching of pessimism and ignorance, the whole structure of thought and feeling which is imbued with the animal fear of the reactionary bourgeoisie in the face of reality.

But in order to organize resistance of thought to the dark forces of reaction, solidarity on the part of the bearers of advanced thought themselves is imperative. That the voice of the progressive intelligentsia sound like a bell throughout the world in defense of peace and democracy is imperative.

Some scientists, writers, and artists imagine that they can preserve their "independence" if they lock themselves in study or laboratory, if they keep away from public affairs.

This is a harmful and vicious illusion. "To live in society and be free from society is impossible," Lenin used to say. The physicist or chemist, whose inventions can be utilized in the production of new weapons of destruction, is not free from society; the composer, whose compositions are beyond the reach of the people and serve the pleasures of satiated judges, is not free from society. The journalist, whose dispatches are distorted by the masters of the bourgeois press to oblige reaction, is not free. The intellectual, who lives in an unjust social order and submits to the laws and regulations governing that order, cannot be free.

"With whom are you, masters of culture?" With this question Maxim Gorky appealed to the intelligentsia of the West in his time. Again and again he exposed in his articles the bankruptcy of bourgeois-individualistic "humanism" and called upon cultural leaders to go along with the toilers, with the people. The image of this great Russian writer serves even to this day as a model for the advanced intellectuals of the West. Romain Rolland at the end of the first world war proposed the illusory motto of "independence of thought," but subsequently, made wiser by the experience of the postwar history of Europe, he wrote: "Independence of thought, as I understood it in 1918, when I called for its defense, is a magnificent tree whose branches reach out to the sky, but whose roots are deprived of soil. It is destined to perish unless it is transplanted into the thick of mankind, into the Working People, into this fertile ground, this human black soil. . . ."

Until now among some elements of the intelligentsia the false thought has been current that engineers and scientists can direct independently the course of history and move mankind forward. Herbert Wells, for example, supported such an illusion. In his conversation with Wells in 1934, I. V. Stalin proved to him convincingly the falsity of his point of view. He said to Wells: "Under certain conditions the technical intelligentsia can create 'wonders' and bring tremendous benefits to mankind. But it can also bring great harm.

" . . . For education is a weapon, whose effect depends on who holds it in his hands and at whom it is aimed. . . . The intelligentsia can be strong only if they unite with the working class. If they go against the working class, they become nothing."

Many progressive leaders of culture in various countries are now convinced of this truth. Sinclair Lewis, who for a long time occupied a middle-of-the road position in the social struggle of our days, shortly before the end of the second world war stated in one of his articles: "An artist or a scientist must know and loudly declare whether he stands on the side of tyranny, cruelty, and mechanical obedience, or on the side of the people, of all the people."

He who does not want to tolerate tyranny and cruelty, must place himself on the side of the people. That means on the side of the working people.

Laurent Casanova justly said at the Congress of the French Communist Party in June of 1947: " . . . When the masses move, the sources of the greatest cultural values are found in the very struggle of the masses. . . . When peoples move, the sources of cultural values and the factors of their development fuse with the very movement of the masses. . . ." All forward-looking masters of culture understand that scientists, writers, and artists must unite with the people, with all mankind, with the entire progressive movement; otherwise they will come face to face with the destruction of science, they will be driven into exile, or they will write only what their masters order them to write. They must become either frightened dwellers in the "ivory tower," or buffoons, or persons standing firmly on their own feet and marching in step with their people.

The experience of the immediate past graphically demonstrates that cultural leaders are powerless in the conflict with reaction, if they are not united with the masses. They are strong if they associate themselves with the struggle of the people.

In Germany during the period of Hitler's coming to power there were not a few scientists and artists who abhorred fascism, but they did not want or did not know how to resist it actively. The democratic forces of the German people were not united, the democratic forces of the German intelligentsia were neither organized nor united with the popular masses. And this led to consequences catastrophic for Germany and grievous for all mankind.

A contrary example can be cited. In France not long before the second world war a popular-front movement emerged and was developing successfully. Such great scientists as Langevin and Joliot-Curie and such great writers as Barbusse and Romain Rolland participated in the work of uniting the democratic anti-fascist forces. When the rulers of France betrayed their country to the fascist usurpers, the progressive French intelligentsia merged with the popular masses into the underground Movement of Resistance. Among the active participants in the Resistance were prominent writers such as Aragon, Eluard, Chamson, and many others. The voice of the progressive French intelligentsia was heard by the people. The Resistance Movement hastened the hour of the liberation of France from German occupation. And in no small measure this must be placed to the credit of the progressive leaders of French culture who were able to be useful to their people. And it is no accident that now, as fascist circles strive to subjugate the political life of France, reactionary forces attempt to defame and slander the progressive warriors of the Resistance.

How many noble hearts were inflamed by that incorruptible and honest voice which sounded unceasingly in the days of war and which, in spite of the slander of enemies, sounds today and is heard throughout the world, the voice of Martin Krasny — our aged and ever youthful Martin Andersen Nexö!

The courageous and incorruptible conduct of Howard Fast went far beyond the bounds of a single demonstration of steadfastness. He is associated with the most forward-looking movement of the contemporary world.

Cultural leaders played a great rôle in the movement for the liberation of the people of Slavic countries from the fascist usurpers. Who does not know of the supreme struggle of a whole galaxy of five Polish writers within their country during the fascist occupation! We all heard resounding from beyond the border the clear and strong voice of the magnificent poet, Julian Tuvim, the significance of whose genius grew immeasurably because he strove with the people against reaction. Everybody knows of the courageous struggle of the writers of Czechoslovakia against the enslavers of their motherland. Never will the name of Vanchur be forgotten! The whole world honors the memory of the national hero of Czechoslovakia, the remarkable writer and journalist, Julius Fuchik.

The example of the heroes of Resistance reveals how much a man of creative thought can achieve if he unites his activity with the organized movement of the popular masses. It is precisely under such conditions that his knowledge, his talent, and his spiritual riches can aid in subduing the forces of reaction and be of real use to the cause of progress.

Prior to the second world war forward-looking intellectuals of various countries were disturbed by the danger of war and attempted to halt fascist aggression. However, the experience of the recent past teaches us: that solidarity of the forces of the progressive intelligentsia in itself is not yet sufficiently effective in the struggle against reaction. A union of the activities of the intelligentsia with the people is essential. Constant daily participation of the leaders of culture in the democratic popular movement is essential.

The USSR — Hope and Bulwark of the Progressive Forces. The defense of culture and the struggle for peace and democracy are the common cause of the peoples of the entire globe. During the three decades of its existence the Soviet state emerged invariably as the defender of peace and culture, as the defender of the independence and freedom of peoples. The struggle of the Soviet Union for peace and culture is determined by the very nature of the Soviet order, which is founded on a genuine socialist democracy embodying the development of the culture of all the peoples of the Soviet Union. Gorky wrote: "In the Union of Soviet Socialist Republics energy works miraculously; its quantity grows and its quality rises from year to year; and this energy continuously throughout the world arouses to activity the energy related to it through the kinship of class. . . . " In the Soviet land culture is a truly people's cause.

"Nowhere," says Lenin, "are the popular masses so interested in genuine culture as in our country; nowhere are questions of this culture treated so profoundly and so consistently as in our country."

In the Soviet Union the century-old gap between the culture and the people is destroyed. Broad access to education and to the enjoyment of art is open to every ordinary Soviet person. A new Soviet intelligentsia has grown up; in the USSR prominent political leaders, scientists, and artists were formerly workers and peasants.

In the Soviet Union every cultural leader is surrounded by universal attention and support. Every intellectual, be he a doctor or a teacher, an architect or a poet, knows that his work is needed by the masses. The halls of universities, the library reading rooms, the picture galleries and theatres are filled with toilers who eagerly master knowledge and enjoy the fruits of culture. Soviet artists and writers have many millions of noble and exacting readers, spectators, and auditors who are capable of evaluating every one of their new creative successes. Every important event in the development of Soviet culture, be it a congress of writers or a congress of composers, a philosophic discussion or an election to the Academy of Science, is conducted with the friendly attention of the wide ranks of Soviet society, for whom the fate of Soviet science and art is a matter of vital concern.

In the Soviet Union a genuine and complete equality of nationalities is realized in state and public life, as well as in the field of culture. Soviet citizens of any nationality can read and study in their native tongue. Suffice it to say that in the USSR books are published in 119 languages, that the works of Gorky and Tolstoy are translated into sixty-six of the languages of the peoples of the Soviet Union. National republics have their own native academies of science where scientific work is developed and their own prominent scientists are promoted.

The Soviet state and the Communist Party show great and daily concern for the development of science and art. Important decisions of Party and state on various questions of culture are adopted as a result of serious discussions in which the creative workers themselves actively participate. Broad constructive discussions of controversial questions in science and art are a matter of daily practice in Soviet cultural life. Representatives of the public organs and the popular masses are drawn into these discussions.

The culture of the Soviet Union is permeated with the noble ideas of the friendship of peoples and of a socialist attitude of one person toward another.

It is not surprising that the eyes of progressive people throughout the world are turned toward the USSR — people who regard the country of socialism as the incarnation of future mankind, as the hope and bulwark of all the progressive forces of world culture. The finest writers, artists, and scientists of the capitalist world invariably have become friends of the USSR. Anatole France, Barbusse, Rolland, Bernard Shaw, Dreiser, Upton Sinclair, Heinrich Mann, Carel Chapel, Pablo Neruda, Martin Andersen Nexö, Langevin, Irène Joliot-Curie, Holdein, Parhon, Prenant — the whole flower of world culture has always been on the side of the USSR, and the achievements of socialist construction and culture in our country have rejoiced and inspired these best people of the world.

"You carry mankind on your shoulders," said Romain Rolland in addressing the Soviet people. "With all my heart I approve it," spoke Theodore Dreiser on socialist construction. In one of his latest works, in a book entitled *Political Gazetteer for All*,[5] Bernard Shaw writes as follows: "In Russia civilization has marched so far ahead that an astonished Europe has lagged far behind. . . . Compare what our government has done with what an efficient and public spirited government could have done during the two centuries of its deplorable existence, or with what the Soviet government has done during 20 years, and all our Whig Macaulayism drops dead before the facts."

On July, 1941, during the cruelest hour of the struggle of the peoples against the fascist enslavers, Bernard Shaw wrote: "When Russia destroys Hitler she will become the spiritual center of the world. . . .

[5] Presumably, *Everybody's Political What's What* (New York, 1944).

Remember that our civilization stands now at a crisis which she has not yet succeeded in surmounting. And this time Russia must lead us forward or we perish."

It is well to recall today the words of the wise Shaw, particularly in connection with that furious campaign of lies and slander against Communism and the Soviet Union which reactionary circles launched at the close of the war. These circles are alarmed by the strengthening of the forces of the democratic camp, at whose head marches the Soviet Union.

The second world war weakened the imperialist camp and increased its internal contradictions. The campaign against Communism which world reaction is conducting today, is an expression of weakness and not of strength. The campaign against Communism is indissolubly linked with the campaign of the warmongers against culture and with attempts to strangle every expression of progressive, free, and independent thought.

The American bourgeoisie view science and reality with alarm because neither promises anything good in the future. With the despair of a man condemned to death it attempts to revive backward views and deny the laws of social development.

The French writer, Claude Morgan, says: "Trembling from fear the bourgeoisie gather all of their strength to halt the rise of the masses of the people. That is why they appeal now to the gravediggers of the republic, to the collaborationists and traitors. It is a question of dire necessity, a question of the mobilization of everybody who can be mobilized."

Enemies of freedom and progress strive to halt or at least delay the march of historic development, to retard the awakening of peoples and the union of the wide masses with culture.

In one of his addresses V. M. Molotov gave a remarkable characterization of the present moment: "Capitalism has become a drag on the progress of mankind, and a continuation of the adventurous policy of imperialism, which already has brought two world wars, is the chief danger to peace-loving peoples. The Great October Socialist Revolution has opened the eyes of the people to the fact that the age of capitalism is coming to an end and that sure roads to universal peace and great popular progress lie ahead. The feverish attempts of imperialists, under whose feet the ground is shaking, will not save capitalism from approaching destruction. We live in an age when all roads lead to Communism."

No artifices and no wild rages of reaction can stop or suppress the growth of the forces of democracy throughout the world.

In every capitalist country by the side of the culture of the misanthropic bourgeoisie is the culture of the people, all of whose forces must be mobilized today for the repulse of reaction. The progressive forces of all countries of the capitalist world must rally to resist the efforts of reaction to strangle the culture of the peoples. The solidarity of the progressive thought of the world in defense of culture, which today is under threat, takes place everywhere. The Soviet Union marches hand in hand with these progressive forces.

Forward, to the struggle against reaction encroaching on free thought and culture!

Forward, to the struggle for the peace, freedom, and happiness of peoples, for the freedom and happiness of mankind!

3

The average unsophisticated American will be shocked by this address of the General Secretary of the Union of Soviet Writers. He will feel that any likeness between this portrait of the United States and his native land is "purely coincidental." But the credentials of Fadeev would appear to be of the highest. He is a self-acknowledged "master of culture," professing to speak for all that is finest and best in the human heritage in the contemporary battle for "peace, progress, and democracy." He was selected by his Party to represent the arts and sciences of his country and people at a supposedly international conference devoted to building understanding among the nations. In this setting his address would seem to be scarcely worthy of the frequent bursts of "tumultuous applause" which it received.

The language and spirit of the speech clearly violate the great humanistic tradition in whose name it was delivered. In dealing with all opponents and critics Fadeev resorted to falsehood without scruple and practiced the art of vituperation with the ease and proficiency of a master. At the same time, whenever he refers to his own cause, to his companions-in-arms, or to actual or prospective fellow travellers, he engages in exaggerated praise, unctuous sentimentalism, and fawning ingratiation. Without the slightest restraint of conscience he turns from vilification to flattery and back again. He quotes out of context, invents motives, falsifies data, and violates all the canons of truth. He always does this of course in the name of the "people."

To the sophisticated mind the form and the content of the address are no shock. Fadeev is a perfect example of the literary "soldier of Communism" and his speech is "Party literature" in the sense in which Bolsheviks have always used the term. In the violence and self-righteousness of its language and morals it imitates the models set in international conferences by Molotov and Vishinsky, and before them by Hitler and Mussolini. But its parentage can be traced back through the decades of the Russian revolutionary struggle by way of such figures as Stalin, Zinoviev, and Lenin to Nechaiev and Bakunin. In this struggle truth was always the first casualty. In fact the very notion of truth assumed the form of that which will contribute to victory. This entire pattern of thought, speech, and ethics has been carried to all nations through the Communist International. The American people must come to recognize it wherever and whenever it appears in the world. It will probably be with them for a long time. To resist the temptation to adopt it themselves will be one of their most difficult tasks.

Fadeev himself may be a victim of that scourge of blindness which for some time now has been sweeping his country. He may actually believe everything contained in his address. He probably knows nothing of the outside world beyond what has reached him through minds as blind and distorted as his own. That he has the slightest conception of the nature of a free society seems unlikely. Thoroughly habituated to life in a totalitarian state in which all media of communication are "co-ordinated" and made to speak with a single voice, he may actually believe that whatever appears in the American press reflects the clearly formulated policy of the "ruling class" with its capital in Wall Street. Yet, as he sat in the Congress at Vroslav, some doubts of the complete truth of his indictment must have intruded themselves into his mind. In attendance were thirty-two "delegates" from the United States, all equipped with American passports. Twenty-three of these people voted to approve the "manifesto" adopted at the meeting which was clearly aimed at their own country. And it is doubtful that any one of them would desire to surrender his citizenship and spend the rest of his days east of the "iron curtain." Fadeev certainly knew also that no Soviet citizen could have attended the Congress on his own initiative or would have dared to question in the slightest the wisdom and justice of the policies of the Kremlin.

One feature of Fadeev's address is somewhat puzzling. He misquoted and misinterpreted authors when this was wholly unnecessary. Anyone familiar with the output of the American press knows that by merely selecting and quoting accurately newspapers, journals, books, and writers he can prove almost any case to the uninformed. He can prove that the United States is on the verge of becoming either fascist or Communist, that it is abandoning or strengthening capitalism, that it is seeking war or peace with the Soviet Union, that it is moving toward race equality or toward the restoration of slavery, or that it is for or against vegetarianism. Fadeev did find a few things in the American press which tended to support his conception that the country is filled with warmongers bent on unleashing a third world war and extending their imperialistic rule throughout the world. But with all the rich possibilities presented to him by the institutions of a free country he still found it necessary to invent and distort. This is incomprehensible. His research staff is either wholly inadequate or incompetent.

He attributes to De Witt Wallace something he never said, misinterprets *Bases Overseas* by George Weller written long before the United Nations was launched, and puts his own meaning into the wholly harmless and "ideologyless" geographical atlases of Richard E. Harrison. But it is his treatment of the one really

solid work to which he refers that merits closer examination —
The Absolute Weapon, prepared by the staff of the Institute of
International Studies of Yale University and published in 1946.
He states categorically that the authors "advocate the launching of
an atomic war against the USSR" and are "a disgrace to science."
It will be enlightening to see just what they actually say.

The discussion of this question is found in the third chapter of
the volume under the title of "The Atomic Bomb in Soviet-
American Relations." If a sober and temperate treatment of the
issue is to be found anywhere in the language, it is to be found
here. Professor Arnold Wolfers, author of the chapter, writes that
"the idea of a preventive war is so abhorrent to American feeling
that no government in this country, to judge from the state of
public opinion today, could hope to gain popular support for
such a venture." [6] Further on he says that "the whole idea of an
offensive use of the bomb during the period of our monopoly can
safely be laid aside as utterly impracticable." [7] In discussing "lines
of defense" he argues that the first line "consists in proper efforts
on our part to settle our disputes with the Soviet Union peacefully and to avoid adding new ones." [8] He believes that "wise
statesmanship will have to seek a mode of conduct which will
neither tempt the Soviet government to overstep the limits we can
in safety and decency concede nor provoke it to undertake actions
out of sheer resentment or suspicion of our intentions." [9] Professor Wolfers strives generously at every point to view the issue
from the Russian standpoint. He even defends the veto on the
ground that the "Soviet Union has good reasons for believing that
the veto constitutes an essential element of her security." [10] Obviously the General Secretary of the Union of Soviet Writers should
read this book. But doubtless he, like other leaders of the All-
Union Communist Party of Bolsheviks, is less than friendly toward
Yale University because the Yale Press published a well-docu-
mented book by David J. Dallin entitled *Forced Labor in Soviet
Russia.* Up to the present moment no one has replied convinc-

[6] Bernard Brodie, Editor, *The Absolute Weapon* (New York, 1946), p. 117.
[7] *Ibid.*, p. 119.   [8] *Ibid.*, p. 131.   [9] *Ibid.*, p. 132.   [10] *Ibid.*, p. 133.

ingly to the materials presented in this volume. Fadeev should have undertaken this assignment at the Congress.

On page 324 of the present volume Fadeev quotes "one of the prominent leaders of American culture," whose name he fails to disclose, on the state of the civil liberties in the United States. The authors submitted this statement to Morris Ernst, a most distinguished American lawyer who has given much of his life to the defense of those liberties. His opinion follows:

It is a shame to have to cut down trees to make paper to reply to the spread of such untruths in the United States. However, it would be worth a real forest of trees if the answer could ever be made available to Russian minds.

There is absolutely no truth in the statement that "expression of any thought which might be regarded as 'dangerous' will be punished with ten years in prison, a fine of ten thousand dollars, and deprivation of citizenship." In the first place, we have seriously limited our definitions even under wartime sedition laws, by requiring the court to find that, as a result of the expression or writing, "a clear and present danger" to the body politic is proven. Except in the case of war situations, there have been practically no cases upheld by the United States Supreme Court convicting anybody for the utterance of any thought or for any written document. I leave out of consideration the application of obscenity laws where the "clear and present danger" rule has not yet been applied, but even here practically no publication, openly published and openly reviewed, is ever bothered or even attacked.

I am quite clear that there has never been any sanction imposed such as indicated in the quote. Furthermore, there never has been a law permitting the deprivation of American citizenship except on the ground that the citizenship was obtained through fraud.

I don't know how to answer the statement that a writer who writes "anything dissenting from the official policy of the government" is threatened with ten years in jail. I assume this thought occurred to Fadeev because he cannot believe that in a democracy like ours, there can be no single governmental defined policy. Needless to say, there has never been a statute in our history which places in a penal area anyone "dissenting from the official policy of the government."

This statement must be born of ignorance or evil intent to deceive people behind the "iron curtain" who have been denied the high privi-

lege of the right to see, to hear, to read — and hence are totally un-
developed in their capacity for critical judgments. It will take decades
to reopen the minds of these millions so long diseased by censorship
and intellectual black-outs.

In his address Fadeev cites the names of a number of distinguished writers as supporters of Soviet practice and ideology.
Among them he includes two living Americans who throughout
their lives have subjected the ways and institutions of their own
country to sharp and fearless criticism — Sinclair Lewis and Upton
Sinclair. The reader will doubtless want to know whether these
men regard themselves as belonging to the Soviet camp. Each was
given an opportunity to express himself on the question.

Fadeev quoted from an alleged article by Sinclair Lewis to the
effect that "an artist or a scientist must know and loudly declare
whether he stands on the side of tyranny, cruelty, and mechanical
obedience, or on the side of the people, of all the people." This
pronouncement he interprets as meaning that the American writer
is marching under the Communist banner. Writing from Italy
Mr. Lewis says that the statement itself "sounds correct," but that
it "of course places me not as standing for the Soviet Union and
its hysterical crusade but against it and its 'tyranny and mechanical obedience.' "

Upton Sinclair asks that the following reply be "published without deletion":

Either Mr. Fadeev has not read my books, or they have been incorrectly translated in their Russian editions. For forty-seven years I have
been advocating free, democratic Socialism, to be obtained by the
method of education and persuasion under our American system of
government by popular consent. I defended the right of the Russian
people to choose their own form of government, but that was when I
believed that they would be given the right to choose. I accepted
Lenin's promise that the state would wither away; but it hasn't. It
has become a reactionary nationalist imperialism, telling the Russian
people even what music they shall listen to and what they shall believe
about the inheritance of acquired characteristics. The rape of the
Czechoslovak democracy destroyed the last trace of hope I had of any

good to come from the Soviet Union. If I have any influence with the Russian people, I will use it to tell them that the present Party Line is bound to lead to another World War, many times more dreadful than the last.

Since the American people for a generation have taken great delight in the eccentric attacks of Bernard Shaw on their institutions, they will be interested in the authenticity of Fadeev's quotation from his *Everybody's Political What's What?* On the whole it is an accurate citation, even though the first sentence quoted is missing. But anyone who has followed the public utterances of the playwright is quite prepared for anything. He has long been fond of making use of the hard-won liberties of his people to ridicule those liberties, and the English seem to like it. One thing that Fadeev fails to note in his reference is that Shaw was making one of his "conventional" attacks on the democratic political process and parliamentary institutions and was placing Stalin in rather unwelcome company. The quotation follows in the same paragraph the sentence: "This lands us in the unexpected conclusion that government by Parliaments modelled on the British Party System, far from being a guarantee of liberty and enlightened progress, must be ruthlessly discarded in the fullest agreement with Oliver Cromwell, Charles Dickens, John Ruskin, Thomas Carlyle, Adolf Hitler, Pilsudski, Benito Mussolini, Stalin and everyone else who has tried to govern efficiently and incorruptly by it, or who has studied its operation with a knowledge of its history and that of the Industrial Revolution." [11] One can understand why Fadeev was not disposed to emphasize at the Congress the common political outlook of Hitler, Mussolini, and Stalin.

4

In order to propagate the myth of Soviet superiority throughout the world the All-Union Communist Party overlooks nothing. It

[11] *Op. cit.*, p. 29.

organizes its outward thrust through its faithful lieutenants in the Third International and its subsidiaries, it limits direct contact with Soviet reality by reducing to a minimum opportunity to visit and see the Union at first hand, it maintains a careful watch on the borders to prevent escape to other lands, it circumscribes the marriage of Soviet citizens to nationals of foreign countries, and prohibits the travel abroad for personal reasons of its own people. Yet one difficulty remains.

Some Soviet citizens do escape and others are sent abroad on state business. The problem is to insure the silence of the former and the return of the latter. The methods employed to achieve this double purpose are revealed in full clarity in the case of two teachers who had been brought to New York to teach in a Soviet school maintained for the children of Soviet officials in the city. When the Russian authorities closed the school in the summer of 1948 these two teachers, Oksana Kasenkina and M. E. Samarin, decided to remain in the United States and sought refuge with American friends. The case of Mrs. Kasenkina reads like a detective story. Having found her way to Reed Farm and placed herself under the care of Miss Alexandra Tolstoy, daughter of the great Russian writer, she was taken into custody by Soviet agents and held captive in the consulate in New York City. To escape again she leaped from a third-story window of the room in which she was confined to the cement pavement below. Had the fall not been broken by telephone wires she probably would have been killed. As it was, she suffered bodily injuries so severe that her life hung in the balance for several days.

The incident had international repercussions. The Soviet authorities demanded her return and also the return of Mr. Samarin to their guardianship. Failing in this, they endeavored to use their power over the surviving members of the Tolstoy family in Russia to mould the minds of their own people and to extend their terror to former citizens who had found refuge in other countries and particularly in the United States. The following incredible "Letter to the Editor" appeared in the issue of *Pravda* for September 21, 1948, under the caption "A Protest of the

Members of the Family of Leo Nikolaevich Tolstoy against the Espionage Activity in America of A. Tolstoy, a Traitor to Her Motherland":

Esteemed Comrade Editor!

With indignation we have learned of the criminal intrigues of the American police directed against Soviet citizens dwelling in the United States of America.

Having read in our papers the correspondence from New York, "The Piratical Morals of the American Police," we have experienced feelings of abhorrence and indignation similar to those we experienced in 1941 when we learned of the barbarous desecration of the great tomb of L. N. Tolstoy by the German fascists.

However, nobody could expect anything else from the German fascists. But from people who had known L. N. Tolstoy and especially from his daughter, A. L. Tolstoy, we rightly expected a more tender attitude toward his name, rightly demanded that it should not be linked with filth, putrefaction, and rottenness. But what can one demand from a person who has severed connections with her native land, who has dishonored the memories, sacred to every Russian, of the name of the great writer.

We protest categorically against the use of the name of L. N. Tolstoy for the so-called "Tolstoy Fund" which is composed of political corpses, spies, and murderers.

Who among us, Soviet people, is not insulted by reading the name of Tolstoy in connection with the filthy story of the activity of the "Tolstoy Fund" which is directed against our great Motherland and to the support of those who yesterday treacherously aided the German usurpers and who today are ready to serve any enemy of their fatherland?

The political gangsters of reactionary America — Mundt, Edgar Hoover, Thomas, and others — are attempting to conceal their dark deeds with the name of the brilliant Russian writer, with the great patriot, Leo Tolstoy. What is there in common between Tolstoy and the traitorous activity of that sink of iniquity, Reed Farm? Beastly hatred toward the Soviet people drove A. Tolstoy, traitress to the Motherland, to flee from the Soviet Union and hide behind the name of the great writer. Revolting is her base attempt to use the name of Tolstoy in the interests of those against whom Tolstoy wrote passionately and pitilessly. Did not Tolstoy in his time call these Beloselsky and Belozersky former counts, these Zenzinov and Weinbaum rogues, these Vonsiatsky bandits, "parasites of life"?

Leo Tolstoy lived and worked in those times now long past when the lords of the present white-guard haunts constituted "order and authority" in the then existing society of Russia. With a clarity permitting no idle talk he expressed his attitude toward them: "As a man denying and repudiating the entire existing system of order and authority, I plainly make my declaration."

With his passionate unmasking activity he assisted in the struggle for a new and just social order! With the penetrating glance of an artistic genius he saw clearly that the "people want, not to submit, but to be free." While professing the "law of non-resistance to evil," Tolstoy at the same time proclaimed the right of the people to defend heroically their fatherland against the attacks of barbarians. American reaction has accepted willingly the service of those who inflame hatred toward the Soviet people, who unashamed of treason defile the social order created by the will of the entire Soviet people.

The great patriot, L. N. Tolstoy, taught us to love and defend our country. It is best that those who do not should forget his name. They do not understand and never will understand the great events of our epoch; they cannot understand us, the Russian people, Soviet patriots, who love their country and give to it all of their strength; they cannot understand the struggle for truth, justice, and lasting peace on earth toward which all progressive mankind strives.

We demand the immediate closing of the organization in America which insults the great Tolstoy, our people, and all democrats who love and appreciate Tolstoy. The name of the organizer of "Reed Farm," A. Tolstoy, has long been forgotten by the Soviet people. Having betrayed the memory of her great father, she is known by her vile deeds against her compatriots; having already lived more than fifteen years in the camp of the most wicked enemies of the Soviet Union she would deserve no attention, were she not supported by the forces of American reaction. More than this, the American warmongers have dragged white-guard corpses into the light of god and are attempting by this means to frighten somebody. But the peoples of the world, and the Soviet people in particular, cannot be deceived and frightened easily. Our great people long ago threw overboard and consigned to oblivion these nobodies who are brought together in the "Tolstoy Fund," are nesting in the "Reed Farm" haunt, and still dare call themselves Russians.

One to whom Tolstoy is dear cannot help loving his own people, cannot betray his own fatherland. In our country the heritage of Tolstoy is preserved for the entire Soviet people.

During the years of Soviet power 27,558,000 copies of the works of Tolstoy in the Russian language and in fifty-nine other languages of the peoples of the Soviet Union were sold in our country. Moreover, some of these languages had not been set to writing before the revolution. At the same time the first full academic collection of the works of Tolstoy, consisting of ninety-six volumes, is being published by a special resolution of the Soviet government. The edition is being printed in accordance with the Tolstoy manuscripts on which a number of great scholars are working.

Five museums honoring Tolstoy have been founded in the Soviet Union. One million objects associated with the life and creative work of the great Russian writer are preserved in these museums — his manuscripts, books and portraits, illustrations for his works, original objects which belonged to Tolstoy and his family. According to a special resolution of the Soviet government under the signature of V. M. Molotov, these museums are placed under the jurisdiction of the Academy of Science of the USSR. Here is carried on profound scientific work on the study of the creative genius and biography of the writer and on the collection and preservation of everything ever associated with Tolstoy.

Two Tolstoy museums are located in Moscow. One of these is the House of Tolstoy with the homestead, the outbuildings, and the huge garden. Here Tolstoy lived for twenty years and wrote approximately ninety works. The entire environment of the house which belonged to the writer and his family is preserved inviolate. Lenin visited this house personally and was concerned about the founding there of a national museum in which everything would be preserved just as it was during Tolstoy's life.

In another building is housed the Central Tolstoy Museum whose exhibits consistently illuminate the stages of the life and creative work of Tolstoy. This museum was badly damaged by a fascist bomb, but the Soviet government restored it even before the end of the war in 1943.

Yasnaia Poliana which was occupied by the Germans and suffered grievously has been restored. Both of the Yasnaia Poliana museums are open: the house in which Tolstoy lived, half-burned by the German fascists, has now assumed its former livable condition, just as it was in the last year of Tolstoy's life. Yasnaia Poliana is a preserve of 400 hectares and is maintained just as it was during his lifetime.

The fifth Tolstoy museum is in the station Astanov. There the room in which Tolstoy died is kept inviolate and the entire house of the station-master is converted into a literary museum of Tolstoy.

Tens of thousands of people from all corners of the Soviet Union daily visit the Tolstoy museums, these places sacred to Soviet people.

We despise and curse those who attempt in the name of the great Russian writer and patriot to conceal their filthy spying man-hating deeds which are directed against peace, progress, and freedom.

We call upon all honorable people of the world to join with us in condemning and branding with infamy the filthy haunt of Alexandra Tolstoy who has disgraced the name of her great father.

The name of Leo Tolstoy cannot stand alongside the names of fascist scum, American gangsters, lynchers of Negroes, murderers, stranglers of democracy, enemies of freedom-loving people.

> Director of the State Museum
> L. N. TOLSTOY
> of the Academy of Science of the USSR
>
> Granddaughter of the writer —
> SOFIA TOLSTOY
>
> Grandsons of L. N. TOLSTOY —
> ILIA ILICH TOLSTOY
> VLADIMIR ILICH TOLSTOY
>
> Great-grandchildren of L. N. TOLSTOY —
> NIKITA ILICH TOLSTOY
> OLEG VLADIMIROVICH TOLSTOY
> ILIA VLADIMIROVICH TOLSTOY

That the members of the Tolstoy family whose names appear at the end of this "letter" ever composed the document or signed it voluntarily is scarcely possible. Had they refused to sign it or protested the use of their names they would probably have found themselves placed in the same category as Alexandra — people without rights, traitors to their Motherland. The language of the "letter" is the language of Fadeev and the Communist Party wherever it operates in the world. In both form and content the communication is an excellent exhibit of "Party literature."

CHAPTER TEN

IN THE PERSPECTIVES OF HISTORY

THE STORY unfolded in these pages adds little that is wholly novel to the human record. This veracious account of resolutions and decrees, of confessions and recantations, of cringing and grovelling, of flattery and sycophancy presents a picture as old as unmitigated tyranny. It should dispel the last illusion, still surviving from the hopes of 1917, that the Bolsheviks have brought anything new and inspiring to man's long search for freedom, justice, and truth. The promise of the Russian Revolution has been wrecked on the rocks of dictatorship and absolutism. The most pessimistic predictions made by Lenin's old comrade, Jules Martov, and other liberal leaders of the "October days" have been fulfilled to the last letter. These words of Peter Lavrov from his appeal to Russian revolutionary youth in 1874 seem to have been written in the light of the events and conditions reported in the foregoing pages: "Falsehood cannot be the means for the dissemination of truth, nor the authoritarian rule of a person the means for the realization of justice."

This is not to say that the Communists have contributed nothing toward perfecting the methods of tyranny and mind control. The contrary is probably the case. Rarely, if ever, has any despotism organized its system of rule with such cool calculation and on such a vast scale. The Soviet leaders have exhibited a measure of genius in the utilization for their purposes of those powerful engines for the moulding of the mind created by modern science and technology — the press, the cinema, the radio, and all forms of mass communication. And with these they have co-ordinated the machine gun and other weapons of war which, when linked with automobiles, railroads, and airplanes, make it possible for the smallest minority to hold unnumbered millions in perpetual subjection without hope and possibly without desire of revolt. Also they have so mastered the allied arts of persuasion and coercion that they are able to employ with equal facility truth and falsehood, love and hatred, honor and shame, worship and terror, rewards and punishments of every description. They have even made literacy an instrument for the establishment of a universal tyranny.

Some will say that this Bolshevik tyranny is unlike all other tyrannies in history because it springs from pure and noble purposes. Is it not dedicated to the fulfilling of the dream of the ages, to the building of an ideal society, to the serving of the people, to peace, progress, and democracy? But this defense will scarcely bear the light of knowledge. Most of the tyrannies of the past have justified their actions in terms of some great good. How often has "true religion" used the torture chamber to vanquish "false religion"? Socrates was condemned to drink the hemlock for "corrupting the youth" of ancient Athens. Bruno was burned at the stake in the name of truth, and women were sent to the hangman in Salem because they were "witches." The Inquisition was dedicated to saving the immortal souls of men through the agonies of their mortal bodies. American slaveholders defended their "peculiar institution" in terms of an ideal society. The tsar sent men and women to prison, into exile, and to the gallows to protect his people from "harmful ideas." Bakunin preached "pandestruction" and Nechaiev assassination, always for the "good of the people," and for no other reason whatsoever. Under the banners of man's loftiest conceptions and aspirations the Bolsheviks have fashioned and established an all-embracing tyranny and a system of mind control which are rapidly converting the Soviet Union into a country of the blind. And every assault they make on individual human beings they make in the interests of an abstract something called the "people." The unparalleled success of the Party of Lenin and Stalin in cloaking despotism in the garb of liberty, justice, and democracy probably constitutes its most unique achievement.

2

The fact must be recognized that all of those Russian liberal and democratic revolutionists, from Nikolai Chernyshevsky, Alexander Hertzen, and Peter Lavrov in the middle of the nineteenth century to George Plekhanov, Paul Axelrod, Victor Chernov, and Jules Martov in 1917, who foresaw tyranny perpetuated through a revolutionary dictatorship, have been proved absolutely correct. It is clear now that Lenin failed to solve the "means and ends" problem and that Stalin never had the slightest interest in it. For twenty years at least the Soviet leaders have been pursuing an increasingly reactionary course. Today they are striving with all the concentrated power of a modern police state to destroy one of the most precious values in our Western civilization — a value which is the creative element in human society — a value which has always led a precarious existence — a value which has cost much in struggle and tears — a value which until recently many thought had finally established itself on the earth — freedom of speech, freedom of thought, freedom of inquiry, freedom of the mind. There are of course other values, but without this one man must lose control of his destiny and return to a condition of blindness and slavery.

This is not the place to review the long struggle of heroic men and women to establish the right of the individual to inquire, think, and speak. It must suffice to point out here that in most lands and ages this right has been severely restricted. But where it has appeared, the human spirit has blossomed and brought forth great and lovely creations which have ever been a source of wonder to less happy nations and epochs. Because the pattern seems to have originated in the West among the ancient Ionians and Athenians and continued among the ancient Romans, the entire world owes to these peoples a vast debt of gratitude. Even among the Athenians, however, the most renowned of all, devotion to freedom of the mind was by no means complete. In the age of Pericles, disturbed by the weakening of old tribal loyalties, they enacted a law against blasphemy. Under this act many dissenters were prosecuted, including such giants as Anaxagoras, Protagoras, and Euripides. And at the age of seventy the greatest philosopher of the ancient world was tried, found guilty, and sentenced to death. Although Socrates might have saved his life by recanting, he preferred to defend the sublime principle by which he had lived and thus left for all subsequent ages an affirmation of freedom of the mind that should be recalled and celebrated today. In the words of Plato he spoke thus to his accusers:

If you propose to acquit me on condition that I abandon my search for truth, I will say: I thank you, O Athenians, but I will obey God, who, as I believe, set me this task, rather than you, and so long as I have breath and strength I will never cease from my occupation with philosophy. I will continue the practice of accosting whomever I meet and saying to him, "Are you not ashamed of setting your heart on wealth and honours while you have no care for wisdom and truth and making your soul better?" I know not what death is — it may be a good thing, and I am not afraid of it. But I do know that it is a bad thing to desert one's post and I prefer what may be good to what I know to be bad.

After the fall of the ancient empires, the invasions of the barbarians, and the triumph of the Christian Church a long era of thought control began. For many generations the power of the state supported ecclesiastical doctrines and beliefs. And through the Inquisition, which was established in the thirteenth century, the Church endeavored by heroic measures to defend its ideas against the inroads of scientific inquiry, geographical discovery, and bold speculation about the nature of things. Through a network of inquisitors and tribunals embracing most of Western Christendom it was able to hold back or retard the rush of modern thought. But in time the old bulwarks gave way and the spirit of the ancient Athenians was revived and, as many hoped, placed on the more enduring foundations of scientific method. The triumph seemed so complete by the beginning of the twentieth century that Professor J. B. Bury could write near the end of his *A History of Freedom of Thought*, published in 1913, as follows: "The struggle of reason against authority has ended in what appears to be a decisive and permanent victory for liberty. In the most civilized and progressive countries, freedom of discussion is recognized as a fundamental principle." [1]

3

One can understand the optimism of this statement from the distant past of 1913. At the time men were still living in the afterglow of the most humane of the centuries, and the great convulsions which were to make a shambles of the world were still in the future. As yet no one had experienced either the First World War or the Second, the term "Bolshevik" was known only to a small circle of revolutionaries, and the word "fascism" was yet to be coined.

But Professor Bury probably wrote much more wisely than he knew in that closing chapter of his account of the long struggle for freedom of thought. After registering the optimism expressed above, he begins to wonder. "Yet history may suggest that this prospect is not assured," he says. And then he asks, "Can we be certain that there may not come a great set-back?" Taking another glance at the past and recalling the recurrent ages of darkness, he writes: "Is it not conceivable that something of the same kind may occur again? that some new force, emerging from the unknown, may surprise the world and cause a similar set-back?" With this he takes a look at the present of 1913 and engages in the following extraordinary speculation or prophecy:

"It is by no means inconceivable that in lands where opinion

[1] J. B. Bury, *A History of Freedom of Thought* (London and New York, 1913), pp. 248–49.

is now free coercion might be introduced. If a revolutionary social movement prevailed, led by men inspired by faith in formulas (like the men of the French revolution) and resolved to impose their creed, experience shows that coercion would almost inevitably be resorted to." [2]

This remarkable forecast has been fulfilled. In the Soviet Union we certainly see a revolution "led by men inspired by faith in formulas . . . and resolved to impose their creed." Although opinion was far from free in the old Russia, it was freer in some respects than it is in the new. And anyone who has read this far in the present volume probably has already been reminded of an earlier age in Western Europe when men were "inspired by faith in formulas" and sought "to impose their creed" on others, employing the combined powers of church and state. How often did the present authors, as they worked over these documents of contemporary Russia, recall the Inquisition, the death of Bruno, the recantation of Galileo, and the entire struggle of the fourteenth, fifteenth, sixteenth, seventeenth, and eighteenth centuries to liberate the human mind from the formulas of the Mediaeval World! Lest men forget, the parallel will be drawn in brief detail.

The Soviet Union has had and doubtless will continue to have its Socrates and Brunos — men and women who because of their ideas are attacked without mercy by the Party and refusing to recant are denied a means of livelihood, perhaps arrested and sentenced by the MVD to penal servitude and oblivion. The names of not a few of these unfortunate people can be found in the pages of this book. But of Galileos and persons of still softer metal, there are many more — men and women who, because of their ideas, feel the displeasure of the Party, confess their sins or mistakes, promise to mend their ways, and suffer merely demotion of rank and a measure of disgrace. The names of many such people appear in the resolutions, counterresolutions, and confessions included in the present volume.

In order that the reader may see Soviet practice in the perspectives of history, the experience of Galileo will be recalled. Born

[2] *Ibid.*, pp. 250–51.

at Pisa in 1564, he was destined to join the great galaxy of thinkers who laid the foundations of modern science and thought. He was influenced in his early years by the brilliant studies and speculations of Copernicus and made original contributions in the fields of mathematics, physics, astronomy, and mechanics. He was aware of the fate of that eccentric genius Giordano Bruno who was arrested in Venice in 1592, taken to Rome in 1593 by officers of the Inquisition, and subjected to seven years of imprisonment and persecution. Failing to force him to recant his heretical views, the Church turned him over to the civil authorities for "correction" with the request that he "be punished as lightly as possible and without bloodshed." Unrepentant, he died at the stake on February 17, 1600. This act of the Inquisition suggests the mercy of the Soviet Government in abolishing capital punishment while continuing to send multitudes to death in the Corrective Labor Camps of the Arctic. Such presumably was the fate of Vavilov, and of many another creative mind in the "first workers' republic of history."

In February, 1616, Galileo, as a result of a visit to Rome to make his peace with the Pope, was "admonished" by His Holiness to abandon his opinions concerning the relations of earth and sun. But he continued his researches and writings and in February, 1632, published his famous *Dialogues on the Two Principal Systems of the World, the Ptolemaic and Copernican*. As a result of the appearance of this work he received a summons the following September to appear before the Inquisition in Rome and defend himself. Borne in a litter, because of his health, the old man reached the Holy City the next February and was immediately brought to trial. On June 22, 1633, in the great hall of a convent in the presence of his judges and a "large assemblage of cardinals and prelates of the Holy Congregation" he heard the judgment of the Inquisition.

Immediately and in the presence of the assembly, Galileo made his recantation. The essence of this statement follows:

Therefore, desiring to remove from the minds of your Eminences, and of all faithful Christians, this strong suspicion, reasonably conceived against me, with sincere heart and unfeigned faith I abjure, curse, and detest the aforesaid errors and heresies, and generally every other error and sect whatsoever contrary to the said Holy Church; and I swear that in future I will never again say or assert, verbally or in writing, anything that might furnish occasion for a similar suspicion regarding me; but that should I know any heretic, or person suspected of heresy, I will denounce him to this Holy Office, or to the Inquisitor and ordinary of the place where I may be.[3]

The Church authorities now proceeded with great vigor to destroy the Copernican heresy root and branch throughout Western Christendom and particularly in Italy. Catholic officials who had been involved in any way with the publication of Galileo's *Dialogues* were punished severely. Without benefit of a daily press, the cinema, the radio, the locomotive, the automobile, the airplane, the telegraph, or the telephone, word of the signal triumph of "truth" over "error" was carried swiftly to the far corners of Europe. Copies of the sentence of the Inquisition and the recantation of Galileo were sent to the official representatives of the Pope in all countries of Europe and to all archbishops, bishops, and inquisitors in Italy. A special effort was made to place these documents in the hands of all "professors of philosophy and mathematics." In the more important cities of Italy and Catholic Europe they were read aloud before assemblies of "counsellors of the Holy Office, canons and other priests, professors of mathematics and friends of Galileo." Neighbors were advised under threat of heavy penalties to report the heresies of neighbors, and members of families to spy on one another. Countless assurances of loyalty poured into Rome, even from distant points of the realm. "The professors of our university," wrote the Rector of the University of Douai, "are so opposed to that fanatical opinion . . . that they have always held that it must be banished from the schools." [4]

The Church turned to the press to crush the heresy. On the

---

[3] Karl Von Gebler, *Galileo Galilei and the Roman Curia* (London, 1879), pp. 243–44.

[4] *Ibid.*, p. 270.

one hand, the printing of both old and new books by Galileo, or
works of similar tendency, was placed under the ban. Also by a
special bull the reading of "all writings which affirm the motion
of the earth" was forbidden. On the other hand, with the voices
of Copernicus, Galileo, Kepler, and their followers silenced, orthodox theologians were called upon to turn their pens to the refuta-
tion of the heretical doctrine. As a result, for years to come there
issued from the press a flood of books and pamphlets designed to confirm the faithful in their faith. It would appear that
victory was never more complete. Doubtless the Central Committee of the Party, as it reads the expressions of devotion and gratitude coming in from all parts of the Soviet Union and from its
official representatives throughout the earth, enjoys a like sense
of triumph.

This ancient pattern of the effort to stifle thought and hold the
human mind in thrall by overwhelming power has been revived
in nearly all its details and has been strengthened in many ways
by the Communist dictatorship in the Soviet Union. In its broad
outlines the case of Galileo can be duplicated in every field of
thought and creative activity in Russia today — in literature, in
the drama, in music, in science, in history, in philosophy and in
organized education in all of its branches. But the reader would
find it particularly profitable and illuminating to turn back to the
case of Zhebrak. His recantation after the Party had spoken and
the hostile response of *Pravda* to his plea to be allowed to remain
in the ranks of Soviet science are profoundly reminiscent of the
experience of Galileo. And as Galileo had his Bruno who was
burned at the stake, so Zhebrak had his Vavilov who died in a
"labor camp." What has happened or will happen to Schmalhausen, Dubinin, and others who seem to have refused to recant
and grovel before the Party authority, time alone will reveal.

4

At the time of the Russian Revolution most thoughtful people of the Western World lived under the comforting illusion expressed by Bury. They believed that "the struggle of reason against authority" had at last ended in a "decisive and permanent victory for liberty." As a consequence, when the Bolsheviks came to power in 1917, repeatedly proclaiming their devotion to freedom, as their successors do to this moment, observers tended to discount the fear that the dictatorship was anything more than a temporary measure necessary to liquidate the tyranny of the tsar. From the pronouncements of Soviet leaders today, it is clear that they at least are intending to maintain and strengthen the dictatorship until the whole earth falls under their sway and they are able to make their "truth the truth of the toiling masses of the entire world." Only then can freedom of the mind be allowed to return to mankind. History provides no support for the hope that success will ever cause the present dictatorship willingly to surrender its authority. Indeed, until the régime itself decays, success is much more likely to strengthen and add lustre to the tyranny.

Clearly the American liberal, or the liberal of any other country, can no longer with good conscience apologize for this régime that repudiates the basic and central postulate of liberalism. If the term has any meaning whatsoever, it means commitment to the liberation of the human mind, it means freedom to think, inquire, and speak. It means *political liberty*. Bronislaw Malinowski, the distinguished Anglo-Polish anthropologist, in his last book, published after his death and devoted to a study of the relation between freedom and civilization, concluded thus: "Although political freedom is not the only type of freedom in culture, yet its absence destroys all other liberties." [5] And perhaps the essence of our American liberalism was given its finest expression in these

[5] Bronislaw Malinowski, *Freedom and Civilization* (New York, 1944), p. 15.

words of Thomas Jefferson: "I have sworn upon the altar of God eternal hostility against every form of tyranny over the mind of man." If by brute power this spirit is ever driven from the earth, man will most certainly enter a dark age, made the darker by the use of the "fruits of science" to subdue and enslave the mind.

A glance at recent history must arouse the fear that the modern day of human liberty is already well advanced, and that the night is coming. And so much of responsibility for the outcome rests with the American people. One wonders whether they possess the understanding, the fortitude, and the strength to avert the catastrophe which the optimism, indifference, and ignorance of the last thirty-five years have brought so near. The two world wars, disastrous as they were, are only a prelude to what may overtake the human race.

If the liberal and democratic forces are to win in the present world-wide struggle with the forces of Communist totalitarianism and of other forms of totalitarianism recently driven beneath the surface of our civilization, they will have to develop a strategy appropriate to and commensurate with the task. The picture of Soviet methods and mentality portrayed in the foregoing pages suggests that nothing short of the best will suffice. The immediate and urgent task is to undertake any and all measures which might persuade the men of the Kremlin that they are mistaken now, as they have been mistaken in the past, and even as Marx and Engels and Lenin were mistaken before them, regarding the imminence of *their* revolution and the universal triumph of Communism on the earth. It can be assumed that the one and only consideration which will lead them to abandon their great hope of the moment and cause them to revive and refurbish the doctrine of the "temporary stabilization of capitalism" is a recognized change in the power relations of the world, and, in the style of Zhdanov, to their disadvantage. As long as their power position and their "revolutionary" wave seem to them to be advancing, they will pursue their present policy with increasing vigor and determination. This is elementary.

If the liberal and democratic forces are successful in achieving this first objective, a still more difficult long-range task will confront them. At the present stage in the history of the Communist drive for world domination, the decision to come to terms with "capitalism" again will not mean final defeat. On the contrary, it will only mean a postponement in the decisive struggle between the systems of liberty and dictatorship. The Soviet leaders will merely adjust their policies to the new realities and await the return of favoring conditions. The long-range strategy of democracy therefore calls for measures which in the course of decades, perhaps generations, will expose to all the world the fallacies in the doctrines of Lenin and Stalin and cause the Communist theologians to doubt the authenticity of their apocalyptic vision. The development and elaboration of this strategy should be the first responsibility of all men and women who make the slightest profession of liberalism and humanism.

The broad outlines of the strategy for the achievement of both the immediate and the more remote aims suggested above are fairly obvious. And the course which the American people should follow is clearly indicated, even though they may not follow it. That course should embrace the following twelve elements, measures, and policies and should be pursued with resourcefulness and tenacity. The free world can win only if it takes the offensive.

The American people should do everything in their power to:

(1) Build the foundations of world peace through international organization. They should become the most vigorous, informed, and loyal supporter on earth of the United Nations. They must drive stubbornly to strengthen its structure and operations; fight to limit the handicap of the veto; accept willingly the necessity of limiting national sovereignty; promote a program of universal and effective reduction· of armaments; take the lead in the effort to establish an international police force adequate to enforce the decisions of the Security Council; advocate on every occasion the enactment, codification, and administration of laws to govern the relations among nations. The United Nations may seem to be a slender reed to lean on in the present crisis, but if it crashes, hope of peace crashes with it. Everything short of sur-

render of fundamental principles to hold Russia in the organization should be done, but if the Politburo continues to sabotage efforts to make it an effective agency for keeping the peace, the free nations should proceed without the Soviet Union.

(2) Keep their country strong. The men of the Kremlin have never shown the slightest respect for weakness. On the contrary, weakness on the part of the opposition has always encouraged their aggressions. They will never be driven to war or peace by public opinion at home, and they will never go to war on their own initiative unless they are sure of victory. Until the United Nations therefore gains sufficient strength and authority to bear the burden of maintaining peace, America must support a powerful military establishment. At the same time she must maintain her economy at full production. An industrial crisis or depression — what the Soviet leaders are counting on — would be fatal to success in this struggle for democracy and human liberty.

(3) Halt the aggressions of the Politburo-controlled Soviet Government. Working through the United Nations and through supplementary measures permitted by its Charter, their representatives should take advantage of every opportunity to expose to the whole world Soviet aims and methods both at home and abroad. No Soviet spokesman should be allowed for a moment to pose before any international tribunal as the champion of human rights, of political liberty, of intellectual freedom, of mercy and justice. Our delegates to the United Nations should revive the Atlantic Charter, make it the touchstone of their own policies, judge all Soviet acts by its principles, and keep before all peoples the many and continued violations of these principles by the Kremlin. America must show no fear of Soviet power, must call every bluff. Every successful threat on the part of the Politburo will only encourage further assaults by them on the peace and security of nations. Also America should enter into military alliances with any and all free nations for the purpose of resisting Russian advance through terror and the threat of war. The speedy ratification of the Atlantic Pact is obviously essential.

(4) Halt the aggressions of the Politburo-controlled Third or

Communist International. Since the day of its announced birth in March, 1919, it has been an international conspiracy dedicated to revolutionary aims and patterned in methods, morals, and principles after the Bolshevik Party and the traditions of revolution by a group of professionals reaching back through Lenin to Tkachev, Nechaiev, Bakunin, Pestel, and perhaps the French Jacobins. Wherever it goes it introduces a profoundly undemocratic ethics — the ethics of war, the ethics of the lie, of deceit, of espionage, of violence, of power. Since the close of the nineteen-twenties it has been directed from the Kremlin, is completely subservient to the Kremlin, and is dedicated to the overthrow by violence or any other means of every government on earth. That it was ever dissolved in May, 1943, is highly improbable, and the changing of its name to the Cominform should deceive no one. The free world should launch a vigorous and relentless offensive against this conspiratorial body by all means compatible with the values of democracy. Vital to the success of this offensive is the removal of the "iron curtain" so that Soviet citizens and citizens of other states may travel freely in and out of Russia and across the borders of all countries. With unrestricted communication the myth about the Soviet Union, on which the Third International thrives, would be quickly dispelled.

(5) Speed the economic recovery of Europe and the world. This is fundamental. Without such recovery all other measures will fail. The power and the aggressiveness of the Soviet Union rise and fall according to the economic conditions among nations. This is precisely the reason for the bitter opposition of the men of the Kremlin to any and all plans for the economic and political unification of Europe. Therefore, America must strive for a united and prosperous Europe.

(6) Support and nourish liberal régimes everywhere. They should refuse assistance to any régime which clearly represents the interests of a privileged class, unless by doing so they could lead that régime in the direction of democratic methods and purposes. Support of fascist or quasi-fascist states will lead to disaster. The Kremlin would undoubtedly pay a high price to maneuver the American

Government into a position of friendly relations with Franco Spain. Also, the blind policy advocated by some American business and political leaders of supporting the mythical system of "capitalism," or of "laissez faire," or of "free enterprise" in the nineteenth-century sense of the term must be abandoned. As a matter of fact, no such system exists anywhere in the world today, not even in the United States. Mixed economies involving a larger or smaller measure of socialization of productive property and of state intervention are the order of the day. This means that *democratic* socialism, that is, a socialism that cherishes and protects civil and political liberties, should be encouraged wherever it shows strength. It probably represents the only hope of halting Communism and other forms of totalitarianism in Europe and perhaps in China and India. The men of the Kremlin undoubtedly fear it more than capitalism because they are confident that the latter will destroy itself.

(7) Liquidate speedily the entire colonial system and mentality. In the United Nations and in all diplomatic relations the Government of the United States should take the lead in wiping out this heritage of five centuries of European aggression and exploitation. America, the first of the great colonies to shake off the rule of the Old World, should assist colonial peoples everywhere to gain political independence, to acquire a mastery of science and technology, to develop their natural resources in their own interests. The vigorous pursuit of such a policy will require unceasing vigilance to prevent predatory interests from manipulating that policy for private profit. And as the world is casting off the remnants of an old imperialism, it should be made aware of the dangers inherent in that new and vigorous brand of imperialism which carries the banners of national liberation and equality to all peoples — the imperialism of the Soviet Union, assisted by the Communist International. It is now obvious that the states behind the iron curtain move under a dominion surpassing in its tyranny the colonial system of the nineteenth century.

(8) Fulfill the democratic promise of their history at home. The only thing that can be counted upon to defeat the false democracy of the Communists is genuine democracy. This calls

for a nation-wide effort of all the friends of liberty to bring to an end those essentially un-American practices of racial discrimination and at the same time extend to all people the rights and freedoms, the benefits and responsibilities, of democracy. It is at this point that the entire American system is most vulnerable to the Soviet shafts of propaganda, and for the simple reason that here is to be found the most conspicuous failure of American democracy. The spokesmen of the Kremlin never miss an opportunity to broadcast and exaggerate all instances of racial injustice in the United States. Every act of discrimination is in a sense morally treasonable because it actually means giving "aid and comfort" to the enemy. In the years ahead, the Report of the President's Committee on Civil Rights, *To Secure These Rights*, should be regarded as a program of action by all Americans who take their democratic professions seriously.

(9) Rebuild the economic foundations of their democracy. This should be a central concern of government, labor, agriculture, and management, as well as of all other citizens either as individuals or in their organized capacities. The fact must be recognized that the original base of wide distribution of land and natural riches on which the republic was built is largely gone and that as yet no other comparable base has been found. Always loyal to the democratic process and guided by the experimental method and temper, the American people must strive to find the road to economic stability and security for all. The history of the present epoch shows that unemployment and fear of unemployment open the gates to dictatorship and the loss of all democratic rights and liberties. And the achievement of economic security must be linked with the elimination of the extremes of poverty and riches and the full utilization of science and technology to raise the standard of living of all the people. In the present world struggle America is being challenged to demonstrate that free men can also be secure in their economic relations. She must demonstrate for all the world to see that the way of liberty is also the way to security and equality. This, the Soviet propagandists are telling the peoples of the earth, is not possible. Even though they have yet to

police tyranny, they proclaim their goal with such dogmatism that many take the proclamation of intent as accomplished fact.

(10) Revive with power one of their most precious traditions. They should open their gates and offer their land as a refuge to all who escape from this twentieth century despotism. Today there are scores of thousands of these people in the camps for displaced persons in Europe, many of them men and women of highest character and great talents, people of sublime courage and idealism. They should be welcomed to this ancient sanctuary of the oppressed and persecuted. And though poverty-stricken and crushed in spirit for the moment, they would not come empty-handed to their adopted country. Having lived so recently under tyranny, they would serve as a powerful bulwark of freedom and might even instruct some Americans of Jamestown and Mayflower lineage in the values of liberty in the present age. They would certainly assist in smashing domestic attempts at totalitarianism in all its forms. Also they would constitute a rich resource in the current struggle with Communism abroad. The more gifted and experienced among them would be invaluable in carrying the democratic offensive behind the iron curtain and into the very camp of dictatorship. They might even be able to make millions of the blind see again.

(11) Strive with utter seriousness to acquire understanding of the increasingly strange world in which they live. Near the close of his *Outline of History,* published in 1921, H. G. Wells observed that "human history becomes more and more a race between education and catastrophe." The next twenty years witnessed the greatest expansion in schools and agencies of mass education of all time. Apparently these agencies either were handmaidens of disaster or were so limited in conception or so remote from the contemporary world that they were ineffective. The thing needed today is a broad educational program for both young and old, and particularly for the mature, which is wholly and profoundly relevant to these times. This program should give systematic attention to the material and spiritual foundations of human liberty and to the sources

of totalitarianism in all of its forms. Both Communism and fascism should be studied thoroughly by the American people. They should be regarded as seriously as plagues threatening to wipe out the entire population. What each of these despotisms says about the other is not far from the truth. Abundant resources should be supplied to establish the finest research institute in the world to study scientifically Russian history, Marxism, Communism, and the entire structure and operation of the Soviet régime. The American people, even in their official capacity, are quite unprepared to confront intelligently the challenge and the threat to their liberties which the cataclysm of the Second World War has brought to their doorstep. The mind of the average politician, businessman, farmer, and even labor leader is almost ideologically empty in relation to the demands of these times. They prize their liberties, but they are ignorant of the foundations of freedom in an age marked by the swift advance of science and technology. And no one knows how long or short may be the time to prepare for or to ward off the approaching catastrophe.

(12) Move speedily and surely to develop an educational program dedicated to the values of freedom and democracy. Understanding of the contemporary world, the totalitarian challenge, and the foundations of liberty in the industrial age is absolutely essential. Only understanding on the part of the people can serve to show the way in both the preparation and the execution of all measures directed toward democratic goals. The experience of the last generation demonstrates that any other procedure, even if conducted in the name of liberty, leads inevitably down the dark road of tyranny to a régime of dictatorship and thought control. To repudiate popular understanding in favor of submission to the will of an "enlightened minority" is to put out the eyes of the common man. But understanding without practical issue, understanding which holds decision in suspense, is not enough. It must bear positive fruit in the form of educational measures designed to cultivate in the young all of those loyalties to equality and justice on which political and intellectual freedom must rest. First of all, class, caste, race, and creed as a foundation of opportunity must be rooted out of American life and particularly out of edu-

cational institutions. Then the practices of schools and other organized agencies for the moulding of the mind must be subjected to pitiless scrutiny in order to eradicate inequalities and disabilities of every kind and to put in their place a system of human relations which expresses a positive affirmation of the democratic faith. The Declaration of Independence, the Federal Bill of Rights, the Gettysburg Address, and the Declaration of Human Rights of the United Nations should give guidance and direction to all measures and institutions engaged in the teaching of young and old. The time has long since passed when the American people could afford to approach such questions in a spirit of complacency and indifference. They must realize that in this day they are being called to judgment by history to honor their democratic professions.

5

If free men succeed in halting Soviet aggression at this time and in escaping fascist dictatorship, the fight against Communist totalitarianism is apparently destined to be long and bitter. In the nineteen-twenties and early thirties there seemed to be reason for believing that the dictatorship would relax, that dogmatic faith in the Soviet apocalypse would decay under the pressure of events, and that the harsher features and more uncompromising doctrines of Leninism would be softened or abandoned. After the war the precise opposite seems to have occurred. The Russian leaders appear to have become more fanatical in their faith, more convinced of the truth of their special revelation, and more confident of their strength than ever before. And there is no evidence that they are likely to lose this confidence in the near future. If the "revolutionary wave," as they understand it, recedes, they may alter profoundly both their strategy and their tactics many times in response to changes in the power patterns of the world. But it seems probable that faith in the ultimate triumph of Communism on the earth will dominate their thoughts and direct their policies for an indefinite period.

It seems probable too that the policy of all-out aggression decided upon and formulated as the war was drawing to its close will not be abandoned soon or lightly. In view of the nature of the Soviet system, with its high command in the Politburo and the Central Committee, that policy must have been the result of much study, deliberation, and calculation. This conclusion is suggested by the thoroughness with which the entire cultural apparatus, from humor to science, has been brought into its service. It is of course true that the "line" of the All-Union Communist Party is in a state of almost perpetual flux and that repercussions of the changes are felt throughout the Soviet system. But only twice before in the history of the revolution has the cultural apparatus been overhauled in a fashion comparable in sweep and depth to the transformation reported in this volume. The first was the occasion of the revolution itself when the Soviet system was being established. The second was associated with the consolidation of Stalin's power, the purging of the Opposition, and the launching of the great program of construction directed toward the industrialization of the economy and the "building of socialism in one country." Such shocks to Soviet folkways and mores, as indeed they must be, are certainly not administered for trivial or ephemeral reasons. At the end of the war, as pointed out in these pages, the men of the Kremlin set a course which they expected to follow for a considerable period of time — perhaps to victory.

Soviet strength should not be underestimated. The power of two hundred million people occupying a geographically strategic position in the world, possessing vast natural resources, and disciplined to act as a single unit should never be taken lightly. The fact must not be forgotten that the Soviet state is a military state, and a military state in a condition psychologically of perpetual war. That state now rules by dictatorial methods a zone in central and eastern Europe inhabited by 150,000,000 people. How far the current sweep in China will go and toward what end will probably not be known for some time. Also the historical analysis of Marx, Lenin, and Stalin by which the Russian people live undoubtedly contains a great deal of truth. Much of the behavior of the "capitalist" states following the revolution and down to the present moment has confirmed the faith of the Soviet leaders in their doctrines. Moreover, vast multitudes of men and women the world over are oppressed and live under conditions of misery and injustice. Today they are in a spirit of revolt and are ready to follow a political will-o'-the-wisp in the hope of finding relief. Not infrequently have the blind followed the blind in the past. The Soviet leaders are straining every nerve to provide leadership in this situation.

The fact must be recognized too that blindness has a certain kind of strength. A mob roused to a high pitch of fear, anger, hatred, or self-righteousness is no less awe-inspiring because it is blind. The men of the Kremlin, themselves blinded by their doctrines and by their ignorance of the rest of the world, have been engaged systematically for a generation and particularly since the end of the war in cultivating in their people precisely this mob mind. They are telling them through every agency of communication that they are the greatest people on earth, that their social system is immeasurably superior to every other, that they are destined to save the world from tyranny, that they and they alone today are marching in the great tradition of human liberation, and that their doctrines and their leaders are without equals in history. They are also telling their people through the same agencies that they are surrounded by warmongers, that all other nations are in the grip of exploiters and vampires, that "bourgeois" civilization is decadent and putrescent, and that enduring peace between the "camp of socialism" and the "camp of capitalism" is not possible. A people thus blinded, if committed unwittingly to a course of aggression, can be a dangerous and terrifying adversary, advancing with the inexorable and pitiless quality of an avalanche. In the long run sight is certainly strength and blindness is weakness; but in a brief clash, the event may prove otherwise. The hope of mankind therefore rests with the possibility of a prolonged and peaceful competition between the system of dictatorship and the system of democracy. The result then would scarcely be in doubt.

The central objective of the statesmanship of the free world should be the establishment of the conditions essential for this peaceful competition.

INDEX OF REFERENCES TO

MARX, ENGELS, LENIN, AND STALIN

GENERAL INDEX